EVALUATING TEACHING

Second Edition

Edited by
James H. Stronge

EVALUATING
TEACHING

Second Edition

A Guide to Current
Thinking and Best Practice

CORWIN PRESS
A SAGE Publications Company
Thousand Oaks, California

For information:

Corwin Press
A Sage Publications Company
2455 Teller Road
Thousand Oaks, California 91320
www.corwinpress.com

Sage Publications Ltd.
1 Oliver's Yard
55 City Road
London EC1Y 1SP
United Kingdom

Sage Publications India Pvt. Ltd.
B-42, Panchsheel Enclave
Post Box 4109
New Delhi 110 017 India

Printed in the United States of America

Library of Congress Cataloging-in-Publication Data

Evaluating teaching: A guide to current thinking and best practice / James H. Stronge, editor.-2nd ed.
    p. cm.
Includes bibliographical references and index.
ISBN 1-4129-0977-5 (cloth)—ISBN 1-4129-0978-3 (pbk.)
    1. Teachers-Rating of-United States. 2. Teacher effectiveness-United States.
I. Stronge, James H.
LB2838.E847 2006
371.14′4-dc22   2005015257

This book is printed on acid-free paper.

05   06   07   08   09   10   9   8   7   6   5   4   3   2   1

Acquisitions Editor:	Elizabeth Brenkus
Editorial Assistants:	Candice L. Ling and Desirée Enayati
Production Editor:	Laureen Shea
Copy Editor:	Kristin Bergstad
Typesetter:	C&M Digitals (P) Ltd.
Proofreader:	Dennis W. Webb
Indexer:	Molly Hall
Cover Designer:	Lisa Miller

Contents

Preface

There is renewed interest in the role of teacher evaluation as a fundamental aspect of school improvement. To a large extent, this interest in teacher evaluation comes from the realization that any significant improvement in schooling must have the teacher at its heart. And, just as there is a rational connection between school improvement and teacher performance, there is a necessary and rational connection between teacher improvement and teacher evaluation.

This volume synthesizes current research and thinking about teacher evaluation and blends that research with practice. Each chapter is rich with illustrations and examples as we attempt to make a strong research-practice connection. In addition, a question and answer format is included in each chapter to enhance the utility of the book and its practical applications.

The book is organized into 13 chapters and three major sections. In the introductory chapter, "Teacher Evaluation and School Improvement," I suggest that "a conceptually sound and properly implemented evaluation system for teachers is a vital component of successful reform efforts." The chapter discusses key features of effective teacher evaluation systems and offers one model for designing a quality teacher evaluation system for school improvement and teacher growth.

Part I, *Designing a Teacher Evaluation System*, begins with a chapter by Patricia Wheeler and Michael Scriven, "Building the Foundation: Teacher Roles and Responsibilities," in which they describe foundations for teacher evaluation and then focus on roles and responsibilities of the teacher as a desirable foundation. In Chapter 3, "Applying the Personnel Evaluation Standards to Teacher Evaluation," Barbara Howard and James Sanders provide background and implications for using the Standards in teacher evaluation. Pamela Tucker and Marguerita DeSander discuss the legal context and parameters for designing and conducting teacher evaluations in Chapter 4, "Legal Considerations in Designing Teacher Evaluation Systems."

Part II, *Assessing Teacher Performance*, provides a rationale and explores application issues for using multiple data sources in assessing teacher performance. In Chapter 5, "Classroom-Based Assessments of Teaching and Learning," Sally Zepeda offers a call for going beyond teacher evaluation by using classroom-based observations for assessing teaching and learning through instructional supervision. In Chapter 6, Laura Ostrander and I offer guidance for using parent, student, and peer feedback in "Client Surveys in Teacher Evaluation."

In Chapter 7, "Student Achievement and Teacher Evaluation," Pamela Tucker and I discuss promising approaches to using student learning data in the evaluation of teachers' work. Kenneth Wolf describes the benefits, liabilities, and applications of portfolios in Chapter 8, "Portfolios in Teacher Evaluation." In Chapter 9, "Teacher Self-Evaluation," Peter Airasian and Arlen Gullickson describe a process in which teachers make judgments about their own performance for the purpose of self-improvement. In the last chapter in Part II, Kenneth Peterson explains the data sources that can provide a more in-depth view of teacher quality.

Part III, *Implementing the Teacher Evaluation System,* explores often neglected but important issues in the successful application of an effective evaluation system. In Chapter 11, "Conducting a Successful Evaluation Conference," Virginia Helm and Henry St. Maurice draw heavily from the business and professional literature to describe how evaluation conferences can serve as a key component in an ongoing communication and feedback cycle. Next, in Chapter 12, Mary Jo McGrath discusses factors that should be incorporated on a day-to-day basis in "Dealing Positively With the Nonproductive Teacher." And finally, in Chapter 13, Stephen Gordon makes a case for the vital connection between teacher evaluation and professional development in the successful school process.

Taken collectively, *Evaluating Teaching: A Guide to Current Thinking and Best Practice* represents our attempt to provide a coherent and comprehensive approach to designing, implementing, and monitoring quality teacher evaluation systems. Our goal is to provide a framework for improvement—improvement of the teacher, improvement of the school, and, ultimately, improvement in student performance. We trust that our intended readers—school practitioners (principals, supervisors, staff development specialists, superintendents), graduate students, and researchers of teacher evaluation—find the text to be true to this purpose and of value in their work.

—James H. Stronge

ACKNOWLEDGMENTS

Corwin Press gratefully acknowledges the contributions of the following individuals:

Lynda Boyer
Principal
Manatee High School
Bradenton, FL

Cheryl B. Henig
Professor
Curry School of Education
University of Virginia
Charlottesville, VA

Margo Kipps
Teacher Supervisor
Department of Education
University of California
Santa Cruz, CA

Edward Lee Vargas
Superintendent
Hacienda La Puente Unified School District
City of Industry, CA

About the Authors

Peter W. Airasian received his PhD from the University of Chicago, with a specialization in assessment, testing, and evaluation. He is a former high school chemistry and biology teacher. His research focuses on classroom assessment and teacher evaluation. He is the author of *Classroom Assessment* and a member of the founding board of CREATE, the Consortium for Research on Educational Accountability and Teacher Evaluation.

Marguerita K. DeSander currently is an independent educational law and human resources administration consultant for public sector organizations. She was the Executive Director of Human Resources for four years with Williamsburg-James City County Public Schools in Virginia and a practicing attorney for five years in the metropolitan Detroit area, focusing on employment issues. She received her PhD in educational policy, planning, and leadership from the College of William and Mary and her JD from Thomas M. Cooley Law School.

Stephen P. Gordon is a Professor of Educational Leadership and Codirector of the National Center for School Improvement at Texas State University. He is author of the book *Professional Development for School Improvement: Empowering Learning Communities* and coauthor of the books *SuperVision and Instructional Leadership* (with Carl D. Glickman and Jovita M. Ross-Gordon) and *How to Help Beginning Teachers Succeed* (with Susan Maxey). He is a former teacher and staff developer. He teaches courses in educational administration and in Texas State's new doctoral program in school improvement. His research interests are instructional supervision, professional development, and school improvement. He received his doctorate in instructional supervision from the University of Georgia.

Arlen Gullickson is Director of The Evaluation Center and professor of education at Western Michigan University. He is a member of the American Educational Research Association, American Evaluation Association, the National Council on Measurement in Education, the National Education Association, and the Consortium for Research on Educational Accountability and Teacher Evaluation (CREATE). He is the current chair of the Joint Committee on Standards for Educational Evaluation, which has developed three books of standards: *The Personnel Evaluation Standards*, *The Program Evaluation Standards*, and *The Student Evaluation Standards*. His doctorate in educational research was received from the University of Colorado.

Virginia M. Helm is Provost and Vice Chancellor for Academic Affairs at the University of Wisconsin-Stevens Point. She has taught high school (Oak Park & River Forest High School in Illinois) as well as graduate courses in Educational Administration at Western Illinois University. Her research interests have focused on legal issues in educational technology and in personnel evaluation, as well as on assessment. She received her PhD in Educational Administration from the University of Iowa.

Barbara B. Howard is Project Director of Educator Assessment in the Education Leadership Program of the SERVE Center of the University of North Carolina at Greensboro. She has been actively engaged in the area of personnel evaluation development and research for a number of years as lead developer of the SERVE models of teacher and principal evaluation. Her work includes research and development in the area of new principal and teacher recruitment and retention. She served as Chair of the Task Force for the second edition of the Personnel Evaluation Standards issued by the Joint Committee on Standards for Educational Evaluation. Prior to coming to the SERVE Center, she was a classroom teacher and administrator in public schools in North Carolina for 13 years. She received her doctorate in Educational Leadership from Appalachian State University in Boone, North Carolina.

Mary Jo McGrath, Attorney at Law, is Founder and President of McGrath Training Systems. She specializes in legally fit and principled professional development programs for elementary, secondary, and higher education school districts, risk management pools, and other public agencies. She and her associates deliver on-site workshops and online distance learning programs on five key topics: (1) Communication, Supervision, Evaluation, and Leadership for Administrators; (2) Anti-Bullying Training for Educators, Staff, Administrators, Parents, and Students; (3) Prevention, Detection, and Investigation of Educator Sexual Misconduct; (4) Valuing and Managing Cultural and Racial Diversity; and (5) Legal Liability for Athletic Coaches and Extracurricular Program Advisors. Since 1989, McGrath Training Systems has trained more than 250,000 administrators, educators, staff, parents, and students throughout the United States and Canada. She also produces three highly acclaimed educational video series for schools: *Sexual Harassment: Minimize the Risk; The Early Faces of Violence: From Schoolyard Bullying and Ridicule to Sexual Harassment;* and *SUCCEED With Supervision, Evaluation and Leadership.* For two years she served as Chair of the U.S. Department of Education Safe, Disciplined, and Drug-Free Schools Expert Panel.

Laura Pool Ostrander worked for the Virginia Beach City Public Schools for more than 25 years as a science teacher, gifted/talented resource teacher, television coordinator, planning specialist, assessment specialist, and organizational development specialist. She was instrumental in developing and implementing a client survey program for public school employees in Virginia Beach, Virginia. She previously worked for Portsmouth City Public Schools and the

Hampton Roads Educational Television Association. She is a graduate of Mary Washington College (BS) and the University of Virginia (MEd and EdD) and currently works as an educational consultant.

Kenneth D. Peterson is Professor of Education at Portland State University in Portland, Oregon. His central instructional duties are in preservice teacher education. He maintains a Web site on teacher evaluation (www.teacherevaluation.net) and on teacher hiring (www.teacherhiring.net).He is the author of *Teacher Evaluation: A Comprehensive Guide to New Directions and Practices* (Corwin, 2000), *Effective Teacher Hiring: A Guide to Getting the Best* (2002), and the forthcoming *Effective Teacher Evaluation: A Guide for Principals* (Corwin, 2006). He has published extensively in the teacher evaluation research literature.

Henry St. Maurice is Director of Field Experiences & Professional Development and Professor of Education at the University of Wisconsin-Stevens Point. He has also taught in elementary, secondary, and rehabilitation programs. His research interests include rhetorical, philosophical, and historical studies of teacher education. He received his doctorate in Curriculum and Instruction from the University of Wisconsin-Madison.

James R. Sanders is Professor Emeritus of Education and former Associate Director of The Evaluation Center at Western Michigan University. He received his master's degree in educational research from Bucknell University and his PhD in educational research and evaluation from the University of Colorado. He has served as a visiting professor at St. Patrick's College (in Dublin, Ireland), Utah State University, and the University of British Columbia. He is coauthor of *Educational Evaluation: Theory and Practice* (1973), *Practices and Problems in Competency-Based Measurement* (1979), *Educational Evaluation: Alternative Approaches and Practical Guidelines* (1987), *Program Evaluation* (1997; 3rd ed., 2004), and author of *Evaluating School Programs* (2nd cd., 2000). He is author or coauthor of numerous articles, monographs, and technical reports in the area of program evaluation.

Michael Scriven took two degrees in mathematics at Melbourne, Australia, before getting a doctorate in philosophy at Oxford. He has taught in the United States, Australia, and New Zealand in departments of mathematics, philosophy, psychology, education, and the history and philosophy of science, including 12 years at the University of California at Berkeley. He has about 350 publications in about 11 fields, including parapsychology, ethics, computer science, and critical thinking. He currently directs the interdisciplinary doctoral program in evaluation at Western Michigan University, a new discipline that he helped to develop. He has served as president of the American Educational Research Association and the American Evaluation Association and as a Fellow of the Center for Advanced Study in the Behavioral Sciences at Stanford University.

James H. Stronge is Heritage Professor in the Educational Policy, Planning, and Leadership Area at the College of William and Mary in Williamsburg, Virginia.

Among his primary research interests are teacher effectiveness and student success and teacher and administrator performance evaluation. Relevant publications include the books *Handbook on Teacher Evaluation: Assessing and Improving Performance* and *Evaluating Professional Support Personnel in Education* (Sage). Most recently he has coauthored the book *Handbook for Qualities of Effective Teachers* for the Association for Supervision and Curriculum Development. He also authored *Qualities of Effective Teachers*. His doctorate is from the University of Alabama in Educational Administration and Planning.

Pamela D. Tucker is an associate professor of education in the Curry School of Education at the University of Virginia in Charlottesville, Virginia. Her research focuses on teacher effectiveness, the nature of the school principalship, and personnel evaluation. Books coauthored with others include *Linking Teacher Evaluation and Student Achievement, Handbook for the Qualities of Effective Teachers* (2004), *Handbook on Teacher Evaluation: Assessing and Improving Performance,* and *Handbook on Educational Specialist Evaluation: Assessing and Improving Performance* (2003), *Educational Leadership in an Age of Accountability* (2003), and *Handbook on Teacher Portfolios for Evaluation and Professional Development* (2000). She has published in professional journals and presented at numerous national conferences on personnel evaluation issues. She has been a classroom teacher and school administrator in a special education setting. She received her doctorate from the College of William and Mary.

Patricia H. Wheeler is the President and Principal Research Associate of EREAPA Associates. She was a Consultant and Senior Research Associate with the federally funded Center for Educational Accountability and Teacher Evaluation at Western Michigan University for five years and a researcher, evaluator, and program administrator at Educational Testing Service for more than 20 years. She has a bachelor's degree in psychology and a master's degree in counseling from the University of Rochester, an MBA in management from Armstrong College, and a PhD in education from the University of California at Berkeley.

Kenneth Wolf is an associate professor in educational psychology in the School of Education at the University of Colorado at Denver. He received his doctorate at Stanford University in Curriculum and Teacher Education, with an emphasis in Language, Literacy, and Culture. His areas of scholarship are in educational assessment and literacy, and his publications have appeared in a variety of scholarly and practitioner journals. He presently teaches classes in research methods and classroom assessment and serves as the faculty fellow for assessment. In this role, he guides academic programs in identifying student learning outcomes, creating effective assessments for measuring student learning, and using the information to inform program improvement to advance student learning. In 1995, he was selected as the university's Teacher of the Year. He has been an English Language Arts teacher and ESL teacher in the Peace Corps and in International Schools in North Africa, South America, and the Mideast.

Sally J. Zepeda is an associate professor and the Graduate Coordinator in the Department of Educational Administration and Policy at the University of Georgia in Athens. One of her primary research interests is in instructional supervision focusing on differentiated and developmental approaches. She has served on editorial boards (*Journal of Curriculum and Supervision*), and she served as the book and review column editor for the *Journal of Staff Development* for ten years. She has written and coauthored several books, book chapters, and articles chronicling the work of principals and teachers in the improvement of instruction. She is a member of the learned society Council of Professors of Instructional Supervision (COPIS), and she is currently working with numerous school systems, state agencies, and professional organization focusing on instructional support systems. In 2004, she guest edited a themed issue on instructional supervision for the National Association of Secondary School Principals, *NASSP Bulletin*. She received her doctorate in curriculum and instruction from Loyola University Chicago and teaches courses including Supervision of Instruction, Trends and Issues in Supervision, Supervision Theory, and Methods of Teacher Evaluation.

Teacher Evaluation and School Improvement

1

Improving the Educational Landscape[1]

James H. Stronge

S o why does teacher evaluation matter? Because teaching matters: "Without capable, high quality teachers in America's classrooms, no educational reform effort can possibly succeed" (Stronge & Tucker, 2003, p. 3). The core of education *is* teaching and learning, and the teaching-learning connection works best when we have effective teachers working with every student every day. While effectiveness can be defined in myriad ways (Cruickshank & Haefele, 2001), the essential issue is that we have the most effective teachers possible guiding the learning of students. And, "without high quality evaluation systems, we cannot know if we have high quality teachers" (Stronge & Tucker, 2003, p. 3).

Teacher evaluation is, first, about documenting the quality of teacher performance; then, its focus shifts to helping teachers improve their performance as well as to holding them accountability for their work.

> In recent years, as the field of education has moved toward a stronger focus on accountability and on careful analysis of variables affecting educational outcomes, the teacher has proven time and again to be the most influential school-related force in student achievement. (Stronge, 2002, p. viii)

Given the emphasis on teacher quality as expressed in No Child Left Behind, as well as legislation, public policy, and practice in every state (and, for that matter, many nations throughout the world), a premium must be placed on high quality teacher evaluation systems to a degree that didn't exist heretofore.

So why does teacher evaluation matter? Because regardless of how well a program is designed, it is only as effective as the people who implement it (Stronge, 1993). Thus, a conceptually sound, well-designed, and properly implemented evaluation system for teachers is an important—indeed, essential—component of an effective school. Despite the fact that proper assessment and evaluation[2] of teachers is fundamental to successful schools and schooling, this key element in school reform is too frequently neglected—due not to the absence of teacher evaluation, but rather to the implementation of poor evaluation systems and poor evaluation practices.

The basic needs in a quality teacher evaluation system are for a fair and effective evaluation based on performance and designed to encourage improvement in both the teacher being evaluated and the school. The purpose of this book is to explore key elements for constructing and implementing fair and effective teacher evaluation systems. This introductory chapter attempts to set the stage by discussing critical components for a quality teacher evaluation system and by identifying how effective teacher evaluation contributes to effective schools. Specifically, the chapter addresses the following questions:

- Why is there a need for quality teacher evaluation?
- What are the basic purposes of a teacher evaluation system?
- What are obstacles to quality teacher evaluation systems?
- What are key features of an effective teacher evaluation system?
- How can a teacher evaluation system be designed for school improvement and personal growth?
- How can self-reflection and feedback improve teaching?

WHY IS THERE A NEED FOR QUALITY TEACHER EVALUATION?

Failures of Educational Reform

Too often, educational reform has produced disappointing results (Clark & Astuto, 1994) or outright failure (Pogrow, 1996). Fullan (1996) noted that one of the reasons for failure of systemic reforms is fragmentation: "Fragmentation occurs when the pressures—and even the opportunities—for reform work at cross purposes or seem disjointed and incoherent" (p. 420). Other reasons for the failure of systemic reforms are that reform efforts are implemented too quickly, from too many directions, and without regard to how the reform effort and the subsequent changes will affect teachers (Bascia & Hargreaves, 2000). Thus, reform efforts fail.

One example of cross-purpose, disjointed, and incoherent reform that is played out in schools on a regular basis is as follows: (1) change school policy for a given innovative teacher program, (2) provide some level of staff development on the prospective innovation, (3) ostensibly implement the innovative practice, and (4) continue to use existing evaluation practices. When reform efforts are disconnected from assessment, there is no way to measure success in the reform effort. Such a disconnect is a formula for failure.

A conceptually sound and properly implemented evaluation system for teachers (and, indeed, for all educators) is a vital component for successful reform efforts. "A rational relationship exists between personnel and programs: If program effectiveness is important and if personnel are necessary for effective programming, then a conceptually sound and properly implemented evaluation system for . . . education personnel is essential" (Stronge, 1993, p. 445).

Balancing the Needs of Teachers and the Needs of the Organization

A dynamic relationship between the teacher and the school exists in a healthy organization: What's good for the organization must also be good for the teacher. This type of synergistic relationship enhances the ability of both the teacher and the school to achieve desired goals. Moreover, balancing individual needs with institutional expectations is essential for fostering productive work environments (March & Simon, 1967, 1993).

An organization's beliefs about performance appraisal are inherent in the assumptions underlying the development of an appraisal system. Castetter (1996) explained that these assumptions "form a basis for achieving integration of individual and organizational interests" (p. 282). If the assumption is correct that individual and institutional goals are intertwined, then it is logical to consider teacher evaluation as a vehicle to facilitate and assess success for both the teacher (e.g., personal growth and performance improvement) and the school (e.g., goal accomplishment and accountability). Thus, teacher evaluation can and should be considered a vital part of the total improvement-restructuring efforts in education.

Improvement can take numerous forms, including

- improvement in performance of individual teachers, and other educators (administrators, support personnel);
- improvement of programs and services to students, parents, and community; and
- improvement of the school's ability to accomplish its mission.

Fostering improvement in teacher evaluation systems means balancing individual and institutional demands. Little (1993) stated that "the language of reform underestimates the intricate ways in which individual and institutional lives are interwoven" (p. 147). As Fullan (1991) noted, "Combining individual and institutional development has its tensions, but the message . . . should be abundantly clear. You cannot have one without the other" (p. 349). In order to accomplish personal and professional goals, the individual needs the institution. In order to accomplish organizational goals, the institution needs the individual.

Purposes of Teacher Evaluation

In addition to the basic function of school, teacher, and, ultimately, student improvement, how can the requisite time, effort, and resources needed to design, implement, and support a quality teacher evaluation system be justified? Why should school divisions develop a teacher evaluation system? The Personnel Evaluation Standards of the Joint Committee on Standards for Educational Evaluation (1988, pp. 6–7) identified ten distinct purposes for high quality teacher evaluation as depicted in Table 1.1.

Table 1.1   Purposes for High Quality Teacher Evaluation From Joint Committee on Personnel Evaluation Standards

- evaluate entry-level educators before certifying or licensing them to teach
- identify promising job candidates
- assess candidates' qualifications to carry out particular assignments
- guide hiring decisions
- assess performance of educators for tenure and promotion decisions
- determine recognition and awards for meritorious contributions
- assist faculty and administrators in identifying strengths and needs for improvement
- plan meaningful staff development activities
- develop remediation goals and activities, and, when necessary
- support fair, valid, and legal decisions for termination

The two most frequently cited purposes of personnel evaluation are accountability and professional growth (see, for example, Danielson & McGreal, 2000; Peterson, 2000). The accountability purpose reflects the need for determining competence of teachers in order to assure that services delivered are safe and effective (McGaghie, 1991) and typically has been viewed as summative in nature. The performance improvement purpose reflects the need for professional growth and development of the individual teacher and typically has been considered to be formative in nature.[3]

There is room in teacher evaluation systems for both accountability and performance improvement purposes. In fact, evaluation systems that include both accountability and personal growth dimensions are both desirable and necessary for evaluation to productively serve the needs of individual teachers and the school and community at large.

Performance improvement and accountability purposes are not competing, but supportive interests—dual interests that are essential for improvement of educational service delivery. These two roles are inextricably intertwined in the total evaluation process. Moreover, a conceptual framework for [teacher] evaluation should emphasize the dynamic relationship between individual and institution where the needs and interests of one fuse with and support the other. (Stronge, 1995, p. 13)

For multiple purposes in teacher evaluation systems to be feasible, however, there must be a rational link between the purposes (Stronge, 1995). McGreal (1988) argued that multiple purposes of evaluation can be met successfully with a single evaluation system when the system is viewed as one component of a larger mission—furthering the goals for the school. This conception of teacher evaluation ties evaluation not only to teacher improvement but also to school improvement. Thus, a comprehensive teacher evaluation system should be rooted in two broad purposes:

- It should be *accountability-oriented*, contributing to the personal goals of the teacher and to the mission of the program, the school, and the total educational organization, and should provide a fair measure of accountability of performance (i.e., summative focus).
- It should be *improvement-oriented*, contributing to the personal and professional development needs of the individual [teacher] as well as improvement within the school (i.e., formative focus). (Stronge, Helm, & Tucker, 1995)

Accountability Orientation

The school or systemwide purposes form the basis of all organizational action. An effective school is one in which the school or systemwide purposes become a unifying agent (Stronge, 1993). A sound evaluation system revolves around the mission and goals of the individual school and of the school district (Danielson & McGreal, 2000; Stronge & Helm, 1991). The evaluation system should facilitate not only accomplishment of the school's goals but also compatibility with and support for individual teacher goals. Given the various implications of the No Child Left Behind Act, accountability to teacher evaluation is required. In addition, if goal accomplishment (both school and teacher) is fundamental to success, then the evaluation system should reflect this orientation (Stronge & Helm, 1992).

Ralph Tyler (1942) reflected the outcome/goal orientation that should serve as a basis for teacher evaluation systems:

A . . . basic assumption involved in evaluation is that the kinds of changes in behavior patterns in human beings which the school . . . seeks to bring about are its educational objectives. The aims of any educational program cannot be stated in terms of the content of the program, or in terms of the methods and procedures followed by the teachers, for these are only means to other ends. Fundamentally, the purposes of education represent these changes in human beings which we hope to bring about through education. (p. 495)

Improvement Orientation

While a teacher assessment and evaluation system should be oriented toward accomplishing the school's goals, it also should be focused on improvement. Goals typically reflect a desired state of being, not an existing state. Therefore, if established goals (for both the individual teacher and the school) are to be achieved, an emphasis on improvement and monitoring of progress toward goal accomplishment is inherent in a sound evaluation system (Stronge & Helm, 1992). Davis, Ellett, and Annunziata (2002) argued that

> School level professionals can choose to either use a system for the evaluation of teaching as a perfunctory and meaningless bureaucratic necessity, or to use the teacher evaluation system as a meaningful process that is viewed as a catalyst for improving teaching and learning in schools. (p. 299)

A teacher performance assessment and evaluation system, properly designed and implemented, supports a balanced relationship between school or districtwide goals and individual teacher professional growth and improvement. For teacher evaluation systems to support professional growth, both organizational barriers (e.g., incompatibility of individual and institutional needs) and personal barriers (e.g., disillusionment, distrust, stress, fear of failure) must be removed (Duke, 1993). Despite the complexities of addressing both improvement and outcome concerns, such a combination is needed. As Saphier (n.d.) surmised,

> There are those who say supervision must be separated from evaluation because it is impossible for teachers to open up and have productive, growth-oriented dialog with one who judges them. In other words, teacher evaluation is incompatible with stimulating teachers' thinking and growth. We reject that notion. The problem is not that evaluators can't supervise, it is that they cannot supervise often enough. (p. 50)

WHAT ARE KEY FEATURES OF AN EFFECTIVE TEACHER EVALUATION SYSTEM?

To achieve a high quality teacher assessment and evaluation system built upon a dynamic balance between school and teacher improvement, several key features are essential. Among these important concepts and criteria are mutually beneficial goals, emphasis on systematic communication, climate for evaluation, technically sound evaluation systems, and use of multiple data sources. Each of these features will be briefly explored on the following pages.

Mutually Beneficial Goals

As described in the previous section of the chapter, goals that are valued by both the individual teacher and the school are vital to successful teacher evaluation systems. Unless the individual and institutional purposes and goals are mutually beneficial, the efforts of the school are likely to be futile, and teacher evaluations based on those efforts will be meaningless. Scriven (1972) described the essence of this position: "It is obvious that if the goals aren't worth achieving then it is uninteresting how well they are achieved" (pp. 126–127). Mutually beneficial and supportive goals make the evaluation process and outcomes more acceptable and beneficial to the school community and the teacher alike. Goals that are mutually beneficial (i.e., compatible) to the individual as well as the institution are essential. Indeed, if goal accomplishment (both for the school and the teacher) is fundamental to success, then the evaluation system should reflect this balanced perspective (Stronge & Helm, 1992).

Emphasis on Systematic Communication

Teacher evaluation systems should reflect the importance that effective communication plays in every aspect of the evaluation process, including aspects that are more public in nature (e.g., public relations) as well as those that require more private communication (e.g., interpersonal relations) (Stronge, 1995).

One aspect of an emphasis on systematic communication in evaluation is that of public disclosure of those elements about which teachers, administrators, and the general public have the right to be informed. Vital elements for public disclosure in teacher evaluation include, among others,

- establishing institutional goals;
- determining evaluation purposes in relation to those goals;
- developing teacher job descriptions and roles and responsibilities;
- identifying acceptable standards of performance;
- delineating procedural guidelines and safeguards embedded in the evaluation system; and
- describing the evaluation timeline.

From the beginning of discussion regarding the identification of the needs/goals of the school through summative evaluations of performance, stakeholders should know as much as possible about the evaluation system. Guidelines should specify "that teachers should be informed about and understand the means by which they will be evaluated and that the evaluation should take into account any factors that affect evaluation results" (Seyfarth, 2002, p. 153).

For teachers and other educators, certain aspects of public communication and disclosure regarding teacher evaluation are codified in law (e.g., state statutory requirements for substantive and procedural due process in evaluation decisions). For the general public, this right to know about the school's evaluation system is reflected both in general public policy and in law. For instance, state open meetings acts typically provide for public disclosure and opportunities for public discussion on all relevant issues of policy and practice being considered by a local school board, with a few narrowly defined exceptions (e.g., personal and confidential information about individuals).

Contrasting with the openness in communication described above, another vital aspect of effective communication is more personal and private in nature—that of ongoing two-way communication between the administrator-evaluator and teacher-evaluatee. Good communication between the evaluator and the evaluatee

- allows for the cooperative development of an evaluation plan;
- provides a systematic opportunity for individual skill enhancement and improved performance;
- provides the teacher with enhanced self-expectations;
- increases the likelihood of changes in performance;
- identifies ways to reach higher standards and correct significant discrepancies; and
- establishes a check and balance system for the evaluation process.

Systematic communication between the evaluator and the evaluatee throughout an evaluation cycle minimizes unintended consequences and maximizes organizationally relevant improvement and performance (Cummings & Schwab, 1973). Since the ultimate goal of any evaluation is to continue successful programs or improve less successful ones, communication in the forms of public disclosure and evaluator-evaluatee communication is essential. Indeed, systematic communication should be viewed as a hallmark of sound evaluation.

Climate for a Quality Evaluation

Evaluation conducted in an environment that fosters mutual trust between the evaluator (representing the school) and the teacher holds the greatest potential for benefiting both parties. Indeed, Castetter (1996) maintained that the quality of the relationship between the evaluator and evaluatee plays a central role in the effectiveness of the evaluation system due to the fact that evaluation is personal and emotional. Although teacher evaluation as a process too frequently has tended to generate suspicion if not outright conflict, trust between evaluator and evaluatee can prevail in an effective personnel evaluation system

(Stronge, 1991). Thus, training for evaluators is critical in developing a sound evaluation system (Castetter, 1996; Seyfarth, 2002).

Satisfaction, an attribute closely associated with the concept of climate (Owens, 1998), should exist if teacher evaluation systems are to fulfill their potential. A critical variable in creating a climate of satisfaction in the workplace is that of consideration (i.e., fair and humane treatment among employees and between employer and employee). George (1987) noted that performance management is based on communications and personal relationships and that, similar to other relationships, "the qualities of empathy, honesty, and esteem need to be consistent" (p. 23).

While a supportive climate is logically related to productive evaluations, there are instances when productive evaluations require less-than-ideal environments. When employees are not measuring up to reasonable performance expectations, and when improvement through remediation will not remedy the problem, then it may be necessary to proceed with meaningful evaluations and, if necessary, to make negative personnel decisions based on the results of those evaluations. It is essential to remember that, ultimately, the best interests of the school's primary clients, the students, must be protected.

Technically Sound Evaluation Systems

While a conceptually sound and technically correct teacher evaluation system will not guarantee effective evaluation, one that is technically flawed and irrational most assuredly *will* guarantee failure. Evaluation systems that are conceptually and technically sound promote the likelihood of achieving desirable outcomes such as those described in the guiding assumptions of the Personnel Evaluation Standards (Joint Committee on Standards for Educational Evaluation, 1988):

- to provide effective service to students and society;
- to establish personnel evaluation practices that are constructive and free of unnecessary threatening or demoralizing characteristics; and
- to facilitate planning for sound professional development experiences.

Technically sound evaluation systems enjoy the benefits of the four basic standards espoused in the Personnel Evaluation Standards:

- *propriety* (i.e., legally and ethically acceptable)
- *utility* (i.e., useful, informative, timely, and influential)
- *feasibility* (i.e., efficient, viable in the context of the organization, and relatively easy to use), and
- *accuracy* (i.e., valid and reliable).

Proper use of the Standards can provide assurances of quality control to stakeholders and can support improvement in the overall personnel evaluation process (Stufflebeam & Brethower, 1987; Stufflebeam & Sanders, 1990).

Use of Multiple Data Sources

An important feature of an effective teacher evaluation system is the use of multiple data sources for documenting performance. The most common method for evaluating teachers is a clinical supervision model consisting of a pre-conference, observation, and post-conference. In fact, as noted in a study conducted by the Educational Research Service (1988), 99.8% of American public school administrators use direct classroom observation as the primary data collection technique. A study conducted in 1996 reached similar conclusions regarding the use of direct classroom observations, with 94.1% of school districts reporting using this technique as a primary method of data collection (Loup, Garland, Ellett, & Rugutt, 1996). However, primary reliance on formal observations in evaluation presents significant problems (e.g., artificiality, small sample of performance).

The creative use of multiple data sources to provide an accurate measure of teacher performance invokes a fuller view of performance than would be available through a more narrowly defined approach to data collection (Peterson, 2000; Stronge & Tucker, 2003). While formal classroom observation can be a significant data source, it is too limiting as a single source of data for teacher evaluation.[4] Thus, teacher performance can be judged best by means more comprehensive and inclusive than merely direct observation.

Using multiple data sources in the teacher evaluation process offers numerous advantages over single source data collection processes (see, for example, Conley, 1987; Dyers, 2001; Peterson, Stevens, & Ponzio, 1998). Among the advantages are those described in Table 1.2.

Table 1.2   Advantages of Using Multiple Data Sources in Teacher Evaluation

- produce a richer textured and more complete portrait of the evaluatee's performance
- collect data in more naturally occurring situations
- integrate primary and secondary data sources in the evaluation
- assure greater reliability in documenting performance
- enhance objectivity in documenting performance
- document performance that is more closely related to actual work
- offer a more legally defensible basis for evaluation decisions

Major sources for teacher evaluation include

- Observation (observation of teachers, e.g., formal classroom/work setting observation, ongoing anecdotal observation of performance, and observation of student work);
- Client feedback (i.e., client interviews or surveys for students, parents, subordinates, and peers);

- Student performance data (i.e., student achievement);
- Portfolios (e.g., actual materials and reflections on performance logs, case notes, lesson plans); and
- Self-evaluation (i.e., self-reflection and analysis of performance).[5]

Integrating multiple data sources in a teacher assessment and evaluation system offers a much more realistic picture of actual job performance and provides a stronger platform upon which to build realistic improvement plans than would be possible with merely a single source of information such as classroom observation. As multiple data sources are properly employed in performance evaluation, the validity and utility of the process can be dramatically enhanced.

WHAT ARE OBSTACLES TO QUALITY TEACHER EVALUATION?

The Joint Committee on Standards for Educational Evaluation identified several prominent criticisms of performance evaluation practices, including those for teachers (Table 1.3).

Table 1.3   Common Failures in Teacher Evaluation Systems

- screening out unqualified persons from certification and selection processes
- providing constructive feedback to individual educators
- recognizing and helping reinforce outstanding service
- providing direction for staff development programs
- providing evidence that will withstand professional and judicial scrutiny
- providing evidence efficiently and at reasonable cost
- aiding institutions in terminating incompetent or unproductive personnel
- unifying teachers and administrators in their collective efforts to educate students

In addition to those common failures noted in Table 1.3, another major obstacle to effective teacher evaluation systems can be the influence of politics. The process is described as both emotionally laden and politically challenging (Stronge & Tucker, 1999). The stakeholders involved in the development of the new evaluation system must buy into the new system.

A study of the evaluation practices in the 100 largest school districts showed that the groups involved in the process represented both external and internal stakeholders (Loup et al., 1996). Groups included business leaders, state department of education staff, central office staff, school site administrators, teachers, teacher organization representatives, parents, and students. "These stakeholders often have conflicting expectations regarding what is good practice and effective reform and, yet, the input and support of these groups is an important aspect of gaining political support for a new evaluation system" (Stronge & Tucker, 1999, p. 339). They have differing views on issues related to both improvement and accountability.

Fullan (1997) stated that "power in school systems is distributed throughout the organization . . . and decision-making is inevitably a bargaining process to arrive at solutions that satisfy a number of constituencies" (p. 5). Bridges and Groves (1999) explained that major decisions must be made regarding ground rules, procedures used in the evaluation system, judgments made through the evaluation system, and the uses of those judgments in an evaluation system. The internal and external stakeholders involved in the development process of an evaluation system have differing views on issues related to both improvement and accountability (Stronge & Tucker, 1999). A major challenge for developing quality teacher evaluation is listening to and accounting for these differing views. Johnson (1997) described the challenge in this way:

> One should not underestimate the difficulties associated with developing and sustaining over time evaluation systems that are valid, reasonably reflective of both teaching and learning literatures, contextually sensitive, politically viable, legitimate, and consistent with what is known about schools as organizations. (p. 85)

In other words, teacher evaluation systems must be legally defensible, useful, feasible, and accurate measures of teacher performance.

HOW CAN A TEACHER EVALUATION SYSTEM BE DESIGNED FOR SCHOOL IMPROVEMENT AND PERSONAL GROWTH?

It is important to consider the unique contributions made by each teacher to the accomplishment of the school's mission if a teacher assessment and evaluation system is to be effective. The goals and roles evaluation (Stronge, 1995; Stronge & Helm, 1990, 1991, 1992)[6] is one evaluation model that offers a practical, research-based model of teacher evaluation that is rooted on the premise of individual-institutional improvement. The model is designed generically for use with a variety of positions, and it may serve well as the basis for an evaluation system not only for teachers but also administrators and support personnel.

The goals and roles evaluation model reflects two phases with six distinct steps in the evaluation process:

Development Phase

1. Identify system needs

2. Develop roles and responsibilities for the job

3. Set standards for job performance

Implementation Phase

4. Document job performance

5. Evaluate performance

6. Improve/maintain professional service

The following provides a brief description of each step as represented in Figure 1.1.

Figure 1.1 Goals and Roles Evaluation Model

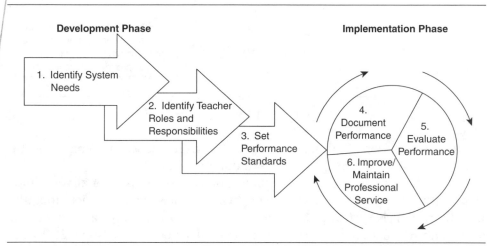

SOURCE: The Goals and Roles Evaluation Model is reprinted with permission from James H. Stronge.

Development Phase

Step 1: Identify System Needs

Each school has specific needs that relate to its mission and that are met through the collective performance of all personnel (e.g., principal, classroom teachers, resource specialists, counselors). A systematic examination of the needs of the school's constituents will help clarify its mission and purpose. Goals should be developed within the context of the greater community and in consideration of relevant variables such as financial and personnel resources. School or districtwide goals often are found in a mission statement, a set of educational goals, a multiyear school plan, or a strategic plan.

Once school goals have been established, attention should turn to the matter of translating those goals into operational terms. One logical way of accomplishing this task is to consider all programs (e.g., math curriculum, guidance-counseling services, athletic program) in light of whether they contribute to the accomplishment of the school's goals and then to relate program objectives to

Figure 1.2 Interconnectivity Among School Goals, Programs, and Personnel

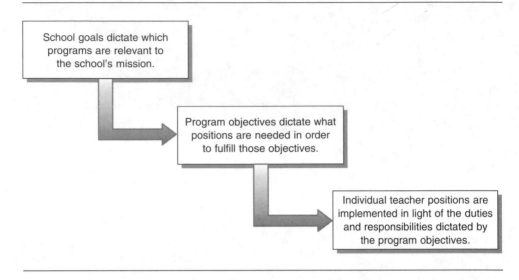

position expectations (Stronge & Tucker, 1995). In essence, a domino effect is initiated in this line of planning and evaluation (Figure 1.2).

Determining the needs of the organization is a prerequisite for all remaining steps if the evaluation process is to be relevant to the school's mission and, ultimately, responsive to public demands for accountability (Castetter, 1996; Connellan, 1978; Goodale, 1992; Locke, 1968; Danielson & McGreal, 2000; Phi Delta Kappa National Study Committee on Evaluation, 1971; Seyfarth, 2002).

Step 2: Identify Teacher Roles and Responsibilities

Accurate and appropriate descriptions of the teacher's roles and responsibilities can be developed only from clear statements of school or district goals and philosophies. Once school goals are determined, then it is only sensible to relate program expectations to position expectations. Typical areas of responsibility might include instructional planning and delivery, assessment, management, and professionalism. These areas of responsibility can serve as a framework for the categorization of more specific responsibilities (or "duties")[7] (Educational Review Office, 1998; Redfern, 1980; Scriven, 1988a, 1988b, 1991; Weiss & Weiss, 1998).

Danielson (1996) explained that "the components of professional practice are a comprehensive framework reflecting the many different aspects of teaching" (p. 2). Danielson's framework includes four domains: planning and preparation, the classroom environment, instruction, and professional responsibilities. This framework can be used to guide both novice and experienced teachers, to provide a structure for reform efforts, and to communicate expectations to the community (Danielson, 1996).

Because job performance must reflect behavior in order to be evaluated, an important addition to the definition of the teacher's role and responsibilities is to identify sample performance indicators. While professional responsibilities are intended to capture the essence of the teacher's job, it is difficult, if not impossible, to document the fulfillment of professional responsibilities without some measurable indication of their accomplishment. Thus, to give meaning to the teacher's professional responsibilities, it is advisable to select a *sampling* of performance indicators that are both measurable and indicative of the job (Bolton, 1980; Cascio, 1998; Keegan, 1975; Redfern, 1980; Sawyer, 2001; Valentine, 1992).

Step 3: Set Performance Standards

Setting standards involves determining a level of acceptable performance. It also may entail determining performance that exceeds acceptable expectations. Because of school needs, available resources, the purpose of a specific position, and a variety of other factors, standards of performance may vary from organization to organization. Although operational definitions for standards may vary from organization to organization, they must be standard and consistently implemented within the school or school district in order to ensure fairness and legal defensibility. This step is important in any goals-oriented personnel evaluation system and should be addressed by both the administrator-evaluator and the teacher (Ellett, Loup, Naik, Chauvin, & Claudet, 1994; Joint Committee on Standards for Educational Evaluation, 1988; Manatt, 1988; McCarthy, Cambron-McCabe, & Thomas, 1998; Phi Delta Kappa National Study Committee on Evaluation, 1971).

Note: Steps 1 through 3 constitute the Development Phase of the goals and roles evaluation model and are intended to be given careful consideration in advance of the Implementation Phase.

Implementation Phase

Step 4: Document Performance

Documentation is the process of recording sufficient information about the teacher's performance to support ongoing evaluation and to justify any personnel decisions based on the evaluation. The basic question is: How will the teacher demonstrate performance of the roles and responsibilities of the job? Documentation procedures need to rely on multiple data sources, as discussed earlier in the chapter (Conley, 1987; Helm, 1994; McGreal, 1988; Peterson, 2000; Stronge & Tucker, 2003; Wilkerson, Manatt, Rogers, & Maughan, 2000).

Step 5: Evaluate Performance

Evaluation is the process of comparing an individual teacher's documented job performance with the previously established roles and responsibilities and acceptable performance standards. While this step clearly entails an end-of-cycle summative evaluation, evaluating performance also must include periodic feedback through formative assessment. By providing feedback throughout the evaluation cycle, the teacher is supported in his or her ongoing efforts to fulfill performance expectations and is able to identify areas of performance that need attention while there is still time to improve. In addition, an opportunity for adequate notice is provided through periodic formative feedback, leading to a fair summative evaluation in which there should be no surprises.

Summative evaluation provides an opportunity to determine individual merit based on performance. Further, the evaluation affords the basis for judging worth, first, by viewing evaluation performance in light of the school's goals and, second, by maintaining compatibility between individual performance and school goals. In an ongoing, systematic evaluation process, identifying system needs and relating those needs to performance ensures that the evaluation is concerned with both the merit (internal value) and worth (external value) of performance (Castetter, 1996; Danielson & McGreal, 2000; Frels & Horton, 1994; Medley, Coker, & Soar, 1984; Scriven, 1973, 1995; Valentine, 1992).

Step 6: Improve/Maintain Professional Service

With an emphasis in the evaluation process on both improvement (i.e., formative) and accountability (i.e., summative) purposes, Step 6 brings the goals and roles evaluation process full circle. Formative aspects of evaluation, intended to provide recognition for noteworthy performance, along with immediate and intermediate feedback for performance improvement and correction where needed, should be ongoing throughout the evaluation process and are implicit in this model. Nonetheless, it is beneficial to provide an explicit step for improving or maintaining professional service as the culmination of the evaluation cycle and as an entrée into the following cycle.[8]

Improving and maintaining professional service may take the form of a variety of personnel decisions, including assisting the teacher in improving performance, personnel transfers, and when necessary, termination. Moreover, this step suggests the importance of professional development with a balance between the interests of the teacher and the interests of the school in a continuous improvement cycle (Little, 1993). After all, the most fundamental purpose of an evaluation is to *improve* both the individual's and institution's performance (Colby, Bradshaw, & Joyner, 2002; Hunter, 1988; Iwanicki, 1990; Johnson, 1997; McGreal, 1988; Stufflebeam, 1983).

While six distinct steps in the goals and roles evaluation model are described, it is important to recognize that the first three steps require intensive attention only during the *Development Phase*. For example, once the organizational goals are established (Step 1), it is not necessary to reassess those goals every year; rather, most schools implement a mid- to long-range systematic plan that is reviewed and updated periodically. In addition, once roles and responsibilities are determined for a given position (Step 2) and performance standards are established (Step 3), there typically exists a need for only review and minor modifications during the *Implementation Phase*. Thus, once the *Development Phase* has been completed, most of the energy and effort are invested in the *Implementation Phase* (the last three steps of the evaluation): documenting performance (Step 4), evaluating performance (Step 5), and improving and maintaining professional service based on that performance (Step 6).

HOW CAN SELF-REFLECTION AND FEEDBACK IMPROVE TEACHING?

A teacher evaluation system that is designed for school improvement and teacher growth can improve teaching. The *value* in evaluation is improving performance. At its most fundamental level, teacher evaluation helps teachers identify the need to improve and then serves as a catalyst for accomplishing those desired improvements. If teacher evaluation is to serve this important function, then there must be a mechanism for communicating why and how to change. Among the viable sources for offering assistance for improving performance are teachers themselves, peers, and supervisors. Each of these sources will be discussed, briefly, in turn.

Teachers Helping Themselves: Self-Reflection

Good teachers don't just teach; rather, they think about what they plan to teach, they teach, and then they think about it again. In essence, they self-reflect. Reflection is a powerful force for improvement. A hallmark of expert teachers is their ability to learn from experience through observation and reflection (Tucker, Stronge, & Gareis, 2002). In fact, expert teachers engage in instructional self-assessment as a mechanism for continual improvement (Covino & Iwanicki, 1996). While experience can be valuable in the teaching profession, "experience without reflection does not improve instruction or teacher effectiveness. Rather, it is the combination of experience and thoughtful analysis that makes teachers more effective" (Tucker et al., 2002, p. 79).

Teachers Helping Teachers: Peer Feedback

Is there value in teachers serving as peer assistants or assessors in a performance evaluation system? The available evidence is quite promising, as suggested in the following references:

- Peer assistance programs offer helpful support to new and veteran teachers in need of improving their skills or knowledge. Most peer review programs have some form of peer assistance in place, thus connecting formative (improvement) and summative (accountability) aspects of teacher evaluation (Hertling, 1999).

- In school districts such as Toledo, Ohio, and Rochester, New York, where peer review programs have been implemented, the percentage of teachers who have received less-than-satisfactory evaluations and, thus, additional assistance and training, has increased dramatically over traditional administrator-only evaluations from 0.1% to 8% (see Pfankuch, 1997).
- Significantly higher percentages of first year teachers have been identified as needing assistance or as not satisfactory through peer-review (Bradley, 1998). Interestingly, "anecdotal accounts suggest that new teachers need and welcome assistance from more-experienced colleagues, even when those colleagues render a negative evaluation" (Ruenzel, 1999, p. 1).
- Consulting teachers typically spend more time observing classrooms, are more thorough in documenting performance, and are able to offer more extensive improvement assistance than traditional administrator evaluators (Pfankuch, 1997).
- "New teachers stay on the job far longer in Columbus, Ohio, than in typical urban districts that lack such programs, where about 50 percent of new hires leave after five years. In Columbus, 80 percent of new teachers remain on the job five years later" (Bradley, 1998, p. 2).
- There is evidence that peer review programs even help satisfactory teachers become better (Pfankuch, 1997).

Administrators Helping Teachers: Supervisor Feedback

Evaluation systems have been criticized for relying merely on observation by an administrator or supervisor as the primary data collection tool (Danielson & McGreal, 2000; Peterson, 2000; Stronge & Tucker, 2003). However, feedback from administrators and supervisors can be used in meeting both the accountability and professional growth purposes of an evaluation system. Supervision, defined in this way, takes the form of instructional leadership (McEwan, 2003).

- "Educators agree that there should be some internal consistency to sequences of subject matter and that there should be articulation between grades of a school and levels of the school system. A supervisor is the one person in a school system who can help achieve these goals" (Oliva & Pawlas, 1997, p. 42).
- "Effective instructional leaders take personal responsibility for making sure that trustworthy research and proven practices are talked about frequently and demonstrated ably in their schools" (McEwan, 2003, p. 36).
- "At the individual school building level, the principal, assistant principal, lead teacher, curriculum coordinator, or curriculum resource teacher can oversee the planning for continuous sequences among courses or grades within a particular school" (Oliva & Pawlas, 1997, p. 42).
- "If supervision is a service designed to help teachers become more effective so that their students will benefit, then staff development is an important domain of supervision" (Oliva & Pawlas, 1997, p. 54).

- "Supervision in the form of curriculum support can be very helpful to the teacher. . . . Curriculum support focuses on materials, objectives, and philosophy of instruction" (Acheson & Gall, 1997, p. 14).

SUMMARY

Effective teacher evaluation is essential for effective schools. The advantages of a quality teacher evaluation system are listed in Table 1.4.

Table 1.4   Advantages of a Quality Teacher Evaluation System

- joint involvement of administrators and teachers in the design process
- inclusion of entire professional staff
- rationally linked school goals and individual responsibilities
- clearly established objectives for the teacher
- a basis for an objective evaluation
- efficiently channeled systemwide resources
- manageable and meaningful evaluator training
- appropriate systematic opportunities for improvement for all professional employees
- more school accountability through meaningful inclusion of all professional employees
- a legally defensible evaluation system in terms of its treatment of teachers and others

In the final analysis, teacher evaluation in its myriad forms is nothing more than a process for determining how an individual, program, or school is performing in relation to a given set of circumstances. When evaluation is viewed as more than this process (i.e., evaluation as an end in itself), it gets in the way of progress and, thus, becomes irrelevant. When evaluation is treated as less than it deserves (i.e., superficial, little or no resource allocation, invalid evaluation systems, flawed implementation designs), the school, its employees, and the public at large are deprived of opportunities for improvement and the benefits that accountability affords. All of us, whatever our relationship to the educational enterprise, deserve high quality evaluation. A teacher assessment and evaluation system that is built squarely upon individual *and* institutional improvement holds the promise of filling this need and better serving our students and our communities.

NOTES

1. Portions of this chapter are derived from an earlier article, "Balancing Individual and Institutional Goals in Educational Personnel Evaluation: A Conceptual Framework," by Stronge (1995).

2. The term *assessment* is used more typically to connote the formative aspects of performance review while *evaluation* is sometimes used to describe the summative aspects. While both terms are used in this chapter, "evaluation" will be considered to be the more inclusive term and, thus, will be used to include both formative and summative aspects of performance review.

3. Please refer to Scriven (1967) for a discussion of the concepts of formative and summative purposes in evaluation.

4. For additional discussion of the limits of classroom observation for teacher evaluation, see Chapter 6, "Using Client Surveys in Teacher Evaluation," in this text.

5. Separate chapters are provided in this text on each of these data sources.

6. Initial work on the model was in the context of evaluation for educational specialists (e.g., school counselor, school psychologist) described as Professional Support Personnel. The model is intended to provide an evaluation paradigm that can be adapted to each individual and institution. Permission is granted for use in this text.

7. Scriven (1991) developed an extensive list of the Duties of the Teacher (DOTT).

8. The length of an evaluation cycle should be determined based on the context of the setting. In some schools and for some teachers (e.g., probationary status), a one-year cycle may be most beneficial, while in other settings, a multiyear cycle may work best.

REFERENCES

Acheson, K. A., & Gall, M. D. (1997). *Techniques in the clinical supervision model: Preservice and inservice applications* (4th ed.). New York: Longman.

Bascia, N., & Hargreaves, A. (2000). Teaching and leading on the sharp edge of change. In N. Bascia & A. Hargreaves (Eds.), *The sharp edge of educational change.* New York: Routledge.

Bolton, D. L. (1980). *Evaluating administrative personnel in school systems.* New York: Teachers College Press.

Bradley, A. (1998, June 3). Peer-review programs catch hold as unions, districts work together. *Teacher Magazine on the Web, 17,* 1–4. Retrieved May 24, 2005, from http://www.teacher magazine.org/ew.vol-7/38peer.h17

Bridges, E. M., & Groves, B. R. (1999). The macro- and micropolitics of personnel evaluation: A framework. *Journal of Personnel Evaluation in Education, 13,* 321–337.

Cascio, W. F. (1998). *Managing human resources: Productivity, quality of work life, profits* (5th ed.). Boston: Irwin McGraw-Hill.

Castetter, W. B. (1996). *The personnel function in educational administration* (6th ed.). Englewood Cliffs, NJ: Prentice Hall.

Clark, D. L., & Astuto, T. A. (1994). Redirecting reform: Challenges to popular assumptions about teachers and students. *Phi Delta Kappan, 75,* 513–520.

Colby, S. A., Bradshaw, L. K., & Joyner, R. L. (2002, April). *Teacher evaluation: A review of the literature.* Paper presented at the Annual Meeting of the American Educational Research Association, New Orleans.

Conley, D. T. (1987). Critical attributes of effective evaluation systems. *Educational Leadership, 44*(7), 60–64.

Connellan, T. K. (1978). *How to improve human performance: Behaviorism in business and industry.* New York: Harper & Row.

Covino, E. A., & Iwanicki, E. F. (1996). Experienced teachers: Their constructs of effective teaching. *Journal of Personnel Evaluation in Education, 10,* 325–363.

Cruickshank, D. R., & Haefele, D. (2001). Good teachers, plural. *Educational Leadership, 58*(5), 26–30.

Cummings, L. L., & Schwab, D. P. (1973). *Performance in organizations—Determinants and appraisal.* Glenview, IL: Scott, Foresman.

Danielson, C. (1996). *Enhancing professional practice: A framework for teaching.* Alexandria, VA: Association for Supervision and Curriculum Development.

Danielson, C., & McGreal, T. L. (2000). *Teacher evaluation: To enhance professional practice.* Alexandria, VA: Association for Supervision and Curriculum Development.

Davis, D. R., Ellett, C. D., & Annunziata, J. (2002). Teacher evaluation, leadership and learning organizations. *Journal of Personnel Evaluation in Education, 16*(4), 287–302.

Duke, D. L. (1993). Removing barriers to professional growth. *Phi Delta Kappan, 74,* 702–712.

Dyers, K. M. (2001). The power of 360° degree feedback. *Educational Leadership, 58*(5), 35–39.

Educational Research Service. (1988). *Teacher evaluation: Practices and procedures.* Arlington, VA: Author.

Educational Review Office. (1998). *The capable teacher.* Retrieved May 24, 2005, from http://www.ero.govt.nz/Publications/eers1998/98no2hl.htm

Ellett, C. D., Loup, K. S., Naik, N. S., Chauvin, S. W., & Claudet, J. G. (1994). Issues in the application of a conjunctive/compensatory standards-setting model to a criterion-referenced, classroom-based teacher certification assessment system: A case study analysis. *Journal of Personnel Evaluation in Education, 8*(4), 349–375.

Frels, K., & Horton, J. L. (1994). *A documentation system for teacher improvement and termination.* Topeka, KS: National Organization on Legal Problems in Education.

Fullan, M. G. (1991). *The new meaning of educational change.* New York: Teachers College Press.

Fullan, M. G. (1996). Turning systemic thinking on its head. *Phi Delta Kappan, 77,* 420–423.

Fullan, M. G. (1997). *What's worth fighting for in the principalship.* New York: Teachers College Press.

George, P. S. (1987). Performance management in education. *Educational Leadership, 44*(7), 32–39.

Goodale, J. G. (1992). Improving performance appraisal. *Business Quarterly, 51*(2), 65–70.

Helm, V. M. (1994, April). *The professional support personnel evaluation model: The use of multiple data sources in personnel evaluation.* Paper presented to the Annual Conference of the American Educational Research Association, New Orleans.

Hertling, E. (1999, May). *Peer review of teachers. ERIC Digest Number 126.* Eugene, OR: ERIC Clearing house on Educational Management. (ERIC Document Reproduction Service No. 429 343)

Hunter, M. (1988). Create rather than await your fate in teacher evaluation. In S. J. Stanley & W. J. Popham (Eds.), *Teacher evaluation: Six prescriptions for success* (pp. 32–54). Alexandria, VA: Association for Supervision and Curriculum Development.

Iwanicki, E. F. (1990). Teacher evaluation for school improvement. In J. Millman & L. Darling-Hammond (Eds.), *The new handbook for teacher evaluation.* Newbury Park, CA: Sage.

Johnson, B. L. (1997). An organizational analysis of multiple perspectives of effective teaching: Implications for teacher evaluation. *Journal of Personnel Evaluation in Education, 11*(1), 69–88.

Joint Committee on Standards for Educational Evaluation (D. L. Stufflebeam, Chair). (1988). *The Personnel Evaluation Standards: How to assess systems of evaluating educators.* Newbury Park, CA: Sage.

Keegan, J. J. (1975). Performance based staff evaluation: A reality we must face. *Educational Technology, 15,* 35–38.

Little, J. W. (1993). Teachers' professional development in a climate of educational reform. *Educational Evaluation and Policy Analysis, 15,* 129–151.

Locke, E. A. (1968). Toward a theory of task motivation and incentives. *Organizational Behavior and Human Performance, 3,* 157–189.

Loup, K. S., Garland, J. S., Ellett, C. D., & Rugutt, J. K. (1996). Ten years later: Findings from a replication of a study of teacher evaluation practices in our 100 largest school districts. *Journal of Personnel Evaluation in Education, 10*(3), 203–226.

Manatt, R. P. (1988). Teacher performance evaluation: A total systems approach. In S. J. Stanley & W. J. Popham (Eds.), *Teacher evaluation: Six prescriptions for success* (pp. 79–108). Alexandria, VA: Association for Supervision and Curriculum Development.

March, J. G., & Simon, H. A. (1967). *Organizations.* New York: John Wiley.

March, J. G., & Simon, H. A. (1993). *Organizations* (2nd ed.). Cambridge, MA: Blackwell Business.

McCarthy, M. M., Cambron-McCabe, N., & Thomas, S. B. (1998). *Public school law: Teachers' and students' rights* (4th ed.). Boston: Allyn & Bacon.

McEwan, E. K. (2003). *Seven steps to effective instructional leadership* (2nd ed.). Thousand Oaks, CA: Corwin.

McGaghie, W. C., (1991). Professional competence evaluation. *Educational Researcher, 20,* 3–9.

McGreal, T. L. (1988). Evaluation for enhancing instruction: Linking teacher evaluation and staff development. In S. J. Stanley & W. J. Popham (Eds.), *Teacher evaluation: Six prescriptions for success.* (pp. 1–29). Alexandria, VA: Association for Supervision and Curriculum Development.

Medley, D. M., Coker, H., & Soar, R. S. (1984). *Measurement-based evaluation of teacher performance.* New York: Longman.

No Child Left Behind Act of 2001, Pub. L. No. 107–110, 115 Stat. 1425 (2002).

Oliva, P. F., & Pawlas, G. E. (1997). *Supervision for today's schools* (5th ed.). New York: Longman.

Owens, R. G. (1998). *Organizational behavior in education* (6th ed.). Boston: Allyn & Bacon.

Peterson, K. D. (2000). Teacher evaluation: A comprehensive guide to new directions and practices (7th ed). Thousand Oaks, CA: Corwin.

Peterson, K. D., Stevens, D., & Ponzio, A. (1998). Variable data sources in teacher evaluations. *Journal of Research and Development in Education, 31*(3), 123–132.

Pfankuch, T. (1997, June 29). Thirty minutes or 30 hours? *Florida Times-Union.* Retrieved May 25, 2005, from http://schoolmatch.com/audit/jacksonville/articles/2a13peer.htm

Phi Delta Kappa National Study Committee on Evaluation. (1971). *Educational evaluation and decision making.* Itasca, IL: F. E. Peacock.

Pogrow, S. (1996). Reforming the wannabe reformers: Why education reforms almost always end up making things worse. *Phi Delta Kappan, 77,* 656–663.

Redfern, G. B. (1980). *Evaluating teachers and administrators: A performance objectives approach.* Boulder, CO: Westview.

Ruenzel, D. (1999, May/June). A jury of your peers? *Teacher Magazine on the Web, 10.* Retrieved May 24, 2005, from http://www.teachermagazine.org/tm/vol-10/08bookes.h10

Saphier, J. (n.d.). *How to make supervision and evaluation really work: Supervision and evaluation in the context of strengthening school culture.* Carlisle, MA: Research for Better Teaching, Inc.

Sawyer, L. (2001). Revamping a teacher evaluation system. *Educational Leadership, 58*(5), 44–47.

Scriven, M. S. (1967). The methodology of evaluation. In R. Tyler, R. Gagne, & M. Scriven (Eds.), *AERA monograph review on curriculum evaluation: No. 1* (pp. 39–83). Chicago: Rand McNally.

Scriven, M. S. (1972). The methodology of evaluation. In C. H. Weiss (Ed.), *Evaluating action programs: Readings in social action and education.* Boston: Allyn & Bacon.

Scriven, M. S. (1973). The methodology of evaluation. In B. R. Worthen & J. R. Sanders (Eds.), *Educational evaluation: Theory and practice.* Belmont, CA: Wadsworth.

Scriven, M. S. (1988a). Duties-based teacher evaluation. *Journal of Personnel Evaluation in Education, 1,* 319–334.

Scriven, M. S. (1988b). Evaluating teachers as professionals: The duties-based approach. In S. J. Stanley & W. J. Popham (Eds.), *Teacher evaluation: Six prescriptions for success* (pp. 110–142). Arlington, VA: Association for Supervision and Curriculum Development.

Scriven, M. S. (1991). *Duties of the teacher (TEMP A Memo).* Kalamazoo, MI: Center for Research on Educational Accountability and Teacher Evaluation, Western Michigan University.

Scriven, M. S. (1995). A unified theory approach to teacher evaluation. *Studies in Educational Evaluation, 21,* 111–129.

Seyfarth, J. T. (2002). *Human resources management for effective schools* (3rd ed.). Boston: Allyn & Bacon.

Stronge, J. H. (1991). The dynamics of effective performance evaluation systems in education: Conceptual, human relations, and technical domains. *Journal of Personnel Evaluation in Education, 4,* 405–411.

Stronge, J. H. (1993). Evaluating teachers and support personnel. In B. S. Billingsley (Ed.), *Program leadership for serving students with disabilities* (pp. 445–464). Richmond: Virginia Department of Education.

Stronge, J. H. (1995). Balancing individual and institutional goals in educational personnel evaluation: A conceptual framework. *Studies in Educational Evaluation, 21,* 131–151.

Stronge, J. H. (2002). *Qualities of effective teachers.* Alexandria, VA: Association for Supervision and Curriculum Development.

Stronge, J. H., & Helm, V. M. (1990). Evaluating educational support personnel: A conceptual and legal framework. *Journal of Personnel Evaluation in Education, 4,* 145–156.

Stronge, J. H., & Helm, V. M. (1991). *Evaluating professional support personnel in education.* Newbury Park, CA: Sage.

Stronge, J. H., & Helm, V. M. (1992). A performance evaluation system for professional support personnel. *Educational Evaluation and Policy Analysis, 14,* 175–180.

Stronge, J. H., Helm, V. M., & Tucker, P. D. (1995). *Evaluation handbook for professional support personnel.* Kalamazoo: Western Michigan University, Center for Research on Educational Accountability and Teacher Evaluation.

Stronge, J. H., & Tucker, P. D. (1995). Performance evaluation of professional support personnel: A survey of the states. *Journal of Personnel Evaluation in Education, 9,* 123–138.

Stronge, J. H., & Tucker, P. D. (1999). The politics of teacher evaluation: A case study of new system design and implementation. *Journal of Personnel Evaluation in Education, 13*(4), 339–360.

Stronge, J. H., & Tucker, P. D. (2003). *Handbook on teacher evaluation: Assessing and improving performance.* Larchmont, NY: Eye on Education.

Stufflebeam, D. L. (1983). The CIPP model for program evaluation. In G. Madaus, M. S. Scriven, & D. L. Stufflebeam (Eds.), *Evaluation models: Viewpoints on educational and human services in evaluation* (pp. 117–141). Boston: Kluwer-Nijhoff.

Stufflebeam, D. L., & Brethower, D. M. (1987). Improving personnel evaluations through professional standards. *Journal of Personnel Evaluation in Education, 1,* 125–155.

Stufflebeam, D. L., & Sanders, J. R. (1990). Using the Personnel Evaluation Standards to improve teacher evaluation. In J. Millman & L. Darling-Hammond (Eds.), *The new handbook of teacher evaluation: Assessing elementary and secondary school teachers* (pp. 416–428). Newbury Park, CA: Sage.

Tucker, P. D., Stronge, J. H., & Gareis, C. R. (2002). *Handbook on teacher portfolios for evaluation and professional development.* Larchmont, NY: Eye on Education.

Tyler, R. W. (1942). General statement on evaluation. *Journal of Educational Research, 35,* 492–501.

Valentine, J. W. (1992). *Principles and practices for effective teacher evaluation.* Boston, MA: Allyn & Bacon.

Weiss, E. M., & Weiss, S. G. (1998). *New directions in teacher evaluation.* Washington, DC: ERIC Clearinghouse on teaching and teacher education. (ERIC Document Reproduction Service No. ED429052)

Wilkerson, D. J., Manatt, R. P., Rogers, M. A., & Maughan, R. (2000). Validation of student, principal, and self-ratings in 360° feedback® for teacher evaluation. *Journal of Personnel Evaluation in Education, 14*(2), 179–192.

Part I

Designing a Teacher Evaluation System

Building the Foundation

2

Teacher Roles and Responsibilities

Patricia H. Wheeler

Michael Scriven

W hen building a teacher evaluation system, the developers are usually aware of the purpose—for example, for accountability or improvement, or a mixture of these. However, once the purpose is specified, the next steps are often taken too quickly. Although it is crucial to write criteria, design assessments, set standards, and prepare procedures, the next step should be selection of an appropriate foundation(s) upon which to build a valid system. The foundation provides "the rationale for the attributes and domains covered by a teacher evaluation system" (Wheeler, 1995, p. 3). Possible foundations include research on teaching, government policies, professional expertise, theories of teaching and learning, and teacher roles and responsibilities.

Once an appropriate type of foundation is identified and tentatively specified, the foundation should undergo a careful review—a descriptive or prescriptive content analysis with substantial input by teachers and administrators. Then the next steps of writing criteria and indicators, selecting and/or designing assessment instruments, determining standards for various levels of performance, and preparing evaluation procedures can begin. These further steps are just as important as identifying the foundation. The use of a suitable foundation is a necessary, but not a sufficient, condition for a valid and legally defensible system. It also helps to ensure that the criteria reflect the school's and district's missions and policies.

The failure to use an appropriate and a solid foundation could have serious consequences for the teacher evaluation system and, hence, for the educational services provided by the school. For example, the criteria could be incomplete or include indefensible requirements, or the standards could be too high or too low, in which case good teachers will be overlooked and poor ones retained and promoted.

PURPOSES OF TEACHER EVALUATION SYSTEMS

The purpose of a particular teacher evaluation system is one key to selecting the appropriate foundation upon which to build that system. There is a multitude of purposes for evaluating teachers, some of which are discussed in Chapter 1 of this volume. Possible purposes include the following:

- Hiring
- Assigning
- Performance evaluation
- Pre-tenure retention/termination
- Tenure
- Post-tenure retention/termination
- Promotion/career ladder
- Salary decisions
- Reduction in force
- Retirement exemption
- Licensing/credentialing
- Awards/recognition
- Self-assessment
- Mentoring appointment

Ten purposes for evaluating teachers are identified in the Personnel Evaluation Standards developed by the Joint Committee on Standards for Educational Evaluation (1988): entry to training, certification/licensing, defining a role, selection, performance reviews, counseling for staff development, merit awards, tenure decisions, promotion decisions, and termination.

Wise, Darling-Hammond, McLaughlin, and Bernstein (1984) list four basic purposes of teacher evaluation, the first two focusing on improvement and the last two on accountability: individual staff development, school improvement, individual personnel decisions, and school status decisions. Wheeler (1991) identifies several uses of teacher evaluation for personnel decisions: hiring, job assignments, formal evaluations, retention and termination, tenure, salary and other compensation, career ladder and promotion, reduction in force, and exemption from age-based retirement. The purposes of the teacher evaluation system must be clearly stated and the users and uses delineated before the determination is made regarding which foundations to use.

WHAT ARE SOME POSSIBLE FOUNDATIONS FOR TEACHER EVALUATION?

Just as there are multiple purposes for a teacher evaluation system, there are several types of foundations upon which a system can be built (Wheeler, 1991, 1992a, 1994b, 1995). The foundations covered in this chapter are of eight types:

1. What teachers are doing or say they are doing as part of their job

2. What administrators and others would like teachers to be doing

3. What others say good teachers do

4. What students, their parents, and other clients and stakeholders like to see in a teacher

5. What research says effective teachers do

6. What theories of teaching and learning say teachers should do

7. What the outcomes of teaching are

8. What the roles and responsibilities of teachers are

Examples of each of these types of foundations are provided below, and some of the problems associated with each are delineated.

What Teachers Are Doing or Say They Are Doing as Part of Their Job

One type of foundation relies on input from teachers about what they are doing as part of their job. Examples are job analysis studies, teacher surveys, teacher consensus about the nature of their job, logs or self-reports of individual teachers about what they do, and the teaching norms and traditions of the school.

Job analysis is a type of research that focuses on the job components of what a teacher is doing. It identifies the tasks and activities as well as the knowledge, skills, and abilities needed to perform those tasks. It can be based on extensive and comprehensive observations of teachers at work or on surveys of teachers about their jobs. An example of a job analysis that looked at the coverage of an assessment for potential teachers was that conducted for the National Teacher Examination (NTE) Core Battery by Rosenfeld, Thornton, and Skurnik (1986). These researchers identified six major professional functions of teachers:

1. Managing and influencing student behavior

2. Clerical, administrative, and other professional functions

3. Assessing, grading, and recording student learning progress and evaluating instructional effectiveness

4. Planning the lessons, selecting the materials, and previewing the instructional program

5. Implementing the planned instructional program, using a variety of techniques

6. Identifying students with individual or similar instructional needs and teaching them accordingly

Based on their own experience, teachers can be asked to delineate their own job functions and professional responsibilities and to identify those areas that affect how a person performs the job of teaching. This can be done in a focus group, to build consensus among the teachers on the nature of their jobs; through self-reports by individual teachers, which later need to be compiled; or by ascertaining the teaching norms and traditions of the school through a close look over time at how the school functions.

What Administrators and
Others Would Like Teachers to Be Doing

The second kind of foundation involves what administrators and others say concerning how teachers should do their job. It is sometimes referred to as style-based evaluation. Examples of evaluation systems based on such foundations are programs requiring the use of certain teaching practices or strategies, the imposition of specific styles on teachers by other educators or policy makers, mandates to use only certain publishers' curriculum materials, and the preferences of those doing the evaluating as well as other individuals or groups.

A teacher evaluation system using this type of foundation focuses on a certain style of or approach to teaching. The criteria reflect what a teacher using that style of teaching ought to be doing. Examples are cooperative learning, whole language instruction, lecturing, and team teaching. The assumptions are that a particular teaching style is best for the students in that school and that only teachers who use that style well are good teachers. Ornstein (1991) pointed out that such assumptions are questionable: "Teacher style is a matter of choice and comfort, and what works for one teacher with one set of students may not work for another" (p. 72). Limiting teachers' choices of curriculum materials can decrease the effectiveness of a teacher and can limit the teacher's use of various instructional and assessment methodologies to those reflected in the curriculum materials.

This foundation for evaluation may be appropriate when a school is trying to implement a new instructional program or strategy and wants to see how well each teacher is doing with this style. However, it is not an appropriate foundation for most teacher evaluation systems and should not be used for personnel decisions. Scriven (1994b) reminded us, "The imposition of style requirements, even if they were based on good evidence overall, imposes a handicap on many individual teachers and hence on the children" (p. 87).

What Others Say Good Teachers Do

The collective professional judgment of a group of experts is commonly used as the foundation for a teacher evaluation system. As a group or individually, these experts identify the criteria and indicators that reflect what they regard as good teaching. Such experts typically include experienced teachers, curriculum specialists, administrators, teacher trainers, other college faculty, and researchers. Frameworks for teaching (e.g., Danielson, 1996) are one example for such a foundation. National organizations have developed standards for teachers that can be used as part of a foundation. These include the Interstate New Teacher Assessment and Support Consortium and the National Board for Professional Teaching Standards. The first of these focuses on new teachers, whereas the second focuses on more experienced teachers seeking nationally recognized professional certification above that required in their state. In addition, some professional associations offer documents that can be helpful in developing a teacher evaluation system (e.g., American Association of School Personnel Administrators, 1995; National Council of Teachers of Mathematics, 1991).

Raths (1999) cautioned educators and the public about using such standards without carefully reviewing and questioning them:

> The pursuit of ways to distinguish competent teachers from incompetent teachers is a noble enterprise. If our profession is to advance, we need to have useful and effective criteria for evaluating our teacher education programs and our teacher candidates. However, we cannot reach this goal merely by stipulating that any particular set of standards is the answer. We need to receive all proposals for teacher standards with respect and challenge the claims made for them. (p. 142)

Such national and regional or state teaching standards, as well as standards from other local education agencies, can be part of the foundation for a teacher evaluation system. However, they should be carefully examined before being adopted as part of a local teacher evaluation system. These standards may be narrowly focused, may reflect the interests and goals of the association, and may not be relevant for the local context.

What Students, Their Parents, and Other Clients and Stakeholders Like to See in a Teacher

One can also ask the clients of teachers—the students, parents, community members, local business leaders, and others—what makes a teacher a good teacher. They will tend to base their responses on the array of teacher behaviors to which they have been exposed throughout their own schooling, on their own educational needs, and on comments about teachers they have heard from others.

At the postsecondary level, student ratings of teacher performance are often used to evaluate faculty (Braskamp, Brandenburg, & Ory, 1984; Centra, 1980). This approach is based on client satisfaction. By looking at characteristics of faculty members receiving high ratings compared to those receiving low ratings, one can infer what characteristics students like in their teachers. At the elementary and secondary levels, not only are students a potential source of information about what teachers do and what constitutes good teaching performance, but so are other stakeholders—parents, community agencies, local employers.

Although this is not likely to be a strong foundation by itself, it can help reinforce or enhance other foundations and, at times, make one aware of areas that may have been overlooked. A teacher evaluation system could be built, in part, based on the input of these various client groups and other stakeholders about what makes a good teacher. There is apt to be more acceptance of the system if this is one of the foundations used; at least, these clients and stakeholder groups will have an opportunity for input on the criteria the system covers.

What Research Says Effective Teachers Do

Another foundation for a teacher evaluation system involves reviewing research on teaching. An evaluation system can be built based on the results of such studies, which typically look at effective and, in some cases, ineffective teachers. The researchers identify the practices and behaviors associated with effective teachers (effective teaching research or process-product studies).

Research on effective teaching has identified a number of teaching practices that are associated with desired results (e.g., Brophy & Good, 1986; Darling-Hammond & Youngs, 2002). A comprehensive review of research on effective teaching has frequently been used as a foundation for teacher evaluation systems. While a research foundation is a highly desirable attribute of a teacher evaluation system, it should be used with caution as a single source for building the evaluation system. As McDonald and Elias (1976) found in the Beginning Teacher Evaluation Study, what worked well in one subject or at one grade level or in one teaching context did not necessarily work well in another. The generalizability of findings from research on effective teaching is questionable; research alone should not be a basis for building a teacher evaluation system. As Scriven (1990) pointed out, "Many researchers who have encouraged the use of this research by schools and colleges—and states and districts—as a basis for a teacher evaluation system have seriously misled their readers and clients" (p. 19).

Shuell (1993), based on his premise that teaching and learning must be addressed simultaneously, identified three considerations that should be taken into account in the use of such research. First, few studies look at "the relationship between specific teaching practices and the consequent learning processes elicited in students" (p. 302). Second, such studies often look at learning and cognition in isolation from other concerns such as metacognitive, affective, motivational, and developmental processes. And finally, "research on teaching and learning should be concerned with teacher evaluation content and context of learning as well as the process of learning" (p. 302).

Research findings are useful in preservice teacher training, inservice staff development, and the review of a teacher evaluation system to ensure that no key areas or criteria and performance indicators have been overlooked. However, effective teaching research and process-product studies should not be a sole foundation for building a teacher evaluation system.

What Theories of Teaching and Learning Say Teachers Should Do

Scriven (1991) defined theories as "general accounts of a field of phenomena, generating at least explanations and sometimes also predictions and generalization" (p. 360). The emphasis in theories is on explanations. These may be based on styles or preferences of key leaders in education or on the findings of research. However, Scriven pointed out that explanatory power is not the only indicator of a sound theory (and thus solid foundations). Other aspects to consider include "predictive power and accuracy, economy of assumptions, fertility of implications, cross-field support (e.g., by analogy), and simplicity of claims" (p. 360).

Theories that are likely to inform teacher evaluation systems are described as middle-range theories grounded in practice. They provide theoretical propositions that shape inquiry and generate further research, but are more limited in scope and longevity than the type of theory described by Scriven (1991). Middle-range theories that could be considered as foundations for teacher evaluation systems include theories of teaching, cognitive theories of teachers' thought processes, and theories of the cognitive development of teachers.

Examples of theories of teaching are provided by Joyce and Weil (1986), who described four models of teaching, each justified by a theory and linked to outcomes of teaching—social interaction models, information processing models, personal models, and behavior modification models. In their theory of teaching, Medley, Coker, and Soar (1984) proposed three levels of teaching—environmental maintenance, implementation of instruction, individualization—all of which occur simultaneously in a classroom.

Theories in cognitive psychology of teaching look at teachers' thought processes. They cover such areas as planning, decision making, judgments, implicit theories, expectations, and attributions (Clark & Peterson, 1986). Cognitive psychologists have developed theories of the cognitive development of teachers. Costa, Garmston, and Lambert (1988), for example, offered a set of benchmarks that teachers should attain with training and experience. The benchmarks are defined by three stages of teacher development (entry, tenure, master) and by four cognitive development areas (learning, doing, valuing, thinking). Such theories are not, by themselves, sufficient as a valid foundation for a teacher evaluation system, although they can supplement other foundations.

What the Outcomes of Teaching Are

As is often done for summative evaluation of educational programs, teachers are sometimes evaluated based on the extent of their attainment of a set of goals and objectives and on the outcomes of their teaching. Examples include management by objectives, professional development goals, student outcomes, and teacher productivity.

In management by objective, the criteria for the evaluation are based on the contributions of each teacher to the overall objectives and common goals delineated by the school. The goals and objectives are set by a local policy group (e.g., the school board, the school site council) or by the school or district administration, although some teachers may be involved in the setting of goals and objectives.

As part of their own professional growth, teachers may be asked to set developmental goals for themselves. These goals are usually written with the assistance of an administrator or a mentor teacher and are agreed on by both parties. Each teacher is evaluated based on his or her own goals. This foundation is more frequently used for formative than summative evaluation.

An array of student outcomes can be used as a foundation to evaluate teachers. They include direct measures of student learning and development (behavioral, physical, social). The rationale behind a student outcomes foundation is that "student learning is both the goal and the product of teaching" (Robinson, 1984, p. 15). Standardized tests are the most frequently used student outcomes measure for evaluating teachers, although such use of these tests can have serious limitations (e.g., Berk, 1988; Haertel, 1986; Millman, 1981; Wheeler, 1995/1996). In the current era of No Child Left Behind, schools are evaluated based on test results in reading and math. In such a high-stakes situation for schools, the focus of teacher evaluation too often becomes test results. Goldberg (2005) felt that, "Schools will not be able to attract high-quality teachers to a system that stifles richness and creativity and emphasizes a narrow band of knowledge and a very restricted set of tests to measure that knowledge" (p. 394). Teachers will focus their teaching on what is measured on the tests if they are used for evaluating teachers. Regarding the No Child Left Behind legislation, Neill (2003) pointed out,

All our children deserve a high-quality education, not classrooms transformed into test-prep centers. In most states, the law will make scores on standardized reading and math tests the sole measure of student progress. Test proponents claim that these exams measure what is most important, but any realistic assessment of state tests reveals that much of what is important is not tested and much of what is tested in not of major importance. (p. 225)

Tests do not measure much of what a teacher does, and some teachers have much more responsibility for promoting students' reading and math learning than do other teachers. It is difficult to link test results to the performance of individual teachers, as there are so many other confounding variables. Droege (2004) pointed out that

The ability to raise test scores is . . . one component of a teacher's quality. . . . Test scores do not reflect the teacher's skills or strategies for assessing students' diverse learning styles, adapting instruction to individual levels or needs within a classroom, observing students for signs of understanding or confusion, and infusing curriculum with personality, excitement, and imagination to make it inspiring. (p. 612)

Sometimes other student outcome measures are used, such as measures of academic, physical, social, and personal development. Examples include grades, promotion and graduation rates, performance on physical tasks (e.g., pull-ups, fine motor coordination tasks), referrals for disciplinary action, attendance, and service hours to the school. Although such indicators may seem objective, they can be difficult to link to the performance of an individual teacher, and they reflect only part of a teacher's array of responsibilities and of the content and skills taught to students by that teacher.

Teacher productivity reflects the accomplishments of a teacher during the period covered by the evaluation. The measures used most often in elementary and secondary schools for teacher evaluation are listed above under student outcomes. Examples of other productivity variables include number of students taught, volume of content covered or number of activities completed in a given period of time, number of articles and books published, amount of resources used, and cost per student. Productivity approaches to teacher evaluation tend to quantify teaching. It must be kept in mind that outcomes-based teacher evaluation systems "can drive instruction and teaching behavior rather than promote diverse instructional approaches and curricular content for different teachers and students" (Wheeler, 1994c, p. 3).

What the Roles and Responsibilities of Teachers Are

Rather than building a teacher evaluation system on a foundation of what teachers are doing or what someone thinks they should be doing, it is more appropriate to consider what teachers are hired to do—that is, their professional roles and responsibilities in given positions. This includes their professional responsibility to fulfill entry-level requirements for the job and to keep current on fulfillment of requirements.

The teacher's roles and responsibilities, including entry-level requirements, should be delineated in a job description or similar document at the time of employment by the school (McConney et al., 1996). A job description should cover the primary function, qualifications, and organizational relationships (Stronge & Tucker, 2003). Professional roles and responsibilities within the primary function can include such areas as being knowledgeable in the subject matter, earning and maintaining current teaching credentials, reviewing and selecting curriculum materials, designing instruction and planning lessons, monitoring and assessing student learning, communicating with parents, maintaining records of student learning, fulfilling applicable laws and government regulations, and participating in professional service and staff development activities.

Evaluation systems for inservice teachers should have built-in procedures for monitoring ongoing fulfillment of applicable licensing and credentialing requirements. Teachers have a professional responsibility to maintain minimal levels for such requirements over time. For example, although when a teacher was licensed there may have been evidence that he or she had a minimally acceptable level of subject-matter knowledge, changes in the field or years of not teaching certain subject areas might indicate the necessity for a teacher evaluation system to monitor subject-matter knowledge with regard to licensure requirements as part of evaluation and job assignment. Or state licensing requirements may have been updated, and changes may apply to all teachers, including those currently teaching.

In addition to the licensure and credentialing requirements, there may be other governmental requirements that affect public employees, including teachers. Usually these are designed to protect the public. For example, they might be concerned with criminal records, federal or state safety codes (e.g., storage of chemicals in the science lab, proper use of safety equipment in the wood shop), or the need for special training (e.g., first aid/CPR for physical education teachers and coaches). Such licensing and governmental requirements should be addressed by a teacher evaluation system, since they are directly related to the roles and responsibilities of teachers.

Scriven (1988b) referred to this type of teacher evaluation system as duties-based teacher evaluation, or DBTE. Table 2.1 contains an outline of the Duties of the Teacher (DOTT) (Scriven, 1988a, 1988b, 1994a), which can provide a good starting point for building an evaluation system on a foundation of roles and responsibilities.

HOW DOES ONE CHOOSE A FOUNDATION?

When choosing a foundation upon which to build a teacher evaluation system, one must consider some of the problems associated with the major types

Table 2.1   Outline of the Duties of the Teacher

1. **KNOWLEDGE OF SUBJECT MATTER**
   A. In the fields of special competence
   B. In across-the-curriculum subjects

2. **INSTRUCTIONAL COMPETENCE**
   A. Communication skills
   B. Management skills
       i. Management of process
       ii. Management of progress
       iii. Management of emergencies
   C. Course construction and improvement skills
       i. Course planning
       ii. Selection and creation of materials
       iii. Use of available resources (a. Local; b. Media; c. Specialists)
       iv. Evaluation of course, teaching, materials, and curriculum

3. **ASSESSMENT COMPETENCE**
   A. Knowledge of student assessment
   B. Test construction/administration skills
   C. Grading/ranking/scoring practices
       i. Process
       ii. Output
   D. Recording and reporting student achievement
       i. Knowledge of reporting achievement
       ii. Reporting process (to: a. Students; b. Administrators; c. Parents; d. Others)

4. **PROFESSIONALISM**
   A. Professional ethics
   B. Professional attitude
   C. Professional development
   D. Service to the profession
       i. Knowledge of the profession

5. **OTHER DUTIES TO THE SCHOOL AND COMMUNITY**
   A. Committee work
   B. Community work
   C. Special school assignments (e.g., lunchroom, coaching)

SOURCE: Michael Scriven, P.O. Box 69, Point Reyes, CA 94956; e-mail scriven@aol.com; fax 415-663-1913. Comments of all kinds are extremely welcome.

NOTE: An expanded version of the outline is in Scriven (1994a), where it is prefaced by a lengthy discussion of concepts, use, and more.

of foundations. Examples of such problems (Wheeler, 1995) are shown in Table 2.2. These problems and others discussed in this chapter should also be addressed when reviewing or revising an existing teacher evaluation system.

Table 2.2   Examples of Problems With Major Types of Foundations

---

FOUNDATION: *What teachers are doing or say they are doing as part of their job*

Problems with this foundation:

Assumes that what teachers say they are doing is an accurate and comprehensive portrayal of their jobs, but such self-reporting is often incomplete or may overlook critical responsibilities that apply in intermittent years.

Needs teachers who can clearly articulate and describe what they do.

Requires careful interpretation of what teachers say and caution in not over- or underemphasizing various aspects of the job.

Assumes that what teachers are doing is best for students, parents, schools, and communities, but this is not always true.

Assumes that the long-standing norms and traditions of the school reflect the needs of current students and effective use of available resources.

Leads to a tendency for new teachers to rely heavily on what they learned during their teacher training programs rather than what is best for the students assigned to them and the context in which they are now working.

FOUNDATION: *What administrators and others would like teachers to be doing*

Problems with this foundation:

Assumes that what works well for one teacher in a given context with certain students works well for other teachers, regardless of teaching context, which is unreasonable.

Evaluates teachers for their style rather than fulfillment of their responsibilities. Teachers should not be penalized for using a particular style unless it violates the law or another style is mandated by law or policy, in which case it becomes a responsibility.

Sprouts from the personal preferences of one or more individuals and may not be in the best interest of the teachers or of the students, parents, and community.

Can discourage the use of diverse instructional approaches and curricular content that may be more appropriate for certain teachers and students. This can especially be true when teachers are limited to using the curriculum materials of certain publishers and are not free to select what they judge is best for their students.

Takes away the responsibility of each teacher as a professional educator to determine how best to meet the needs of students in order to promote student learning and improve student behavior effectively.

Is clearly invalid for evaluating many teachers, even if the approach works well for some teachers.

FOUNDATION: *What others say good teachers do*

Problems with this foundation:

Tends to encourage too much reliance on external standards and guidelines.

May be narrowly focused and/or reflect the interest of a certain association or political agenda.

May be irrelevant to the local teaching context and teacher roles and responsibilities.

FOUNDATION: *What students, their parents, and other clients and stakeholders like to see in a teacher*

Problems with this foundation:

Sprouts from the experience, needs, and personal preferences of the individuals giving input and may not be in the best interest of the teachers or the students, parents, and communities.

Needs input from individuals who can clearly articulate what they would like to see in a teacher.

May focus on characteristics of teachers not associated with good teaching, for example, type of rewards given, or use of time for noninstructional activities.

Bases satisfaction levels on limited interaction of a client with a teacher. Does not look at other things that teachers do that do not involve the clients directly.

Is based on a marketing model where industries evaluate their products and services based on client satisfaction (e.g., student and parent ratings) and sales (e.g., student enrollment requests for a given teacher). This model is not appropriate for the teaching profession.

Results in skewed input, ratings, and results due to low levels of participation. Can be costly to get high levels of participation in obtaining input on what they want to see in a teacher.

FOUNDATION: *What the research says effective teachers do*

Problems with this foundation:

Assumes that the same variables that correlate positively with what is regarded as good teaching or with student outcomes are themselves sound bases for evaluating teachers.

May overlook some key variables, because the teaching variables examined usually are determined by the researcher or the sponsor of the research.

Is based on research results that imply guilt by association, using designated teacher characteristics and generalizing those qualities associated with certain types of teachers—such as gender, height, ethnicity, college attended, academic major, or primary language—to all teachers.

Encourages the tendency to generalize research findings across teachers and different teaching contexts when it is inappropriate or unjustifiable to do so.

Makes it easy to overlook the fact that the measures for assessing students and teachers yield only estimates of their levels of performance and that often steps are not taken to minimize error of measurement or to consider error factors when interpreting results.

Promotes the tendency to infer causality from correlational research when there is no basis for assuming direct or even indirect causality.

Can result in adverse impact when used for career decision and personnel actions, and lead to decisions and actions that are legally indefensible and/or technically unsound.

(Continued)

Table 2.2 (Continued)

FOUNDATION: What theories of teaching and learning say teacher should do

 Problems with this foundation:

As with styles, is often based on the preferences of key leaders in the field rather than what works well for a given teacher and his or her students.

Is limited to the aspect of teaching and learning under consideration.

Is based on a certain orientation or way of thinking about teaching and learning, such as constructivism or cognitive psychology, that may be inappropriate for the teacher and school and that limits the ways of looking at teaching and learning.

Can be easily overlooked as only being attempts to explain phenomena and can tend to give theories more emphasis than warranted.

FOUNDATION: What the outcomes of teaching are

 Problems with this foundation:

Limits the primary focus of the teacher evaluation system to the designated outcome variables.

Becomes more difficult to give meaningful and constructive feedback to teachers on their teaching behaviors because evaluation results shed little light on the teaching behaviors and processes that led to those outcomes.

Is unable to control for all the confounding factors when student outcome measures are used, such as test scores, absentee rates, and misconduct referrals. Examples of such confounders are missing test data, lack of appropriate tests for disabled or non-English-proficient students, irregular test administration and scoring practices, a schoolwide flu epidemic, tampering with student record computer files, and loss of key records in a fire.

Is impossible to isolate the impact that a given teacher has had on the learning and behavior outcomes of individual students, due to the many context features beyond the control of the teacher and the school that affect student outcomes.

Encourages teachers to focus their energies on those outcomes that will be assessed rather than the needs of the students and the teachers' responsibilities. Especially in high-stakes situations, the use of this type of foundation can lead to such unintended consequences as teaching to the test, various forms of cheating when administering and scoring the tests, or not implementing the student conduct policy if misconduct referrals are used for evaluation instead of keeping disruptive students in class.

May be inappropriate or irrelevant for teachers who are confronted with challenging situations, difficult teaching contexts, or students with extensive behavior and learning problems.

Leads to basing evaluation criteria on outcomes that do not clarify the role of the teacher and the teacher's responsibilities.

Assumes that attaining the designated outcomes is the primary function of the teacher.

FOUNDATION: What the roles and responsibilities of teachers are

Problems with this foundation:

Tends to focus on the general responsibilities of all teachers, and might overlook additional responsibilities or specific ones applicable to a few teachers.

May not come with adequate resources for teachers to implement or government regulations may be short-lived, reflecting current political agendas.

May lack delineated teacher responsibilities—either general ones for all teachers or specific ones for each teaching position—in job descriptions or elsewhere.

Requires fully informing teachers about the state, district, and school procedures, policies, and curriculum frameworks, as teachers will be evaluated for their implementation of these.

Requires delineation of teacher responsibilities as well as familiarity with pertinent laws and regulations and with state, district, and program requirements.

The choice of the wrong foundation can have serious consequences. First, the attributes of teaching and the areas covered by the evaluation system may be incomplete and/or poorly defined. Second, the criteria and standards will lack validity and will not provide a justifiable basis for career actions and personnel decisions regarding teachers.

The problems with the eighth type of foundation, roles and responsibilities, are weaknesses that should be overcome by a school or district before it develops or revises a teacher evaluation system, whereas many of the problems listed for the other seven types of foundations cannot be easily overcome or are, in and of themselves, inherent weaknesses that can lead to an invalid system. Despite the potential and real problems with these types of foundations, all foundations can be useful in some aspect of teacher evaluation by providing enlightening perspectives for some of the evaluation tasks or by helping to ensure that key areas are not overlooked.

A system designed to evaluate a teacher's performance on the job would be invalid if it did not address roles and responsibilities. That type of foundation is the keystone for a system used to make personnel decisions, such as retention, dismissal, promotion, transfer, or compensation. The other seven types of foundations can be useful for such purposes as professional development, teacher self-evaluation, teacher preparation, licensure and credentialing, professional certification, and special awards or recognition. Again, it is critical to keep in mind what the professional roles and responsibilities of the teacher are and to ensure that the system addresses them, even if it relies heavily on one or more other types of foundations.

HOW ARE TEACHER ROLES AND RESPONSIBILITIES DETERMINED?

If the primary purpose of the teacher evaluation system is to determine how well each teacher is performing his or her job, then the most solid and valid foundation to use is the eighth: what teachers should be doing—that is, their roles and responsibilities. Ultimately, we must be concerned with the question of whether teachers are doing what they have been hired to do, that is, fulfilling their assigned roles and responsibilities.

The development of a list of roles and responsibilities can be a challenging and time-consuming process. However, it is essential to the development of a sound teacher evaluation system with valid criteria. One place to start is with the job descriptions, which should cover position title, qualifications, general job responsibilities, specific job responsibilities, physical and mental demands, and working conditions. An example of a partial job description for a middle school science teacher is shown in Table 2.3.

Table 2.3   Sample of a Partial Job Description

1. Position Title: Middle School Science Teacher.

2. Qualifications: State science teacher credential, either life or physical/earth science.

A minimum of four college-level courses in both life sciences and physical/earth sciences and at least four upper-division courses in either life sciences or physical sciences. Fluency in standard English; proficiency in a second language desirable, especially Spanish.

3. Generic Job Responsibilities:

The teacher shall participate as a faculty member in the activities of the school in ways that contribute to the attainment of the purposes and goals of the school district.

The teacher shall design and implement instructional plans for the student group or groups assigned to him/her.

The teacher shall instruct students in a manner that will enable them to perform their best on the district testing program.

The teacher shall accept responsibility for continuing enhancement of his/her professional knowledge, skills, and performance.

The teacher shall make and keep proper records of student work and the progress of students in his/her charge.

The teacher shall serve as a school-community liaison person in contacts with parents of students and other members of the community.

The teacher shall be aware of and observe legal mandates, Board policy, administrative procedures, and contractual agreements as they pertain to his/her position.

The teacher shall perform all other duties of the position as assigned by the principal and his/her designee within the limits agreed upon by contract and the State Education Code.

4. Specific Job Responsibilities:

The teacher shall inventory and maintain science lab equipment, materials, and live specimens.

The teacher shall store and use chemicals in accordance with state safety codes and Occupational Safety and Health Administration (OSHA) regulations.

The teacher shall implement the State's science curriculum framework for grades 6–8.

The teacher shall plan and coordinate the school's annual science fair.

The teacher shall advise the Science Club.

The teacher shall serve on the district's science curriculum committee as requested by the Superintendent.

5. Physical and Mental Demands:

Physical:

Maintain high level of physical stamina to supervise students throughout the day, including classes, labs, recesses, all-day field trips, special duties, night meetings, etc.

Some light lifting (up to 40 pounds).

Mental:

Ability to communicate, both orally and in written form, in standard English.

Ability to enforce safety standards in large-group setting (e.g., lab safety).

Ability to maintain emotional control under stress and to use judgment, patience, and sensitivity in dealing with students.

Ability to respond to injuries and administer first aid as needed.

6. Working Conditions:

Will have own classroom, but may have to share classroom space with other teachers (summer/night school).

Daily work hours at school site, 7:30 AM to 3:45 PM; traditional school year schedule, but must be willing to change to year-round schedule if required by district.

Requires evening and weekend time commitments for special activities.

Work environment may be physically isolated from coworkers (for example, portables).

May have to cope with physically dangerous situations (for example, handling of hazardous chemicals, potential violence in school and nearby neighborhood).

SOURCE: McConney et al. (1996). Used with permission.

Many schools and districts lack job descriptions for teachers, or if they have them, they tend to be minimal, generic, incomplete, and out of date. Reasonable job descriptions can be developed using some of the foundations discussed earlier in this chapter as well as input from teachers. In addition to improving the comprehensiveness and validity of the teacher evaluation system, the development of thorough job descriptions delineating teachers' roles and responsibilities can result in many other benefits (McConney et al., 1996). Job descriptions help communicate to individual teachers the requirements of their job assignments and those responsibilities for which they will be held accountable. They contain information for preparing job announcements, developing job descriptions for new positions, and informing job applicants about the expectations of the position. They offer individual teachers ideas for use in self-evaluation, and can be helpful to supervisors and mentors who must conduct informal monitoring of individual teachers' performances for purposes of formative evaluation and professional development. They give educators and other stakeholders a better grasp on and understanding of the job of teaching and its demands and challenges. They can be one vehicle for informing preservice teacher education programs, inservice training programs, and licensing boards about the nature of teachers' jobs and for helping boards identify areas or requirements that they should address. When a personnel decision is appealed or a case is presented before a court of law or an arbitrator, they offer documentary evidence of the nature of the job and the roles and responsibilities the job incumbent is expected to fulfill.

WHAT ARE THE NEXT STEPS IN DEVELOPING A TEACHER EVALUATION SYSTEM?

Once teachers' roles and responsibilities have been delineated, the next three steps are as follows:

- Develop the criteria for the evaluation and the indicators for those criteria.
- Determine which assessment methods and data sources to use.
- Set standards for evaluating performance.

Danielson and McGreal (2000) noted that

As part of defining good teaching, we need to establish the relative importance of the different criteria ("Are they all equally important?"); the level of performance ("What does it look like when it is done well?"); and standards for acceptable, or exemplary, performance ("How good is good enough and how good is very good?"). (p. 22)

Developing Criteria and Indicators

A criterion provides a general dimension along which performance, such as teaching, is rated or judged as meeting a standard or as successful or meritorious (Wheeler & Haertel, 1993). Indicators are the more specific and observable types of knowledge, skills, abilities, behaviors, and attributes that are empirically or by definition connected to the criterion. Descriptors are specific examples of the performance being assessed. They are useful for training people to implement the evaluation system and for informing teacher about the types of performance being assessed. However, they represent only examples of performance for an indicator and not the full scope of potential performance related to an indicator. Both indicators and descriptors must be stated specifically and in measurable or observable terms. Examples of some indicators and descriptors are provided in Table 2.4.

Table 2.4   Examples of Criteria, With Indicators and Descriptors

Criterion: The teacher keeps parents informed about their children's academic progress and behavior in school.

Indicators:

- The teacher contacts each family by telephone or mail within the first month of school.
- The teacher contacts all parents of Title I students at least once a month to inform them of their children's progress in the reading program and to monitor the students' home reading activities.
- The teacher notifies parents whenever their children receive an award for good behavior from the school staff.

Descriptors:

- The teacher's log indicates that parents of seven children had not been contacted by the end of the first month of school, and that for five of these students, no effort had been made to contact the parents.
- Notes were sent by the teacher to parents of six Title I students during the first week of November with a list of books they read in class in October, and copies were placed in the students' folders in the office.
- A copy of the letter to the parents of the science fair winner is in the teacher's portfolio.

Criterion: The teacher maintains a physically safe environment with regard to equipment, materials and supplies, facilities, and numbers of people present.

Indicators:

- The teacher has the students use safety equipment (e.g., approved eye protection devices when working with hazardous materials, suitable safety gear and equipment for designated athletic activities).

(Continued)

Table 2.4 (Continued)

- Chemicals are stored in accordance with compatibility groupings.
- Chemicals are stored in appropriate, locked cabinets, off the floor.
- All chemicals are labeled, including preparation or receipt date.
- The teacher spreads students out in the lab or workshop so they are not working in overcrowded or unsafe conditions.
- Emergency supplies, including a well-stocked first aid kit, a spill kit, and a fire extinguisher, are readily available at all times.

Descriptors:

- One parent wrote a letter to the principal complaining that the physical education teacher did not allow his daughter to ride with the school's Bike Club on October 4 because she did not have a suitable helmet. (School policy requires that all persons on school bike trips wear helmets that meet Snell standards.)
- The teacher has arranged all chemicals in one collection by alphabetical order, not by compatibility groupings.
- The chemicals are stored in locked cabinets under lab counters designed for such use.
- Three bottles of chemicals on the third shelf of the second cabinet are not labeled.
- There are 33 students in a physics lab of 1,200 square feet, considered overcrowding by the National Science Teachers Association's recommended standard of 45 square feet per student.
- Students report that their music teacher always has a supply of water bottles available on hot days before the marching band practices on the field.

Criterion: The teacher continually acquires updated and expanded knowledge of the subject area(s) he or she teaches or is eligible to teach.

Indicators:

- The teacher satisfactorily completes relevant courses in higher-education institutions.
- The teacher attends school and district workshops and seminars.
- The teacher systematically reads professional literature and periodicals.
- The teacher participates in job-related studies, projects, and professional activities.
- The teacher goes to subject-matter conferences and meetings.
- The teacher writes papers and articles, conducts workshops, and makes presentations for colleagues in the same subject area.

Descriptors:

- The university transcript shows a grade of B+ in Russian History for the fall term.
- The teacher's professional development log indicates that she went to two workshops on reading strategies and one on promoting students' writing skills.
- The teacher reports regularly reading two math journals to which he subscribes.
- The teacher has been an essay reader for the state assessment program this year, participating in the reader training program in August.
- The teacher attended the state's English teachers conference in November this year.
- The teacher did a workshop on integrating reading and writing instruction for the teaching staff at three schools in the district this summer.

Each indicator should focus on one aspect of teaching; that is, an indicator should *not* be multidimensional. An example of a multidimensional indicator—one that looks at two aspects of teaching performance—is, "The teacher speaks clearly to the class and responds to students' questions in a timely manner."

The use of a solid foundation will help to ensure that valid criteria for evaluating teacher performance are delineated. The criteria should cover all the major areas of teaching (e.g., the five major categories in Table 2.1).

The term *standards* is sometimes used in lieu of *criteria*. Although standard can mean criterion, the terms should represent two different phenomena. "Criteria are names of variables that are relevant to making decisions; standards specify the 'amount' of each variable that is needed to decide whether or not a standard has been met" (Raths, 1999, p. 137). Clearly differentiating between criteria and standards should make clearer to all the basis upon which a teacher is being evaluated; that is, the standards. The criteria show the areas being considered in the evaluation.

Determining Assessment Methods and Data Sources

Once the criteria and indicators are identified, the methods for assessing performance for each of them and the sources for data can be ascertained. Numerous assessment methods may be considered (Wheeler, 1994a); several possibilities are discussed in this book. There are also numerous possible sources of data, including educators and other people, existing records and data, teacher products, and other products (Wheeler, 1992b).

In some cases, the methods and data sources are readily apparent. For example, if teachers are to communicate with the parents or guardians of each student at least once a quarter, then two obvious data sources are teachers and parents. Assessment methods could include a review of the teacher records (phone logs and written communication files) and a survey of parents.

In other cases, the methods and data sources are not so readily apparent. For example, a teacher should be able to use the audiovisual equipment and computer technologies appropriate for his or her teaching assignment. To observe a teacher using all the possible equipment and technologies could be very time-consuming and would have to be done by a person knowledgeable about them. It would have to be determined which equipment and technologies are appropriate for a given teacher's assignment (both subject matter and types of students) and which are available for the teacher's use within the teaching context and work setting. Teachers could be required to maintain logs of their use of various equipment and technologies or could be given knowledge tests about the equipment and technologies; students could be asked about their teachers' use of various types of equipment and forms of technologies; or various pieces of equipment and technologies could be chosen at random, and teachers could be asked to demonstrate their use and discuss their role in instruction.

Using the set of criteria derived from the list of roles and responsibilities and the indicators of performance, one can identify potential assessment methods and data sources. As Shulman (1988) noted in his discussion of several methods,

Each of these several approaches to the assessment of teachers is, in itself, as fundamentally flawed as it is reasonably suitable, as perilously insufficient as it is peculiarly fitting. What we need, therefore, is a union of insufficiencies, a marriage of complements, in which the flaws of individual approaches to assessment are offset by the virtues of their fellows. (p. 38)

Wheeler (1994a) reminded us of two reasons for using multiple assessment methods: "(1) No one instrument or method is appropriate for all aspects of teaching performance covered by the evaluation system. (2) The use of multiple assessment methods for one domain or indicator allows for verification of data and triangulation of results" (p. 4).

Setting Standards for Evaluating Performance

Criteria and *standards* are used differently in this chapter, although many use these terms interchangeably. In her article on standards, Noddings (1997) pointed out that "Some see standards as a flag of sorts—something to rally around. Others see it as a goal to be reached, and still others see it as a description of various proficiency levels" (p. 184). The third definition is the one used in this chapter. It is important to differentiate between *criterion* and *standard* (Glass, 1978). Teachers need to understand that they will be evaluated, or judged, against the standards, not the criteria. Satisfactory levels of performance on criteria are specified by standards and are linked to the results on the assessments used to measure performance. Standards indicate what level of performance is considered minimally acceptable for a specified purpose and in a given teaching context. They should be set after assessment methods are developed and prior to the implementation of the evaluation system. Procedures should be in place to ensure that the standards are reviewed regularly (at least every five years) and systematically to ensure that they remain appropriate, especially if the teaching context or school environment changes. For example, an influx of non-English-speaking students, a change from a standard school year to a year-round schedule, changes in staff configuration (e.g., eliminating all counselors, adding a reading specialist), or the acquisition of several computers for each classroom could affect the appropriateness of current standards.

There are several types of standards (Wheeler & Haertel, 1993):

- *Developmental* standards are often used for professional improvement, mentoring, training, self-evaluation, and formative evaluation. They indicate the level of growth or change to be attained by teachers, individually or as a group, and apply to new as well as more experienced teachers.
- *Minimum* standards designate the level of performance that must be met to satisfy some requirement, and below which performance is not acceptable. Such standards are used for licensure and credentialing, hiring, and personnel decisions such as job assignments and retention or termination. There may be different minimum standards for new and

for experienced teachers, or for teachers working in different contexts (e.g., at schools in low-income areas, with students who have physical disabilities, at schools with no counselors or libraries).

- *Desired* performance standards reflect exemplary or meritorious levels of performance.

These various types of standards apply to such uses as promotions, awards, and special recognition. Examples of these types of standards are shown in Table 2.5.

Table 2.5   Examples of Different Types of Standards for Three Criteria (with possible assessment methods)

Criterion: *The teacher gives appropriate assignments, in and out of class, to students.*

Developmental: The teacher becomes better able to modify assignments in the teacher's guides for non-English-proficient students as shown by progressively better adaptations of five different assignments each, over a three-month period, in language arts, mathematics, and science. (portfolio)

Minimum for New Teacher: The teacher selects appropriate classroom activities and homework assignments from the teacher's guide or instructional kit for use with his or her own students. Appropriateness considers students' needs and abilities, instructional program goals and objectives, and available resources. (observation, portfolio)

Minimum for Experienced Teacher: The teacher selects and modifies appropriate classroom activities and homework assignments from the teacher's guide or instructional kit, and develops new ones for use with his or her own students. Appropriateness considers students' needs and abilities, instructional program goals and objectives, and available resources. (observation, portfolio)

Desired Performance: The teacher develops new, innovative, and appropriate classroom activities and homework assignments for use with his or her own students and by other teachers. Appropriateness considers students' needs and abilities, instructional program goals and objectives, and available resources. (observation, portfolio)

Criterion: *The teacher manages student misbehavior in the classroom and elsewhere at school.*

Developmental: The teacher acquires skills in anger management and conflict resolution by completing this year's training program. (professional development log, certificate from the trainer)

Minimum for New Teacher: The teacher maintains enough control of his or her students so that no student is physically injured or emotionally abused. (observation, office records)

Minimum for Experienced Teacher: The teacher maintains enough control of his or her students so that there are few and insignificant disruptions to learning and other activities. (observation, office records)

Desired Performance: The teacher is able to quickly handle an actual violent situation on the school campus. (peer reports, observation, simulated work sample)

(Continued)

Table 2.5 (Continued)

Criterion: *The teacher adapts instructional content and concepts to address students' understanding of the subject matter and their misconceptions.*

Developmental *(for a more experienced teacher)*: The teacher plans and conducts a workshop for the teaching staff to impart expertise that will help them address common student misconceptions about weather and climate. (peer feedback, science test of student understanding)

Minimum for New Teacher: The teacher assumes that students will understand the content and concepts being presented in class and explains the material in the same manner to all students. (observation)

Minimum for Experienced Teacher: The teacher realizes during instruction that some students are confused by the content and concepts presented in class and explains the materials in more than one way to improve student understanding. (observation)

Desired Performance: The teacher anticipates in advance what misconceptions the students will have and what content and concepts might be confusing to them and prepares explanations prior to instructing the students. (observation, portfolio)

An array of methods, both empirical and judgmental, exists for setting standards (Cizek, 1996; Livingston & Zieky, 1982). Most methods employed to set standards for evaluating teaching performance rely heavily on professional judgment. The process of establishing standards should involve key stakeholders—teachers, administrators, school board representatives, and others. These individuals must be carefully selected and thoroughly trained. They should be familiar with and well informed about the array of teaching positions and job assignments to be covered, the roles and responsibilities associated with those positions, the teaching context, the criteria and indicators to be covered, the nature of the assessment methods, how the assessments will be scored, and who will use the evaluation results and for what purposes. Cizek (1995) warned of the importance of training those involved in setting standards:

> [An] area in desperate need of attention is the training provided to standard setting participants. In the legal arena, it can take months to select a jury and to educate them about the task they will be asked to perform. Indeed, in other areas such as athletics, music, or drama, the vast majority of time is spent in training for but a fleeting moment of performance. In contrast, the training provided to standard setting participants is often minimal compared to the task they will be asked to perform. (pp. 10–11)

Whatever methods are used, the standards should not be set so low that they have the unintended consequence of dragging down the quality of teaching. They must be fair, reasonable, attainable, and clear to all persons involved in the evaluation process, including the teacher. They must be designed to encourage good teaching, promote student learning, and improve student behavior. Above all, they must protect the interests and well-being of the students, their families, the school, and the community.

SUMMARY

In the selection of a foundation on which to build a teacher evaluation system, the first question that must be asked is, "What is the purpose of the evaluation system?" Some of the foundations discussed in this chapter are much more appropriate than others—or may even be required—for some purposes, as in the case of state laws and governmental regulations. Other factors that must be considered include (a) the availability of the information and of the people needed to use a particular foundation (e.g., local or applicable job analysis data, well-constructed lists of teacher duties and job descriptions, someone to conduct a review of the research literature), (b) the quality of this information, and (c) the qualifications of people who would provide input and judgment. More than one foundation will have to be employed for one or another use, even if the evaluation system builders rely heavily on one foundation for most purposes.

The use of a combination of foundations results in a more comprehensive and solid basis for a multipurpose teacher evaluation system than the use of any single foundation alone, no matter how strong that foundation is. This will lead to teacher evaluation systems that permit better decisions to be made and that will be more apt to improve the overall quality of a wider array of teaching or teaching-related performances. It can also strengthen the technical, professional, and legal quality of the system.

Through the use of appropriate foundations, valid criteria and indicators of teaching performance can be derived. Based on the performance indicators, suitable and feasible methods of assessment can be selected or developed, and sources of data can be identified. Standards for minimally acceptable performance for each criterion can be set. Ultimately, these standards should reflect the purpose of the teacher evaluation system, incorporate the assessment methods, and protect the interests and well-being of all concerned parties, especially the students.

REFERENCES

American Association of School Personnel Administrators. (1995, April). *Most critical knowledge & skills of a future educator.* Sacramento, CA: Author. (Prepared by the 1994–95 Teacher of the Future Committee, A. May, Chair).

Berk, R. A. (1988). Fifty reasons why student achievement gain does not mean teacher effectiveness. *Journal of Personnel Evaluation in Education, 1,* 345–363.

Braskamp, L. A., Brandenburg, D. C., & Ory, J. C. (1984). *Evaluating teaching effectiveness: A practical guide.* Newbury Park, CA: Sage.

Brophy, J. E., & Good, T. L. (1986). Teacher behavior and student achievement. In M. C. Wittrock (Ed.), *Handbook of research on teaching* (3rd ed., pp. 328–375). New York: Macmillan.

Centra, J. A. (1980). *Determining faculty performance*. San Francisco: Jossey-Bass.

Cizek, G. J. (1995, April). *Standard setting as psychometric due process: Going a little further down an uncertain road*. Paper presented at the annual meeting of the National Council on Measurement in Education, San Francisco.

Cizek, G. J. (1996, Summer). Setting passing scores (NCME Instructional Module). *Educational Measurement: Issues and Practice, 15*(2), 20–31.

Clark, C. M., & Peterson, P. L. (1986). Teacher's thought process. In M. C. Wittrock (Ed.), *Handbook of research on teaching* (3rd ed., pp. 255–296). New York: Macmillan.

Costa, A. L., Garmston, R. J., & Lambert, L. (1988). Evaluation of teaching: The cognitive development view. In S. J. Stanley & W. J. Popham (Eds.), *Teacher evaluation: Six prescriptions for success* (pp. 145–172). Alexandria, VA: Association for Supervision and Curriculum Development.

Danielson, C. (1996). *Enhancing professional practice: A framework for teaching*. Alexandria, VA: Association for Supervision and Curriculum Development.

Danielson, C., & McGreal, T. L. (2000). *Teacher evaluation to enhance professional practice*. Alexandria, VA: Association for Supervision and Curriculum Development and Princeton, NJ: Educational Testing Service.

Darling-Hammond, L., & Youngs, P. (2002, December). Defining "highly qualified teachers": What does "scientifically based research" tell us? *Educational Researcher*, pp. 12–25.

Droege, K. L. (2004, April). Turning accountability on its head: Supporting inspired teaching in today's classroom. *Phi Delta Kappan, 85*(8), 610–612.

Glass, G. V. (1978). Standards and criteria. *Journal of Educational Measurement, 15*, 237–262.

Goldberg, M. (2005, January). Test mess 2: Are we doing better a year later? *Phi Delta Kappan, 86*(5), 389–395.

Haertel, E. (1986). The valid use of student performance measures for teacher evaluation. *Educational Evaluation and Policy Analysis, 8*(1), 45–60.

Joint Committee on Standards for Educational Evaluation. (1988). *The personnel evaluation standards: How to assess systems for evaluating educators*. Newbury Park, CA: Sage.

Joyce, B., & Weil, M. (1986). *Models of teaching* (3rd ed.). Englewood Cliffs, NJ: Prentice Hall.

Livingston, S. A., & Zieky, M. J. (1982). *Passing scores*. Princeton, NJ: Educational Testing Service.

McConney, A. (Ed.), Wheeler, P. H., Wiersma, W., Millman, J., Stufflebeam, D., Gullickson, A., Airasian, P., Vicinanza, N., Haertel, G. D., Barry, K., & Cullen, K. (1996). *Teacher evaluation kit and database of CREATE products* [CD-ROM]. Kalamazoo: Western Michigan University, Evaluation Center.

McDonald, F. J., & Elias, P. (1976). *The effects of teaching performance on pupil learning* (Final Report, Beginning Teacher Evaluation Study, Phase II, Vol. I). Princeton, NJ: Educational Testing Service.

Medley, D. M., Coker, H., & Soar, R. S. (1984). *Measurement-based evaluation of teacher performance: An empirical approach*. New York: Longman.

Millman, J. (1981). Student achievement as a measure of teacher competence. In J. Millman (Ed.), *Handbook of teacher evaluation* (pp. 146–166). Beverly Hills, CA: Sage.

National Council of Teachers of Mathematics. (1991). *Professional standards for teaching mathematics*. Reston, VA: Author.

Neill, M. (2003, November). Leaving children behind: How No Child Left Behind will fail our children. *Phi Delta Kappan, 85*(3), pp. 225–228.

Noddings, N. (1997). Thinking about standards. *Phi Delta Kappan, 79*(3), 184–189.

Ornstein, A. C. (1991). Teacher effectiveness research: Theoretical considerations. In H. C. Waxman & H. J. Walberg (Eds.), *Effective teaching: Current research* (pp. 63–80). Berkeley, CA: McCutchan.

Raths, J. (1999, October). A consumer's guide to teacher standards. *Phi Delta Kappan, 81*(2), 136–142.

Robinson, G. E. (1984). *Incentive pay for teachers: An analysis of approaches*. Arlington, VA: Educational Research Service.

Rosenfeld, M., Thornton, R. F., & Skurnik, L. S. (1986). *Analysis of the professional functions of teachers: Relationships between job functions and the NTE Core Battery* (Research Report 86–8). Princeton, NJ: Educational Testing Service.

Scriven, M. (1988a, July). Duty-based teacher evaluation. *Journal of Personnel Evaluation in Education, 1*(4), 319–334.

Scriven, M. (1988b). Evaluating teachers as professionals: The duties-based approach. In S. J. Stanley & W. J. Popham (Eds.), *Teacher evaluation: Six prescriptions for success* (pp. 110–142). Alexandria, VA: Association for Supervision and Curriculum Development.

Scriven, M. (1990). Can research-based teacher evaluation be saved? *Journal of Personnel Evaluation in Education, 4*(1), 19–32. (Reprinted in R. L. Schwab [Ed.], [1990]. *Research-based teacher evaluation: A special issue of the "Journal of Personnel Evaluation in Education"* (pp. 19–32). Boston: Kluwer).

Scriven, M. (1991). *Evaluation thesaurus* (4th ed.). Newbury Park, CA: Sage.

Scriven, M. (1994a, July). Duties of the teacher. *Journal of Personnel Evaluation in Education, 8*(2), 151–184.

Scriven, M. (1994b). Using the duties-based approach to teacher evaluation. In L. Ingvarson & R. Chadbourne (Eds.), *Valuing teachers' work: New directions in teacher appraisal* (pp. 70–95). Melbourne: Australian Council for Educational Research.

Shuell, T. J. (1993, Fall). Toward an integrated theory of teaching and learning. *Educational Psychologist, 28*(4), 291–311.

Shulman, L. S. (1988, November). A union of insufficiencies: Strategies for teacher assessment in a period of educational reform. *Educational Leadership, 46*(3), 36–41. (ERIC Document Reproduction Service No. EJ 385 344)

Stronge, J. H., & Tucker, P. D. (2003). *Handbook on teacher evaluation: Assessing and improving performance.* Larchmont, NY: Eye on Education.

Wheeler, P. (1992a, July). Foundations for building teacher evaluation systems. *CREATE Newsletter, 2*(2), 4–5.

Wheeler, P. (1992b, October). *Sources of data for evaluating teachers* (TEMP B Memo 7). Kalamazoo: Western Michigan University, Evaluation Center.

Wheeler, P. (1994a, August). *Assessment methods for use in evaluating educators* (TEMP C Memo 12). Kalamazoo: Western Michigan University, Evaluation Center.

Wheeler, P. H. (1991, November). *Building a teacher evaluation system: Finding the right foundation.* Paper presented at the annual meeting of the California Educational Research Association, San Diego, CA.

Wheeler, P. H. (with Scriven, M.). (1994b, July). Duties of the teacher . . . An essential foundation for a teacher evaluation system. *AASPA Report, 1*(7), 2–3.

Wheeler, P. H. (1994c). *Foundations upon which to build a teacher evaluation system* (TEMP C Memo 18). Kalamazoo: Western Michigan University, Evaluation Center.

Wheeler, P. H. (1995, July 10). *Building and rebuilding teacher evaluation systems: Selecting the appropriate foundation.* A paper presented at the fourth annual National Evaluation Institute, Kalamazoo, MI. (Also available as EREAPA Publication Series 95–1, EREAPA Associates, Livermore, CA)

Wheeler, P. H. (1995/1996, December/January). Consider these issues . . . Before you use student tests in teacher evaluation. *AASPA Report, 3*(3), 12–13.

Wheeler, P., & Haertel, G. D. (1993). *Resource handbook on performance assessment and measurement: A tool for students, practitioners, and policymakers.* Chico, CA: Owl Press. (ERIC Document Reproduction Service No. ED 367 686)

Wise, A. E., Darling-Hammond, L., McLaughlin, M. W., & Bernstein, H. T. (1984). *Teacher evaluation: A study of effective practices.* Santa Monica, CA: Rand.

Applying the Personnel Evaluation Standards to Teacher Evaluation

3

Barbara B. Howard

James R. Sanders

Educational standards have long played a significant role in protecting and promoting public trust by ensuring the quality and integrity of the programs and professional activities to which they are applied (Björk & Rinehart, 2004). As such, standards serve as guides to best practices in a variety of endeavors associated with systems of accountability, including the evaluation of personnel.

Although the standards-based movement in accountability has seemingly moved to the forefront of educational reform only during the last decade or so, in fact, educational accountability has a long history of controversy involving its use and misuse dating back to the beginning of publicly funded education (Herrington, 1993; Kirst, 1990). During the 1980s, in response to such landmark reports as *A Nation at Risk: The Imperative for Educational Reform* (National Commission on Excellence in Education, 1983) and *Time for Results* (National Governors' Association, 1986), the nation moved toward the most recent wave of standards-based performance expectations for students and those who teach them with state and national systems of accountability (Adams & Kirst, 1999).

Recent federal legislation (No Child Left Behind, 2001) emphasizes student achievement, particularly Adequate Yearly Progress (AYP), as a cornerstone of its accountability system. With the inclusion of "highly qualified teachers" as part of this same legislation, there is the acknowledgment that the skills and knowledge of the individual teacher have an impact on student achievement. At the state and national levels, regardless of whether for accountability or recognition (such as through the National Board for Professional Teaching Standards), measurement of a teacher's skill and knowledge must rely heavily on standardized tests of knowledge, licensure requirements such as degrees or coursework, or other means of external evaluation. Individual schools and districts, however, monitor teacher performance on a more continuous and individual basis through systems of personnel evaluation. The approach these systems take varies widely from those based solely on classroom observation and rating scales to those centered on the use of some kind of performance rubric with multiple data sources. Many incorporate a measurement of student performance. While Shinkfield and Stufflebeam (1995) cautioned that "there is no topic on which opinion varies so markedly as that of the validity of basing teacher effectiveness on student learning" (p. 7), Sanders (2000) asserted that modeling student progress over time with value-added analyses controlling for confounding factors provides an accurate quantitative measurement that can be directly attributed to the professional practice of individual teachers.

Regardless of the system of teacher evaluation in place within a school or district, the evaluation system should provide its users (both the evaluators and those being evaluated) with information that will not only ensure quality of performance of each teacher but also guide the school leaders in making critical decisions. While these decisions inevitably will include those associated with hiring and dismissal, they must also involve an even more crucial area—professional development. It is logical to surmise that without the highest possible caliber of teacher in the classroom, a school is far less likely to attain its academic goals for students. While not intended to provide actual procedures or forms for evaluation, the Personnel Evaluation Standards, developed and issued by the Joint Committee on Standards for Educational Evaluation (1988), address attributes of systems of personnel evaluation that will provide users with guidance in developing and/or implementing a valid and reliable system.

This chapter begins with background information on the Standards and a brief history of their development. Following this is a description of their content and implications for teacher evaluation. In this era of high-stakes accountability and the necessity of ensuring that all children have the most effective teacher available, a crucial section of this chapter will address the application of these standards and their importance to teacher evaluation. Although these standards are meant to apply to the evaluation of *all* personnel engaged in educational activities (teachers, support staff, school nurses, guidance counselors, administrators, professors, etc.), this chapter will focus on the evaluation of the classroom teacher.

WHAT IS THE PROCESS OF STANDARD DEVELOPMENT BY THE JOINT COMMITTEE?

The Joint Committee on Standards for Educational Evaluation was created in 1975 in response to the growing need to establish expectations for evaluations in education. It is a coalition of 16 professional associations[1] that meet annually to review issues in educational evaluation. Currently, there are three sets of standards issued by the Joint Committee to address educational evaluations in the following key areas: program, personnel, and student. During the development phase of its first set of standards, Program Evaluation Standards, the Joint Committee constructed a set of operating procedures to guide all subsequent work on standards (Sanders, 1994). A fundamental piece of the entire process is the way the Joint Committee defines the concept of a standard. According to the Joint Committee, a standard is a principle "*commonly agreed to by people engaged in the professional practice of evaluation for the measurement of the value or the quality of an evaluation*" (Joint Committee, 1981, p. 12). In this chapter, those standards pertain to the evaluation of personnel or, more specifically, teachers.

To meet this definition, the standards-setting process for all types of educational evaluation used by the Joint Committee is open, public, and participatory. The Joint Committee follows all required reporting and validation procedures specified by the American National Standards Institute (ANSI) for approval as American National Standards for each set of standards (Section 5.3.7, Operating Procedures of the Joint Committee on Standards for Educational Evaluation, 2002). It is essential that evaluation standards describe those practices to which all will agree are appropriate and acceptable. To meet this goal, the Joint Committee takes the following steps:

1. *Identification of issues:* Educators and all other interested parties are invited to identify those issues that need to be addressed. A review of the literature supplements any reported issues.

2. *Development of a first draft:* A task force of writers who are experienced in the topic is appointed or commissioned by the Joint Committee to develop initial versions of the standards or to revise current ones. These initial drafts are reviewed, critiqued, and rewritten by members of the Joint Committee prior to being released as a first draft.

3. *National and international reviews:* The first draft is critiqued by reviewers identified by each of the Joint Committee's member associations. Beyond this group of reviewers, anyone who requests it may review it. The criteria used for these reviews include (a) the need for the document, (b) responsiveness to concerns in the field, (c) courage, (d) validity of the content, (e) practicality, (f) legality, (g) clarity, and (h) depth of treatment. Based on reviews, the Joint Committee, through the Task Force, creates a second draft.

4. *Field trials:* Trial use of the second draft is arranged through the member associations in as broad an application as possible to capture critical issues addressed by the standards. The Joint Committee considers results of the field trials in developing a third draft to offer at the national public hearings.

5. *National public hearings:* Hearings are organized to provide an open forum for anyone wishing to comment on the standards. Those who cannot provide testimony in person are encouraged to submit written comments. Reactions collected through these national hearings guide the development of a fourth draft.

6. *American National Standards Institute (ANSI) review:* This fourth draft is submitted to ANSI for announcement in *Standards Action,* a bulletin disseminated to all who are interested in the setting of voluntary standards. The Joint Committee must address any reactions resulting from this announcement.

7. *Finalization of the standards:* Once the final draft of the standards has reached this point, the Joint Committee reviews, revises, and votes on the final version prior to submission for publication.

It should be obvious from the process described above that every effort is made to solicit reviews and comments from anyone who would be directly affected by the set of standards under development. In addition to the task force directly involved in the work, the Joint Committee appoints an independent validation panel of educators to oversee the process, thus ensuring that all procedures have been followed faithfully. The resulting product is a compilation of best practices, warnings of common errors encountered in the field, and guidelines for use of each standard.

The Joint Committee reviews each set of standards every three years with recommendations for revisions based on these reviews. There is no better source to use in a review of evaluation practices in schools and other organizations engaged in educational endeavors.

WHAT ISSUES DRIVE THE NEED FOR PERSONNEL EVALUATION IN EDUCATION?

At the time of the development of the first edition of the Personnel Evaluation Standards in the mid- to late 1980s, there was widespread concern about the quality of teacher evaluation (Joint Committee, 1988, p. 6, App. A). One group of researchers noted that teacher evaluations were often "subjective, unreliable, open to bias, closed to public scrutiny, and based on irrelevancies" (Soar, Medley, & Coker, 1983, p. 246). This assertion was supported by research conducted by the RAND Corporation that concluded that most teacher evaluation systems were illogical, simplistic, unfair, counterproductive, or simply unproductive (Darling-Hammond, Wise, & Pease, 1983).

The Joint Committee concluded that a major problem was the lack of widespread agreement concerning the characteristics of good personnel evaluation practices, so it set out to fill that void with the publication of *The Personnel*

Evaluation Standards (Joint Committee on Standards for Educational Evaluation, 1988). The primary purpose for sound personnel evaluation in all institutions of education remains to educate students effectively and achieve all other educational goals. Therefore, sound systems of personnel evaluation are still needed to "select, retain, and develop qualified personnel and to manage and facilitate their work" (Joint Committee, 1988, p. 5). The standards do not specify procedures to be used in personnel evaluation, but, rather, provide a framework for designing, conducting, and judging personnel evaluation reports and the systems that produced them.

WHAT ARE THE ATTRIBUTES OF SOUND PRACTICES FOR TEACHER EVALUATION?

The Personnel Evaluation Standards are organized into four categories or attributes that also apply to program and student evaluations although the content and number of standards vary according to the set of standards. These four attributes are as follows:

1. *Propriety:* Seven standards intended to facilitate the protection of rights of all individuals directly affected by the evaluation;

2. *Utility:* Six standards intended to guide evaluations so that they are informative, timely, and influential or useful to all parties involved;

3. *Feasibility:* Three standards intended to recognize that all personnel evaluations must occur within a real context and may be affected by certain factors such as availability of resources that are unrelated to the process itself;

4. *Accuracy:* Eleven standards intended to guide the collection of adequate and appropriate information upon which sound judgments and decisions regarding personnel issues may be formed.

HOW DOES AN EDUCATIONAL INSTITUTION APPLY THESE STANDARDS?

The 27 standards found within the four attributes provide specific guidance for all who are engaged in the evaluation of personnel, including board members who may use the results of the evaluation to make program and personnel decisions, those being evaluated, and those conducting the evaluations. These standards may be applied at the institution or district level when considering the overall system of evaluation. In that case, the following suggested steps may be useful:

1. Identify as many stakeholder groups (administrators, teachers, parents, taxpayers, district office personnel, teacher unions or organizations, etc.) directly affected by personnel evaluation as possible and involve representatives from these groups in the process.

2. Ensure that these representatives have the opportunity to become generally acquainted with the standards and their application.

3. Clarify your purposes for applying the standards (e.g., to develop a new system of evaluation or to review and revise an existing one).

4. Review and apply each set of standards to the pertinent parts of the evaluation procedures either as a whole group or in smaller subgroups.

5. Decide upon and implement the appropriate course of action to correct any deficiencies.

This process requires numerous meetings over the course of a year or so with or without the help of an external consultant. A primary outcome of this effort will be that members of all stakeholder groups will support a system of teacher evaluation aligned with the goals and beliefs of the district. The results of a well-designed teacher evaluation system include a much higher likelihood of fidelity of implementation by evaluators and a positive impact on teacher performance.

The Personnel Evaluation Standards: How to Assess Systems of Personnel Evaluation (Joint Committee on Standards, 1988) provides additional information and guidance in applying the standards. For each standard, an explanation and rationale are followed by a set of guidelines and common errors. In addition, cases from actual practice are included to illustrate positive and negative applications of the standards. An analysis and discussion of each illustrative case follows. For example: "U2—Defined Uses—'Both the users and intended uses of a personnel evaluation should be identified at the beginning of the evaluation so that the evaluation can address appropriate questions and issues'" (Joint Committee on Standards, 1988).

The following is an illustrative case with the accompanying analysis and suggestions for this standard:*

Illustrative Case Description

Members of a school board charged a new superintendent with devising a plan for awarding merit pay to teachers. While the current system of evaluation appeared fair and accepted by the teachers, principals, and teacher organizations, it had not been used for merit pay in the past. In reviewing the process, the superintendent and district administrators determined that the evaluation system had been used primarily to provide teachers with feedback. No teachers had ever been dismissed in the district solely as a result of poor performance, and, in

---

*SOURCE: Joint Committee on Standards for Educational Evaluation (1988). Used with permission.

fact, no teachers in the district had been rated on this evaluation system as being less than satisfactory in all areas. Most teachers were rated at the exemplary level in all areas.

In reviewing these documents, this puzzled the superintendent who knew the district struggled with 3 of its 15 schools designated as low performing schools on state accountability measures in the past year. How could the students of "exemplary" teachers be falling so far behind? The superintendent decided that the evaluation process did not need to change; its use and implementation did.

The superintendent and his district office administrative team began a thorough review of all the evaluation documentation of the past two years. They found that in many cases, principals were dating observations all on one day—the day before the records were due in the central office. The comments from some principals appeared to be the same for most if not all teachers they supervised. In some cases, the principal rated all teachers as exemplary in all areas with little or no differentiation of scores. This indicated to the superintendent that a lack of a system for oversight had resulted in the evaluations being used merely as paperwork to be completed and turned in with no follow up. The evaluations certainly were not being used for their intended purposes as stated in the current district policy—that of differentiating between effective and ineffective teachers and identifying specific teacher strengths and weaknesses. Based on these evaluations, there were no means of improving teacher quality, let alone identifying teachers for merit pay.

The superintendent modeled the evaluation process with each principal through the principal evaluation system. Each principal received feedback on individual strengths and weaknesses as well as ratings that differentiated performance among the principals. The superintendent also provided specific feedback to each principal on the implementation of the teacher evaluation system at his or her school. All principals received additional training in the process with the assurance that a system of oversight at the district office would be in place.

Through a series of meetings and discussions with all involved in the evaluation process, the superintendent garnered support for the plan that merit pay would apply to principals as well as teachers based on the summative evaluation process. Before this plan went into effect, the district policy was changed to reflect the use of the teacher and principal evaluation processes would change to include merit pay as well as the original purposes of identifying strengths and weaknesses and identifying incompetent teachers.

Illustrative Case Analysis

It can happen that the intended uses of an evaluation system are well defined in district policy but the actual implementation does not meet these expectations. In this case, the principals had been allowed through a lack of oversight and feedback to simply complete forms and meet deadlines thus short circuiting the intended use of identifying and addressing weaknesses in teacher practice. This resulted in inflated evaluation scores that may have masked poor instructional practices thus impacting student achievement.

The superintendent recalled the intended uses of the evaluation and added merit pay, but she did so involving all those involved in the process. By clearly identifying these uses, she increased the level of implementation within the schools and districts and made personnel evaluation a top priority rather than perfunctory paperwork. (Joint Committee on Standards for Educational Evaluation, 1988)

For both organizations and individuals, a series of critical questions (see Table 3.1) is a good start in the application of these standards. While any application must start with a thorough understanding of the scope of each standard, these critical questions can provide useful insight in the implementation of any system of personnel evaluation.

Table 3.1   Linking Standard Statements to Key Questions of Teacher Evaluations

Attribute	Standard Statement	Key Questions
PROPRIETY	P1—SERVICE ORIENTATION Personnel evaluations should promote sound education, fulfillment of institutional missions, and effective performance of job responsibilities, so that the educational needs of students, community, and society are met.	Are teacher job descriptions clearly written and understood by both teachers and evaluators? Are these job expectations aligned with district goals and sound educational practice?
	P2—APPROPRIATE POLICIES AND PROCEDURES Guidelines for personnel evaluations should be recorded and provided to evaluatees in policy statements, negotiated agreements, and/or personnel evaluation manuals, so that evaluations are consistent, equitable, and fair.	Are written policies regarding all aspects of teacher evaluation written, adopted by governing boards, and available to all teachers and evaluators as well as other stakeholders? Is there an oversight of the process to ensure consistency and fairness of judgment of the evaluator?

(Continued)

Table 3.1 (Continued)

Attribute	Standard Statement	Key Questions
PROPRIETY	P3—ACCESS TO EVALUATION INFORMATION Access to an evaluatee's evaluation information should be limited to the persons with established legitimate permission to review and use the information, so that confidentiality is maintained and privacy protected.	Is the information gathered during an evaluation protected and held confidential? Is there a process in place to ensure that only those with a legitimate purpose have access to personnel evaluations?
	P4—INTERACTIONS WITH EVALUATEES Evaluators should respect human dignity and act in a professional, considerate, and courteous manner, so that evaluatees' self-esteem, motivation, professional reputations, performance, and attitude toward personnel evaluation are enhanced or at least not needlessly damaged.	Are there safeguards and oversights in place to ensure that evaluators conduct all interactions (both written and verbal) in a professional, constructive manner? Is there a process in place to address incidences of unprofessional interactions with evaluatees?
	P5—BALANCED EVALUATION Personnel evaluations should provide information that identifies both strengths and weaknesses, so that strengths can be built upon and problem areas addressed.	Do procedures and expectations allow the identification of strengths and weaknesses rather than focusing solely on the deficits of performance? Are there structures in place to address specific areas of weakness?
	P6—CONFLICT OF INTEREST Existing and potential conflicts of interest should be identified and dealt with openly and honestly, so that they do not compromise the evaluation process and results.	Are there safeguards and oversights in place to ensure that preexisting conditions or events would not compromise the evaluator's ability to be fair and unbiased?

Attribute	Standard Statement	Key Questions
PROPRIETY	**P7—LEGAL VIABILITY** Personnel evaluations should meet the requirements of all federal, state, and local laws, as well as case law, contracts, collective bargaining agreements, affirmative action policies, and local board policies and regulations or institutional statutes or bylaws, so that evaluators can successfully conduct fair, efficient, and responsible personnel evaluations.	Does the evaluation process meet all federal, state, and local laws and guidelines including those established through collective bargaining? Do all those involved generally agree that the evaluations are fair and efficient?
UTILITY	**U1—CONSTRUCTIVE ORIENTATION** Personnel evaluations should be constructive, so that they not only help institutions develop human resources but encourage and assist those evaluated to provide excellent services in accordance with the institution's mission statements and goals.	Does the evaluation process include structures that allow the data to be used not only for personnel decisions, but also for professional development?
	U2—DEFINED USES Both the users and intended uses of a personnel evaluation should be identified at the beginning of the evaluation so that the evaluation can address appropriate questions and issues.	Have *all* users (teacher, administrators, School Board members, etc.) of the evaluation process been clearly identified from the beginning of the evaluation cycle? Have the uses for the information (dismissal, tenure, merit pay, etc.) been clearly identified?
	U3—EVALUATOR CREDIBILITY The evaluation system should be developed, implemented, and managed by persons with the necessary qualifications, skills, training, and authority so that evaluation reports are respected and used.	Have all the evaluators received appropriate training in the evaluation process? Have those who manage the records received appropriate training and hold appropriate credentials?

(Continued)

Table 3.1 (Continued)

Attribute	Standard Statement	Key Questions
UTILITY	**U4—EXPLICIT CRITERIA** Evaluators should identify and justify the criteria used to interpret and judge evaluatee performance, so that the bases for interpretation and judgment are clear and defensible providing a clear rationale for results.	Is the process as objective as possible with easily defined criteria? Does the process encourage evaluators to collect and record specific types of data?
	U5—FUNCTIONAL REPORTING Reports should be clear, timely, accurate, and germane, so that they are of practical value to the evaluatee and other appropriate audiences.	Is there a system of oversight to ensure that all reports generated by the evaluator meet deadlines and provide useful, accurate information?
	U6—PROFESSIONAL DEVELOPMENT Personnel evaluations should inform users and evaluatees of areas of the job assignment in need of professional development to ensure that all educational personnel can better address the institution's missions and goals, fulfill their roles and responsibilities, and meet the needs of students. Appropriate action based on this information should follow all evaluations.	Is there a structure in place to allow the use of data generated by teacher evaluation in developing professional development plans? Are there procedures in place that allow oversight to ensure appropriate follow-up of evaluation results?
FEASIBILITY	**F1—PRACTICAL PROCEDURES** Personnel evaluation procedures should be practical, so that they produce the needed information in an efficient, nondisruptive way.	Are procedures for collecting data as simple and job-embedded as possible to prevent undue overburdening of either the teacher or the evaluator?
	F2—POLITICAL VIABILITY Personnel evaluations should be planned and conducted with the anticipation of questions from evaluatees and others with a legitimate right to know, so that their questions can be addressed and their cooperation obtained.	What is the process in place that allows all stakeholders the opportunity to question the procedures or results of an evaluation? Is there a process to determine the outcome of questions asked concerning an evaluation?

Attribute	Standard Statement	Key Questions
FEASIBILITY	**F3—FISCAL VIABILITY** Adequate time and resources should be provided for personnel evaluation activities, so that evaluation can be effectively implemented, the results fully communicated, and appropriate follow-up activities identified.	Can the district afford the resources to conduct the teacher evaluation in the way that will maximize its effect?
ACCURACY	**A1—VALIDITY ORIENTATION** The selection, development, and implementation of personnel evaluations should ensure that the interpretations made about the performance of the evaluatee are valid and not open to misinterpretation.	Are safeguards in place that ensure that all comments about a teacher's performance are clearly communicated and directly related only to the specified duties of the teacher?
	A2—DEFINED EXPECTATIONS The qualifications, role, and responsibilities of the evaluatee should be clearly defined, so that the evaluator can determine the evaluation data and information needed to ensure validity.	Are the expectations and scope of work for the teacher clearly defined and understood not only by the evaluator, but also by the teacher as well?
	A3—PERSONAL AND CONTEXTUAL ANALYSIS Personal and contextual variables that influence performance should be identified, described, and recorded, so that they can be considered when interpreting an evaluatee's performance.	Whenever data are collected, is there a structure or expectation in place that the details regarding the circumstances also be recorded (i.e., notation on observation forms)?
	A4—DOCUMENTED PURPOSES AND PROCEDURES The evaluation purposes and procedures, both planned and actual, should be documented, so that they can be clearly explained and justified.	Is there a structure in place for ensuring that all evaluators and teachers clearly understand the purposes and procedures to be followed?
	A5—DEFENSIBLE INFORMATION The information collected for personnel evaluations should be defensible, so that the information can be reliably and validly interpreted.	Is there oversight in place to ensure that the results of any given evaluation would be the same regardless of evaluator?

(Continued)

Table 3.1 (Continued)

Attribute	Standard Statement	Key Questions
ACCURACY	**A6—RELIABLE INFORMATION** Personnel evaluation procedures should be chosen or developed and implemented to assure reliability, so that the information obtained will provide consistent indications of the performance of the evaluatee.	Is there oversight to ensure that the procedures of evaluation are the same for all teachers regardless of the evaluator?
	A7—SYSTEMATIC DATA CONTROL The information collected, processed, and reported about evaluatees should be systematically reviewed, corrected as appropriate, and kept secure, so that accurate judgments about the evaluatee's performance can be made and appropriate levels of confidentiality maintained.	Is there a structure in place that ensures that all evaluation information is held in a secure place?
	A8—BIAS IDENTIFICATION AND MANAGEMENT Personnel evaluations should be free of bias, so that interpretations of the evaluatee's qualifications or performance are valid.	Is there oversight to ensure that the results of any evaluation are not influenced by preconceived ideas of the evaluator that may be unrelated to the actual job performance of the teacher?
	A9—ANALYSIS OF INFORMATION The information collected for personnel evaluations should be systematically and accurately analyzed, so that the purposes of the evaluation are effectively achieved.	Is there oversight of the evaluator's final reports and disposition to ensure continued accuracy and use of data?
	A10—JUSTIFIED CONCLUSION The evaluative conclusions about evaluatee performance should be explicitly justified, so that evaluatees and others with a legitimate right to know can have confidence in them.	Is there a structure in place that requires the evaluator to justify the disposition of an evaluation based on documentation of performance?
	A11—METAEVALUATION Personnel evaluation systems should be examined periodically using these and other appropriate standards, so that mistakes are prevented or detected and promptly corrected, and sound personnel evaluation practices are developed and maintained over time.	Is there a system in place to allow the periodic review of the teacher evaluation system to ensure its continued usefulness?

WHAT ARE THE POTENTIAL BENEFITS OF APPLYING THE PERSONNEL EVALUATION STANDARDS?

The Personnel Evaluation Standards are an essential resource for educators who recognize that teacher evaluation is a valuable tool for moving educational practices toward excellence. By providing teachers with expectations, clear direction, and credible feedback on performance through well-designed systems of teacher evaluation, evaluators are able to hold teachers accountable for the high standards demanded by the public, resulting in instruction that best benefits the children. If used as suggested, the Personnel Evaluation Standards will enable schools to develop and conduct teacher evaluations that move beyond bureaucratic paperwork to become a critical piece of school reform.

NOTE

1. The sponsoring organizations of the Joint Committee (listed alphabetically) are: American Association of School Administrators (AASA); American Counseling Association (ACA); American Educational Research Association (AERA); American Evaluation Association (AEA); American Psychological Association (APA); Association for Supervision and Curriculum Development (ASCD); Canadian Evaluation Society (CES); Canadian Society for the Study of Education (CSSE); Consortium for Research on Educational Accountability and Teacher Evaluation (CREATE); Council of Chief State School Officers (CCSSO); Council on Recognition of Postsecondary Accreditation; National Association of Secondary School Principals (NASSP); National Association of Elementary School Principals (NAESP); National Council on Measurement in Education (NCME); National Education Association (NEA); National Legislative Program Evaluation Society (NLPES); and National School Boards Association (NSBA).

REFERENCES

Adams, J. E., Jr., & Kirst, M. W. (1999). New demands and concepts for educational accountability: Striving for results in an era of excellence. In J. Murphy & K. S. Louis (Eds.), *Handbook of research on educational administration* (2nd ed.; pp. 463–489). San Francisco: Jossey-Bass.

Björk, L. G., & Rinehart, J. (2004, June). Alternative and conventional certification for education administrators in *AEL Policy Briefs.* Charleston, WV: Appalachia Education Laboratory.

Darling-Hammond, L., Wise, A. E., & Pease, S. R. (1983). Teacher evaluation in the organizational context: A review of the literature. *Review of Educational Research, 53,* 285–328.

Herrington, C. D. (1993). Accountability, invisibility and the politics of numbers: School report cards and race. In C. Marshall (Ed.), *The new politics of race and gender* (pp. 36–47). Washington, DC: Falmer.

Joint Committee on Standards for Educational Evaluation. (1981). *Standards for evaluations of educational programs, projects, and materials.* New York: McGraw-Hill.

Joint Committee on Standards for Educational Evaluation. (1988). *The Personnel Evaluation Standards: How to assess systems of evaluating educators.* Newbury Park, CA: Sage.

Joint Committee on Standards for Educational Evaluation. (2002). Operating procedures. Retrieved May 24, 2005 from http://www.wmich.edu/evalctr/jc/

Kirst, M. W. (1990). *Accountability: Implications for state and local policy-makers.* Washington, DC: U.S. Government Printing Office.

National Commission on Excellence in Education. (1983). *A nation at risk: The imperative for educational reform.* Washington, DC: U.S. Government Printing Office.

National Governors' Association. (1986). *Time for results.* Washington, DC: Author.

Sanders, J. R. (1994). The process of developing national standards that meet ANSI guidelines. *Journal of Experimental Education, 63*(1), 5–12.

Sanders, W. L. (2000). Value-added assessment from student achievement data: Opportunities and hurdles. *Journal of Personnel Evaluation in Education, 14*(4), 329–339.

Shinkfield, A. J., & Stufflebeam, D. L. (1995). *Teacher evaluation: Guide to effective practice.* Boston: Kluwer Academic.

Soar, R. S., Medley, D. M., & Coker, H. (1983). Teacher evaluation: A critique of currently used methods. *Phi Delta Kappan, 65,* 239–246.

Legal Considerations in Designing Teacher Evaluation Systems

4

Pamela D. Tucker

Marguerita K. DeSander

The legal context for teacher evaluation has its underpinnings in the U.S. Constitution, federal and state statutes, and case law. Fundamentally, the law strives to balance the legal rights of the individual teacher against the rights and needs of society and, by extension, its schools (Cambron-McCabe, McCarthy, & Thomas, 2004). The rights of the individual teacher to due process are weighed against the obligation of the school board to ensure the quality of instruction that students receive. Although the courts are often viewed as favoring the rights of teachers over those of school boards, which act on behalf of students, analysis of dismissal cases has shown that school districts have prevailed in the majority of cases (Cain, 1987; Rossow & Tate, 2003). Typical of many legal decisions, the court in *Childs v. Roane County Board of Education* (1996) commented that "courts are reluctant to substitute their judgment for that of a school board where its exercise of judgment does not violate the law" (p. 365).

Despite a record of support by the courts in cases where there has been proper due process, school administrators are often leery of the legal ramifications of teacher evaluation in cases where there is potential for nonrenewal or dismissal (Frels & Horton, 2003; McGrath, 1993; Zirkel, 1996). As noted by Perry Zirkel (1996), "professional lore" is often confused with "pertinent law" (p. 18) regarding what are the minimal legal requirements. The courts, as well as researchers in the field of teacher evaluation, however, have observed that school districts have *a responsibility* to "hold teachers accountable to standards of practice that compel them to make appropriate instructional decisions on behalf of their students" (Wise, Darling-Hammond, McLaughlin, & Bernstein, 1984, p. 80).

Our purpose in this chapter is to define the legal context and parameters for designing and conducting teacher evaluation in a reasonable and fair manner. We begin with an overview of the purposes of teacher evaluation and the sources of legal standards for evaluation, which is followed by discussion of statutory and case law examples of the desirable elements of evaluation procedures and processes. The discussion focuses primarily on the practical features of an evaluation system and procedures for implementation. Finally, we recommend some principles for designing and implementing an evaluation system, drawn from various legal sources.

WHY EVALUATE?

The importance and centrality of teacher effectiveness has never been more widely asserted than in today's demanding context of educational accountability (Darling-Hammond, 2000; Rice, 2003). It is "the most important school-related factor influencing student achievement" (Rice, 2003, p. v) and is widely viewed as the bedrock upon which educational reform must take place. Although curricula and other variables play an important part in the educational experience, instructional expertise of teachers is at the heart of the learning enterprise (Corcoran & Goertz, 1995; Darling-Hammond, 2000; Rice, 2003; Wang, Haertel, & Walberg, 1993). The ability to judge teacher effectiveness accurately is essential to all personnel processes (e.g., selection, promotion), but most especially to the ongoing evaluation of classroom teachers. For administrators, teacher evaluation can be one of the primary means of ensuring a quality educational program for students, and yet many are hesitant to conduct honest and meaningful evaluations with staff for fear of the potential legal ramifications in cases of unsatisfactory performance (McGrath, 1993).

As the most visible professional within the school environment, the classroom teacher has been evaluated in some manner for as long as we have had schools. Over the years, evaluation has evolved into the highly structured and prescribed procedures used in most school systems today (Shinkfield & Stufflebeam, 1995). Much of the current prescriptiveness is a result of public attention and legislation passed during the 1970s and 1980s (Fuhrman, 1994). Beginning in the 1970s with a push for accountability, the general public demanded more rigorous performance assessments of school programs and personnel to demonstrate educational effectiveness (Harris, 1981). The pressure to improve the quality of teaching was heightened by reports such as *A Nation at Risk* (National Commission on Excellence in Education, 1983), and many state legislatures began to mandate evaluation not only of teachers but also of all certificated employees; subsequently, evaluation became *the* primary tool of accountability in the schools (McLaughlin & Pfeifer, 1988). This expansion of the "state role in defining and developing evaluation systems for teachers" (Sclan, 1994, p. 2) resulted in the implementation of teacher evaluation systems by most states.

Personnel evaluation, in general, and teacher evaluation, in particular, are typically viewed as serving the dual purposes of accountability (i.e., decision making regarding teacher quality) and professional development and improvement (Duke, 1990; Stronge, 1997). Thus conceptualized, they encompass the whole range of personnel functions from selection and hiring to promotion and compensation (Wheeler & Scriven, 1997). Other authors (Millman, 1981; Scriven, 1967) have categorized the purposes as primarily formative and summative. Most legal references on personnel evaluation use *formative* to indicate the developmental process of collecting and sharing information on the teacher's performance and *summative* to indicate the final synthesis of the documentary material for the personnel file; these are treated as distinct stages and components of the evaluation process (Beckham, 1985a; Cambron-McCabe et al., 2004).

Hiring and selection of teachers is an area in which a majority of superintendents (78%) and principals (71%) are satisfied with the freedom and autonomy they have to perform this task (Public Agenda, 2001). Evaluation of candidates typically relies on an interview and review of credentials, primarily professional certification and reports of prior performance (Peterson, 2002). Certification typically reflects the completion of required coursework, satisfactory performance during field experiences, and passage of tests, such as Praxis.

Once a teacher is hired, observation of classroom lessons is by far the most common means of determining contract renewal and promotion. In a study by the National Association of Secondary School Principals ([NASSP], 2001), 89% of the principals reported *always* using classroom observation as a means of evaluation and the remaining 11% used observation sometimes. This widely accepted evaluation strategy is in striking contrast to the examination of lesson/unit plans, which is always used by only 34% of principals and the examination of teacher assessments, assignments, and tasks, which is always used by 27% of principals. Practice has changed little since a 1988 study of teacher evaluation by the Educational Research Service (ERS), which found that 99.8% of the responding school districts reported using direct observation as part of the evaluation process. Based on these data sources, 92% of the principals in the NASSP study reported that they could "evaluate effectiveness of teachers accurately," and 71% thought that their teachers "routinely used their teacher evaluation results and feedback to improve their teaching" (p. 23).

Almost all secondary principals (99%) believe that "teachers are the most important school-related influence on student achievement" (NASSP, 2001, p. 26) and, as a result, view their role in personnel matters as very important and rate this task second only to the establishment of a learning climate in their schools (NASSP, 2001). Teacher evaluation is also a task for which 56% of the principals bear full responsibility; yet 67% of secondary principals report spending *less than* five hours a week engaged in the activity (NASSP, 2001). Despite the belief in the importance of teacher evaluation, the minimal time investment probably reflects the realities of today's busy secondary principalship (NASSP, 2001).

The areas of teacher evaluation in which frustrations appear to arise are around dismissal and compensation. In a Public Agenda (2001) survey of superintendents and principals, 71% of the superintendents and 67% of the principals expressed a need for more autonomy and freedom in removing ineffective teachers from the classroom. Given that less than 1% of teachers are dismissed per year and 5% of teachers are estimated to be ineffectual (Tucker, 1997), it is not surprising that this is an area of concern for administrators. On the upper end of the continuum, 76% of the superintendents and 67% of the principals wanted greater capacity to reward outstanding teachers and staff.

WHAT ARE THE SOURCES OF LEGAL REQUIREMENTS IN TEACHER EVALUATION?

Teacher evaluation is a process conducted within and constrained by the application of legal principles. It is the consideration of those principles that dictates the framework for development of evaluation criteria and procedures and determines the requisite accommodations applicable in cases of unsatisfactory performance. The legal parameters of teacher evaluation derive from several sources: federal constitutional law and state statutory law and the judicial decisions that interpret and apply them. The outcome in any particular case will, of course, turn on the unique circumstances of the case, including specific statutes, local policies, negotiated agreements, and existing case law; thus, differences may exist in what constitutes an acceptable evaluation procedure from state to state and from circuit to circuit (Frels, Cooper, & Reagan, 1984). Nonetheless, it is possible to define the structural underpinnings common to a legally sound system of public teacher evaluation.

Constitutional Foundation

The due process clause embodied in the Fifth and Fourteenth Amendments of the U.S. Constitution are the foundation for the guiding principles of fairness and equity in the evaluation process. Specifically, the due process clause of the Fourteenth Amendment prohibits state governmental action that would deprive individuals of "life, liberty, or property without due process of law." In the context of teacher evaluation, teachers would have a liberty interest in their professional reputation and a property interest in reappointment to teach (Alexander & Alexander, 2005; Cambron-McCabe et al., 2004). As public schools are state entities, school boards are required to ensure and safeguard those rights that are guaranteed by law.

There are two fundamental forms of due process that are considered by the courts: substantive and procedural (Alexander & Alexander, 2005; Cambron-McCabe et al., 2004; Fischer, Schimmel, & Stellman, 2003; La Morte, 1996). Due process necessitates *substantive* protections against arbitrary and capricious government action and *procedural* protections when the government endangers an individual's life, liberty, or property interests afforded by the U.S. Constitution (Cambron-McCabe et al., 2004).

Substantive due process ensures equity and protects individuals from the development of laws and policies that have a potential for a "chilling effect" on individual freedoms and liberty. Moreover, it requires that laws (regulations, rules, and policies) are enacted on a rational basis with means reasonably related to achieving a legitimate objective, such as the use of job-related criteria for the evaluation of teacher performance. Substantive due process safeguards protect individuals against arbitrary government action by the state that seeks to diminish life, liberty, or property interests. Simply stated, substantive due process refers to the legitimacy or propriety of laws or policies. While there have been challenges to laws and policies based on a violation of substantive due process requirements, most legal challenges focus on procedural due process infringements. This is due primarily to the legal threshold the state must meet for substantive due process scrutiny: It merely requires a *rational basis* for the law with means *reasonably related* to achieve a *legitimate* government purpose (Cambron-McCabe et al., 2004). In most cases, there is a rational basis for the actions of schools districts relative to teacher evaluation.

Procedural due process safeguards seek to ensure procedural fairness or the actual procedures followed when government power is used to deprive an individual of life, liberty, or property (Alexander & Alexander, 2005; Cambron-McCabe et al., 2004; Fischer et al., 2003; La Morte, 1996; Nowak & Rotunda, 1995; Valente, 1998). This would involve, for example, notice of concerns and an opportunity to respond by a teacher to an unsatisfactory evaluation. The notion of procedural due process is primarily a "balancing" act by the courts of the individual and government interests that are affected in each unique circumstance. In the case of *Mathews v. Eldridge* (1976), the U.S. Supreme Court set forth the following considerations for a thorough review of procedural due process claims:

> [F]irst, the private interest that will be affected by the official action; second, the risk of an erroneous deprivation of such interest through the procedures used, and the probable value, if any, of additional or substitute procedural safeguards; and finally, the government's interest, including the function involved and the fiscal and administrative burdens that the additional or substitute procedural requirement would entail. (p. 335)

When applied to teacher evaluation, for example, the above considerations would require significant due process safeguards for matters impairing the rights of a *tenured* versus *nontenured* teacher (Alexander & Alexander, 1995, 2005; Cambron-McCabe et al., 2004; Imber & van Geel, 1993; La Morte, 1996; Valente, 1998).

Yet, despite the requirement of procedural due process safeguards, the "[c]ourts have noted that no fixed set of procedures apply under all circumstances" (Cambron-McCabe et al., 2004, p. 402), as each state's due process procedures may vary. Likewise, the level of due process safeguards provided to public school teachers may vary depending on whether the individual has attained *tenure* status—a vested property right in one's position. When the government acts as employer, however, there are special issues with respect to the existence of liberty or property rights in employment. As state agents, public schools must provide due process when an employee's liberty or property rights may be impaired or denied. Although "all the procedural rights can drag a case out for years" (Schweizer, 1998, p. 41), due process safeguards do not shield employees from termination.

Landmark Case Law

Adams (1988/1989) asserted that prior to 1950, it was the courts' philosophy to abstain from interference with or substitute judgment for that of local school boards to dismiss incompetent teachers. In 1950, that philosophy began to change and courts commenced a policy of reviewing school boards' decisions that had gone virtually unchecked until that time. This was the precursor to the current state of public teacher evaluation and termination procedures. From 1958 through 1987, the U.S. Supreme Court granted certiorari to a number of landmark cases that are still the guiding precedent for matters of teacher termination. A discussion of selected cases follows below.

In *Board of Regents v. Roth* (1972), the U.S. Supreme Court clarified the meaning of liberty and property rights in the context of nontenured teaching positions. Roth was an assistant professor hired for a one-year term at Wisconsin State University at Oshkosh. He had no tenure rights, and under state law the decision whether to rehire a nontenured teacher was left fully to the discretion of university officials. The Court stated that a nontenured teacher has a liberty interest not to be stigmatized or to have anything said about his or her good name or reputation. Thus, the violation of a liberty interest requires some evidence that the teacher's "good name, reputation, honor, or integrity" has been negatively affected or that the personnel decision has "imposed on him a stigma or other disability that foreclosed his freedom to take advantage of other employment opportunities" (pp. 572–573), which the court did not find in this case.

The court ruled that the mere dismissal from a particular position does not implicate a liberty interest because having one form of government employment foreclosed does not constitute the kind of deprivation of freedom encompassed by the term *liberty*. Only if, in dismissing the teacher, the government also forecloses his or her chances of employment in a wide range of activities might the dismissal encompass a deprivation of liberty sufficient to require that the individual receive due process safeguards (Alexander & Alexander, 2005; Cambron-McCabe et al., 2004; Nowak & Rotunda, 1995). Because personnel matters are typically considered confidential, teachers are rarely able to establish a violation of liberty interests.

The violation of property interests is a more viable claim in teacher dismissal cases, especially when the teacher has a continuing contract (i.e., tenure with vested property interests). In *Roth,* the Court established that for a property right to exist, one must have a "legitimate claim of entitlement" (p. 577) to some benefit, and in its companion case, *Perry v. Sindermann* (1972), the Court explained that there must be some "mutually explicit understanding" (p. 601) of the benefit. Thus, a person will have a constitutionally recognizable property right in a government benefit, such as public employment, if the person can be deemed to be "entitled" to the benefit. The applicable federal, state, or local law that creates the benefit must define the interest in such a way that there is a mutual expectation that the individual should continue to receive the benefit under the terms of the law in order for there to be a recognizable claim of entitlement (Alexander & Alexander, 2005; Cambron-McCabe et al., 2004; Fischer et al., 2003; Nowak & Rotunda, 1995). Based on these standards, Roth had no property interest because he had only a one-year contract, whereas Sindermann, who, though not tenured, was in fact entitled by Texas state law to continuing reemployment absent nonrenewal for cause, was found to have an implied or de facto property right based on administrative policies and practices.

State statutes often speak to the issue of whether a property interest is granted by the probationary or continuing contract. Case law has further clarified that a tenured teacher's teaching position and salary increments *do* constitute property rights, but additional duties such as extracurricular work and textbook selection are held at the will and pleasure of the school board. As such, they are not constitutionally protected interests (*Needleman v. Bohlen,* 1979). In addition, to establish a denial of either liberty or property rights, the teacher must also establish that the deficiencies that were given as grounds for dismissal were "arbitrary and capricious and not supported by credible evidence" (Delon, 1982, p. 62).

We will continue to use case law that addresses the issues of teacher evaluation throughout this chapter to provide examples of how the intersection of state laws, negotiated agreements, and local school board policies has been interpreted by the courts. Due to the myriad possible combinations, each decision is unique to its specific circumstances. However, the interpretations from various courts across the country are generally consistent in the basic expectations concerning the teacher evaluation process, and they will be discussed in the final section of this chapter. When the basic elements of due process have been present, the courts have typically ruled in the school district's favor (Adams, 1988/1989; Cain, 1987; Rossow & Tate, 2003).

Statutory Law

By 1950, all states had enacted statutes addressing the dismissal of incompetent teachers (Adams, 1988/1989). The grounds for dismissal vary from state to state, ranging from the single, general criterion of "good and just cause" used in Michigan to multiple causes for dismissal, such as the 19 used in Nevada. Although all the statutory law is based on the Tenth and Fourteenth

Amendments, the particular history of each statute and its interpretation by the courts has had a major influence on the resulting case law, so that substantial variations exist across states. Despite the variance in the law among the states, one common thread tends to prevail: When school boards prove teacher incompetence through tangible, corroborated evidence, and demonstrate that appropriate due process safeguards have been afforded to the teacher, courts typically will defer to the decision of the school board (Jackson & Riffel, 1998).

In addition to the state's involvement in defining the broad statutory terrain for dismissal, state legislatures also provide guidance on the specifics of personnel evaluation. As a result of the public demand for quality instruction, discussed earlier, and the courts' growing reliance on school districts' evaluation policies, state legislatures increasingly have played a role in defining the broad parameters for personnel evaluation based on local policies and procedures (Frels et al., 1984). A national survey conducted by Stronge and Tucker (1995) indicated that 79% of the responding states legally mandate evaluation of school personnel by state law, state board of education policy, or state superintendent directive. In some states, a combination of mandates exists. In Hawaii, Texas, and New York, for example, all three sources of legal requirements for personnel evaluation are in place.

Statutory law is the most common source of mandatory teacher evaluation. Of the states responding to the Stronge and Tucker survey, 69% cited statutory requirements; 52% reported a supplemental or independent state board of education policy. Only 12% of the states reported the use of state superintendent directive regarding personnel evaluation. In all of these states, except New York, a superintendent's directive existed in addition to statutes or board policies. Of the 42 responding states, only 8 (19%) indicated they had no state-level legal mandate for personnel evaluation.

In addition to legislating evaluation procedures, a few states have taken the even bolder step of tying satisfactory evaluations to continuing teacher certification. To illustrate, provisions of the Children First Act in Louisiana set forth that teaching certificates can be revoked based on unsatisfactory evaluations. When the law's constitutionality was challenged in *Eiche v. Louisiana Board of Elementary and Secondary Education* (1991), the Supreme Court of Louisiana ruled that provisions of the act relating to revocation of teaching certificates based on the teachers' failure to obtain satisfactory evaluations are not in violation of the state constitution.

State statutes typically define two levels of teachers—those on probationary contracts and those with continuing contracts. Because the due process rights afforded teachers differ based on the level of commitment that the state has made to them for continuing employment, the resulting due process procedures also differ based on the designation of probationary or continuing contract. Nonrenewal of a probationary teacher's contract typically requires only notification that a contract will not be offered for the upcoming year, whereas dismissal of a teacher who is on continuing contract requires full due process, including a statement of specified deficiencies, an opportunity to improve, and an opportunity to question and respond to reasons for dismissal

(Alexander & Alexander, 2005; Cambron-McCabe et al., 2004; Fischer et al., 2003). An unusual provision in the state code of Texas allows school districts to choose between offering teachers continuing or fixed-term contracts. Case law in Texas has further clarified that teachers have no implied property interest in continued employment under the fixed-term contract system (*Texas Education Code Annotated,* 2004). In most states, the general evaluation process and criteria tend to be similar for both probationary and continuing contract teachers, with the exception of how often evaluations are conducted and the requirement to provide an opportunity to improve.

In contrast to Texas, with its weaker protection for teachers with continuing contracts, Ohio offers considerable protection for teachers (Petrie & Black, 1983). The standard for termination in the *Ohio Revised Code* is that of "gross incompetency," which has come to be interpreted as "extreme, flagrant, or complete" inefficiency by the teacher (p. 1050) through Ohio case law. This standard has placed a substantial burden of proof on local school districts compared with the usual standard of "incompetency" and has resulted in some daunting termination cases. "The most extreme case of attenuated teacher termination proceedings on record" (Petrie & Black, 1983, p. 1041) dragged on in the courts for more than ten years (*Jones v. Mt. Healthy Board of Education,* 1983). Unfortunately, the *Ohio Revised Code* provides little guidance to the local school system on how to conduct teacher evaluation, although case law has helped to define what constitutes "gross incompetency." A comparison of the statutorily defined grounds for dismissal in the states of Texas, Ohio, California, Virginia, and Michigan is presented in Table 4.1.

Table 4.1   Examples of Statutory Grounds for Dismissal

California *(California Education Code, 2004, § 44932)*

1. immoral or unprofessional conduct
2. commission, aiding, or advocating the commission of acts of criminal syndicalism
3. dishonesty
4. unsatisfactory performance
5. evident unfitness for service
6. physical or mental condition unfitting him or her to instruct or associate with children
7. persistent violation of or refusal to obey the school laws of the state or reasonable regulations
8. conviction of a felony or any crime involving moral turpitude
9. violation of Section 51530 of this code
10. knowing membership by the employee in the Communist Party
11. alcoholism or other drug abuse which makes the employee unfit to instruct or associate with children

(Continued)

Table 4.1 (Continued)

Ohio *(Ohio Revised Code Annotated, 2004, § 3319.16)*

1. gross inefficiency or immorality
2. willful and persistent violations of reasonable regulations of the board of education
3. other good and just cause

Texas *(Texas Education Code Annotated, 2004, §§13.109, 13.110)*

1. immorality
2. conviction of any felony or other crime involving moral turpitude
3. drunkenness
4. physical or mental incapacity preventing performance of the contract of employment
5. repeated and continuing neglect of duties
6. incompetency in performance of duties
7. failure to comply with reasonable requirements prescribed by the school district for achieving professional improvement and growth
8. willful failure to pay debts
9. habitual use of addictive drugs or hallucinogens
10. excessive use of alcoholic beverages
11. necessary reduction of personnel
12. for good cause
13. failure to perform satisfactory on examination

Michigan *(Michigan Compiled Laws Annotated, 2004, § 38.101)*

1. good and just cause

Virginia *(Code of Virginia, 2004, § 22.1-307)*

1. immorality
2. noncompliance with school laws and regulations
3. disability
4. conviction of a felony or crime of moral turpitude
5. incompetency
6. other good and just cause

Table 4.2 is a second comparison of these five states and the presence of possible due process safeguards. The X's in the state columns of the table indicate the explicit presence of given items in the state codes. The omission of any of these items does not suggest that they are not addressed specifically in the codes.

Table 4.2   Evaluation Components of State Statutes

	CA	OH	TX	MI	VA
State guidelines	X				X
Frequency of evaluation	Annually probationary; every other year permanent; every five years if highly qualified	Twice per year if the intention is not to reemploy	Annually	Annually	Annually
Assessment categories	X	X	X		X
Use of standardized tests					
Written evaluation	X	X	X	X	X
Opportunity to respond	X	X		X	X
Conference	X	X		X	X
Notice of unsatisfactory performance	X	X	X	X	X
Specific recommendations for remediation	X	X	X	X	X
Assistance	X	X		X	X
Hearing	X	X		X	X
Training for evaluators	X				X
Special features	Expressly excludes the use of standardized exams	Uses gross inefficiency as a standard for dismissal	Rating scale prescribed in statutes, one year probation if conditions met in §13.306	Finding of incompetence requires evidence of harmful impact on students	Incompetency defined as performance documented through evaluation that is consistently less than satisfactory §22.1-307

Negotiated Agreements

Teacher unions or associations have negotiated agreements (collective bargaining) that affect the employment of teachers in most states. Negotiated agreements typically address conditions of employment such as salary, benefits, class size, preparation time, and instructional time. The evaluation procedures have also been interpreted to affect the work and welfare of employees; thus, state courts have permitted the negotiations of procedural aspects of the evaluation process (e.g., *Wethersfield Board of Education v. Connecticut State Board of Labor Relations*, 1986; Alexander & Alexander, 2005; Cambron-McCabe et al., 2004). The specific evaluation criteria have been considered by most courts to be management rights or prerogatives (e.g., Ohio Revised Code) and are not negotiable items (Cambron-McCabe et al., 2004). Likewise, collective bargaining procedures and negotiations cannot change or diminish statutory mandates (Cambron-McCabe et al., 2004).

In addition to providing procedural protections in the evaluation process, negotiated agreements can play a substantial role in the dismissal process by making it subject to grievance procedures (Cambron-McCabe et al., 2004; Johnson, 1984). In the event of a negative evaluation, an unsatisfactory rating, or a recommendation for dismissal, a teacher can file a grievance. Typically, during the grievance procedure, the teacher is provided with union representation at a structured hearing or series of hearings to review the procedures used in the evaluation process and sometimes the actual contents of the evaluation document (Frels et al., 1984). "Typically, as the appeal moves up the steps of the grievance procedure, the hearings become more formal and adversarial" (Johnson, 1984, p. 121). Finally, unless specifically prohibited by law, some negotiated agreements may provide nontenured teachers with a higher level of due process protections than are required by state law or the Fourteenth Amendment (Cambron-McCabe et al., 2004).

PROBATIONARY STATUS VERSUS TENURE STATUS

According to Alexander and Alexander (1995) "[t]enure is a privilege bestowed upon the teaching profession by the legislature. The privilege may be prospectively altered by legislative action, but not by local school boards" (p. 348). School districts have the authority to grant tenure; however, school districts cannot alter the provisions of tenure as defined by legislation (Alexander & Alexander, 2005; Cambron-McCabe et al., 2004).

Depending upon the jurisdiction, the concept of "tenure" has many designations, including, but not limited to, the following: continuing contract teacher, permanent teacher, master teacher, career teacher, and professional teacher. It is a designation that denotes permanence in one's position. Moreover, it is a status that is attached to teachers who have successfully demonstrated, during a probationary period, that they are competent and able to carry out the essential functions of the position (Alexander & Alexander, 2005; Valente, 1998).

Modern history suggests the primary purposes for establishing tenure for public school teachers were to (1) eliminate political abuse from the teaching profession; (2) eliminate arbitrary and capricious actions by school boards; (3) create a stable and *competent* teaching force; and (4) safeguard *competent* professionals through job security (Alexander & Alexander, 2005; La Morte, 1996; Rebore, 1997; Valente, 1998; Yudof, Kirp, Imber, van Geel, & Levin, 1982). Protecting and enhancing competence was at the core of establishing tenure for public school teachers.

Typically, beginning teachers are referred to as "probationary teachers" and generally do not enjoy the same protections afforded to teachers who have attained tenured status (Alexander & Alexander, 2005; Alexander & Alexander, 1995; Dawson & Billingsley, 2000; La Morte, 1996; Neill & Custis, 1978; Rebore, 1997; Valente, 1998; Ward, 1995; Yudof et al., 1982). A probationary period, usually defined by state statute as three years, is provided to beginning teachers. The intent of the probationary period is to allow for the acquisition and refinement of teaching skills necessary to become a competent teaching professional. It is also a phase that allows for the critical assessment of those skills and the potential for success by the school district.

Probationary Teachers

Unlike their tenured counterparts, probationary status teachers may be *nonrenewed* at the end of the contract period for any reason or no reason; hence school districts generally are not required to provide evidence of incompetence or make available strategies for remediation so long as the teacher is informed of the nonrenewal decision as specified by law (Alexander & Alexander, 2005; Larson, 1983; Rebell, 1990; Rebore, 1997). However, probationary status teachers have limited protections *during the term* of the contract, and as such, school districts must provide evidence of incompetence or other just and reasonable cause for dismissal actions commenced when the contract is in full force and effect (Alexander & Alexander, 2005; Dawson & Billingsley, 2000; La Morte, 1996; Neill & Custis, 1978; Rebore, 1997; Valente, 1998; Ward, 1995; Yudof et al., 1982).

Tenured Teachers

Typically, teachers automatically attain tenure status *after* the conclusion of the probationary period, provided a decision for nonrenewal has not been exercised. Some state codes allow for extending the probationary period under limited circumstances, but as a general rule, tenure is bestowed after the conclusion of the initial probationary period (Alexander & Alexander, 1995; Dawson & Billingsley, 2000; La Morte, 1996; Neill & Custis, 1978; Rebore, 1997; Valente,

1998; Ward, 1995; Yudof et al., 1982). Once attained, dismissal proceedings may be commenced only for grounds outlined within a state code (Alexander & Alexander, 1995; La Morte, 1996; Larson, 1983; Cambron-McCabe et al., 2004; McGrath, 1993; Rebore, 1997).

In addition, tenure status provides teachers with due process rights—in other words, a vested property interest in the position. Due process requirements (which vary from state to state) squarely place the burden of proof for dismissal on the school board (Alexander & Alexander, 2004; La Morte, 1996; Cambron-McCabe et al., 2004; McGrath, 1993, 1995; Rebore, 1997; Valente, 1998; Ward, 1995; Yudof et al., 1982). Due process requirements also create a higher threshold for dismissal (and other disciplinary actions) that is much more difficult to sustain (Alexander & Alexander, 2005; Bridges, 1992; Frase & Streshly, 2000; La Morte, 1996; Cambron-McCabe et al., 2004; McGrath, 1995; Rebore, 1997; Sullivan & Zirkel, 1998; Valente, 1998; Ward, 1995; Yudof et al., 1982).

WHAT ARE THE RECOMMENDED COMPONENTS OF AN EVALUATION SYSTEM?

Because the combination of mandates varies by school district, there is no one evaluation system that conforms to the unique circumstances existing in all localities (Gessford, 1997), but some general principles can be recommended. Evaluation procedures must

1. be clearly articulated and uniformly applied to meet the judicial standard of "reasonableness" and "fairness" (Beckham, 1985a),

2. address both the general substantive and procedural aspects of the law, and

3. provide "notice" to teachers of the conditions of employment, which will be clearly articulated, explained, and distributed to every teacher.

To satisfy these basic principles, evaluation systems typically include the following components:

a. A statement of purpose,

b. Performance criteria,

c. A rating scale that defines standards of performance,

d. A description of the procedures used to collect information on performance, and

e. A formal means of summarizing the information on performance, such as an evaluation summary. (Beckham, 1985a; Frels & Horton, 2003; Gessford, 1997; Stronge & Tucker, 2003).

A handbook describing the entire evaluation system, inclusive of the above items, should be distributed to all teachers before implementation (Frels et al., 1984). Such a handbook should provide notice of both the expectations and possible rewards or disciplinary action for performance. Each component is described in more detail below.

Statement of Purpose

Evaluation policies and procedures *must* conform to statutory mandates, state and local school board regulations, and the terms of collective bargaining agreements. All policies of a local school board, including the evaluation policy, have the force of law, and the board *must* comply with its own rules (*Iverson v. Wall Board of Education,* 1994). Because the evaluation policy has the force of law, it should be written with care and should reflect principles that the board is capable of fulfilling. An evaluation policy should include a clear statement of purpose.

The statement of purpose in an evaluation policy can set the tone for the school system's approach to evaluation, establish its rational relationship to the state's purpose, and stipulate the possible consequences of the evaluation process (Bosher, Kaminski, & Vacca, 2004; Delon, 1982; Frels et al., 1984; Gessford, 1997). As noted earlier, educational authors have emphasized the dual purposes of teacher evaluation as accountability and professional development (Darling-Hammond, 1990; Duke, 1990; Stronge, 1997). Translated into practice, these purposes can include tenure decisions, promotion, merit pay increases, and termination. A clear statement of the tangible consequences of the evaluation process provides employees with "notice" of the potential state action, an important element of procedural due process. In addition to delineating the uses of the evaluation process, the policy should state when it is to take effect and whether it supersedes in part or whole a previous policy (Frels et al., 1984).

Criteria

The most critical issue in the assessment process is the development of the criteria against which a teacher's performance will be measured (Frels et al., 1984). There should be "sufficient specificity in the elaboration of assessment standards so as to inform a reasonably prudent person of the applicable criteria" (Beckham, 1985a, p. 9). Case law and most state statutes require that performance criteria be objective and job related (Beckham, 1985a). The courts, however, have acknowledged and accepted that there is a subjective quality to evaluation that is unavoidable (Rossow & Tate, 2003; Zirkel, 1996). For example, in *Rogers v. Department of Defense* (1987), the court found that although the evaluation required some subjective judgment, the overall process (including meetings and written instructions) was sufficiently objective to inform the teacher of areas in need of improvement. The subjectiveness of the judgments is permissible so long as the criteria are job related, observable, and uniformly applied to all teachers (Beckham, 1985a; Rossow & Tate, 2003).

In *Eshom v. Board of Education of School District No. 54* (1985), a tenured teacher argued that the principal's evaluation of her teaching was invalid because he compared her with other teachers in the building instead of to objective standards. The Supreme Court of Nebraska ruled that teacher performance could not be "measured in a vacuum nor against a standard of perfection but, instead, must be measured against the standard required of others performing the same or similar duties" (p. 13). Therefore, performance criteria must be applied in a manner that balances an absolute and normative interpretation of their meaning. This process is, of course, less than objective, but it is legally permissible by the courts if there is uniform application.

If some criteria are considered more important than others, this should be indicated in the written evaluation manual (Beckham, 1985b). The relative importance of various criteria was also addressed in the *Rogers v. Department of Defense* (1987) case. The school stipulated that two of the five job elements were "critical for satisfactory job performance," specifically those of "student assessment" and "instructional program." The teacher claimed that he was rated unsatisfactory on only a few of the subitems in each of these categories and that his overall performance did not warrant an unsatisfactory rating. The court held that the school could satisfy its burden of proof regarding an overall unsatisfactory rating based on fewer than all of the subitems of a critical job element if (a) the teacher was given adequate notice of the importance of these elements or (b) evidence was provided that supported the critical nature of unsatisfactory subitems in the overall job performance. In this case, both conditions were met and the teacher's dismissal was upheld.

Although a few states, such as Virginia and Tennessee, have promulgated specific performance standards, these are typically left to the discretion of the local school board, with minimal guidance from state law (Rossow & Tate, 2003). For example, the *California Education Code* (§ 44662) states that local school districts should evaluate certificated employees in the following areas: (a) progress of students toward established standards, (b) instructional techniques and strategies, (c) adherence to curricular objectives, and (d) establishment and maintenance of a suitable learning environment *(California Education Codes Annotated,* 2004). In addition to performance standards that address specific classroom duties, including disciplinary practices *(Sargent v. Selah School District No. 119,* 1979), criteria can include items that assess responsibilities such as coaching, supervision of yearbook development, and professional conduct. If performance criteria can be justified as job related and a nexus, or connection, exists between the identified behavior to be evaluated and proper fulfillment of the professional role, they are generally acceptable to the courts (Cambron-McCabe et al., 2004).

California's inclusion of the criterion of student progress represents a relatively new and controversial development in teacher evaluation (Farmelo, 2000). Although it is assumed that student learning has been implicit in the educational enterprise since the beginning, explicit inclusion of some measure of student achievement is a more recent practice. Researchers in the area of educational evaluation and teachers' unions have criticized the practice, arguing that student progress cannot be measured in a vacuum (Darling-Hammond, 1997; Kupermintz, 2003; Sykes, 1997). Student achievement has been found to be influenced by individual differences in ability and a multiplicity of other variables that are often beyond the control and influence of classroom teachers (Alkin, 1992; Nye, Konstantopoulos, & Hedges, 2004). Nonetheless, several states include provisions similar to California's, and a number of court decisions, using the rational basis standard, have upheld the use of tests to assess student progress as a reasonable basis for unsatisfactory evaluations (Farmelo, 2000; Petrie & Black, 1983; Rossow & Tate, 2003).[1]

A second controversial area in the selection of performance criteria for teacher evaluation is the use of standardized testing results for teachers. Opinions vary on this issue, as exemplified by California statutes that explicitly preclude the use of teacher testing *(California Annotated Code,* 2004, § 44662) and Texas statutes that require it *(Texas Education Code Annotated,* 2004, § 13.047). In *United States v. South Carolina* (1978), the U.S. Supreme Court upheld the use of the National Teacher Examination (NTE) as permissible to establish a minimal level of knowledge within a subject area, but noted that the examination does not measure teaching skills or teaching effectiveness. Therefore, although valid tests such as the NTE, and now the Praxis, may be used for assessing content-area knowledge, they have not been accepted as indicative of actual teaching performance (Rossow & Tate, 2003).

Rating Scales

"A rating system must have definition and meaning to all [parties] involved in the assessment process" (Frels et al., 1984, p. 5). The ratings given to a teacher should be consistent with any directives for improvement. In *Long v. School District of University City* (1989), a teacher received an overall rating of "good" but was informed that her performance in specific areas needed to improve or she would not receive a raise the following year. According to the administrator, the teacher did not improve in the specified areas the following year, was given an unsatisfactory rating, and subsequently did not receive a salary raise. When she requested a hearing before the school board, her request was denied. When the teacher took the case to court, a lower court ruled that she had been denied due process rights, especially in the form of a hearing, and the Missouri Court of Appeals upheld the decision. In this case, the incongruity between the overall rating of "good" one year and the consequence of a salary freeze the following year raised the question of arbitrary and capricious action. Rating scales or systems are usually developed at the local level, but in some states, such as Texas, rating scales are prescribed by state statute *(Texas Education Code Annotated,* 2004, § 13.306). In either case, the more precise the definition for each rating, the more objective and credible the rating scales generally will be perceived to be by teachers and the courts (Gessford, 1997).

Procedures

A description of evaluation procedures should identify who will be evaluated, by whom, and how often. According to the 1988 Educational Research Service (ERS) survey, 99.6% of the 909 reporting school districts had formal evaluation procedures for probationary teachers, and 98.7% had such procedures for tenured teachers. However, the quality of the procedures and their utility in achieving the stated purposes vary substantially (Sclan, 1994). Even the frequency of evaluations varies based on the district and on the longevity of service. Probationary teachers were evaluated at least once a year in more than 98% of the school districts responding to the ERS survey, but tenured teachers were evaluated less than once a year in the majority of the school districts. Most states stipulate the frequency of evaluations in state statutes (Stronge & Tucker, 1995). The states of Texas, Michigan, and Ohio, for example, require annual evaluations of both probationary and tenured teachers. Distinctions based on employment status (probationary or tenured) need to be addressed in the procedures. In addition, individual teachers should be notified that they will be evaluated in a given year for the sake of clarity.

The principal is the supervisor who typically conducts evaluations of staff within his or her building, with observations by assistant principals and department heads in some cases (NASSP, 2001). Some states require that only certified administrators conduct evaluations, but unless a state statute stipulates otherwise, anyone in the school system with the skills and training to make assessments could fulfill that role. Ideally, evaluators should be trained in the chosen assessment techniques and should be familiar with the overall evaluation system (Beckham, 1985a; Frels et al., 1984; Schwartz, 1997). Stronge and Tucker (1995) found that 36% of the states responding to their survey provided state-sponsored formal training in teacher evaluation for administrators. In addition, an increasing number of local school systems are addressing the issue of better training for supervisors (Petrie & Black, 1983). The ERS (1988) found that 84.8% of the local school districts surveyed provided training to evaluators prior to their assessing teacher performance. Ten years earlier, only 61.4% of the school systems had provided similar training. The increased effort to provide more training, coming from the state level in some cases, was attributed to concerns with the credibility and effectiveness of teacher evaluation (ERS, 1988).

In addition to identifying the participants in the evaluation process, evaluation procedures should provide an approximate timeline for the evaluation process, forms to be used, the steps to be taken (minimum number of observations), and how they will be accomplished (Frels et al., 1984; Petrie & Black, 1983). Although the courts have not required school systems to adhere to every aspect of their written evaluation procedures in cases of dismissal, they "have been notably less deferential to school boards in procedural than in substantive matters" (Zirkel, 1996, p. 11). In general, school districts are expected to follow procedures specified in state laws and school board policies (Cambron-McCabe et al., 2004). Therefore, it is important that the evaluation procedures be realistic and somewhat flexible in nature so that compliance is easy to attain. For example, a range of dates versus a rigid timeline provides adequate notice for teachers and yet allows for unexpected events and conflicts.

The majority of schools still rely on observation as the primary data collection method for teacher evaluation, although alternative methods are being tried in some school systems (NASSP, 2001). As noted by Frels et al. (1984), it would be difficult to "justify and defend an evaluation of a teacher's performance that did not include some classroom observation" (p. 10). The use of additional data sources increases both the validity and the legal credibility of a teacher evaluation, and it is especially important in cases of unsatisfactory evaluation. In *Rosso v. Board of School Directors (1977)*, the court commended the school system's "model" evaluation procedures in a dismissal case wherein the principal, the superintendent, and three other administrators observed and rated the teacher's performance with similar results. The court found that multiple perspectives lessened the influence of personal bias and prejudice. The court also noted that the superintendent's method of recording what was going on in the classroom at five-minute intervals gave the "best picture of the learning atmosphere in a classroom that [the court had] seen to date in the anecdotal record" (p. 1330).

Evaluation Summary

The evaluation summary should provide a comprehensive history of the teacher's performance relative to all of the major evaluation criteria. It should note improvement and lack of improvement in specified areas of performance. Examples of specific events and factual information should be used to support conclusions, especially in cases of outstanding or unsatisfactory performance (Frels & Horton, 2003). The focus of the summary should be on patterns of behavior, not isolated incidents, and the impact of that behavior on students or others (Stronge & Helm, 1991). Any personnel decisions made, whether positive or negative, should be substantiated by the summarized record of performance contained in the report (Frels & Horton, 2003).

WHAT ARE THE IMPLEMENTATION ASPECTS OF AN EVALUATION SYSTEM?

Most school districts have relatively broad latitude in how they shape their evaluation criteria and procedures, but this is not the case with implementation. To survive judicial review, it is imperative that all teachers be informed of the procedures and that all teachers be treated in a consistent manner. Less-than-uniform treatment of all teachers could suggest arbitrary treatment, especially when found in conjunction with evidence of discrimination; this variable treatment would be actionable by a teacher (Cambron-McCabe et al.,

2004; Rossow & Tate, 2003). As suggested by Frels et al. (1984), teachers should be treated as the principal would want to be treated if he or she were in the same position, and a climate should be established in which the personal dignity of teachers is preserved.

Just as a curriculum is no better than the teachers who deliver it, an evaluation system is no better than the administrators/evaluators who implement it. Implementation requires ongoing decision making and wisdom in striking the proper balance between encouraging professional growth and requiring accountability for student learning (Stronge, 1997). Effective implementation requires consideration of the following elements:

a. Documentation,

b. Notice of performance concerns,

c. Recommendations for improvement,

d. Time frame for remediation, and

e. Grounds for dismissal (Frels & Horton, 2003; Rossow & Tate, 2003).

Documentation

The primary purpose of the documentation process in most evaluation systems is to provide teachers with useful feedback on their professional responsibilities within the school setting (Frels, Horton, & Brooks, 1997). In cases of unsatisfactory performance, however, the documentation process serves as an important record of the school's actions in a personnel matter. Although documentation is not required on every aspect of an unsatisfactory teacher's performance, it is important that a sufficient sampling of the problems be documented at the time they occur so that it is not necessary to rely only on recall at a later date (Frels et al., 1984). The cumulative weight of relevant and credible evidence is needed to justify a negative personnel decision (Frels & Horton, 2003).

A relevant and credible documentation system should include (a) routine memoranda to the file (minor events of note), (b) specific incidents memoranda (noteworthy events or behavior), (c) visitation memoranda, and (d) summary memoranda (Frels & Horton, 2003). Such records provide principals with factual information on which to base final evaluations, provide teachers with adequate notice regarding potential problem areas, and provide concrete evidence in the event of a termination. To achieve these goals, the principal must engage in ongoing communication with the teacher through conferences and follow-up copies of file memoranda. In fact, Frels and Horton (2003) state that "the cardinal rule of documentation is to conference first and write second" (p. 10), because if an event is important enough to document, it is important enough to warrant seeking the teacher's perception of the situation. A teacher should also be given an opportunity to respond in writing with a memorandum to the file if he or she disagrees with the principal's comments (Frels & Horton, 2003).

Good communication skills are central and fundamental to the evaluation process at all stages (Helms, 1997; McGrath, 1993). Frels and Horton (2003) recommended that communication be "direct, specific, to the point, and be free of educational jargon" (p. 11). The more prompt and specific the feedback to the teacher, the greater the opportunity can be for improvement and avoidance of a termination. Specific feedback is facilitated by the collection of factual data reflecting teacher behaviors and consequences, versus judgments and conclusions, which should be reserved for the final summative evaluation. According to the court in *Gwathmey v. Atkinson* (1976), a termination "decision must be based upon fact and supported by reasoned analysis" (p. 1117).

Effective documentation, ideally, "substantiates the fundamental fairness of the process, establishes a reasonable predicate for the employment decision, and elaborates the procedural integrity of the process" (Beckham, 1985a, p. 1). It can be used to support the integrity of a termination decision even if there are possible charges of discrimination or free speech violations. If there is adequate documentation of deficiencies despite free speech activity, such as involvement in union activities, remediation can continue and termination remains an option if necessary. When evaluations are used as evidence in litigation, the judicial standard is that the documentation be "reliable, probative [i.e., must actually prove the facts at issue], and substantial" (Petrie & Black, 1983, p. 1050).

Notice of Performance

Whatever the source or sources of information used to judge teacher performance, a written record of the information should be shared with the teacher within a short period of time so that he or she is informed of problems and given a chance to respond and improve if necessary *(Needleman v. Bohlen, 1979)*. In the case of classroom or other similar observations, specific facts, not conclusions, should be noted (Frels & Horton, 2003; Rossow & Tate, 2003). Factual reporting based on observation and other sources allows for more specific and focused commendations for superior performance as well as suggestions for improvement in cases of unsatisfactory performance. Short, informal observations can be used to supplement the more traditional, full class period observation. Other sources of information might include parent surveys, student surveys, peer evaluations, and portfolios (Bridges, 1992; Peterson, 2000; Stronge, 1997; Stronge & Tucker, 2003).

When teachers are informed of both the positive and negative findings of the evaluation process, areas of weakness especially must be clearly identified and their relative importance to the overall evaluation must be explained. Teachers should be advised of the fact that failure to improve may lead to termination (Frels & Horton, 2003; Rossow & Tate, 2003). In West Virginia, the court of appeals reinstated a probationary teacher due to a board of education's failure to inform the teacher how he had performed in his job *(Wilt v. Flanigan,* 1982). However, in *Rogers v. Department of Defense* (1987), the issuance of a warning letter that stated the critical nature of four deficiencies that needed to be corrected within two months to achieve a satisfactory performance level was viewed as a proper notice procedure by the court. In the event of unsatisfactory improvement, the specific consequences must be delineated.

Teachers must also be given an opportunity to respond to the grounds for dismissal by presenting evidence on their own behalf prior to discharge *(see,* for example, *Cantrell v. Vickers,* 1980; *Needleman v. Bohlen,* 1979). A major case addressing this issue was brought on behalf of terminated school employees in Ohio, challenging the proper accordance of their due process rights. The U.S. Supreme Court, on certiorari, held that terminated employees were entitled to an opportunity to respond to charges against them *(Cleveland Board of Education v. Loudermill,* 1985).

Recommendations for Improvement

Once unsatisfactory performance has been documented, weaknesses need to be identified, a growth plan developed with specific directives for improvement, and assistance in meeting the directives provided, assuming the unsatisfactory performance is considered to be remediable (Frels & Horton, 2003; Frels et al., 1984; Rossow & Tate, 2003). This is usually done with both oral and written communication to ensure that the teacher understands precisely what behaviors need to be improved, what behaviors are expected, and what the consequences will be if the teacher does not improve in the specified time period. These steps should provide a teacher with reasonable opportunity to improve and substantiate fair treatment by the principal (Schwartz, 1997). Any deficiencies from previous years that have not been remedied should be included in the recommendations, or it can be assumed that they are no longer a concern.

In *Iverson v. Wall Board of Education* (1994), a tenured teacher of ten years was rated unsatisfactory by her new principal; she brought charges based on personal bias and a violation of policy regarding the lack of a plan of assistance. The Supreme Court of South Dakota found that the principal had not acted arbitrarily, capriciously, or unreasonably, but he had failed to provide the teacher with adequate opportunity to improve due to the absence of a plan of assistance. Some states specifically require remediation assistance and others do not, but the courts typically expect it as a component of due process, and concerns are given greater credence when they have been identified and attempts have been made to improve the teacher's performance through a plan of assistance (Rossow & Tate, 2003; Schwartz, 1997).

Time Frame for Remediation

As Adams (1988/1989) has noted, "very little research on the effectiveness of remediation programs for teachers has been reported to date" (p. 24). Frase

(1992) suggested that "only 10% of the teachers found to be incompetent ever achieve competency" (p. 70). This low success rate may be a reflection of the fact that remediation is used as a strategy only in the most extreme cases, but nonetheless, it is important for schools to provide an opportunity for and assistance in remediation to demonstrate a commitment to fairness. Redfern (1983), and later Frase (1992), recommended similar four-phase processes that are thorough and fair, providing the unsatisfactory teacher ample opportunity to seek assistance and to improve, if possible. The process described by both authors consists of the following steps: (a) early diagnosis, (b) performance improvement plan, (c) notification of corrective action, and (d) implementation of termination. The entire process takes 28 to 34 weeks of focused attention and documentation. Although this is more prolonged than what is probably required, it ensures full due process safeguards.

State statutes typically require that a reasonable time period be allowed for the remedy of a deficiency. "Reasonableness" will depend on the specific facts of the case, such as the nature of the deficiency and its impact on children. The Federal Circuit Court upheld a termination of a tenured teacher of eight years that provided only two months for remediation in *Rogers v. Department of Defense* (1987), but the Supreme Court of Minnesota, in *Ganyo v. Independent School District* (1981), disallowed eight weeks as a reasonable time for a teacher of 17 years to remedy teaching practices that had been labeled deficient for the first time. In *Rogers* there had been ongoing difficulties and explicit identification of the expected performance criteria, whereas in *Ganyo* there was no history of problems. These two cases illustrate how different circumstances can render highly discrepant court rulings. Whereas two months was deemed an acceptable time frame for remediation in *Rogers,* a year, as suggested by Frase (1992) and Redfern (1983), is probably a more realistic period.

Grounds for Dismissal

Although dismissals are necessary in a very small minority of cases, a majority of school districts are involved in them on a regular basis. In the 1988 ERS survey, 71.9% of the school districts reported the resignation or termination of a probationary teacher for an unsatisfactory evaluation during the previous two years, and 42% of the school systems reported similar experiences with a tenured teacher. Once a decision for termination has been made, the teacher should be advised of this decision and of his or her right to appeal, informed of the possible consequences of a resignation, and given an opportunity to resign (Frels & Horton, 2003). Because teachers are often afforded the choice to resign, unsatisfactory evaluations frequently result in resignations rather than terminations (McGrath, 1993).

Grounds for dismissal are set forth in most state statutes and typically include incompetency, insubordination, immorality, and failure to improve deficiencies as requested (Rossow & Tate, 2003). Specific examples of the grounds for dismissal from the five states of California, Ohio, Texas, Michigan, and Virginia are given in Table 4.2. Incompetency is "the most time-consuming and demanding of documentation. Nevertheless, it remains one of the most often-used grounds for removing teachers" (Rossow & Tate, p. 21). Incompetency is assumed to entail a lack of both the required knowledge to teach a given subject and the instructional skills to impart that knowledge. The terms may also be used in reference to other areas of responsibility, such as classroom management, student assessment, and duties or actions outside the classroom. Incompetency "ordinarily manifests itself in a pattern of behavior, rather than in a single incident" (Tigges, 1965, p. 1095). Thus, it is essential to have an evaluation system that can document patterns of behavior. Failure by the teacher to remedy deficiencies once identified constitutes permissible grounds for dismissal *(Community Unit School District No. 60 v. Maclin, 1982)*.

In summary, when an evaluation system is implemented, the evaluation procedures should be communicated to teachers before the process is begun and should be applied uniformly and systematically (Cambron-McCabe et al., 2004). The use of multiple sources of information based on different data collection strategies or different evaluators is important for reducing bias and corroborating findings (Bridges, 1992; Peterson, 2000; Stronge, 1997). The preliminary specification of job-related criteria, fair notice of the implementation procedures and evaluation findings, opportunities to discuss and remediate identified deficiencies, and a thorough documentation system constitute a fair and reasonable evaluation system. An evaluation system that embraces the principles described above is one that is likely to be viewed as fair to the teacher and as according due process safeguards while also supporting a termination decision if necessary (Frels & Horton, 2003; Gessford, 1997; Rossow & Tate, 2003; Schwartz, 1997).

WHAT ARE THE GENERAL PRINCIPLES FOR TEACHER EVALUATION?

In essence, the due process and equal protection clauses of the Fourteenth Amendment protect individuals from discriminatory practices by the state. Statutory law further defines the rights of individuals under state law. Compliance with the law and fundamental fairness can be achieved through the adoption of professionally relevant standards of performance and the uniform application of evaluation procedures (Cambron-McCabe et al., 2004; Joint Committee on Standards for Educational Evaluation, 1988; Rossow & Tate, 2003).

Most legal challenges have focused on the procedural aspects of the personnel evaluation process versus actual findings (Cambron-McCabe et al., 2004; Rossow & Tate, 2003). The courts typically have been reluctant to overrule the judgment of a supervisor unless there has been a lack of sufficient documentation to support the conclusions reached, the decisions are deemed "arbitrary or capricious," or there has been evidence of retribution for actions unrelated to job performance (such as the exercise of free speech regarding public issues). As noted in *Parker v. Board of School Commissioners of Indianapolis*

(1984), the court's task "is not to assess the 'wisdom' of employment decisions, but rather to determine whether an employer's selection procedures comport with the law" (p. 529).

The legal context for teacher evaluation provided by the foregoing review of key aspects of the U.S. Constitution, state statutes, and case law collectively suggests the principles summarized in Table 4.3 to guarantee due process in teacher evaluation. These principles not only meet the general legal requirements of a fundamentally fair evaluation process, but also they provide the framework for one that is ethical and supportive of professional growth.

Table 4.3   Legal Principles for Teacher Evaluation

1.	*Written policy*	The criteria for evaluation and the exact procedures to be followed should be formalized in a written policy.
2.	*Legal compatibility*	Any written policy should satisfy state statutory mandates and collective bargaining agreements.
3.	*Prior notification*	All employees must be fully informed of the criteria for evaluation and the exact procedures to be followed before the evaluation process begins.
4.	*Trained evaluators*	Evaluators should be knowledgeable about job requirements and trained to collect data in the manner stipulated by policy.
5.	*Job-related criteria*	Evaluation criteria should be as objective as possible, reflect actual job requirements and school system goals.
6.	*Equitable treatment*	Evaluation procedures should treat all employees in an equitable manner as prescribed by state and local requirements.
7.	*Pattern of performance*	The evaluation procedures should assess a broad sampling of each employee's job responsibilities over a sufficient period of time to identify a pattern or patterns of behavior.
8.	*Documentation*	A record of all written communications regarding the performance of the teacher should be maintained.
9.	*Opportunity to improve*	If job performance is unsatisfactory, there must be adequate notice of concerns, clear directions for improvement, and assistance in improvement (statutory law clearly defines this aspect of due process in some states).
10.	*Substantiation for decisions*	Evaluation summaries must be consistent with and provide sufficient documentation to substantiate personnel decisions.

CONCLUSION

Although administrators could easily be intimidated by the legal requirements inherent in personnel evaluation, there is no need for this to occur. The basic principles set forth in law provide a fundamentally fair and rational system for designing a sound evaluation system and making personnel decisions based on the proper implementation of the system. The courts have supported school districts' personnel decisions when teachers have been accorded fundamental due process rights. The protection of these rights requires time and commitment of resources to the evaluation process, but the provision of fair personnel practices and quality education demand nothing less. The professional development of the vast majority of teachers and the dismissal of the few incompetent teachers are well worth this heightened level of commitment and effort to provide meaningful evaluation. A legally defensible evaluation system is one that provides a useful process for the professional development of most teachers and is ethically sound and fair to all parties.

NOTE

1. Based on the rational basis test, "a court will uphold a law as valid under the Equal Protection Clause or Due Process Clause if it bears a reasonable relationship to the attainment of some legitimate governmental objective" (Black, 2000, p. 1015).

REFERENCES

Adams, F. E. (1988/1989). Legal aspects of teacher dismissal for incompetence in the public schools (Doctoral dissertation, University of Alabama at Birmingham, 1988). *Dissertation Abstracts International, 50,* 311.

Alexander, K., & Alexander, M. D. (1995). *The law of schools, students, and teachers.* St. Paul, MN: West.

Alexander, K., & Alexander, M. D. (2005). *American public school law* (6th ed.). Belmont, CA: ThomsonWest.

Alkin, M. C. (1992). *Encyclopedia of educational research* (6th ed.). New York: Macmillan.

Beckham, J. C. (1985a). *Legal aspects of employee assessment and selection in public schools.* Topeka, KS: National Organization on Legal Problems of Education.

Beckham, J. C. (1985b). Legally sound criteria, processes and procedures for the evaluation of public school professional employees. *Journal of Law and Education, 14,* 529–551.

Black, H. C. (2000). *Black's law dictionary* (7th ed.). St. Paul, MN: West.

Board of Regents v. Roth, 408 U.S. 564 (1972).

Bosher, W. C., Kaminski, K. R., & Vacca, R. S. (2004). *The school law handbook: What every leader needs to know.* Alexandria, VA: Association for Supervision and Curriculum Development.

Bridges, E. M. (1992). *The incompetent teacher: Managerial responses.* Washington, DC: Falmer.

Cain, B. L. (1987). Nonformal teacher discipline (Doctoral dissertation, University of Houston, 1987). *Dissertation Abstracts International, 48,* 1066–1067.

California Education Codes Annotated. §§ 33039, 44662–44664 (2004).

California Education Codes Annotated § 44932 (2004).

Cambron-McCabe, N. H., McCarthy, M. M., & Thomas, S. B. (2004). *Public school law: Teachers' and students' rights* (5th ed.). Boston: Pearson Education.

Cantrell v. Vickers, 495 F. Supp. 195 (N.D. Miss. 1980).

Childs v. Roane County Board of Education, 929 S.W.2d 364 (Tenn. Ct. App. 1996).

Cleveland Board of Education v. Loudermill, 470 U.S. 532 (1985).

Code of Virginia §22.1-307 (2004).

Community Unit School District No. 60 v. Maclin, 106 Ill. App.3d 156, 435 N.E.2d 845 (Ct. App. 1982).

Corcoran, T., & Goertz, M. (1995). Instructional capacity and high performance schools. *Educational Researcher, 24*, 27–31.

Darling-Hammond, L. (1990). Teacher evaluation in transition: Emerging roles and evolving methods. In J. Millman & L. Darling-Hammond (Eds.), *The new handbook of teacher evaluation: Assessing elementary and secondary school teachers* (pp. 17–34). Newbury Park, CA: Sage.

Darling-Hammond, L. (1997). Toward what end? The evaluation of student learning for the improvement of teaching. In J. Millman (Ed.), *Grading teachers, grading schools: Is student achievement a valid evaluation measure?* (pp. 248–263). Thousand Oaks, CA: Corwin.

Darling-Hammond, L. (2000). Teacher quality and student achievement: A review of state policy evidence. *Education Policy Analysis Archives, 8*(1). Retrieved January 3, 2005, from http://epaa.asu.edu/epaa/v8n1/

Dawson, T. C., & Billingsley, K. L. (2000). *Unsatisfactory performance: How California's K-12 education system protects mediocrity and how teacher quality can be improved.* San Francisco: Pacific Research Institute for Public Policy. (ERIC Document Reproduction Service No. ED453152)

Delon, F. G. (1982). *Legal issues in the dismissal of teachers for personal conduct.* Topeka, KS: National Organization on Legal Problems of Education.

Duke, D. L. (1990). Developing teacher evaluation systems that promote professional growth. *Journal of Personnel Evaluation in Education, 4*, 131–144.

Educational Research Service (ERS). (1988). *Teacher evaluation: Practices and procedures.* Arlington, VA: Author.

Eiche v. Louisiana Board of Elementary and Secondary Education, 582 So.2d 186 (La. 1991).

Eshom v. Board of Education of School District No. 54, 364 N.W.2d 7 (Neb. 1985).

Farmelo, D. A. (2000). Using student test results to evaluate educational professionals and institutions: What the law instructs. In National School Boards Association, *Student testing and assessment: Answering the legal questions* (pp. 50–59). Alexandria, VA: Author.

Fischer, L., Schimmel, D., & Stellman, L. (2003). *Teachers and the law* (6th ed). Boston: Allyn & Bacon.

Frase, L. E. (1992). *Maximizing people power in schools.* Newbury Park, CA: Corwin.

Frase, L. E., & Streshly, W. (2000). *Top ten myths in education: Fantasies Americans love to believe.* Lanham, MD: Scarecrow.

Frels, K., Cooper, T. T., & Reagan, B. R. (1984). *Practical aspects of teacher evaluation.* Topeka, KS: National Organization on Legal Problems of Education.

Frels, K., & Horton, J. L. (2003). *A documentation system for teacher improvement or termination* (5th ed.). Dayton, OH: Education Law Association.

Frels, K., Horton, J. L., & Brooks, K. J. (1997). Documentation of teacher performance. In National School Board Association, *Termination of school employees: Legal issues and techniques* (pp. 1–13). Alexandria, VA: Author.

Fuhrman, S. H. (1994). Legislatures and education policy. In R. F. Elmore & S. H. Fuhrman (Eds.), *The governance of curriculum* (1994 ASCD yearbook) (pp. 30–55). Alexandria, VA: Association for Supervision and Curriculum Development.

Ganyo v. Independent School District No. 832, 311 N.W.2d 497 (Mn. S.Ct. 1981).

Gessford, J. B. (1997). Evaluation. In National School Board Association, *Termination of school employees: Legal issues and techniques* (pp. 15–30). Alexandria, VA: Author.

Gwathmey v. Atkinson, 447 F. Supp. 113 (E.D. Va. 1976).

Harris, W. U. (1981). Teacher command of subject matter. In J. Millman (Ed.), *Handbook of teacher evaluation* (pp. 58–72). Beverly Hills, CA: Sage.

Helms, V. M. (1997). Conducting a successful evaluation conference. In J. H. Stronge (Ed.), *Evaluating teaching: A guide to current thinking and best practice* (pp. 251–269). Thousand Oaks, CA: Corwin.

Imber, M., & van Geel, T. (1993). *Education law.* New York: McGraw-Hill.

Iverson v. Wall Board of Education, 522 N.W.2d 1988 (S.D. 1994).

Jackson, W. W., & Riffel, J. A. (1998). Teacher incompetence: A cautionary note. *Education Canada, 28*(4), 12–18.

Johnson, S. M. (1984). *Teacher unions in schools.* Philadelphia: Temple University Press.

Joint Committee on Standards for Educational Evaluation. (1988). *The Personnel Evaluation Standards: How to assess systems of evaluating educators.* Newbury Park, CA: Sage.

Jones v. Mt. Healthy Board of Education, No. A-7305247 (C.P. Hamilton County, Ohio, April 8, 1983).

Kupermintz, H. (2003). Teacher effects and teacher effectiveness: A validity investigation of the Tennessee Value Added Assessment System. *Educational Evaluation and Policy Analysis, 25,* 287–298.

La Morte, M. W. (1996). *School law: Cases and concepts* (5th ed.). Needham Heights, MA: Allyn & Bacon.

Larson, D. H. (1983). Dismissing incompetent staff. *The School Administrator, 40*(2), 28–37.

Long v. School District of University City, *777* S.W.2d 944 (Mo. App. 1989).

Mathews v. Eldridge, 408 S.Ct. (1976).

McGrath, M. J. (1993). When it's time to dismiss an incompetent teacher. *School Administrator, 50*(3), 30–33.

McGrath, M. J. (1995). Effective evaluation. *Thrust for Educational Leadership, 24*(6), 36–39.

McLaughlin, M. W., & Pfeifer, R. S. (1988). *Teacher evaluation: Improvement, accountability, and effective learning.* New York: Teachers College Press.

Michigan Compiled Laws Annotated § 38.101 (2004).

Millman, J. (1981). Introduction. In J. Millman (Ed.), *Handbook of teacher evaluation* (pp. 12–13). Beverly Hills, CA: Sage.

National Association of Secondary School Principals. (2001). *Priorities and barriers in high school leadership: A survey of principals.* Reston, VA: Author; Milken Family Foundation.

National Commission on Excellence in Education. (1983). *A nation at risk: The imperative for educational reform.* Washington, DC: U.S. Government Printing Office.

Needleman v. Bohlen, 602 F.2d 1 (1st Cir., 1979).

Neill, S. B., & Custis, J. (1978). *Staff dismissal: Problems and solutions* (AASA Critical Issues Report). Arlington, VA: American Association of School Administrators. (ERIC Document Reproduction Service No. ED172417)

Nowak, J. E., & Rotunda, R. D. (1995). *Constitutional law.* St. Paul, MN: West.

Nye, B., Konstantopoulos, S., & Hedges, L. V. (2004). How large are teacher effects? *Educational Evaluation and Policy Analysis, 26*(3), 237–257.

Ohio Revised Code Annotated. §§ 3319.11–3319.16. (2004).

Parker v. Board of School Commissioners of Indianapolis, 729 F.2d 524 (7th Cir. 1984).

Perry v. Sindermann, 408 U.S. 593 (1972).

Peterson, K. D. (2000). *Teacher evaluation: A comprehensive guide to new directions and practices* (2nd ed.). Thousand Oaks, CA: Corwin.

Peterson, K. D. (2002). *Effective teacher hiring: A guide to getting the best.* Alexandria, VA: Association for Supervision and Curriculum Development.

Petrie, B. I., Jr., & Black, T. S. (1983). Teacher termination in Ohio for "gross inefficiency": The role of teacher evaluation. *Ohio State Law Journal, 44,* 1041–1050.

Public Agenda. (2001). *Trying to stay ahead of the game: Superintendents and principals talk about school leadership. A report from Public Agenda prepared for the Wallace-Reader's Digest Funds.* New York: Author.

Rebore, R. W. (1997). *Personnel administration in education: A management approach* (5th ed). Needham Heights, MA: Allyn & Bacon.

Redfern, G. B. (1983). Dismissing unsatisfactory teachers: A four phase process. *ERS Spectrum, 1*(2), 17–21.

Rice, J. K. (2003). *Teacher quality: Understanding the effectiveness of teacher attributes.* Washington, DC: Economic Policy Institute.

Rogers v. Department of Defense, 814 F.2d 1549 (Fed. Cir.1987).

Rosso v. Board of School Directors, 33 Pa. Cmwlth.175, 380 A.2d 1328 (1977).

Rossow, L. F., & Tate, J. O. (2003). *The law of teacher evaluation.* Dayton, OH: Education Law Association.

Sargent v. Selah School District No. 119, 599 P.2d 25 (Wash. App. 1979).

Schwartz, R. A. (1997). Remediation. In National School Board Association, *Termination of school employees: Legal issues and techniques* (pp. 31–61). Alexandria, VA: Author.

Schweizer, P. (1998). Firing offenses: Why is the quality of teachers so low? Just try getting rid of a bad one. *National Review, 50*(15), 41–48.

Sclan, E. M. (1994, July). *Performance evaluation for experienced teachers: An overview of state policies.* Paper presented at the annual conference of the National Evaluation Institute, Gatlinburg, TN.

Scriven, M. (1967). The methodology of evaluation. In R. E. Stake (Ed.), *Perspectives on curriculum evaluation* (pp. 39–83). Chicago: Rand McNally.

Shinkfield, A. J., & Stufflebeam, D. L. (1995). *Teacher evaluation: Guide to effective practice.* Hingham, MA: Kluwer Academic.

Stronge, J. H. (Ed.). (1997). *Evaluating teaching: A guide to current thinking and best practice.* Thousand Oaks, CA: Corwin.

Stronge, J. H., & Helm, V. M. (1991). *Evaluating professional support personnel in education.* Newbury Park, CA: Sage.

Stronge, J. H., & Tucker, P. D. (1995). Performance evaluation of professional support personnel: A survey of the states. *Journal of Personnel Evaluation in Education, 9,* 123–137.

Stronge, J. H., & Tucker, P. D. (2003). *Handbook for teacher evaluation: Assessing and improving performance.* Larchmont, NY: Eye on Education.

Sullivan, K. A., & Zirkel, P. A. (1998). The law of teacher evaluation: Case law update. *Journal of Teacher Evaluation in Education, 11,* 367–380.

Sykes, G. (1997). On trial: The Dallas value-added accountability system. In J. Millman (Ed.), *Grading teachers, grading schools: Is student achievement a valid evaluation measure?* Thousand Oaks, CA: Corwin.

Texas Education Code Annotated. §§ 13.047, 13.103-13.115, 13.302-13.306, 21.201-21.205 (2004).

Tigges, J. H. (1965). What constitutes "incompetency" or "inefficiency" as a ground for dismissal or demotion of public school teachers. In *American Law Reports* (4 ALR 3d. 1090). Rochester, NY: Lawyers Co-operative.

Tucker, P. D. (1997). Lake Wobegon: Where all teachers are competent. *Journal of Personnel Evaluation in Education, 11,* 103–126.

United States v. South Carolina, 445 F. Supp. 1094 (D.S.C. 1977), *aff'd mem.,* 434 U.S. 1026 (1978).

Valente, W. D. (1998). *Law in the schools.* Upper Saddle River, NJ: Prentice Hall.

Wang, M. C., Haertel, G. D., & Walberg, H. J. (1993). Toward a knowledge base for school learning. *Review of Educational Research, 63,* 249–294.

Ward, M. E. (1995). Teacher dismissal: The impact of tenure, administrator competence, and other factors. *School Administrator, 52*(5), 16–19.

Wheeler, P. H., & Scriven, M. (1997). Building the foundation: Teacher roles and responsibilities. In J. H. Stronge (Ed.), *Evaluating teaching: A guide to current thinking and best practice* (pp. 27–58). Thousand Oaks, CA: Corwin.

Wethersfield Board of Education v. Connecticut State Board of Labor Relations, 519 A.2d 41 (Conn. 1986).

Wilt v. Flanigan, 294 S.E.2d 189 (WV. Ct. App. 1982).

Wise, A. E., Darling-Hammond, L., McLaughlin, M. W., & Bernstein, H. T. (1984). *Teacher evaluation: A study of effective practices.* Santa Monica, CA: RAND Corporation.

Yudof, M. G., Kirp, D. L., Imber, M., van Geel, T., & Levin, B. (1982). *Educational policy and the law* (2nd ed.). Berkeley, CA: McCutchan Publishing Corporation.

Zirkel, P. A. (1996). *The law of teacher evaluation: A self-assessment handbook.* Bloomington, IN: Phi Delta Kappa Educational Foundation.

Part II

Assessing Teacher Performance

Classroom-Based Assessments of Teaching and Learning

5

Sally J. Zepeda

The process of teaching and learning is complex, and teachers encounter uncertainties while providing instruction to meet students' diverse needs. Similarly, administrators work with diverse pools of teachers relative to experience, preparation, and content and subject matter expertise. Both teachers and students face the call for higher expectations; teachers are expected to do more as are students relative to performance on high-stakes tests. With the reauthorization of the *Elementary and Secondary Education Act of 1965* (ESEA), more widely known as the *No Child Left Behind Act of 2001* (NCLB), school districts across America are striving to hire and retain highly qualified teachers for every classroom. The reauthorization of this legislation calls for scrutiny, for the most part, of teacher knowledge and quality at the front end of teachers' careers while school personnel gauge teacher quality based on the ongoing assessment of teaching through such means as professional development and evaluation.

Assessing teaching in classrooms can and should take many forms involving the stakeholders—teachers and administrators—who have primary responsibility for the instructional program (Danielson & McGreal, 2000; Glickman, Gordon, & Ross-Gordon, 1998; Sullivan & Glanz, 2004; Stronge & Tucker, 2003; Zepeda, 2003a). Assessing teaching and learning is complex because "teachers' knowledge is contextual, interactive, nonroutine, and speculative" (Blase & Blase, 1998, p. 88). For many, to be highly qualified has been equated with proving content knowledge by "searching through the attic" for artifacts that demonstrate in "retro" fashion the qualifications to teach or "by achieving what all but a tiny fraction of teachers routinely achieve: a satisfactory mark on their annual evaluations" (Walsh & Snyder, 2004, p. 2).

The assessment of teaching must be elevated as a proactive and supportive approach (Coppola, Scricca, & Connors, 2004) to assist teachers in further developing the instructional practices that can perhaps enhance learning (Firestone, 1999; Stronge, Tucker, & Hindman, 2004) while proactively involving teachers in self-assessment (Barber, 1990; Peterson & Chenoweth, 1992), and reflection (Laursen, 1996). To engage teachers in such proactive processes would elevate assessment beyond what Darling-Hammond (1997b) characterized as "inspectors who make occasional forays into the classroom to monitor performance and dispense advice without an intimate knowledge of the classroom context, the subject matter being taught, the goals of instruction, and the development of individual children" (p. 67).

Given the importance of teacher quality for improving student achievement, the assessment of teaching *in classrooms* becomes a first step in improving instruction and in assisting teachers in examining their practices one classroom at a time. The supervision of instruction must now take center stage as more than a strategy, as more than a way of evaluating teachers, and as more than a way to ensure compliance. Instructional supervision, regardless of its form (clinical, peer coaching, action research, portfolio development), needs to become a priority because quality teaching emerges in an atmosphere of professional support.

In this chapter, I examine the assessment of teaching by focusing on the formative aspects of instructional supervision, classroom observation techniques, and the differentiated approaches supervision can take to enhance classroom observations. Although covered in depth in subsequent chapters of this book, the use of action research, peer coaching, and the portfolio are examined in light of how these processes can be used to enhance the assessment of teaching. Teaching and learning are at the heart of the instructional program, and it is what teacher do on a daily basis that will make a difference in what and how students learn; thus, it is necessary to examine first what we know about teaching and the standards that have evolved to frame teaching to enhance learning.

WHAT DO WE KNOW ABOUT TEACHING THAT ENHANCES LEARNING?

To be effective, principals and others who work with teachers need understanding of the research on effective teaching. Familiarity and understanding of the research base will produce a more informed basis for the ongoing work needed to strengthen teachers' instructional practices. Research conducted in the past decade demonstrates that teacher quality is one of the most important predictors of student achievement (Darling-Hammond, 1997a, 1997b), and teachers' knowledge of the content area and effectiveness in teaching methods correlate to student achievement (Strahan, 2003; Stronge et al., 2004). With the No Child Left Behind legislation, each state must guarantee a teacher is highly qualified before being hired, and by 2006, teachers in the system must be certified as highly qualified in the subjects and grade levels that they teach.

Teaching is the primary work of teachers and should be the basis for the in-class assessment of teaching and learning for both teachers and students. Assessment of teaching should occur solely on what a teacher does in the classroom as instruction unfolds or as a sum result over time with students. One only has to observe and converse with teachers to understand the complexities of their work. Perhaps viewing what the framers of the National Board for Professional Teaching Standards (1989) enumerated as "the fundamental requirements for proficient" teaching can provide a quick overview on the range, breadth, and depth of skills needed to teach:

> A broad grounding in the liberal arts and sciences; knowledge of the subjects to be taught; of the skills to be developed, and of the curriculum arrangements and materials that organize and embody that content; knowledge of general and subject-specific methods for teaching and for evaluating student learning; knowledge of students and human development; skills in effectively teaching students from racially, ethnically, and socio-economically diverse backgrounds; and the skills, capacities and dispositions to employ such knowledge wisely in the interests of students. (p. 13)

The range of skills and the deep knowledge needed to be a proficient, accomplished teacher is far-reaching, as are the ways in which teachers learn how to teach. Recognizing these complexities in building and further developing the range of skills, competencies, and dispositions teachers need and the work needed to engender the momentum for teachers to want to continue to grow and develop, the National Board for Professional Teaching Standards offered,

> This enumeration suggests the broad base for expertise in teaching, but conceals the complexities, uncertainties, and dilemmas of the work. The formal knowledge teachers rely on accumulates steadily, yet provides insufficient guidance in many situations. Teaching ultimately requires judgment, improvisations and conversation about means and ends. Human qualities, expert knowledge and skill, and professional commitment together compose excellence in this craft. (p. 13)

Because teaching is complex with myriad factors that influence instruction, supervisors are encouraged not to think in absolutes about what is effective or to fall back to the adage, "good teaching is good teaching" while assessing teaching.

To frame thoughts about effective teaching and the work administrators are being called to do to assess teaching, the following is offered: "Teachers learn best by studying, doing, and reflecting; by collaborating with other teachers; by looking closely at students and their work; and by sharing what they see" (Darling-Hammond, 1998, p. 6).

Much of the early research on teaching centers on the effects of teaching, and the major factors that consistently point to effective teaching include

- Sustained time on task (Brophy, 1986; Rosenshine, 1980; Walberg, 1988)
- Pacing of the curriculum and instruction (Berliner, 1984)
- Allocation of time and mindful management of time (Good & Brophy, 1986)
- High expectations (Edmonds, 1986; Guskey, 1982)
- Skillful transitions (Emmer, Evertson, & Anderson, 1980; Kounin, 1970; Kounin & Doyle, 1975)
- Clear classroom management and discipline strategies that are fairly and consistently applied (Emmer et al., 1980; Good & Brophy, 1986)

The next generation of effective teaching principles emerged, which situated the teacher as decision maker and problem solver (Hunter, 1988). Effective teachers "looked for a fit" so that they could "vary their instructional plans and procedures to accommodate not only differences in students, but also differences in subject matter, various learning goals within a subject area, available instructional resources, and available time for teaching" (Schalock, Schalock, Cowart, & Myton, 1993, p. 110).

The release of *A Nation at Risk: The Imperative for Educational Reform* by the National Commission on Excellence in Education in 1983 elevated the discussion of teacher effectiveness and quality, and the premise that teacher knowledge is critical for increasing student learning began to take root in the late 1980s. Following the publication of *A Nation Prepared: Teachers for the 21st Century* (Carnegie Forum on Education, 1986), the National Board for Professional Teaching Standards (NBPTS) was established (Danielson, 1996). The belief and vision of NBPTS was that teacher quality and student achievement could be improved by raising the standards, strengthening educational preparation programs, requiring teachers to participate in performance-based assessments, and more recently focusing on the outcomes of teaching. Five core propositions (see Table 5.1) were developed to aid in the identification and recognition of teachers who "effectively enhance student learning and demonstrate the high level of knowledge, skills, dispositions, and commitments" (p. 12).

Table 5.1   Core Propositions About National Board Certified Teachers

1. Teachers are committed to students and their learning.
2. Teachers know the subjects they teach and how to teach those subjects to students.
3. Teachers are responsible for managing and monitoring student learning.
4. Teachers think systematically about their practice and learn from reflection.
5. Teachers are members of learning communities.

SOURCE: National Board for Professional Teaching Standards, 1989, pp. 10–11.

Darling-Hammond (1989) reported numerous findings pointing to increased levels of student achievement associated with teacher expertise, education, ability, and experience. In 1992, the Interstate New Teacher Assessment and Support Consortium (INTASC) released standards for what beginning teachers should know and be able to do relative to teaching, framing the learning environment, and developing professional roles. The INTASC standards offer an expanded view of knowledge across 10 principles, and embedded within each principle there is a range (8 to 15) of standards divided into knowledge, disposition, and performance standards. Although the INTASC standards (see Table 5.2) are primarily geared for

Table 5.2   INTASC Standards

Standard 1—Subject Matter

The teacher understands the central concepts, tools of inquiry, and structure of the discipline(s) he or she teaches and can create learning experiences that make these aspects of subject matter meaningful for students.

Standard 2—Student Learning

The teacher must understand how students learn and develop and must provide learning opportunities that support a student's intellectual, social, and personal development.

Standard 3—Diverse Learners

The teacher must understand how students differ in their approaches to learning and create instructional opportunities that are adapted to students with diverse backgrounds and exceptionalities.

Standard 4—Instructional Strategies

The teacher must understand and use a variety of instructional strategies to encourage student development of critical thinking, problem solving, and performance skills.

Standard 5—Learning Environment

The teacher must be able to use an understanding of individual and group motivation and behavior to create learning environments that encourage positive social interaction, active engagement in learning, and self-motivation.

Standard 6—Communication

The teacher must be able to use knowledge of effective verbal, nonverbal, and media communication techniques to foster active inquiry, collaboration, and supportive interaction in the classroom.

Standard 7—Planning Instruction

The teacher must be able to plan and manage instruction based upon knowledge for subject matter, students, the community, and curriculum goals.

Standard 8—Assessment

The teacher must understand and be able to use formal and informal assessment strategies to evaluate and ensure the continuous intellectual, social, and physical development of the student.

Standard 9—Reflection and Professional Development

The teacher must be a reflective practitioner who continually evaluates the effects of choices and actions on others, including students, parents, and other professionals in the learning community, and who actively seeks out opportunities for professional growth.

Standard 10—Collaboration, Ethics, and Relationships

The teacher must be able to communicate and interact with parents or guardians, families, school colleagues, and the community to support student learning and well-being.

SOURCE: Interstate New Teacher Assessment and Support Consortium (1992).

beginning teachers, the standards parallel the basis for effective teaching across the career continuum.

Concomitant with the development of the INTASC standards, content and performance standards emerged across disciplines (e.g., math, science, and social studies); embedded within these standards are scientific assumptions about teaching and learning within content areas (Zepeda & Mayers, 2004). Because subject area content standards also represent learning objectives and performance assessment across grade levels, supervisors are encouraged to gain familiarity with them.

Danielson (1996) presented a comprehensive view of teaching in her book, *Enhancing Professional Practice: A Framework for Teaching*, which was based on research on teacher effects. Danielson's framework encompasses four primary domains as the overall standards that frame teaching: (1) planning and preparation, (2) the classroom environment, (3) instruction, and (4) professional responsibilities. Similarly, Stronge et al. (2004) reported the research base for organizing instruction, and they concluded from this research that effective teachers organize more effectively to increase student learning and engagement by

- Focusing on instruction
- Maximizing instructional time
- Expecting students to achieve
- Planning and preparing for instruction (p. 94)

Teaching and learning have also been influenced by several other developments, applications, and constructs such as

- Differentiated instruction (Tomlinson, 1999, 2001; Tomlinson & Allan, 2000)
- Multiple intelligence theory (Gardner, 1993, 1999)
- Brain research (Berninger & Richards, 2002; Wolfe, 2001)
- Constructivist approaches (Brooks & Brooks, 1993; Fosnot, 1996)
- Learning styles (Keefe, 1987; Kolb, 1984; Silver & Hanson, 1998)

Although unique, these constructs have several commonalities that, when incorporated into instruction and assessment practices, can enhance student learning. Moreover, these strategies can be observed and assessed in the classroom. The instructional practices associated with these constructs are important. These practices make opportunities available for student engagement in the learning process based on individual needs, for students to demonstrate learning in different ways that complement and accommodate student differences, and for students to build knowledge from engagement in more authentic ways through problem solving and working in small and large groups (Darling-Hammond, 1997c; Erickson, 2001; Tomlinson & Allan, 2000).

Because teaching occurs in the context of the classroom, its assessment, in part, occurs as instruction unfolds within that context. To assess instruction and to assist teachers in developing their skills, the following forms of instructional and teacher assessments will be examined: formative and summative evaluation and supervision and highlights of in-class assessments that hold promise for improving teaching and learning—primarily for the teachers who have been entrusted to educate children. These assessments can lead to providing more than mere snapshots of teaching and support increasing "teachers' awareness of the learning of students and the creativity of teaching" (Laursen, 1996, p. 54).

WHAT IS MEANT BY FORMATIVE AND SUMMATIVE ASPECTS OF TEACHER ASSESSMENT?

Replete in the literature on teacher evaluation and instructional supervision are the concepts of formative and summative assessments (Bradshaw & Glatthorn, 2001; Barber, 1990; Iwanicki, 1998; McGreal, 1988; Scriven, 1981; Zepeda, 2003a). Formative evaluation practices are concerned with the ongoing growth and development of teachers, whereas summative evaluation practices are generally associated with an overall assessment related to decision making and personnel actions (Hazi, 1994; Scriven, 1981). Formative evaluation, according to Barber (1990), is

> a helping, caring process that provides data to teachers for making decisions about how they can best improve their own teaching techniques, styles or strategies. Formative evaluation must occur in close collaboration with the person being evaluated—he or she must agree to it, be an intensive part of it, participate willingly in it, and, in the case of experienced teachers, even direct it, thus a new dimension of self-assessment. (p. 216)

Formative evaluation situates the teacher as an active and self-directing professional and includes "all activities associated with growth and development including: self-assessment, goal setting, and feedback from such sources as peer review, peer coaching, and portfolio development" (Howard & McColskey, 2001, p. 48). The construct of formative evaluation of teaching will continue to evolve with learning opportunities made available for teachers to develop as professionals (e.g., reflective assessment of student work).

At the other end of the spectrum is summative evaluation that is more concerned with accountability and the legal aspects of teacher competence, rendering final judgments on performance and assisting in making other decisions, including the granting of tenure, removing probationary status, continuing contracts, and dismissal (Scriven, 1987). To this end, summative evaluation helps administrators answer the question, "Will this teacher work here next year?" (McGreal, 1983).

Formative assessments can include a variety of processes and data from in-classroom observations and the examination of artifacts including lesson plans, student work samples, the results of formal and informal student assessments (teacher-developed and standardized tests), artifacts from portfolios, and findings from action research. The rub is that these same data can be used to frame summative judgments about overall teacher performance. The reality is that formative and summative evaluation both detail teacher instructional effectiveness, with the latter culminating in "an overall and final judgment" (e.g., S = satisfactory, E = excellent, NI = needs improvement) (Zepeda, 2003a, p. 19).

Although different in intent and purpose, summative and formative evaluation can and do coexist (Zepeda, 2001), and it is almost impossible, perhaps unadvisable, to try to separate the two in that these forms of evaluation act in complementary and reciprocal fashion. In fact, Stodolsky (1984) offered the caveat, "formative and summative evaluations cannot be seen as two discrete categories" (p. 11). Ongoing assessments provide the basis for summative evaluation, and summative evaluation can inform the types of assistance and professional learning opportunities needed to assist with *formative* development. Although there are numerous ways to assess teaching, one key authentic way to capture data is from classroom observations (clinical and peer).

There are several inherent tensions between the fields of instructional supervision and teacher evaluation. The primary tension includes the belief that the same person cannot provide both formative support (e.g., supervision and coaching) and then later evaluate the overall performance of the teacher for purposes of continued employment (Goldsberry, 1997; Waite, 1997). Another tension with the supervision-evaluation or formative-summative tug-of-war is the fact that in many schools, evaluation is practiced as instructional supervision (Ponticell & Zepeda, 2004); however, "the purposes of evaluation and supervision need not be in direct opposition; both can support the improvement of instruction" (Zepeda, 2003a, pp. 21–22). In an extensive review of the research and theoretical literature on teacher evaluation, Colby, Bradshaw, and Joyner (2002) detailed that effective evaluation systems included both accountability (summative evaluation) and opportunities for professional growth (formative evaluation).

Peterson (2000) offered the following 12 "new directions" (p. 4) for teacher evaluation that can assist in clarifying and showing the interrelated nature of formative and summative aspects of teacher development. These new directions also embrace approaches to evaluation systems supporting teacher growth and development. The comparisons that Peterson made between these new directions and the current practices and rationales can provide local systems with perspectives for examining existing evaluation systems and for framing why supervision is an important aspect for both formative and summative assessments of teaching.

1. *Emphasize the function of evaluation to seek out, document, and acknowledge the good teaching that already exists.* Current practice is to emphasize

Figure 5.1   The Cyclical Nature of the Clinical Model of Supervision

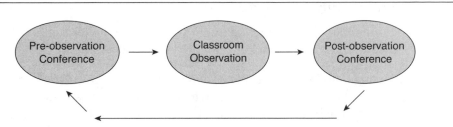

develop follow-up plans for the next observation. Figure 5.1 illustrates the cyclical nature of the clinical model of instructional supervision.

In the pre-observation conference, the teacher and observer discuss a variety of elements including, for example, the objective of the lesson—what will be taught and the methods used, the characteristics of the learners, the assessments that will be used by the teacher, and perhaps more important, the focus of what the teacher wants—feedback. The more the observer understands about the classroom environment and the teacher's instructional objectives prior to the observation, the more informed the observer will be when collecting data that can assist teachers in understanding the dynamics of their work within the classroom environment (Zepeda, 2003a). Evaluation systems that rely more heavily on in-class observations vary in the number of observations conducted per year, whether the pre- and post-observations must be conducted, the length of the classroom observation, and whether classroom observations must be announced in advance.

Although time intensive, one of the original intents of the clinical model was that the observer would engage teachers in several cycles of classroom observations throughout the year. Without negating the call for differentiated supervision and options for professional learning opportunities for teachers made by Glatthorn (1984), part of the rationale for differentiated approaches was that (1) not all teachers needed this type of intensive approach, and (2) the administrative time needed to provide multiple cycles of clinical supervision was daunting for the administrator.

The lynchpin of in-class observations is the data collected and then the analysis of these data by the teacher and administrator (or perhaps a peer in the case of peer coaching). McGreal (1988) made the following points about the relationship between the focus of the observation and data collection to the post-observation conference:

1. The reliability and usefulness of classroom observation is related to the amount and types of information supervisors have prior to the observation.

2. The narrower the focus supervisors use in observing classrooms, the more likely they will be able to describe the events related to that focus.

3. The impact of observational data is related to the way the data is recorded during the observation.

4. The impact of observational data on supervisor-teacher relationships is related to the way feedback is presented to the teacher. (pp. 21–22)

Acheson and Gall (1997) have refined and extended the clinical model through the development of extensive data collection tools, and they indicate that the supervisor's main responsibility is to serve as "another set of eyes" so that the teacher can examine more closely specific classroom behaviors. Data would be collected using either a narrow or a wide lens to frame data collection. It is during the pre-observation conference that the agreement of the focus of the observation would be determined. Agreement on the observation focus is central for the observer to determine which data collection tool to use—selective verbatim, verbal flow, class traffic, interaction analysis, at-task, or anecdotal notes (Acheson & Gall, 1997).

As an example, using a narrow lens and the selective verbatim method, the administrator would be able to track specific words that were said by either the teacher or the students. This form of data collection could be important in the case of the teacher who wants to analyze the types of questions asked during a lecture. As another example of using the narrow lens and the verbal flow method, the administrator would be able to track the frequency of who spoke, how often, and when. At the other end of the spectrum are the wide-angle lens and more anecdotal methods, in which the observer would be able to track overall what was occurring in the classroom. Again, the focus of the observation developed during the pre-observation conference dictates mainly what data are collected during the classroom observation.

Given the contextual nature of schools and the purposes of classroom observations, the observer in consultation with the teacher are in the best position to dictate the best technique to use. Table 5.3 shows the methods in which data can be gathered during informal and formal classroom observations.

The final phase of the clinical model is the post-observation conference where the teacher and observer discuss what was observed. A formal classroom observation that does not include the post-observation conference is counter-productive because the conference is *the* learning opportunity and supports McGreal's (1983) notion that the more teachers talk about teaching, the better they get at it. It is during the post-observation conference that opportunities are given for teachers to talk, inquire, and reflect on their practices. The purpose of the post-observation conference is for the teacher and supervisor to review the data collected in the observation and then to develop a working plan for ongoing growth and development.

HOW DOES AN ADMINISTRATOR DIFFERENTIATE AND EXTEND IN-CLASS ASSESSMENTS OF TEACHING?

The value of conducting in-class assessments of teaching is that multiple types of data can be collected and analyzed by the teacher as a means of improving

Table 5.3   Classroom Observation Data Collection Methods

Method	Description
Behavior Category	A narrow set of behaviors is determined and then tracked. Focus is more on the teacher than the student.
Checklist	A standardized form allows the evaluator to check what activities and/or behaviors are present, absent, or in need of improvement.
Classroom Diagramming	Classroom tracking of certain behaviors and/or movement of teachers and students are recorded in short increments of time.
Selected Verbatim Notes	Words, questions, and interaction are recorded exactly.
Open Narrative	Anecdotal notes with or without a focus are recorded.
Teacher Designed Instrument	Teacher develops an instrument to audit certain teaching and/or learning behaviors.
Audiotape	The teacher and/or the evaluator can audio record teaching and then later listen to the events of the classroom.
Videotape	With the assistance of another person, the teacher can videotape a lesson and then watch the lesson at a later time.

SOURCE: Zepeda, S. J. (2003b). *The Principal as Instructional Leader: A Handbook for Supervisors.* Larchmont, NY: Eye on Education, p. 127. Used with permission.

classroom practice. Three alternatives to the clinical model of teacher observation include using the portfolio (St. Maurice & Shaw, 2004; Zepeda, 2002), action research (Glanz, 1998, 1999; Sullivan & Glanz, 2000, 2004; Zepeda, 2003a), and peer coaching (Arnau, Kahrs, & Kruskamp, 2004; Joyce & Showers, 1983). Either extending the clinical model to include these processes or using the processes in combination with other forms of observation can glean even richer portrayals of teaching and learning.

Through alternatives that extend traditional classroom observation efforts and the use of emergent technology (e.g., videotape analysis, electronic portfolios), data from classroom observations, portfolio artifacts, and video-footage of classrooms can be examined in reciprocal fashion, helping to shape future learning opportunities to "place the teacher at the center of teacher evaluation activity" (Peterson, 2000, p. 4). Extending classroom observations to include such practices as peer coaching, portfolio development, and action research aligns with Peterson's new directions for teacher evaluation enumerated earlier in this chapter.

Action Research

Action research promotes inquiry and is a way in which teachers can be systematically engaged in actively examining their classroom practices through a process of "doing" and learning based on their own investigations of practices. Noffke (1997) reported "the main benefits of engaging in action research as lying in areas such as greater self-knowledge and fulfillment in one's work, a deeper understanding of one's own practice, and the development of personal relationships through researching together" (p. 306). Because action research situates teachers as primary investigators, they benefit from this practice in that the teachers are the "doers" in coming to some deeper meaning about their practices (Patterson & Shannon, 1993). Through active inquiry, reflection, and insights gained through extended conversations with others, teachers are in a better position to make more informed decisions about practices based on discoveries (McKay, 1992), leading to improvements in practice (Grady, 1998).

Most notably, Glanz (1998, 1999) has enumerated a four-phase model of action research that includes selecting a focus, collecting data, analyzing and interpreting data, and taking action. Similar to the clinical model of supervision, action research is cyclical, with the results and discoveries made about practice informing subsequent and ongoing phases of action research. Inherent in each phase of Glanz's model is the reflection teachers engage in before returning to practice and evaluating data derived from practice.

Peer Coaching

Peer coaching originated from the early work of Joyce and Showers (1983) and has evolved from its original application as a follow-up to staff development to a means of collegial supervision in which teachers engage in classroom observations. Peer coaching has also been modified through such forms as cognitive coaching (Costa & Garmston, 2002) that include a planning conference, lesson observation, and a reflection conference. Due to the job-embedded nature of peer and cognitive coaching, teachers are able to observe one another, share strategies, engage in guided practice as follow-up to professional development, and reinforce learning through feedback, reflection, and ongoing inquiry (Zepeda, 2003a).

The research on the practice of peer coaching has been positive (Arnau et al., 2004; Sullivan & Glanz, 2000). In their work with school systems, Sullivan and Glanz (2000) offered that peer coaching is about "helping teachers reflect on and improve teaching practices and/or implement particular teaching skills needed to implement knowledge gained through faculty or curriculum development" (p. 212). In an extended case study, Arnau et al. (2004) reported promising findings in a peer coaching program in which veteran teachers sustained effort to examine their practices over time because coaching offered them multiple opportunities to receive meaningful feedback. The teachers in this peer coaching program reported that they were able to direct their own learning, despite the "extra work" this program placed on their hectic workday, because "they anticipated gains from meaningful feedback, . . . and they believed they would learn something meaningful from their teaching" (p. 38).

Coaching is an important tool for teacher development and increases the likelihood that what is learned is transferred to practice. Joyce and Showers (1983, 1995) related that the level of application after training alone without coaching is about 5%, whereas when peer coaching is included as part of the training design, the level of application increases to about 90%.

Portfolio Development

The use of portfolios in assessing teaching has evolved in practice due to many currents, including the work with preservice teachers and initial certification, the emergence of the portfolio in the process for applying for National Board Certification, and as the evolution of more authentic forms of student assessment has taken hold (St. Maurice & Shaw, 2004). A portfolio is a means for teachers to chronicle and assess their teaching, and the portfolio can be used as a means to extend teacher evaluation (Bird, 1990; Wolf & Dietz, 1998; Zepeda, 2002).

More than a collection of paperwork and discrete artifacts, the portfolio involves teachers in

1. developing goals;

2. selecting artifacts that offer rich portrayals of teaching;

3. receiving feedback on the artifacts as they relate to "live" teaching;

4. reflecting on the impact of the artifacts through data collected in classroom observations; and,

5. chronicling changes in practice based on accumulating artifacts over time (this is achieved by examining notes/memos on earlier artifacts). (Zepeda, 2002)

Based on the research of the author (Zepeda, 2002, 2003a) in an extended two-year case study, a model of portfolio supervision of the practices of teachers in an elementary school was fleshed out. Figure 5.2 illustrates the model and shows how portfolio development can become a vital part of the clinical supervisory process.

Figure 5.2 Portfolio Supervision

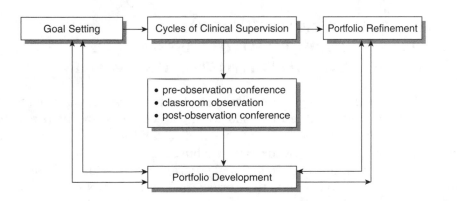

SOURCE: From *Instructional Supervision: Applying Tools and Concepts*, by Sally J. Zepeda, published by Eye on Education, 6 Depot Way West, Larchmont, NY 10538, (914) 833-0551, www.eyeoneducation.com.

Figure 5.3 portrays the reciprocal nature of skill application when the portfolio is used as a complement to the clinical supervision model of teacher observation. The skills work together as teachers explore their practices while constructing knowledge through the practices inherent in the contents of the artifacts included within the portfolio.

Figure 5.3   Skills Inherent in Portfolio Supervision

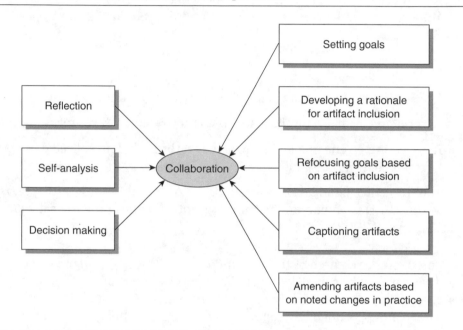

SOURCE: From *Instructional Supervision: Applying Tools and Concepts*, by Sally J. Zepeda, published by Eye on Education, 6 Depot Way West, Larchmont, NY 10538, (914) 833-0551, www.eyeon education.com.

PULLING IT ALL TOGETHER: THE CASE FOR PRESSING FORWARD WITH CLASSROOM OBSERVATION AND DIFFERENTIATED ASSESSMENTS

The assessment of teaching is not a linear, lockstep process that can be reduced to prescriptive methods due to variability in the contexts in which teaching occurs. This premise must become the mantra for the personnel who hold formal and informal authority to assess teaching and learning. The wake-up call for those responsible for the instructional program is to provide multiple opportunities for teachers to examine their practices, to reflect on those practices, to collaborate with others as they are assessing practices, and then to empower these professionals to act on the many lessons learned from these endeavors. It will continue to fall to administrators to render summative judgments based on teaching to fulfill system, state, and federal provisions; however, there needs to be a wide range of latitude between what occurs before and during the process of rendering that final judgment.

Effective administrators are savvy enough to figure out that teachers are and should be at the center of the evaluation process (Peterson, 2000) and that differentiated practices—both supervisory and evaluative—are suggested as ways to work closer with teachers as they develop their practices. Action research, peer coaching, and the portfolio are but a few ways to link both formative and summative assessments of teachers.

Ellen Bernstein (2004), a National Board Certified teacher and the president of the Albuquerque Teachers Federation, in the article, *What Teacher Evaluation Should Know and Be Able to Do: A Commentary*, made the case for the development of five propositions for supervision and evaluation. These propositions can provide a reflective beginning for framing teacher evaluation systems that elevate teacher evaluation to its rightful place in schools—a growth-oriented system. These propositions include

Proposition 1: Supervision and evaluation procedures are committed to teacher growth.

Proposition 2: Supervision and evaluation support teachers to learn content and employ a wide variety of pedagogical techniques.

Proposition 3: Supervision and evaluation procedures are responsible for managing and monitoring teacher growth.

Proposition 4: Supervision and evaluation procedures are designed to support teachers to think systematically about their practice and learn from experience.

Proposition 5: Supervisors (*and evaluators*) are members of learning communities. (pp. 85–87, emphasis denotes text added by this writer)

The possibilities are endless, and a starting point for thinking about these possibilities is to look within the context of the school and to involve those closest to the instructional program in the process of teacher improvement. Many lessons can be learned from within the classrooms as teachers and administrators continue their work to improve teaching and learning for the adults and students who comprise the learning community.

REFERENCES

Acheson, K. A., & Gall, M. D. (1997). *Techniques in the clinical supervision of teachers: Preservice and inservice applications* (4th ed.). White Plains, NY: Longman.

Aleamoni, L. M. (1999). Student rating myths versus research facts from 1924 to 1998. *Journal of Personnel Evaluation in Education, 13*(2), 153–166.

Arnau, L., Kahrs, J., & Kruskamp, B. (2004). Peer coaching: Veteran high school teachers take the lead on learning. *NASSP Bulletin, 88*(639), 26–41.

Barber, L. W. (1990). Self-assessment. In J. Millman & L. Darling Hammond (Eds.), *The new handbook of teacher evaluation: Assessing elementary and secondary school teachers* (pp. 216–240). Newbury Park, CA: Sage.

Berliner, D. (1984). The half-full glass: A review of research on teaching. In P. Hosford (Ed.), *Using what we know about teachers* (pp. 51–84). Alexandria, VA: Association for Supervision and Curriculum Development.

Berninger, V. W., & Richards, T. L. (2002). *Brain literacy for educators and psychologists.* Amsterdam: Academic Press.

Bernstein, E. (2004). What teacher evaluation should know and be able to do: A commentary. *NASSP Bulletin, 88*(639), 80–88.

Bingham, R. D., Heywood, J. S., & White, S. B. (1991). Evaluating schools and teachers based on student performance. *Evaluation Review, 15*(2), 191–218.

Bird, T. (1990). The schoolteacher's portfolio: An essay on possibilities. In J. Millman & L. Darling-Hammond (Eds.), *The new handbook of teacher evaluation: Assessing elementary and secondary teachers* (pp. 241–256). Newbury Park, CA: Sage.

Blase, J. R., & Blase, J. (1998). *Handbook of instructional leadership: How really good principals promote teaching and learning.* Thousand Oaks, CA: Corwin.

Bradshaw, L. K., & Glatthorn, A. A. (2001). *Teacher evaluation for better learning.* Lancaster, PA: Pro>Active Publications.

Brauchle, P., Mclarty, J., & Parker, J. (1989). A portfolio approach to using student performance data to measure teacher effectiveness. *Journal of Personnel Evaluation in Education, 3*(1), 17–30.

Brooks, J. G., & Brooks, M. G. (1993). *The case for constructivist classrooms.* Alexandria, VA: Association for Supervision and Curriculum Development.

Brophy, J. (1986, April). *Teacher effects research and teacher quality.* Paper presented at the annual meeting of the American Educational Research Association, San Francisco.

Carnegie Forum on Education and the Economy's Task Force on Teaching as a Profession. (1986). *A nation prepared: Teachers for the 21st Century.* Washington, DC: The Task Force on Teaching as a Profession.

Cederblom, D., & Lounsbury, J. (1980). An investigation of user-acceptance of peer evaluations. *Personnel Psychology, 33*(3), 567–579.

Cogan, M. (1973). *Clinical supervision.* Boston, MA: Houghton Mifflin.

Colby, S. A., Bradshaw, L. K., & Joyner, R. L. (2002). *Teacher evaluation: A review of the literature.* Paper presented at the 2002 annual meeting of the American Educational Research Association. New Orleans.

Coppola, A. J., Scricca, D. B., & Connors, G. E. (2004). *Supportive supervision: Becoming a teacher of teachers.* Thousand Oaks, CA: Corwin.

Costa, A. L., & Garmston, R. J. (2002). *Cognitive coaching: A foundation for renaissance schools* (2nd ed.). Norwood, MA: Christopher-Gordon.

Danielson, C. (1996). *Enhancing professional practice: A framework for teaching.* Alexandria, VA: Association for Supervision and Curriculum Development.

Danielson, C., & McGreal, T. (2000). *Teacher evaluation to enhance professional practice.* Alexandria, VA: Association for Supervision and Curriculum Development.

Darling-Hammond, L. (1989). Accountability for professional practice. *Teachers College Record, 91*(1), 59–80.

Darling-Hammond, L. (1997a). *Doing what matters most: Investing in quality teaching.* New York: National Commission on Teaching and America's Future.

Darling-Hammond, L. (1997b). *The right to learn: A blueprint for creating schools that work.* San Francisco: Jossey-Bass.

Darling-Hammond, L. (1997c). School reform at the crossroads: Confronting the central issues of teaching. *Educational Policy, 11*(2), 151–167.

Darling-Hammond, L. (1998). Teacher learning that supports student learning. *Educational Leadership, 55*(5), 6–11.

Downey, C., Steffy, B., English, F., Frase, L., & Poston, W. (2004). *The three-minute classroom walk-through.* Thousand Oaks, CA: Corwin.

Driscoll, A., Peterson, K., Crow, N., & Larson, B. (1985). Student reports for primary teacher evaluation. *Educational Research Quarterly, 9*(3), 43–50.

Edmonds, R. (1986). Characteristics of effective schools. In U. Neisser (Ed.), *The school achievement of minority children: New perspectives* (pp. 93–104). Hillsdale, NJ: Lawrence Erlbaum.

Emmer, E., Evertson, C., & Anderson, L. (1980). Effective classroom management at the beginning of the school year. *The Elementary School Journal, 80*(5), 219–231.

Erickson, H. L. (2001). *Stirring the head, heart, and soul: Redefining curriculum and instruction.* Thousand Oaks, CA: Corwin.

Firestone, A. (1999). *The assessment of teaching competence: Rethinking the observation & evaluation of classroom teachers.* Monroe Township: New Jersey Principals and Supervisors Association.

Fosnot, C. (1996). Constructivism: A psychological theory of learning. In C. Fosnot (Ed.), *Constructivism: Theory, perspectives, and practice* (pp. 8–33). New York: Teachers College Press.

Gardner, H. (1993). *Frames of mind: The theory of multiple intelligences.* New York: Basic Books.

Gardner, H. (1999). *Intelligence reframed: Multiple intelligences for the 21st Century.* New York: Basic Books.

Glanz, J. (1998). *Action research: An educational leader's guide to school improvement.* Norwood, MA: Christopher-Gordon.

Glanz, J. (1999). Action research. *Journal of Staff Development, 20*(3), 22–25.

Glatthorn, A. A. (1984). *Differentiated supervision.* Alexandra, VA: Association for Supervision and Curriculum Development.

Glickman, C. D., Gordon, S. P., & Ross-Gordon, J. M. (1998). *Supervision of instruction: A developmental approach* (4th ed.). Boston, MA: Allyn & Bacon.

Goldhammer, R. (1969). *Clinical supervision: Special methods for the supervision of teachers.* New York: Holt, Rinehart & Winston.

Goldsberry, L. (1997). Do teachers benefit from supervision? Yes. In J. Glanz & R. F. Neville (Eds.), *Educational supervision: Perspectives, issues, and controversies* (pp. 44–55). Norwood, MA: Christopher-Gordon.

Good, T. L., & Brophy, J. E. (1986). School effects. In M. C. Wittrock (Ed.), *Handbook of research on teaching* (3rd ed.; pp. 570–602). New York: Macmillan.

Grady, M. P. (1998). *Qualitative and action research: A practitioner handbook.* Bloomington, IN: Phi Delta Kappa.

Guskey, T. (1982). The effects of change in instructional effectiveness on the relationship of teacher expectations and student achievement. *Journal of Educational Research, 75*(6), 345–349.

Hazi, H. M. (1994). The teacher evaluation-supervision dilemma: A case of entanglements and irreconcilable differences. *Journal of Curriculum and Supervision, 9*(2), 195–216.

Holland, P. E., & Adams, P. (2002). Through the horns of a dilemma between instructional supervision and the summative evaluation of teaching. *International Journal of Leadership in Education, 5*(3), 227–247.

Howard, B. B., & McColskey, W. H. (2001). Evaluating experienced teachers. *Educational Leadership, 58*(5), 48–51.

Hunter, M. (1988). Create rather than await your fate in teacher evaluation. In S. J. Stanley & W. J. Popham (Eds.), *Teacher evaluation: Six prescriptions for success* (pp. 32–54). Alexandria, VA: Association for Supervision and Curriculum Development.

Interstate New Teacher Assessment and Support Consortium. (1992). *Model standards for beginning teacher licensing, assessment and development: A resource for state dialogue.* Washington, DC: Author.

Iwanicki, E. F. (1998). Evaluation in supervision. In G. R. Firth & E. F. Pajak (Eds.), *Handbook of research on school supervision* (pp. 138–199). New York: Simon & Schuster Macmillan.

Iwanicki, E. F. (2001). Focusing teacher evaluations on student learning. *Educational Leadership, 58*(5), 48–51.

Joyce, B., & Showers, B. (1983). *Power in staff development through research on training.* Alexandria, VA: Association for Supervision and Curriculum Development.

Joyce, B., & Showers, B. (1995). *Student achievement through staff development: Fundamentals of school renewal* (2nd ed.). White Plains, NY: Longman.

Keefe, J. W. (1987). *Learning style: Theory and practice.* Reston, VA: National Association of Secondary School Principals.

Kolb, D. A. (1984). *Experiential learning: Experience as the source of learning and development.* Englewood Cliffs, NJ: Prentice Hall.

Kounin, J. S. (1970). Observing and delineating techniques of managing behavior in classrooms. *Journal of Research and Development in Education, 4*(1), 62–72.

Kounin, J. S., & Doyle, P. H. (1975). Degree of continuity of a lesson's signal system and the task involvement of children. *Journal of Educational Psychology, 67*(2), 159–164.

Laursen, P. F. (1996). Professionalism and the reflective approach to teaching. In M. Kompf, R. Bond, D. Dworet, & R. T. Boak (Eds.), *Changing research and practice: Teachers' professionalism, identities and knowledge* (pp. 48–55). Bristol, PA: Falmer.

Manatt, R. P., & Daniels, B. (1990). Relationships between principals' ratings of teacher performance and student achievement. *Journal of Personnel Evaluation in Education, 4*(2), 189–202.

McGreal, T. L. (1983). *Successful teacher evaluation.* Alexandria, VA: Association for Supervision and Curriculum Development.

McGreal, T. L. (1988). Evaluation for enhancing instruction: Linking teacher evaluation and staff development. In S. J. Stanley & W. J. Popham (Eds.), *Teacher evaluation: Six prescriptions for success* (pp. 1–29). Alexandria, VA: Association for Supervision and Curriculum Development.

McKay, J. A. (1992). Professional development through action research. *Journal of Staff Development, 13*(1), 18–21.

National Board for Professional Teaching Standards. (1989). *Toward high and rigorous standards for the teaching profession.* Southfield, MI: Author.

National Commission on Excellence in Education. (1983). *A nation at risk: The imperative for educational reform.* Washington, DC: U.S. Department of Education.

No Child Left Behind Act of 2001, Pub. L. No. 107–110, 115 Stat. 1425 (2002).

Noffke, S. (1997). Professional, personal, and political dimensions of action research. *Review of Research in Education, 22*, 305–343.

Patterson, L., &, Shannon, P. (1993). Reflection, inquiry, action. In L. Patterson, C. M. Santa, K. Short, & K. Smith (Eds.), *Teachers are researchers: Reflection and action* (pp. 7–11). Newark, DE: International Reading Association.

Peterson, K. (2004). Research on school teacher evaluation. *NASSP Bulletin, 88*(639), 60–79.

Peterson, K. D. (2000). *Teacher evaluation: A comprehensive guide to new directions and practices* (2nd ed.). Thousand Oaks, CA: Corwin.

Peterson, K. D., & Chenoweth, T. (1992). School teachers' control and involvement in their own evaluation. *Journal of Personnel Evaluation in Education, 6*(2), 177–189.

Peterson, K. D., Stevens, D., & Ponzio, R. C. (1998). Variable data sources in teacher evaluation. *Journal of Research and Development in Education, 31*(3), 123–132.

Ponticell, J. A., & Zepeda, S. J. (2004). Confronting well-learned lessons in supervision and evaluation. *NASSP Bulletin, 88*(639), 43–59.

Popham, W. (1971). Performance tests of teaching proficiency: Rationale, development, and validation. *American Educational Research Journal, 8*(1), 105–117.

Popham, W. J. (1984). Teacher competency testing: The devil's dilemma. *Teacher Education and Practice, 55*(3), 5–9.

Rosenshine, B. (1980). How time is spent in elementary classrooms. In C. Denham & A. Lieberman (Eds.), *Time to learn* (pp. 107–126). Washington, DC: U.S. Department of Education, and Singapore: National Institute of Education.

Schalock, H. D., Schalock, M. D., Cowart, B., & Myton, D. (1993). Extending teacher assessment beyond knowledge and skills: An emerging focus on teacher accomplishments. *Journal of Personnel Evaluation in Education, 7*(2), 105–133.

Scriven, M. (1981). Summative teacher evaluation. In J. Millman (Ed.), *Handbook of teacher evaluation* (pp. 244–271; National Council on Measurement in Education series). Beverly Hills, CA: Sage.

Scriven, M. (1987). Validity in personnel evaluation. *Journal of Personnel Evaluation in Education, 1*(1), 9–24.

Scriven, M. (1994). Using student ratings in teacher evaluation. *Evaluation Perspectives, 4*(1), 4–6.

Silver, H. F., & Hanson, J. R. (1998). *Learning styles and strategies* (3rd ed.). Woodbridge, NJ: Thoughtful Education Press.

Soar, R. S., Medley, D. M., & Coker, H. (1983). Teacher evaluation: A critique of currently used methods. *Phi Delta Kappan, 65*(4), 239–246.

Stansbury, K. (1998). *What is required for performance assessment of teaching?* San Francisco: WestEd.

St. Maurice, H., & Shaw, P. (2004). Teacher portfolios come of age: A preliminary study. *NASSP Bulletin, 88*(639), 15–25.

Stodolsky, S. S. (1984). Teacher evaluation: The limits of looking. *Educational Researcher, 13*(9), 11–18.

Stodolsky, S.S. (1990). Classroom observation. In J. Millman & L. Darling-Hammond (Eds.), *The new handbook of teacher evaluation: Assessing elementary and secondary teachers* (pp. 175–190). Newbury Park, CA: Sage.

Strahan, D. (2003). General patterns and particular pictures: Lessons learned from reports from "beating the odds" schools. *Journal of Curriculum and Supervision, 18(4),* 296–305.

Stronge, J. H., & Tucker, P. D. (2000). *Teacher evaluation and student achievement.* Washington, DC: National Education Association.

Stronge, J. H., & Tucker, P. D. (2003). *Handbook on teacher evaluation: Assessing and improving performance.* Larchmont, NY: Eye on Education.

Stronge, J. H., Tucker, P. D., & Hindman, J. L. (2004). *Handbook for qualities of effective teachers.* Alexandria, VA: Association for Supervision and Curriculum Development.

Sullivan, S., & Glanz, J. (2000). Alternative approaches to supervision: Cases from the field. *Journal of Curriculum and Supervision, 15*(3), 212–235.

Sullivan, S., & Glanz, J. (2004). *Supervision that improves teaching: Strategies and techniques* (2nd ed.). Thousand Oaks, CA: Corwin.

Tomlinson, C. A. (1999). *The differentiated classroom: Responding to the needs of all learners.* Alexandria, VA: Association for Supervision and Curriculum Development.

Tomlinson, C. A. (2001). Standards and the art of teaching: Crafting high-quality classrooms. *NASSP Bulletin, 85*(622), 107–114.

Tomlinson, C. A., & Allan, S. D. (2000). *Leadership for differentiating schools and classrooms.* Alexandria, VA: Association for Supervision and Curriculum Development.

Waite, D. (1997). Do teachers benefit from supervision? No. In J. Glanz & R. F. Neville (Eds.), *Educational supervision: Perspectives, issues, and controversies* (pp. 56–66). Norwood, MA: Christopher-Gordon.

Walberg, H. J. (1988). Synthesis of research on time and learning. *Educational Leadership, 45*(6), 76–85.

Walsh, K., & Snyder, E. (2004). *Searching the attic: How states are responding to the nation's goal of placing a highly qualified teacher in every classroom.* Washington, DC: National Council on Teacher Quality.

Wolf, K., & Dietz, M. (1998). Teaching portfolios: Purposes and possibilities. *Teacher Education Quarterly, 25*(1), 9–22.

Wolfe, P. (2001). *Brain matters: Translating research into classroom practice.* Alexandria, VA: Association for Supervision and Curriculum Development.

Zepeda, S. J. (2001). At odds: Can supervision and evaluation co-exist? *Journal of Cases in Educational Leadership: University Council of Educational Administration, 4*(1), 1–13.

Zepeda, S. J. (2002). Linking portfolio development to clinical supervision: A case study. *Journal of Curriculum and Supervision, 18*(1), 83–102.

Zepeda, S. J. (2003a). *Instructional supervision: Applying tools and concepts.* Larchmont, NY: Eye on Education.

Zepeda. S. J. (2003b). *The principal as instructional leader: A handbook for supervisors.* Larchmont, NY: Eye on Education.

Zepeda, S. J., & Mayers, R. S. (2004). *Supervision across the content areas.* Larchmont, NY: Eye on Education.

Client Surveys in Teacher Evaluation

6

James H. Stronge

Laura Pool Ostrander

T eachers play an essential role in the success of schools and schooling. Research supports the premise that teachers are among the most powerful determinants of student learning (see, for example, Goodlad, 1984; Mendro, 1998; Northwest Regional Educational Laboratory, 1990; Rowan, Correnti, & Miller, 2002; Stronge & Tucker, 2000). Moreover, budget allocations for teacher salaries, the size of the teaching force, and dependence on teachers as the primary workforce of schools point to teachers as a central figure in school success and, for this reason alone, the evaluation of teaching deserves high priority (Harris, 1986).

Teacher evaluation is a critical factor in any effort to validate teaching and learning and the success of schools. Although teacher evaluation has gained attention in recent years, it remains a neglected area of educational research. Evaluation practices have been labeled meaningless (Danielson & McGreal, 2000), described as chaotic (Medley, Coker, & Soar, 1984), and referred to as a disgrace (Scriven, 1981). Regarding the state of the art of teacher evaluation, Frase and Streshly (1994) summarized the opinions of several writers when they stated, "Research and learned opinion strongly support the contention that teacher evaluation has been of little value" (p. 48).

In an era when accountability is the mantra, educational policy makers, educational leaders, legislators, and the American public in general view improving teacher assessment as an important step in ensuring educational

NOTE: The authors would like to express appreciation to and acknowledge permission for using client surveys from the Greenville County (South Carolina) School District, the Lenawee (Michigan) Intermediate School District, and the Virginia Beach (Virginia) School Division.

quality. Consistent with other chapters in the text, this chapter provides a ratio-nale for seeking new approaches to teacher evaluation and explores some potential benefits of collecting data from parents, students, and peers for the assessment of teacher proficiency and for improving classroom instruction and other areas of teacher performance. Specifically, the following six questions are explored:

1. Why should client data be used in teacher evaluation?

2. What are the benefits of including parents in the teacher evaluation process?

3. Can students provide reliable and useful measures of teaching effectiveness?

4. How can feedback from peers be used most effectively in teacher evaluation?

5. What are technical issues to consider in using client surveys?

6. Putting it all together: How can client surveys be used as part of a mul-tiple data source system in teacher evaluation?

WHY SHOULD CLIENT DATA
BE USED IN TEACHER EVALUATION?

The teacher evaluation methods used in the majority of school districts today are based on a model that requires administrators to diagnose weaknesses and subsequently to prescribe solutions. In many American school districts, the primary teacher assessment comes from classroom observations, which may or may not be announced in advanced (Educational Research Service, 1988). In a study of the 100 largest school districts, 94% of those school districts respond-ing to a survey about evaluation practices used direct systematic observation and 87% used informal observation of teachers (Loup, Garland, Ellett, & Rugutt, 1996). Although this single-source method of assessing teacher performance has serious shortcomings (McGreal, 1994; Medley et al., 1984; Peterson, 2000; Scriven, 1981), it is entrenched in American schools.

Medley and colleagues (1984) related the condition of teacher evaluation to continued reliance on a practice filled with opportunities for human error. "The whole art of teacher evaluation up to the present," they summarized, "consists of obtaining someone's subjective judgment of how good a teacher is, a judgment based on the assumption that the judge knows what good teaching is and can recognize it when he [she] sees it" (p. 4). Furthermore, there is con-siderable disagreement on what constitutes the best practices with regard to the complex act of teaching (Scriven, 1981; Tetenbaum & Mulkeen, 1988). Often, minimal teaching competencies based on direct instruction models are used to evaluate teachers (Weiss & Weiss, 1998).

This subjective-judgmental teacher evaluation model that makes "observation" virtually synonymous with "evaluation" has changed little in the past century (Stronge & Helm, 1991). Prevailing practices do not reflect research in effective teaching, nor do they support ongoing educational reform efforts or restructured environments (McGreal, 1994; Peterson, 2000). Weiss and Weiss (1998) explained, "Traditional summative evaluation models are not necessarily structured to support dynamic, regenerative school environments" (p. 1). The most serious indictment against business-as-usual in assessing the job performance of classroom teachers is that the process has done little to improve instruction (Frase & Streshly, 1994).

Classroom Observation Does Not Equal Good Evaluation

Classroom observations are conducted on the premise that seeing a teacher in action provides the best data source for judging teaching effectiveness. These visits, although typically narrow in scope, are important in that they allow the evaluator to assess classroom climate, observe teacher-student interactions, observe instruction directly, and see classroom functioning as no other strategy can (Evertson & Holly, 1981). Direct classroom observation can be a useful way to collect information on teacher performance; as a stand-alone data collection process, however, it has major limitations. If the purpose of a teacher evaluation system is to provide a comprehensive picture of performance in order to guide professional growth, then classroom observations should be only one piece of the information collected.

Scriven (1981) provided an explanation for the low reliability of ratings made during classroom visits. First, the number and length of observations are almost always inadequate for making generalizations. Second, evaluators focus attention on their own personal interests; thus, what gets noticed reflects their personal viewpoints. Third, poor recording systems force the observer to rely on recollections that are influenced by preexisting conceptions. Fourth, any personal relationships or alliances between the evaluator and the subject present confounding factors. Finally, the visit itself alters the behaviors of teachers and students, narrowing the chances of seeing a representative sample of teaching—a factor that preannounced visits only exacerbate.

Additional concerns for classroom observations include

- the artificial nature of scheduled observations,
- the limited focus of the observation,
- the infrequency of the observations (e.g., two visits every two years for classroom teachers),
- only a portion of the full repertoire of teacher duties and responsibilities can be observed (e.g., selected teacher responsibilities may not be performed during the classroom visit), and
- other teacher responsibilities occur entirely outside of the classroom (Stronge, Helm, & Tucker, 1995).

Given the above concerns, the fallacy of making classroom observation the sole source for assessing teachers becomes clearer.

Although classroom observation can be a meaningful and vital aspect of a comprehensive teacher evaluation system, it has major drawbacks as a single source methodology. Teachers often are rated in terms of their *perceived* performance rather than on their *actual* performance, and the observer's perceptions can be affected by preferred teaching styles and beliefs about social roles reflecting biases (Frase & Streshly, 1994; Peterson, 2000). These factors are unrelated to the quality of instruction. There is, in fact, little agreement among evaluators in assessing classroom performance. Like *beauty*, instructional quality seems to be in the eye of the beholder. All too frequently, whim and caprice color judgments (Haefele, 1993), and, although unintentional, prejudice or bias can be factors as well (Wise, Darling-Hammond, McLaughlin, & Bernstein, 1984). Also, it is difficult to separate a teacher's value to the organization from responsibilities directly linked to classroom effectiveness (Scriven, 1981).

Despite the continued reliance on data from principals, many teachers do not perceive principals as competent evaluators of classroom performance, and there is considerable evidence to indicate that principals' ratings tend to be inflated (Frase & Streshly, 1994). Peterson and Kauchak (1982) blamed the failure to develop more effective evaluation procedures on the state of the art, the need to satisfy diverse audiences who compete for information, and the fact that other data sources have been neglected.

Frase and Streshly (1994) reported a study involving six school districts where paid auditors reviewed tenured teachers' evaluation data and made classroom observations. The auditors described many incidents of poor instructional practices (e.g., exclusive use of seatwork, extensive copying of exercises from chalkboards or overheads, students left unattended by their teachers) in classrooms where instructors received high ratings. They concluded that the principals' ratings were grossly inflated and offered little helpful information for teacher improvement.

Root and Overly (1990) reached similar conclusions. They described teacher evaluation as "a bureaucratic requirement that is conducted perfunctorily and does little to improve teacher performance" (p. 35). All too frequently teachers do not receive constructive information from administrators and they view the process as useless. Frase and Streshly (1994) described the principal's performance in teacher evaluation as an "abrogation of duty [that is] malpractice in its worst form" (p. 55).

Bridges (1986) speculated that one explanation for the high ratings principals commonly give teachers is that they are unable to devote enough time to do the job adequately and, thus, are reluctant to be critical of the teacher's performance. Many are defensive about the whole issue of performance assessment. Furthermore, some principals may want to avoid conflict, fear repercussions, and wish to avoid the high cost of litigation if they are challenged in court.

An even more serious criticism for heavy or sole reliance on one-shot observations for teacher evaluation is the contention that teachers seldom use evaluation data from principals to make meaningful changes in classroom practice (Frase & Streshly, 1994) and that current evaluation procedures protect less competent staff members from dismissal (Haefele, 1993). Likewise, there is evidence that principals seldom utilize evaluation data for personnel matters (e.g., hiring, firing, promoting) (McGreal, 1994).

There are two commonly stated arguments against continued reliance on formal observation as the sole assessment of teaching quality. First, the practice places the teacher's fate in the hands of a single judge (Peterson, 2000; Harris, 1986), and second, it is a model that no longer reflects the way American schools operate (McGreal, 1994; Ellet & Garland, 1987). Recent reform movements that foster stakeholder empowerment, collaboration, collegiality, and increased teacher accountability require better ways to validate teacher effectiveness (Dixon, 1994).

Collaboration in Teacher Evaluation

One reason for the uncertainty surrounding current evaluation methods involves the relative isolation in which teachers work. Bruce Joyce (cited in Costa, 1993) described teaching as one of the most private acts in which humans engage, and Peterson (2000) cited isolation and independence as major sociological constraints on evaluation practices. Fullan (1994) called for a move from isolation to collaboration for implementing the successful change strategies that current reform movements demand. He maintained that if organizations do not collaborate externally as well as internally, change does not occur.

One school reform movement that has significant implications for collaboration in teacher evaluation is Total Quality Management (TQM; Deming, 1986). Adopted by many school districts as a framework for educational reform, TQM offers techniques for assessing and improving all components of school operations (Bonstingl, 1992; Bayless et al., 1992). The application of TQM principles to education parallels a growing interest in applying successful strategies from the business world to the management of schools. Two elements drawn from an emphasis on organizational quality significant to the evaluation of teaching are an emphasis on pride of workmanship and customer service.

Pride of workmanship places the responsibility for service improvement on the supplier and requires constant monitoring through feedback from customers. Using this model, teachers are the service providers (or suppliers) and the customers (or clients) include students, parents, other teachers, other institutions, and the community. Client surveys are the primary source of customer feedback.

As more school districts have embraced reform efforts that focus on quality improvement, a concern for *customer service* and client satisfaction has emerged (Bonstingl, 1992). Teachers have identified both internal clients (e.g., principals, students, other teachers, department chairpersons) and external clients (e.g., parents, higher education, employers). Feedback information from one or more of the teachers' clients can help fill a serious gap in the performance review arena.

Table 6.1   Clients as Data Sources for Teacher Evaluation by School Level

Data Source	Elementary School (%)	Middle School/ Junior High (%)	High School (%)
Principals	95.3	93.4	90.8
Assistant principals	43.8	67.3	71.3
Department chairs	5.7	14.1	23.5
Supervisors	30.4	29.9	29.9
Peers	6.4	6.2	6.2
Students	2.8	3.0	3.4
Parents	1.2	1.1	1.1
Self-assessment	23.2	22.6	21.7

SOURCE: Adapted from Educational Research Service, 1988.

A summary of the use of client feedback in teacher evaluation is provided in Table 6.1.

The following sections of the chapter explore issues and implications of incorporating data from three key client sources in a comprehensive teacher evaluation system: parents, students, and peers.

WHAT ARE THE BENEFITS OF INCLUDING PARENTS IN THE TEACHER EVALUATION PROCESS?

Numerous educational reform efforts of the past two decades have called for increased parental involvement in education and increased empowerment of parents for decision making. There is substantial evidence that good parent-teacher relationships and effective home-school communications have positive effects on school success (Becher, 1984). Traditionally, however, most teacher-initiated interactions with parents result from problems that occur at school (Mager, 1980). Some responsibility for this state of affairs can be attributed to educators who have become "gun-shy" because of experience with groups who oppose specific causes (e.g., sex education or outcome-based education), but the failure of parents to demand school accountability is undoubtedly a factor as well.

One vital aspect of enhancing parental involvement in education is to invite parents into the educational enterprise as partners in decision making. Peterson (2000) contended that parent input must be systematic, not haphazard. Haphazard solicitation of parent input results in inaccurate and unreliable information. In a discussion of the value of involving stakeholders (e.g., parents) in evaluation, Mark and Shotland (1985) noted that benefits include empowerment. Once invited to participate in the teacher assessment process, parents can offer a perspective and insight otherwise not available.

Epstein (1985) undertook one of the more comprehensive efforts to investigate the potential contributions of parents in teacher evaluation. In a study involving 77 elementary school teachers, ratings from parents and principals were compared and analyzed to isolate variables that influenced judgments about teacher merit and to assess the efficacy of parent involvement in the evaluation process.

The study revealed that principals and parents emphasized different components of teaching. For example, principals were more aware of how well teachers performed extra duties than about changes in classroom practice; thus doing a good job on noninstructional tasks may have resulted in higher marks from principals than exemplary teaching. Parents, however, were more knowledgeable about special efforts the teacher made to help their children, and this insight had more impact on parents' ratings of teacher performance. Epstein (1985) maintained that parents may, in fact, be more cognizant than principals of some aspects of teacher quality.

> They [the parents] may be knowledgeable about how the teacher interacts with the child and family, responds to the student's needs and skills, assigns appropriate challenges in books and in homework, and inspires the student to continue commitment to school work at home—all indicators of effective teaching. With unique interests and investments in both teacher effectiveness and school organization, parents may be legitimate and important contributors among multiple judges in the evaluation of teachers and school programs. (p. 4)

One of the most important variables identified in Epstein's 1985 work involved the teacher's interpersonal skills. Increased parental involvement, more teacher-initiated communications for parents, and good classroom discipline earned higher ratings for the teachers in this study. Epstein suggested that inclusion of parents in the evaluation process would result in "more teachers [who are] recognized as good teachers for different skills and teaching abilities than if only principals rated the teachers" (p. 9).

Peterson (1988) examined the use of parent surveys as an optional data source. Forty-eight percent of the eligible teachers in two school districts ($n =$ 701) chose parent surveys as a source of data for merit pay consideration. The survey they used was research based, but "addressed only information for which the parents could be expected to have first-hand information" (p. 243). The unit of analysis for this study was the class mean on one global item assessing parents' overall satisfaction with their children's classroom experience. Teachers received a mean rating of 4.49 on a 5-point scale. Both the teachers' mean rating and the return rate declined at higher grade levels. In follow-up interviews, 76.6% of the participating teachers described the parent surveys as "valuable feedback" that was "pertinent, specific, and ultimately credible" (p. 247). They suggested that the parents' open-ended comments were especially helpful.

Peterson's (1988) findings corroborated Epstein's work (1985) with regard to ratings by parents of elementary students but left questions about the use of parent ratings for secondary teachers. He suggested "less contact and communication results in more global or halo ratings for the teachers of older students" (p. 247).

Faucette, Ball, and Ostrander (1995) reported one of the most extensive uses of client surveys in teacher assessment in a large suburban school district ($n = 75,000$) in which teachers were encouraged to voluntarily participate in a customer service project. For three years, survey forms called the Parent Perception Survey (see Figure 6.1), which were developed by teachers, were mailed directly to the parents of students of the participants and returned to an external agency by mail. The confidential data summaries that were provided were intended for the teachers' personal and professional improvement.

Figure 6.1   The Parent Perception Survey

PARENT PERCEPTION SURVEY

> Teacher:
>
> Grade or Subject:
>
> School:

The teacher named above has volunteered to take part in the Parent Perception Survey. This teacher values your opinion. Please be sure your responses apply only to this teacher.

Start Here:

> Since the beginning of the school year, have you . . .
>
> - Attended a general school meeting, for example,   Yes ☐   No ☐
>   back to school night or a meeting of a parent-teacher
>   organization?
>
> - Attended a school or class event such as a play,   Yes ☐   No ☐
>   sports event, or science fair?
>
> - Acted as a volunteer at the school or served   Yes ☐   No ☐
>   on a school committee?

INSTRUCTIONS

Please answer the three questions above. Then, carefully consider each of the following statements as it relates to your impressions about your child's teacher. Decide if you STRONGLY AGREE, AGREE, DISAGREE, or STRONGLY DISAGREE with the statement and fill in the appropriate block. If you are unable to make a judgment for any reason, mark the NO ANSWER block. Please do not leave any items blank.

If you have additional comments, please use the space on the back of this survey. To ensure confidentiality of your response, tear off the section of the survey with your name and address. Then, please fold and return the completed survey to Continental Research by using the enclosed envelope. Please respond within one week.

Thank you very much for your time.

My child's teacher:	Strongly Agree	Agree	Disagree	Strongly Disagree	No Answer
1. Communicates with me	☐	☐	☐	☐	☐
2. Makes me feel comfortable contacting him/her	☐	☐	☐	☐	☐
3. Provides helpful information during conferences	☐	☐	☐	☐	☐
4. Informs me about my child's progress	☐	☐	☐	☐	☐
5. Is courteous	☐	☐	☐	☐	☐
6. Listens to what I have to say	☐	☐	☐	☐	☐
7. Has my respect	☐	☐	☐	☐	☐
8. Informs me about classroom expectations	☐	☐	☐	☐	☐
9. Informs me of classroom grading procedures	☐	☐	☐	☐	☐
10. Makes classroom rules known to students	☐	☐	☐	☐	☐
11. Uses fair disciplinary procedures	☐	☐	☐	☐	☐
12. Challenges my child	☐	☐	☐	☐	☐
13. Builds on my child's strengths	☐	☐	☐	☐	☐
14. Recognizes improved achievement	☐	☐	☐	☐	☐
15. Recognizes positive behaviors	☐	☐	☐	☐	☐
16. Is respected by my child	☐	☐	☐	☐	☐
17. Fosters growth in areas needing improvement	☐	☐	☐	☐	☐
18. Encourages classroom participation	☐	☐	☐	☐	☐
19. Uses a variety of instructional methods	☐	☐	☐	☐	☐
20. Grades my child's overall classroom performance	☐	☐	☐	☐	☐
21. Relates instruction to everyday life	☐	☐	☐	☐	☐

My child's teacher:	Strongly Agree	Agree	Disagree	Strongly Disagree	No Answer
22. Assigns homework that supports classroom learning	☐	☐	☐	☐	☐
23. Explains the homework assignment	☐	☐	☐	☐	☐
24. Offers additional help when necessary	☐	☐	☐	☐	☐
25. Provides an inviting environment	☐	☐	☐	☐	☐
26. Creates a safe learning environment	☐	☐	☐	☐	☐
27. Provides an environment that promotes learning	☐	☐	☐	☐	☐

SOURCE: Virginia Beach City Public Schools, © March 1995. Used with permission.

The results were consistently positive for individual participants and for the school district as a whole. More than 70% of all teachers in the district utilized the survey at least once, and many volunteered all three years. Each year the grand mean[1] increased slightly (see Table 6.2), suggesting that teachers used the information they received from the parents to improve the services they provided. The highest impact appeared to be in the area of communications. Teachers reported that the primary modifications they made in their teaching practices (in response to the parent feedback) were increases in both the quantity and quality of communications with the parents of their students.

Table 6.2   1993–1995 Parent Perception Survey

Category	No. of Teacher Participants	Range of Item Means	No. of Surveys Mailed	Response Rate	Grand Mean
1993	1,610 (37%)	1.8–3.6	40,128	NA	3.40
1994	2,380 (52%)	3.3–3.6	69,102	39.3%	3.46
1995	1,740 (38%)	3.4–3.6	51,972	31.4%	3.53

SOURCE: Ostrander (1995).

In a study involving a sample ($n = 93$) of the parent survey participants, Ostrander (1995) compared the ratings of the parents to teacher self-assessments and to students' and principals' ratings of the teachers on the items in the Parent

Perception Survey. Data were disaggregated for six subcategories including classroom environment, grading, homework, communication, instruction, and interpersonal relationships. While all ratings were generally quite high, there were some subtle differences. Principals consistently rated the teachers higher than any of the other respondents on all subcategories except homework, where the teacher self-assessments were higher. The students gave the teachers the lowest ratings in all of the areas and the parents gave them the second lowest. In addition, parent ratings showed a higher correlation with the students' ratings than with the teachers' or principals'.

The notion that parents favor being involved in the evaluation process and that they appreciate being asked to provide feedback concerning teacher effectiveness has been validated in several projects (Faucette, Ball, & Ostrander, 1994; Peterson & Mitchell, 1985). Teacher participants in these studies found the parent data especially helpful for personal and professional growth. In the 1995 Faucette, Ball, and Ostrander project, teachers reported that they were not previously aware that parents possessed either the quality or quantity of information about classroom practices that the surveys confirmed. They generally accepted the parent data as informative, accurate, and useful. The comment section of the survey was particularly valuable. The parent respondents in this study also reported positive reactions regarding the opportunity to provide the teachers with feedback. The following parent statement is indicative of this finding: "I am proud that my child attends school in a place where educators care about my opinion. I welcome this wonderful opportunity to help my child's teacher."

Figure 6.2 provides another example of a parent survey currently being used by one school district.

CAN STUDENTS PROVIDE RELIABLE AND USEFUL MEASURES OF TEACHING EFFECTIVENESS?

The practice of involving students in teacher evaluation has a long history and appears to be gaining attention (Aleamoni, 1981; Harris, 1986; Follman, 1995). It is one of the most frequently investigated topics in teacher evaluation (Peterson & Kauchak, 1982); however, most of these investigations have been conducted at the college level (Follman, 1996). Some posit "student ratings constitute better feedback than the ratings of others when the focus is student performance" (Wilkerson, Manatt, Rogers, & Maughan, 2000, p. 190).

One of the arguments for including students as evaluators is that they are the primary consumers of the teacher's services. Student attitudes toward school and toward classroom practices can contribute to the teacher's overall effectiveness or can cause disruption (Northwest Regional Educational Laboratory, 1990). As direct recipients of the teaching-learning process, students are the major clients of teachers, and they are in the key position to provide information about teacher effectiveness. Most important, students are

Figure 6.2   Sample of a Parent Survey

LENAWEE INTERMEDIATE SCHOOL DISTRICT

Parent Survey

LISD Itinerant

School Receiving Service   School Year

DIRECTIONS: *Please read the following statements carefully, then circle "Yes" or "No." If the statement does not apply to the itinerant, circle "NA." If you wish to explain your responses, write your comments in the space provided after each item.*

The itinerant:

1. Sought my input to identify my child's needs.   YES   NO   NA

COMMENT: _____

_____

2. Gave me a copy of an evaluation report   YES   NO   NA
    and explained the report to me.

COMMENT: _____

_____

3. Communicated clearly and explained technical terms.   YES   NO   NA

COMMENT: _____

_____

4. Explained various service/program options for   YES   NO   NA
    me to consider for my child.

COMMENT: _____

_____

5. Made me feel comfortable about asking for information. YES   NO   NA

COMMENT: _____

_____

6. Listened with an open mind to my suggestions and information.   YES   NO   NA

COMMENT: _____

_____

7. Has been helpful in providing me with   YES   NO   NA
   information/suggestions on how I can help my child.

COMMENT: _____

_____

8. Communicated effectively with me about my child's progress.   YES   NO   NA

COMMENT: _____

_____

9. Has supported my child in meeting IEP goals   YES   NO   NA
   and objectives for this year.

COMMENT: _____

_____

_____   _____
        Signature of Parent (Optional)   Date

Please return to: _____   by: _____
                  LISD Supervisor   Date

SOURCE: Lenawee Intermediate School District. Used with permission.

the only ones of the teacher's clients who have direct knowledge about classroom practices on a regular basis. Student perceptions of quality, therefore, may be more meaningful to the teacher than judgments by any other client group (Peterson & Kauchak, 1982).

Follman (1992) observed that "no other individual or group has [the] breadth, depth, or length of experience with the teacher . . . [and] . . . teachers look to their students rather than to outside sources for indications of their teaching performance" (p. 169). Evidence regarding teacher and principal support for the practice of involving students is mixed, but some see student involvement as beneficial from the student's perspective as well as from the teachers (Aleamoni, 1981; Follman, 1992). Students can provide information on the teacher's ability to motivate and the degree of communication and rapport that is present. Equally important, student observations of the teacher are unobtrusive (Peterson & Kauchak, 1982). The fact that there is a positive relationship between student ratings and learning is viewed by some as a convincing reason for involving students in the evaluation process (Aleamoni, 1981).

Use of Student Feedback in Teacher Evaluation

Student Age and Client Surveys

As far back as 1925, Flinn (cited in Follman, 1992) found more agreement among the ratings by four groups of high school students than among three groups of principals regarding teacher performance. Follman reviewed more than 20 studies, spanning 70 years, and concluded that secondary students "have and can rate teachers reliably" (p. 171). He also found that variables such as age, gender, and ethnicity did not significantly affect the students' ratings (see Figures 6.3 and 6.4 for sample rating scales designed for different age groups of students).

Figure 6.3   Sample of a Student Survey for Grades 1-2

Greenville County Public Schools

1-2 Student Survey

Directions: As your teacher reads the sentence color the face that shows what you think.

Teacher				School Year	
Example: I ride a school bus to school.		☺	☺	☹	
1. My teacher listens to me.		☺	☺	☹	
2. My teacher gives me help when I need it.		☺	☺	☹	
3. My teacher shows us how to do new things.		☺	☺	☹	
4. I know what I am supposed to do in class.		☺	☺	☹	
5. I am able to do the work in class.		☺	☺	☹	
6. I learn new things in my class.		☺	☺	☹	

COMMENTS:

SOURCE: Greenville County Public Schools. Used with permission.

Figure 6.4   Sample of a Student Survey for Grades 9-12

Greenville County Public Schools

9-12 Student Survey

The purpose of this survey is to allow you to give your teacher ideas about how this class might be improved.

DIRECTIONS: *DO NOT PUT YOUR NAME ON THIS SURVEY. Write your class period in the space provided. Listed below are several statements about this class. Indicate your agreement with each statement. If you strongly disagree, circle 1, if you strongly agree circle 5. If you wish to comment, please write your comments at the end of the survey.*

Teacher's Name	School Year	Class Period			
		Strongly Disagree	Disagree	Neutral	Agree	Strongly Agree

		Strongly Disagree	Disagree	Neutral	Agree	Strongly Agree
Example: I like listening to music.		1	2	3	4	5

In this class, my teacher . . .

		Strongly Disagree	Disagree	Neutral	Agree	Strongly Agree
1.	gives clear instructions.	1	2	3	4	5
2.	treats everyone fairly.	1	2	3	4	5
3.	is available for help outside of class time.	1	2	3	4	5
4.	clearly states the objectives for the lesson.	1	2	3	4	5
5.	grades my work in a reasonable time.	1	2	3	4	5
6.	relates lesson to other subjects or the real world.	1	2	3	4	5
7.	allows for and respects different opinions.	1	2	3	4	5
8.	encourages all students to learn.	1	2	3	4	5
9.	uses a variety of activities in class.	1	2	3	4	5
10.	communicates in a way I can understand.	1	2	3	4	5
11.	manages the classroom with a minimum of disruptions.	1	2	3	4	5
12.	shows respect to all students.	1	2	3	4	5
13.	consistently enforces disciplinary rules in a fair manner.	1	2	3	4	5
14.	makes sure class time is used for learning.	1	2	3	4	5
15.	is knowledgeable about his/her subject area.	1	2	3	4	5
16.	clearly defines long-term assignments (such as projects).	1	2	3	4	5
17.	sets high expectations.	1	2	3	4	5
18.	helps me reach the high expectations that she/he sets.	1	2	3	4	5
19	assigns relevant homework.	1	2	3	4	5
20.	communicates honestly with me.	1	2	3	4	5

COMMENTS:

SOURCE: Greenville County Public Schools. Used with permission.

Haak, Kleiber, and Peck (1972) suggested that Grade 4 and above should be the limit for involving students in the evaluation process; however, students as young as kindergarten age have demonstrated adequate reliability for inclusion in the process (Driscoll, Peterson, Browning, & Stevens, 1990). In a study of the use of student surveys, younger students tended to place more emphasis on how they were treated while older students tended to focus on how supportive the teacher was in the learning process (Peterson, Wahlquist, & Bone, 2000). Follman (1992) contended that the issue should ultimately be "whether students have the experience, knowledge, wisdom, judgment, and poise to discriminate and/or evaluate anybody on anything, let alone a professional person such as a teacher, on their performance" (p. 175).

Student Ability to Assess Teacher Performance

A frequent perception among teachers is that student ratings are easily influenced and that they are based on popularity, but there is evidence that this concern is unwarranted (Peterson & Kauchak, 1982). Ebmeier, Jenkins, and Crawford (1991) compared high school students' ratings of meritorious and nonmeritorious teachers with ratings from expert practitioners. They concluded that the students were able to discriminate between the two groups as well as the qualified evaluators. Peterson and colleagues (2000) found in a study of the use of client surveys that high school students were able to distinguish between teacher-centered and student-centered approaches to teaching and learning.

If ability to assess teacher performance is indicated by student achievement, then students provide valid feedback on teacher performance. Wilkerson, Manatt, Rogers, and Maughan (2000) studied the validity of ratings by students, principals, and the teachers themselves. Of the three sources of feedback, student ratings of teachers were the best predictor of student achievement on both reading and mathematics criterion-referenced tests. Student ratings were also a significant predictor of student achievement in language arts. The researchers concluded, "Students can discriminate teacher performance in relation to their own learning" (p. 190).

Despite the potential value of using student feedback in teacher evaluation, some cautions should be noted. McGreal (1994) and Harris (1986) suggested that student involvement in teacher assessment should be limited to descriptions of life in the classroom rather than ratings of teacher worth. Peterson and Kauchak (1982) and McNeil and Popham (1973) recommended restricting student data to discrete and visible behaviors as a way to increase reliability. Although Larson (1984) reported research that "shows that the most valid and reliable opinions regarding teacher performance are solicited from students" (p. 16), he maintained that it should be up to the teachers to decide if student ratings should be shared with their supervisors.

Purposes of Student Ratings

Aleamoni (1987) argued that the practice of involving students in teacher evaluation should be restricted to formative evaluation, but the evidence for this restriction is not conclusive. At the very least, Peterson and Stevens (1988) suggested that student data for several years are needed to establish patterns of performance. As students participate year after year in teacher evaluation, the validity and reliability of student surveys increase. And, even then, they advocated teacher choice concerning the use of student ratings for summative evaluations. Peterson (2000) explained, "Years of experience for both students and teachers are required for teacher evaluation systems to acquire their full functioning and utility" (p. 120). Student ratings serve the purpose of providing an additional window through which to gauge a teacher's effectiveness.

In the 1995 Ostrander study described earlier, the correlation between student and parent ratings was strong. This correlation indicates that collecting data from both groups simultaneously may provide redundant data. Therefore, if both student and parent surveys are to be conducted, it is better for parents and students to respond to different questions.

HOW CAN FEEDBACK FROM PEERS BE USED MOST EFFECTIVELY IN TEACHER EVALUATION?

While the use of client input from students and parents can provide important feedback for use in teacher assessment, as with classroom observations this information offers only a partial view of teacher performance. If the intent of the teacher evaluation system is to achieve a full and accurate picture of performance in order to guide improvement and to make personnel decisions, then the inclusion of feedback from peers should be considered. Feedback from peers can offer valuable and valid insights into teacher performance.

The Case for Peer Feedback

Earlier in the chapter a description was provided regarding the importance of collaboration in effective teacher evaluation systems—especially if evaluation is used as a tool to enhance quality and support improvement. As a key component of quality improvement efforts, American business and industry have widely adopted the concept of "360-degree" assessment in which all individuals who interact (e.g., customers, coworkers, supervisors) with an employee provide input into that person's personnel evaluation. Lepsinger and Lucia (1997) explained that 360-degree feedback "provides a complete portrait of behavior on the job—one that looks at people from every angle and every perspective" (p. 9). The 360-degree concept closely parallels the movement to seek continuous performance improvement by using peer feedback in teacher evaluation. One superintendent in Massachusetts explained that the use of 360-degree feedback in his school district resulted in professional improvement precipitated by changes in behavior (Santeusanio, 1998).

Teachers often interact with and, in a real sense, serve other teachers and educators in much the same way teachers serve students. Consider, for example, the typical workday of a special education resource consulting teacher. While the special education teacher may have a caseload for working directly with students, it is likely that a significant portion of the day will be spent interacting directly with peers in ways such as coteaching with classroom teachers; conferencing with support staff such as the school counselor or school social worker; and planning with the school principal, teachers, and other staff.

The above scenario is far from unusual; indeed, collaboration as a primary mode of educational service delivery has come to be the norm rather than the exception for many educators, including special education teachers, gifted/talented resource teachers, reading teachers, and a host of other educators (e.g., library/media specialists, counselors). Moreover, in recent decades classroom teachers have assumed increasingly collaborative responsibilities and are spending a growing amount of time collaborating directly with other educators.

Given the collaborative nature of the contemporary teacher/educator, it would be unfair and ill advised to ignore peers as a vital source for performance feedback. Collaborating educators can attest to the quality and quantity of work of the teacher in ways that no one else can. Indeed, "the most complete picture of an employee's performance will be obtained by questioning at least a representative sampling from all of the various constituencies with whom the person works" (Stronge & Helm, 1991, p. 180). Teachers realize that both administrators' and colleagues' expectations are significant.

In addition to providing accurate feedback on performance, including peers in a collegial model of assessment can provide professional growth opportunities and encouragement for teachers (see Figure 6.5 for an example of a survey used to gather peer feedback in one school district). As McGreal noted, "We know that adults respond primarily to positive reinforcement, that they prefer to operate in a collegial and collaborative environment. And traditional teacher evaluation violates many of these new understandings" (cited in Brandt, 1996, p. 30). The advantages of peer review include lessening teacher isolation and encouraging professional behavior as teachers assume a new role within the school (Peterson, 2000). Moreover, in a collegial model approach to evaluation, "teachers are encouraged to form relationships that enable school change to be based on . . . what is really best for the students" (Haefele, 1992, p. 25).

A Caution in Using Peer Feedback

While peer feedback is a promising practice for use in evaluating teachers, there are pitfalls that must be avoided if peer information is to be meaningful. To begin, evaluators should recognize that inviting peers (or for that matter, students or parents) to provide feedback regarding teacher performance is merely that—feedback. Peer feedback is not the same as peer evaluation. In a qualitative study of one school district's experience with peer review, Goldstein (2004) found that while teachers welcomed the opportunity to solicit peer feedback, the same teachers believed that peer feedback should be used only as a part of formative evaluation. The teachers felt that the administrator should make final, summative judgments. Information generated by peers through a

Figure 6.5 Sample of a Peer Survey

LISD | **LENAWEE INTERMEDIATE SCHOOL DISTRICT**

Teacher Survey

_____

~ LISD Itinerant

_____   _____

School Receiving Service   School Year

DIRECTIONS: _Please read the following statements carefully, then respond to the statements about the behavior of the itinerant during any meeting or consultative session you have had with him or her. If the statement does not apply to your work with the itinerant, circle "NA." Please write a brief comment regarding each item._

1. Works collaboratively with me and other school personnel   YES   NO   NA
   to arrange acceptable times for service delivery within time
   allotted for my building.

COMMENT: _____

   _____

2. Communicates effectively regarding the schedule for   YES   NO   NA
   services and any necessary departures from that schedule.

COMMENT: _____

   _____

3. Is helpful in identifying eligible students in the   YES   NO   NA
   pre-referral process.

COMMENT: _____

   _____

4. Communicates effectively the findings and   YES   NO   NA
   recommendations of student assessments.

COMMENT: _____

   _____

5. Provides me with feedback on my referrals   YES   NO   NA
   within a reasonable amount of time.

COMMENT: _____

   _____

(Continued)

Figure 6.5 (Continued)

6. Obtains additional information from me about students as needed.	YES	NO	NA

COMMENT: _____

_____

7. Works cooperatively with me and other school personnel to identify and achieve student goals and objectives.	YES	NO	NA

COMMENT: _____

_____

8. Communicates effectively with me regarding student progress.	YES	NO	NA

COMMENT: _____

_____

9. Enlists the support of other school personnel, parents, and community resources when necessary to meet the needs of students.	YES	NO	NA

COMMENT: _____

_____

10. Demonstrates appropriate professional conduct.	YES	NO	NA

COMMENT: _____

_____

11. Is considerate of my time.	YES	NO	NA

COMMENT: _____

_____

12. Makes me feel comfortable about asking for help in the future.	YES	NO	NA

COMMENT: _____

_____

_____   _____
Signature of Teacher (Optional)   Date

Please return to: _____   by: _____
                   LISD Supervisor   Date

SOURCE: Lenawee Intermediate School District. Used with permission.

client survey or another data collection format is only one data source as part of a comprehensive teacher evaluation system.

Peterson (2000) identified additional concerns with peer-generated information in teacher evaluation. He noted that problems associated with peer review "stem from lack of reliable procedures, credibility to outside audiences, precedent, teacher preparation, and a negative culture for peer evaluation" (p. 123). If peer feedback faces these types of difficulties, then there is no value added to the evaluation process. Failure to account for and minimize (if not eliminate) these concerns not only could yield inappropriate/invalid information, but also could be detrimental to the total teacher evaluation effort.

Ethical issues related to the use of peer review in teacher evaluation systems must be examined. Peterson, Kelly, and Caskey (2002) call for the development of ethical guidelines and codes for teachers in evaluating one another. The purpose of these guidelines and codes is to provide clear expectations for teacher reviewers and to support the professional judgment of teachers. Establishing an ethical code further professionalizes teaching and could serve to mitigate concerns associated with peer review.

WHAT ARE TECHNICAL ISSUES TO CONSIDER IN USING CLIENT SURVEYS?

If client surveys—parents, students, or peers—are to be used in the data collection process for teacher evaluation, several issues should be considered if concerns are to be overcome and the value of client feedback is to be maximized. In particular, the issues of validity, reliability, sampling procedures, factual data, and confidentiality will be explored briefly.

Validity Considerations

The validity of client ratings, in particular those of students, is probably the most important question to consider in their use for assessing teacher performance. Alkin (1992) operationalized the validity of teacher rating scales based on three factors: (a) how well the rating scales capture the nature of effective teaching, (b) the evaluator's ability to accurately perceive what is going on in the classroom, and (c) any biases that might affect the accuracy of the evaluator's judgment. In summarizing the available studies, Aleamoni (1981) concluded that "students are discriminating judges" (p. 112). While less research has been conducted regarding the validity of parent and peer ratings, the same issues undoubtedly apply.

As with anything, a client survey is valid only to the extent that it actually measures what it purports to measure. One simple way to increase validity of client feedback is to ask only job-related questions that the respondents are in a position to answer. For example, evaluators should not ask a peer-teacher how well he or she feels the evaluated teacher-colleague is performing in the area of classroom management if the peer has no direct knowledge of performance. For another example, don't ask parents about classroom instruction, as they are not in a position to have direct knowledge about what transpires in the classroom; rather ask this type of information of students, who are in a position to know.

Reliability Considerations

Reliability, the degree to which a measure produces consistent results, is another issue that deserves attention in the use of client feedback in teacher evaluation. The aspects of reliability of concern for client feedback, especially student ratings, are internal consistency and stability. Various studies (see, for example, Abrami, Perry, & Leventhal, 1982; Marsh & Bailey, 1993) have found students to be fairly consistent in their assessments of specific teachers and their instruction. In a review of research studies, Peterson (2000) concluded that "student ratings of teachers are consistent among students and reliable from one year to the next" (p. 105).

Generally, the larger the sample, the higher the reliability, assuming it is a good (i.e., representative) sample. One of the major drawbacks of formal classroom observation is the extremely small sample size; with only one or two observations, the results of the observations would be suspect. Client feedback typically avoids this low sample size problem since multiple responses are provided in a client survey. However, the reliability of client surveys also is affected by the extent of past use. The results of one or two sets of surveys may be suspect, but as client surveys are administered repeatedly over time, more confidence typically can be placed in the findings. Thus, evaluators should look for patterns in survey results produced over time and be more cautious in placing too much trust in the results of a single data set.

Sampling Procedures

Client surveys are virtually useless without a good sample. One cannot assume that the findings are indicative of performance without reasonably good sampling procedures. With inappropriate sampling procedures, a problem similar to the one that Goldilocks encountered in her visit to the Three Bears would occur: Would the inferences drawn from the sample be too positive, too negative, or just about right? This concern, in fact, holds true for classroom observations, analysis of artifacts of performance, or any other data source. Thus, if any type of client survey is to be conducted, give careful attention to who will be surveyed and how that information will be collected.

Factual Data

In eliciting evaluation data from parents, students, or peers, "the single most important consideration is to focus on obtaining factual descriptions of the person's behavior or performance" (Stronge & Helm, 1991, p. 193). An important consideration for avoiding unfounded perceptual information is to invite feedback only from individuals who work directly with or have direct knowledge of the teacher's performance. For example, ask parents only about issues they are in a position to know about (e.g., communication between the school and home); if you want to know what occurs in the classroom, ask those who are in the classroom—the students. The survey items should focus on feedback regarding specific behaviors rather than general judgments (Lepsinger & Lucia, 1997; Stronge & Helm, 1991). Feedback regarding specific behaviors is more useful to the teacher who is receiving the feedback because the teacher can focus on the specific behaviors that should be changed.

Confidentiality

Parents, students, and peers should be guaranteed anonymity, and the teacher should be assured of confidentiality in the collection and use of client feedback. Trust is a critical element to the teacher evaluation process. Dyer (2001) identified confidentiality and feedback data belonging to the receiver as essential factors. Otherwise, "few individuals will respond with candor—especially subordinates or peers who might be concerned about jeopardizing their own working relationship with the employee" (Stronge & Helm, 1991, p. 181). One approach to confidentiality is the assurance that only the teacher will see the results of the client surveys. While this approach precludes the use of the data in summative evaluation, it is less costly, less threatening, and meets less resistance (Stronge & Tucker, 2003).

PUTTING IT ALL TOGETHER: HOW CAN CLIENT SURVEYS BE USED AS PART OF A MULTIPLE DATA SOURCE SYSTEM IN TEACHER EVALUATION?

Contemporary research on teacher evaluation has emphasized the importance of developing multiple and variable lines of evidence of teacher performance to improve the state of teacher evaluation (Darling-Hammond, Wise, & Pease, 1983; Harris, 1986; Peterson, Wahlquist, Bone, Thompson, & Chattertson, 2001; Scriven, 1994; Stronge, 1995; Stronge & Tucker, 2003; Wilkerson et al., 2000). This movement parallels the national trend toward increased client involvement in school governance and decision making.

The knowledge base regarding effective multiple lines of evidence is, however, inadequate, and many potential data sources are relatively untested (Epstein, 1985; Peterson, Gunne, Miller, & Rivera, 1984; Peterson 2000; Scriven, 1981). Abrami and d'Apollonia (1990) approached the question of the validity of client ratings from two perspectives. If assessments correctly reflect the client's opinions about service quality, then her or his views are worth knowing and thereby provide a valid measure of satisfaction. On the other hand, the same client's opinions may not provide a valid measure of the effectiveness of the service. For example, parent ratings may provide a teacher with valid information about client satisfaction with a course but not supply meaningful information about teaching quality. Abrami and d'Apollonia recommended correlating judgments from multiple sources to establish validity for client information.

Ostrander's (1995) study provided evidence that the use of multiple judges may provide unique perspectives on teacher performance. The findings of the study are consistent with Epstein's (1985) conclusion: "Because there is not a single set of skills that perfectly define effective teaching, measures of many aspects of teaching by multiple judges are likely to yield the fairest and most comprehensive evaluation of teachers" (p. 8).

It is unrealistic to expect any one person to be fully cognizant of how effectively all subordinates carry out assigned duties and responsibilities. Using multiple data sources allows administrators to better focus time invested in evaluation and to cultivate more accurate decisions about competency (Tucker, Bray, & Howard, 1989). Lepsinger and Lucia (1997) likened feedback from multiple data sources to "having a full length portrait, a profile, a close-up shot of the face, and a view from the back all in one" (p. 10).

SUMMARY

Scriven (1994) contended that to be a good teacher, one must have a commitment to success and to improvement. This can be accomplished by "using serious self-evaluation and, for objectivity, subjecting yourself to evaluation by others chosen or accepted by you." He added, "Accountability obliges you to be able to demonstrate your success to third parties—not merely to your own satisfaction" (p. 159).

While additional empirical evidence is needed to determine how multiple measures of performance received from multiple sources contribute to the process of teacher evaluation (Epstein, 1985; McGreal, 1994; Mannatt & Benway, 1998; Ostrander, 1995; Peterson, 1987), it is clear that the use of a multifaceted data collection process can improve overall data quality. In addition, the use of client surveys as part of a comprehensive teacher evaluation system can provide administrators and teachers with better feedback and assessment information both for personal and professional improvement and for ensuring accountability in performance.

NOTE

1. The grand mean is an overall average of all item means calculated out of a possible 4.0.

REFERENCES

Abrami, P. C., & d'Apollonia, S. (1990). The dimensionality of ratings and their use in personnel decisions. In M. Theall & J. Franklin (Eds.), *Student ratings of instruction: Issues for improving practice* (pp. 97–103). San Francisco: Jossey-Bass.

Abrami, P. C., Perry, R. P., & Leventhal, L. (1982). The relationship between student personality characteristics, teacher ratings, and student achievement. *Journal of Educational Psychology*, 74(1), 111–125.

Aleamoni, L. (1981). Student ratings of instruction. In J. Millman (Ed.), *Handbook of teacher evaluation* (pp. 110–145). Beverly Hills, CA: Sage.

Aleamoni, L. (1987). Student rating myths versus research facts. *Journal of Personnel Evaluation in Education, 1,* 111–119.

Alkin, M. C. (1992). *Encyclopedia of educational research* (6th ed.). New York: Macmillan.

Bayless, D. L., Massaro, G., Bailey, E., Coley, D., Holladay, R., & McDonald, D. (1992). The quality improvement management approach as implemented in a middle school. *Journal of Educational Psychology, 6,* 191–209.

Becher, R. M. (1984). *Parent involvement: A review of research and principles of successful practice* (Report No. PS 014 563). Urbana, IL: National Institute of Education. (ERIC Document Reproduction Service No. ED 247 032)

Bonstingl, J. J. (1992). *Schools of quality: An introduction to total quality management in education.* Alexandria, VA: Association for Supervision and Curriculum Development.

Brandt, R. (1996). On a new direction for teacher evaluation: A conversation with Tom McGreal. *Educational Leadership, 53*(6), 30–33.

Bridges, E. (1986). *The incompetent teacher.* Philadelphia: Falmer.

Costa, A. (Speaker). (1993). *Leadership: Protecting the intellectual ecology of the school* (Cassette Recording No. 93-4134). Washington, DC: Association for Supervision and Curriculum Development.

Danielson, C., & McGreal, T. L. (2000). *Teacher evaluation to enhance professional practice.* Alexandria, VA: Association for Supervision and Curriculum Development.

Darling-Hammond, L., Wise, A. E., & Pease, S. R. (1983). Teacher evaluation in the organizational context: A review of the literature. *Review of Educational Research, 53*(3), 285–328.

Deming, W. E. (1986). *Out of the crisis.* Cambridge: MIT Press.

Dixon, R. G. D. (1994). Future schools: And how to get there from here. *Phi Delta Kappan, 75,* 360–365.

Driscoll, A., Peterson, K., Browning, M., & Stevens, D. (1990). Teacher evaluation in early childhood education: What information can young children provide? *Child Study Journal, 20,* 67–69.

Dyer, K. M. (2001). The power of 360-degree feedback. *Educational Leadership, 58*(50), 35–38.

Ebmeier, H., Jenkins, R., & Crawford, G. (1991). The predictive validity of student evaluations in the identification of meritorious teachers. *Journal of Personnel Evaluation in Education, 4,* 341–347.

Educational Research Service. (1988). *Teacher evaluation: Practices and procedures* (Report). Arlington, VA: Educational Research Service.

Ellett, C., & Garland, J. (1987). Teacher evaluation practices in our largest school districts: Are they measuring up to "state-of-the-art" systems. *Journal of Personnel Evaluation in Education, 1,* 69–92.

Epstein, J. (1985). A question of merit: Principals' and parents' evaluation of teachers. *Educational Researcher, 14*(7), 3–10.

Evertson, C. M., & Holley, F. M. (1981). Classroom observation. In J. Millman (Ed.), *Handbook of teacher evaluation* (pp. 90–109). Beverly Hills, CA: Sage.

Faucette, S., Ball, D., & Ostrander, L. (1994). Parents as valued customers: The Virginia Beach Parent Perception Survey. *ERS Spectrum, 12*(2), 3–9.

Faucette, S., Ball, D., & Ostrander, L. (1995). *Client satisfaction surveys* (Unpublished Executive Summary). Virginia Beach City Public Schools.

Follman, J. (1992). Secondary school students' ratings of teacher effectiveness. *High School Journal, 75,* 168–178.

Follman, J. (1995). Elementary public school pupil rating of teacher effectiveness. *Child Study Journal, 25,* 57–78.

Follman, J. (1996). *Pupil ratings of teacher effectiveness.* Paper presented at the CREATE National Evaluation Institute, Bethesda, MD.

Frase, L., & Streshly, W. (1994). Lack of accuracy, feedback, and commitment in teacher evaluation. *Journal of Personnel Evaluation in Education, 1,* 47–57.

Fullan, M. (Speaker). (1994). *Harnessing the forces of educational reform* (Cassette Recording No. 94-GS03). Alexandria, VA: Association for Supervision and Curriculum Development.

Goldstein, J. (2004). Making sense of distributed leadership: The case of peer assistance and review. *Educational Evaluation and Policy Analysis, 26*(2), 173–197.

Goodlad, J. I. (1984). *A place called school.* New York: McGraw-Hill.

Haak, R. A., Kleiber, D., & Peck, R. (1972). *Student evaluation of teacher instrument, II.* Austin: University of Texas, Research and Development Center for Teacher Education. (ERIC Document Reproduction Service No. ED 080 574)

Haefele, D. (1992). Evaluating teachers: An alternative model. *Journal of Evaluation in Education, 5,* 335–345.

Haefele, D. (1993). Evaluating teachers: A call for change. *Journal of Personnel Evaluation in Education, 7,* 21–31.

Harris, B. (1986). *Developmental teacher evaluation.* Boston: Allyn & Bacon.

Larson, R. (1984). Teacher performance evaluation—What are the key elements? *NASSP Bulletin, 68*(469), 13–18.

Lepsinger, R., & Lucia, A. D. (1997). *The art and science of 3600 feedback.* San Francisco: Pfeiffer.

Loup, K. S., Garland, J. S., Ellett, C. D., & Rugutt, J. K. (1996). Ten years later: Findings from a replication study of teacher evaluation practices in our 100 largest school districts. *Journal of Personnel Evaluation in Education, 10*(3), 203–226.

Mager, G. M. (1980). The conditions which influence teachers in initiating contacts with parents. *Journal of Educational Research, 73,* 276–282.

Mannatt, R. P., & Benway, M. (1998). Teacher and administrator performance evaluation: Benefits of 360-degree feedback. *ERS Spectrum, 16*(2), 18–23.

Mark, M. M., & Shotland, R. L. (1985). Stakeholder-based evaluation and value judgments. *Evaluation Review, 9,* 605–626.

Marsh, H. W., & Bailey, M. (1993). Multidimensional students' evaluations of teaching effectiveness. *Journal of Higher Education, 64*(1), 1–18.

McGreal, T. L. (Speaker). (1994). *The next generation of teacher evaluation* (Cassette Recording No. 94–4625). Chicago: Association for Supervision and Curriculum Development.

McNeil, J. D., & Popham, W. J. (1973). The assessment of teacher competence. In R. W. M. Travers (Ed.), *Second handbook of research in teaching* (pp. 218–243). Chicago: Rand McNally.

Medley, D. M., Coker, H., & Soar, R. S. (1984). *Measurement-based evaluation of teacher performance: An empirical approach.* New York: Longman.

Mendro, R. L. (1998). Student achievement and school and teacher accountability. *Journal of Personnel Evaluation in Education, 12,* 257–267.

Northwest Regional Educational Laboratory. (1990). *Effective schooling practices: A research synthesis.* Portland, OR: Author.

Ostrander, L. P. (1995). *Multiple judges of teacher effectiveness: Comparing teacher self-assessments with the perceptions of principals, students, and parents.* Unpublished doctoral dissertation, University of Virginia, Charlottesville.

Peterson, K. (1987). Teacher evaluation with multiple and variable lines of evidence. *American Educational Research Journal, 24,* 311–317.

Peterson, K. (1988). Parent surveys for school teacher evaluation. *Journal of Personnel Evaluation in Education, 2,* 239–249.

Peterson, K. (2000). *Teacher evaluation: A comprehensive guide to new directions and practices* (2nd ed.). Thousand Oaks, CA: Corwin.

Peterson, K., Gunne, G., Miller, P., & Rivera, O. (1984). Multiple audience rating form strategies for student evaluation of college teaching. *Research in Higher Education, 20*(3), 309–321.

Peterson, K., & Kauchak, D. (1982). *Teacher evaluation: Perspectives, practices, and promises* (Report No. SP 022 900). Salt Lake City, UT: Center for Educational Practice. (ERIC Document Reproduction Service No. ED 233 996)

Peterson, K., Kelly, P., & Caskey, M. (2002). Ethical considerations for teachers in the evaluation of other teachers. *Journal of Personnel Evaluation in Education, 16*(4), 317–323.

Peterson, K., & Mitchell, A. (1985). Teacher-controlled evaluation in a career ladder program. *Educational Leadership, 43*(3), 44–47.

Peterson, K., & Stevens, D. (1988). Student reports for school teacher evaluation. *Journal of Personnel Evaluation in Education, 2*, 19–31.

Peterson, K. D., Wahlquist, C., & Bone, K. (2000). Student surveys for school teacher evaluation. *Journal of Personnel Evaluation in Education, 14*(2), 135–153.

Peterson, K. D., Wahlquist, C., Bone, K., Thompson, J., & Chattertson, K. (2001). Using more data sources to evaluate teachers. *Educational Leadership, 58*(5), 40–43.

Root, D., & Overly, D. (1990). Successful teacher evaluation—Key elements for success. *NASSP Bulletin, 74*(527), 34–38.

Rowan, B., Correnti, R., & Miller, R. J. (2002). What large-scale survey research tells us about teacher effects on student achievement: Insights on the prospects study of elementary schools. *Teachers College Record, 104*(8), 1525–1568.

Santeusanio, R. (1998). Improving performance with 360-degree feedback. *Educational Leadership, 55*(5), 30–32.

Scriven, M. (1981). Summative teacher evaluation. In J. Millman (Ed.), *Handbook of teacher evaluation* (pp. 244–271). Beverly Hills, CA: Sage.

Scriven, M. (1994). Duties of the teacher. *Journal of Personnel Evaluation in Education, 8*, 151–184.

Stronge, J. H. (1995). Balancing individual and institutional goals in educational personnel evaluation: A conceptual framework. *Studies in Educational Evaluation, 21*, 131–151.

Stronge, J. H., & Helm, V. M. (1991). *Evaluating professional support personnel in education.* Newbury Park, CA: Sage.

Stronge, J. H., Helm, V. M., & Tucker, P. D. (1995). *Evaluation handbook for professional support personnel.* Kalamazoo: Western Michigan University, Center for Research on Educational Accountability and Teacher Evaluation.

Stronge, J. H., & Tucker, P. D. (2000). *Teacher evaluation and student achievement.* Washington, DC: National Education Association.

Stronge, J. H., & Tucker, P. D. (2003). *Handbook on teacher evaluation: Assessing and improving performance.* Larchmont, NY: Eye on Education.

Tetenbaum, T., & Mulkeen, T. (1988). Assessment of educational personnel in the twenty-first century. *Journal of Personnel Evaluation in Education, 1*, 235–244.

Tucker, N. A., Bray, S. W., & Howard, K. C. (1989). Using a client–centered approach in the principal's evaluation of counselors. *Journal of Personnel Evaluation in Education, 2*, 335–353.

Weiss, E. M., & Weiss, S. G. (1998). *New directions in teacher evaluation.* Washington, DC: U.S. Office of Educational Research and Improvement.

Wilkerson, D. J., Manatt, R. P., Rogers, M. A., & Maughan, R. (2000). Validation of student, principal, and self-ratings in 360 degree feedback for teacher evaluation. *Journal of Personnel Evaluation in Education, 14*(2), 179–192.

Wise, A. E., Darling-Hammond, L., McLaughlin, M., & Bernstein, H. (1984). *Teacher evaluation: A study of effective practices.* Santa Monica, CA: Rand Corporation.

Student Achievement and Teacher Evaluation

7

Pamela D. Tucker

James H. Stronge

The ever-increasing emphasis on accountability has defined the educational reform dialogue for more than three decades. Analysis has taken place at the national, state, and local levels by policy makers in an attempt to leverage available resources in the most advantageous manner possible (Rice, 2003). While there has always been some level of accountability at the classroom level, it is only recently that systematic data collection has been conducted. During the mid-1990s, a number of school systems began looking at student achievement in a formal manner and using it as one component in their teacher evaluation systems (Tucker & Stronge, 2005).

WHAT IS THE CONTEXT FOR TEACHER QUALITY?

While accountability as a concept has historical roots dating back centuries in the form of civil service exams (Madaus, 1990), its most recent incarnation is attributed to President Richard Nixon (Wynne, 1972). It was during his administration that the first nationwide, congressionally mandated testing program, National Assessment of Educational Progress (NAEP), was launched. NAEP, also known as the Nation's Report Card, has provided a national yardstick for assessing student learning based on a representative sampling of students in Grades 4, 8, and 12 in a variety of subject areas (Heinecke, Curry-Corcoran, & Moon, 2003). In addition, during the early 1970s, minimum competency tests were developed simultaneously in a majority of the states and used as a requirement for graduation (Bowers, 1991).

The growing enthusiasm for educational accountability was reinforced by the release in 1983 of *A Nation at Risk* (National Commission on Excellence in Education [NCEE]), which

> called for more testing, but it also called for consequences attached to test scores, recommending that educators and elected officials be held responsible for providing the leadership necessary to accomplish the reform agenda. The report was a clarion call for tying student performance to instruction and assigning the responsibility for improvement in student performance to those most responsible for educating American's children. (Heinecke, et al., p. 15)

While the earlier emphasis on minimum competency tests placed the weight of accountability on students, *A Nation at Risk* redirected some of the responsibility—or accountability—for improvement to educators and policy makers. This tension among these contributing factors in the learning process is at the heart of the debate about using student achievement measures in teacher evaluation. On the one hand, there is compelling evidence that teachers have a substantial effect on student achievement (see, for example, Mendro, 1998; Nye, Konstantopoulos, & Hedges, 2004; Sanders & Horn, 1998) and yet, it is equally evident that student characteristics and instructional resources of all types have an effect on the learning process.

Schalock (1998) has referred to this interdependency of responsibility for the learning enterprise by stakeholders as the collective nature of accountability. Clearly, parents, principals, superintendents, school board members, teachers, and students all play a significant role in building successful educational environments. Holding any one participant solely responsible for academic progress without recognition of the roles played by the other partners would be unfair. Nonetheless, students, as the beneficiaries of the educational process, have the most to gain or lose based on the quality of their schooling.

There has been an evolving effort to apportion responsibility for educational reform to all parties in the education process, from schools of education that prepare future teachers and administrators, to whole school districts and the individuals that work within them. The No Child Left Behind legislation (2001) reflects this distributed responsibility by states, school districts, and individual schools with its requirements for state-level testing programs, adequate yearly progress (AYP) at the district and school level, district- and school-level report cards, and "highly qualified" teachers. All layers of the educational enterprise are addressed by the legislation, but many see the linchpin of these reform efforts as the push to improve teacher quality. In particular, given the emphasis on content knowledge over instructional practice, Emerick, Hirsch, and Berry (2004) argued that *highly qualified* does not mean high quality or even basic competence in some cases.

The emphasis on the teacher seems justified, however, particularly in light of recent analyses of teacher effects and school effects on student achievement gains. Nye et al. (2004) found that teacher effects explain 12% to 14% of the variance in mathematics achievement gains and approximately 7% of the variance in reading. The variance in student achievement gains attributable to teachers was two to three times as great as that of the schools students attended, suggesting that policies addressing teacher effectiveness would yield greater gains than those addressing school improvement efforts.

HOW IS TEACHER QUALITY ASSESSED?

Given the pivotal role of teachers in improving educational outcomes for children, it follows that the enhancement of teacher quality should be the objective of all hiring, development, and evaluation activities within a school system. If this premise is accepted, then the fundamental question that we must answer is, What is teacher quality?

How teacher quality is conceptualized affects our understanding of the term and the manner in which it can be assessed for important personnel decisions. Figure 7.1 represents a conceptual framework for teacher quality that is helpful in analyzing *what quality* means and how it can be assessed.

Medley and Shannon (1994) identified three facets of teacher quality: teacher competence, teacher performance, and teachers' effectiveness in their work. For greater clarity in the terminology, we have chosen to refer to these three components as teacher qualifications, behaviors, and outcomes, respectively. *Teacher qualifications* would include the knowledge, skills, and dispositions viewed as necessary to teach and are addressed, to some extent, by the "highly qualified" requirements of No Child Left Behind (2001). These characteristics typically would be assessed in the certification and hiring process, but would continue to evolve over the course of a teacher's professional service. Certification, including the associated tests such as Praxis I and II, would assess the necessary knowledge base, and interviews are often used to judge teaching candidates' dispositions. *Teacher behaviors* involve the much more complex domain of skills and knowledge necessary for the act of teaching as well as the many other tasks that are required of teachers in today's schools, such as assessment expertise and collaboration. *Teacher outcomes* address the results of teaching. Observation strategies, portfolio material, and client surveys could be used to judge teacher qualifications and behaviors, but direct measures of student learning would be needed to judge the teacher outcomes (Dunkin, 1997; Stronge & Tucker, 2003; Tucker & Stronge, 2005).

Efforts have been made to assess teachers in the three areas of teacher qualifications, teacher behaviors, and teacher outcomes, and yet there is limited research linking the three. How do educational background, teacher preparation, and certification influence teacher behaviors or teacher outcomes? How do teacher behaviors influence teacher outcomes? Despite a significant public

Figure 7.1   Framework for Teacher Quality

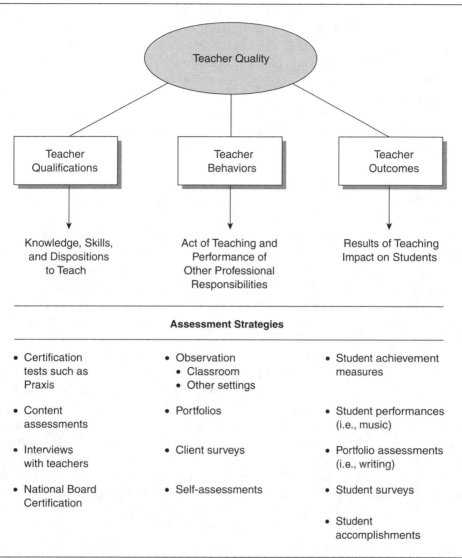

SOURCE: Adapted from Medley & Shannon (1994) and Dunkin (1997).

investment in teacher compensation, roughly $192 billion in teacher pay and benefits during 2002 (Rice, 2003), researchers (Nye et al., 2004; Rice, 2003) have lamented the "absence of a strong, robust and deep body of research" on the specific effect of teacher characteristics on teacher outcomes (Rice, 2003, p. v). Acknowledging the inconsistent nature of the research and methodological concerns, a number of authors have summarized what we do know about teacher quality (Darling-Hammond, 2000; Rice, 2003; Stronge, 2002), and there is no question that "the research suggests that investing in teachers can make a difference in student achievement" (Rice, 2003, p. vii). The accumulated empirical evidence on teacher characteristics has been used to inform educational policy at the local and state level in terms of teacher certification and hiring practices (Darling-Hammond) as well as teacher evaluation (Dunkin, 1997; Stronge & Tucker, 2003), but the focus has been on teacher qualifications and teacher behaviors. It is now time to systematically assess teacher outcomes with the same level of attention.

The assessment of teacher outcomes entails data on student progress toward educational goals, most notably instructional goals. As controversial as this concept remains, many school systems have used measures of student learning for years. In 1988, an Educational Research Service study of teacher evaluation in 909 school districts found that 67% of the school systems surveyed relied on some measure of learner gains. As Alkin noted in 1992, the "idea of basing decisions about teachers on measures of how much students learn from them is one that the public and its elected representatives find very appealing" (p. 1349), and this observation continues to hold true today. The challenge for this approach lies in creating a systematic, fair, and valid methodology that acknowledges the many variables affecting student learning.

The premise of this chapter is that the use of student learning data in some form is necessary to truly measure teacher effectiveness, specifically teacher outcomes, and it is a valuable means of providing feedback in the evaluation process. Given the assumption that evaluation serves the dual purposes of professional accountability and teacher improvement presented elsewhere in this book, information on student learning would serve to ensure a minimal level of teacher competence (accountability) and could offer diagnostic feedback to teachers on the impact of their instruction (improvement) as well. In the following sections, we offer support for the use of student achievement data in teacher evaluation, discussion of implementation challenges, descriptions of working models that use student achievement data, and recommendations for the effective implementation of this approach to teacher evaluation.

WHY SHOULD STUDENT LEARNING DATA BE INCLUDED IN TEACHER EVALUATION?

There are many persuasive arguments for including student achievement information in the teacher evaluation process. Here are some of the most compelling:

1. *There is an abundant research base substantiating the claim that teacher quality is the most important school-related factor influencing student achievement* (Nye et al., 2004; Rivkin, Hanushek, & Kain, 2001). Analysis of data from the Tennessee Value Added Assessment System (Wright, Horn, & Sanders, 1997), the Dallas Independent Public Schools (Mendro, 1998), and other value-added approaches offers compelling evidence regarding

the influence of the classroom teacher on student learning (Stronge & Tucker, 2000; Wenglinsky, 2002). Without a doubt, there are many powerful influences on student academic success, many of which are beyond the direct influence of the school. However, of those factors within the direct influence of the school, the teacher emerges as the most influential on student achievement gains.

2. *Using measures of student learning in the evaluation process provides the "ultimate accountability" for educating students* (Tucker & Stronge, 2001). The mainstay of teacher evaluation has been classroom observation, and yet this approach assesses only one aspect of teacher quality—that of teacher behaviors. There has been an assumption that teacher outcomes can be inferred from limited samples of teacher behavior, but the more direct approach to assessment would be a growth measure of student learning. A diagnostic review of student learning using instructionally useful assessments, whether they are paper-and-pencil tests or student performances of another sort, would open up the "black box" of teaching. Some teachers routinely use student achievement measures informally to assess their effectiveness, but we contend that it should be routine for all teachers as part of the teacher evaluation process.

3. *There is a growing shift in our collective thinking about tests, away from standardized achievement tests to "instructionally beneficial" tests* (Popham, 2003). For example, Stiggins (2004) made the fundamental distinction between "assessment of learning" and "assessment for learning." One source of guidance on test development to support both instruction and accountability was provided by a national commission in 2001 (Commission on Instructionally Supportive Assessment). The testing industry, in turn, is responding as evidenced by the test contract signed by Wyoming in 2004 in which state-level tests will reflect the state content standards, results will be reported by standards for each student, and online, formative assessments will be available anytime for use by teachers in assessing student learning (Olson, 2004a). Tools like this will "provide accurate accountability evidence, yet at the same time nurture improved classroom practice" as noted by W. James Popham (as cited in Olson, 2004a, p. 20). Given the push for better tests, the availability of tools for accurately and fairly measuring learning gains is becoming a reality.

4. *Another requirement for the fair determination of learning gains is a defensible methodology for analyzing measures of student learning.* In cases of student performances (i.e., art, music) or portfolio work, professional judgment is the accepted strategy. For the analysis of test results, researchers have used measures of achievement status and achievement gains (see, for example, Nye et al., 2004). Achievement status refers to the metric used to capture the percentage of content mastered or the score achieved on a given scale. Achievement gain would be the increase in the percentage or score earned on the assessment. Unfortunately, the requirements for adequate yearly

progress under No Child Left Behind are based on the achievement status of students, not progress or growth, to the frustration of many educators (Olson, 2004b).

Clearly, if the intent is to measure school or teacher outcomes, analysis of achievement gains represents a closer approximation of the effects of teaching than achievement status. The currently popular model of measuring achievement gains is value-added assessment, which was pioneered by William Sanders, formerly of the University of Tennessee (Sanders & Horn, 1994). Value-added assessment is based on the amount of academic progress students make from year to year analyzed at the individual level. The mandate for annual testing under the No Child Left Behind Act will permit the tracking of individual student growth from year to year and, according to *Education Week,* many states are moving toward the implementation of value-added growth measures, including Ohio, Pennsylvania, Arizona, Florida, and North Carolina (Olson, 2004b). In addition, the Council of Chief State School Officers sponsored a national meeting in November 2004 to discuss the technical aspects of value-added assessment and plans to continue working with states on this issue (Olson, 2004c).

5. *Work by Nye et al. (2004) and Sanders and Horn (1998) has demonstrated that the variance in student achievement gains explained by teacher effects is greater in low SES schools than in high SES schools.* In other words, there are greater differences in the effects of individual teachers on student achievement in poor schools than richer ones. Other authors (Darling-Hammond, 2000; Krei, 1998) have provided evidence for this phenomenon and advocated for strategies to redistribute high quality teachers. Kevin Carey (2004) of the Education Trust advocated for the use of teacher effectiveness information to ensure equal educational opportunity for students of poverty by improving the effectiveness of current teachers and getting "more effective teachers into the classrooms of the low-income children who rely on them the most for their learning" (p. 3).

WHAT ARE THE IMPLEMENTATION CONCERNS?

1. *The use of student learning measures is not supported by most teachers,* as evidenced by the results of a debate in *NEA Today* back in March 1999 (National Education Association, 1999). Despite a balanced presentation of the arguments on both sides, the April issue of *NEA Today* revealed that members voted 13% in favor of the idea and 87% against it (National Education Association, 1999). Some groups of educators, like the Ohio Federation of Teachers and the Ohio Education Association, however, have embraced the value-added model as *one component* of teacher evaluation (Olson, 2004b).

2. *The impact on student learning must be assessed in multiple ways over time, not by using just one test, to reliably and accurately measure teacher influence.* In addition, measures of student learning reflect just one aspect of teacher quality—that of outcomes. While this is important, other characteristics also contribute to teacher quality, such as knowledge of content and students, instructional skills, assessment skills, and passion for teaching. Other assessment strategies are needed as part of a broader approach using multiple data sources to more accurately judge teacher quality and be legally defensible (National School Boards Association, 2000). In addition, methodological concerns regarding value-added models suggest that they should not be used in isolation for high-stakes purposes (McCaffrey, Lockwood, Koretz, & Hamilton, 2003).

3. *Testing programs in many states and school districts do not reflect the taught curriculum and, therefore, do not accurately reflect the efforts of teachers.* Tests should be aligned with the curriculum and instructionally useful (Popham, 2003). Unless, the tests, the curriculum, and the actual instruction are aligned, students' opportunity to learn (OTL) is minimized. Furthermore, the impact of teachers' efforts to instruct can't possibly be assessed with any degree of confidence.

4. *While the argument has been made for the use of achievement gains versus achievement status for judging teacher outcomes, it is unclear what the fairest and most accurate methodology is for determining gains.* Value-added assessment is currently enjoying widespread popularity, but substantially more research is needed to address value-added application issues, including construct validity (Kupermintz, 2002, 2003; Kupermintz, Shepard, & Linn, 2001; McCaffrey et al., 2004). For instance, Kupermintz et al. expressed concerns regarding the "soundness of inferences drawn from the TVAAS estimates of teacher effectiveness" (p. 19) due to the confounding effects of other independent factors and the "generalizability of multiple-choice test results as indicators of instructional impact" (p. 19).

HOW MIGHT STUDENT LEARNING DATA BE INCLUDED IN TEACHER EVALUATION?

While any type of outcome measure is not sufficient to judge the whole of student learning or teacher effectiveness, outcome measures can provide information on various dimensions of learning, such as the acquisition of knowledge and skills. The information provided by student performances or tests seems to be a good starting point for identifying students who are having difficulty learning material or teachers who are having difficulty teaching specific material. Diagnostically analyzing the problem and providing the needed assistance requires professional understanding of the dynamics of teaching and learning. Student learning data should not be used as a final judgment of failure or success by the student or the teacher, but as an indicator or source of information of possible problems that can be carefully unraveled by experienced educators.

A number of school systems and states have begun the process of linking student learning to the evaluation of teachers. Methodologies vary widely from highly systemic approaches to more individually tailored ones. The four accountability systems highlighted in Table 7.1 reflect this continuum. Each system has unique features that were developed to enhance the fairness of using student learning measures as part of teacher evaluation, and they are described in greater detail below (Tucker & Stronge, 2005).

The Oregon Teacher Work Sample Methodology

The ambitious goal of the Oregon Teacher Work Sample Methodology (TWSM) is to find better ways to assess complex processes of teaching and their connection to student learning. Thus, as the name of this methodology implies, a substantial *sample of teacher work* is designed, implemented, and then assessed for its impact on student learning (student gain scores) using practical, in-classroom assessment data. "TWSM has been designed to portray the learning progress of pupils *on outcomes desired by a teacher* and *taught by a teacher* over a sufficiently long period of time for appreciable progress in learning to occur" (Schalock, Schalock, & Girod, 1997, pp. 18–19). This means TWSM requires that teachers document an extended sample of their work that includes

- descriptions of the context of the teaching and learning,
- desired learning outcomes,
- instructional plans and resources,
- assessments used, and, finally,
- the growth in learning achieved by students.

Furthermore, the process requires teachers to reflect on their own teaching and its effects in terms of the learning achieved by each of their students.

A Standards-Based Approach

The teacher assessment program of Colorado's Thompson School District is a straightforward teacher assessment system designed to provide a practical connection between teacher instruction and student achievement. The standards-based evaluation system uses student achievement as only one factor in the teacher's performance review. The process works as follows:

- benchmarks for student learning goals are set with standardized tests;
- informal assessments are used to measure performance; and
- student achievement is measured using pre- and post-instruction measures that are selected based on content standards.

Table 7.1 Summary of Models for the Use of Student Achievement Measures in Teacher Evaluation

Characteristics	Oregon: Work Sample Methodology Model	Thompson School District (CO): Standards Based Model	Alexandria School District (VA): Student Achievement Goal Setting Model	Tennessee: Value Added Assessment System
How is student learning measured?	Student growth is measured with pre- and post-instruction measures developed or selected by the teacher that are context-specific and selected based on desired outcomes.	Benchmarks for student learning goals are set with standardized tests and then informal assessments are used pre- and post-instruction to measure performance.	Measures of student learning are selected by teachers to capture their primary instructional goals. A menu of options is provided that includes an evolving list of curriculum-based assessments.	Student achievement is measured annually by the Tennessee Comprehensive Assessment Program and gains are compared to each student's own previous growth rate.
How is the information used in teacher evaluation?	The Oregon TWSM, to date, has been used in initial teacher licensure. It has proven to be a viable tool for screening candidates for entry into the teaching profession.	Teacher performance standards are clearly delineated, assessed partially on student learning, and then tied to professional development. The focus of the system is on performance assistance and improvement.	The goal-setting process is an integral part of the overall teacher evaluation system, which places an emphasis on the improvement of student learning, but the focus is on professional development.	Test results by classroom are shared informally by the principal with the teacher and serve as one data source for the summative evaluation. The assessment information is used for remediation when needed.
How is the information used to promote professional development?	The TWSM is designed to foster individualized reflection and self-evaluation based on the critical analysis of teaching episodes.	The overall performance assessment is used to guide the teacher's professional development needs in the upcoming evaluation cycle.	Specialists work with teachers individually to articulate their goals for development and inform teachers about the available resources to support them in achieving their student learning goals.	Principals work with teachers on an individual basis to connect their professional development activities with enhanced student achievement in their classes.

161

When it comes time for an annual evaluation conference between the teacher and the principal, the teacher submits evidence of student learning based on gain scores, and this evidence is reviewed as part of the evaluation cycle. Results of the evaluation cycle are then connected to the teacher's professional growth for the following year. Thus, the improvement cycle in teacher performance is the hallmark of the system.

A Goal-Setting Approach

Alexandria City, Virginia, Public School System's Performance Evaluation Program (PEP) is a comprehensive evaluation system designed to portray the complex nature of teaching. The evaluation system consists of four main components: formal observations, informal observations, portfolios, and academic goal setting. It is the latter component, academic goal setting (i.e., student achievement goal setting), that seeks to link teacher instruction to student achievement by requiring teachers to set annual quantifiable goals related to their students' academic progress. PEP is a more informal value-added student growth model in which the student achievement goal-setting process can be customized for each class and teacher. The process places emphasis upon professional development and is closely linked to mastery learning practices (i.e., feedback-corrective teaching). To determine which academic goals to set, teachers follow the subsequent guidelines:

- identify the content area to be addressed,
- collect baseline data for student performance using the best available means,
- establish student performance goals based on the baseline data,
- determine instructional strategies for meeting the specified student performance goals,
- provide instruction based on the selected instructional strategies,
- assess student performance at the end of the course or year, and
- measure student progress by comparing end results with beginning results.

Value-Added Assessment

The Tennessee Value-Added Assessment System (TVAAS) was developed by William Sanders using a statistical model based on growth or gains in student achievement scores rather than on fixed standards. The Tennessee Comprehensive Assessment Program provides yearly measures of student learning in Grades 2 through 8. Based on this rich resource of student achievement data, the TVAAS compares each individual student's growth to his or her own previous growth rate. That is, this year's gains for each individual student are compared to the gains made in previous years. With TVAAS, each student serves as his or her own control for learning gains and, in this process, it is assumed that the same potential for learning exists each year.

RECOMMENDATIONS FOR IMPLEMENTING VALUE-ADDED TEACHER EVALUATION

The evaluation of teachers and other educators must conform to professional standards of practice as defined by the Joint Committee on Standards for Educational Evaluation (1988). Those standards have been broadly organized around propriety, utility, feasibility, and accuracy (see Chapter 3 in this volume for detailed information regarding the standards). We believe that student achievement data can be used in teacher evaluation while satisfying concerns for legal and ethical practice, useful feedback, feasible management of information, and accurate information.

While there are numerous concerns about the quality of test data now available for use in schools (Popham, 2003), properly constructed tests, better databases, improved methodologies for analyzing test data, proper administrative use, and a climate of trust have the potential to maximize the benefits and minimize the liabilities in the connection of student learning and teacher effectiveness. Thus, based on our analysis of the models described above, we propose the following practices to increase the fairness, accuracy, and usefulness of including student achievement data in the teacher evaluation process:

1. *Use student learning as only one component of a teacher assessment system that is based on multiple data sources.* Measures of student learning are fundamentally necessary to judge the effectiveness of teachers and schools, but they should be used in concert with professional judgment about teacher qualifications and behaviors. Other data collection strategies in teacher evaluation, such as classroom observation, portfolios, and client surveys, can inform professional judgment about teacher abilities. The use of multiple data sources helps to compensate for the limitations of each, and this practice is far more legally defensible (National School Boards Association, 2000; Stronge & Tucker, 2003).

2. *Use fair and valid measures of student learning.* Reliability, validity, freedom from bias, and fairness are obvious concerns and conditions for connecting student assessment to teacher evaluation. These criteria for test selection are essential conditions for a proper testing program and become doubly important when they may have implications for personnel decisions. In addition, the assessment measures should be closely aligned with the curriculum to accurately gauge student learning and be more instructionally beneficial.

3. *Recognize that gain scores have inherent liabilities.* While we support the use of value-added gain score methodologies, we also encourage users to recognize that gain scores have statistical liabilities that need to be acknowledged. One issue to consider is regression to the mean—a statistical artifact that results in student test scores moving toward the mean without any attributable learning (or lack thereof) being responsible for the change in test scores. In addition, when tests are not adequately

robust to measure top-end performance, a ceiling effect can depress learning gain scores because there simply isn't adequate room on the testing instrument to document growth.

4. *Use measures of student gain or growth versus a fixed achievement standard or achievement status, but recognize that value-added models of teacher effects need further research and have limitations.* A growth orientation requires the use of pre- and posttesting to determine progress versus the attainment of predetermined pass rates or proficiency levels based on a single sample of performance. True measures of learning should focus on growth in knowledge and skills, not on inherent student aptitude. Although value-added models that use a growth approach are in their infancy and require continued research, they clearly show promise. A comprehensive study of value-added models was conducted by the Rand Corporation that enumerates the primary concerns for value-added teacher assessment, including the impact of different methods of constructing and scaling tests, student-related covariates, missing data, and contributions of prior-year teachers to current-year scores. At the same time, the Rand report indicated that "given the current state of knowledge about VAM [value-added modeling] we expect that some efforts to estimate teacher effects could provide useful information on teachers" (McCaffrey et al., 2004, p. 114).

5. *When judging teacher effectiveness, consider the context in which teaching and learning occur.* There are conditions related to teaching and learning that simply are beyond the control of the teacher. When teachers have done everything possible at the classroom level to enhance instruction but teaching conditions, such as the lack of materials or student turnover, prevent maximum benefit for children, these conditions need to be recognized and accounted for in any evaluation system that attempts to connect teacher effectiveness and student learning. Consideration always should be given for the wide array of variables beyond the control of individual teachers that impact student learning.

6. *Compare learning gains from one point in time to another for the same students, not different groups of students.* Measuring achievement of different groups of students at different times for a given course (e.g., end-of-course testing for Algebra I for groups of students taught in 2003-2004, 2004–2005, etc.) can be useful in determining trends or patterns of achievement in the given subject area. However, this approach to student achievement measurement *does not* satisfy the requirements for connecting teacher evaluation and student achievement because it doesn't account for the gains in learning for a single group of students that can be attributed to a teacher. Implicit in the concept of student achievement gain scores is the assumption that similar tests will be used to measure student learning across time on an individual basis. In addition, it is essential that achievement gains for

the same group of students be disaggregated to show the impact of a given teacher on their achievement; otherwise, there is no basis for connecting the achievement of students to the teacher responsible for teaching them.

7. *Use a time frame for teacher assessment that allows for patterns of student learning to be documented.* If teachers are to be held accountable for student learning, then it is critical that patterns of student learning over time be established. Single measures of learning provide only a snapshot of performance on a given day, whereas multiple measures over the course of a year are more reliable in providing information on growth patterns.

8. *Use measures of student learning to focus on improvement in teaching, learning, and schooling as a whole.* Measures of student learning have the potential to provide valuable feedback on the learning by individual students, the instructional effectiveness of specific teachers, and the effectiveness of instructional strategies and programs. Thus, student learning measures should be used in a constructive manner to help everyone in schools to improve and grow.

CONCLUSION

Current educational reform efforts have focused squarely on the pivotal role of teachers in delivering rigorous instructional programs to all children. While we cannot ignore the myriad factors that impede student learning, teachers are the strongest school-related factor affecting student learning and it is imperative that we continue our efforts to better understand and assess the construct of teacher quality. In this chapter, we have offered a framework for teacher quality that includes teacher qualifications, behaviors, and outcomes. The assessment of these components requires a multipronged approach that includes scrutiny of a teacher's knowledge, skills, and dispositions to teach; assessment of on-the-job behaviors both in and out of the classroom; and learning outcomes attributable to the teacher. Any of these approaches in isolation is limited and would not provide a complete picture of a teacher's value.

Traditional teacher evaluation has emphasized teacher behaviors in the classroom to the virtual exclusion of other indicators of teacher quality. This overreliance on observation by administrators has fundamental limitations, as noted elsewhere in other chapters. The addition of student learning measures as one data source among others can serve to strengthen the accuracy of judgments and provide helpful feedback for instructional improvement. The development of tests that are most closely aligned with curriculum and of new methodologies to analyze test results provides the foundational requirements for more fairly and accurately using student learning measures in teacher evaluation than ever before. The time has come for considering student learning as an essential element in the quest for teacher quality.

REFERENCES

Alkin, M. C. (1992). *Encyclopedia of educational research* (6th ed.). New York: Macmillan.

Bowers, J. J. (1991). Evaluating testing programs at the state and local levels. *Theory Into Practice, 30*(1), 52-60.

Carey, K. (2004). The real value of teachers: Using new information about teacher effectiveness to close the achievement gap. *Thinking K-16, 8*(1), 6.

Commission on Instructionally Supportive Assessment. (2001). Building tests that support instruction and accountability: A guide for policymakers. Washington, DC: Author. Retrieved January 5, 2005, from http://www.nea.org/accountability/buildingtests.html

Darling-Hammond, L. (2000). Teacher quality and student achievement: A review of state policy evidence. *Education Policy Analysis Archives, 8*(1). Retrieved January 3, 2005, from http://epaa.asu.edu/epaa/v8n1/

Dunkin, M. J. (1997). Assessing teachers' effectiveness. *Issues in Educational Research, 7*(1), 37–51.

Educational Research Service (ERS). (1988). *Teacher evaluation: Practices and procedures.* Arlington, VA: Author.

Emerick, S., Hirsch, E., & Berry, B. (2004). Does highly qualified mean high-quality? *ASCD Infobrief, 39.* Retrieved October 30, 2004, from http://www.ascd.org/publications/infobrief/issue39.html

Heinecke, W. F., Curry-Corcoran, D. E., & Moon, T. R. (2003). U.S. schools and the new standards and accountability initiative. In D. L. Duke, M. Grogan, P. D. Tucker, & W. L. Heinecke (Eds.), *Educational leadership in an age of accountability.* Albany: State University of New York Press.

Joint Committee on Standards for Educational Evaluation. (1988). *The personnel evaluation standards: How to assess systems of evaluating educators.* Newbury Park, CA: Sage.

Krei, M. S. (1998). Intensifying the barriers: The problem of inequitable teacher allocation in low-income urban schools. *Urban Education, 33,* 71–94.

Kupermintz, H. (2002). Value-added assessment of teachers: The empirical evidence. In A. Molnar (Ed.), *School reform proposals: The research evidence.* Retrieved February 14, 2002, from http://www.asu.edu/educ/epsl/EPRU/documents/EPRU%202002-101/epru-2002-101.htm

Kupermintz, H. (2003). Teacher effects and teacher effectiveness: A validity investigation of the Tennessee Value Added Assessment System. *Educational Evaluation and Policy Analysis, 25,* 287–298.

Kupermintz, H., Shepard, L., & Linn, R. (2001, April). *Teacher effects as a measure of teacher effectiveness: Construct validity considerations in TVAAS (Tennessee Value Added Assessment System).* Paper presented at the annual meeting of the National Council on Measurement in Education, Seattle, WA.

Madaus, G. F. (1990). *Testing as a social technology: The inaugural Boisi lecture in education and public policy.* Boston: Boston College, Center for the Study of Testing, Evaluation, and Educational Policy.

McCaffrey, D. F., Lockwood, J. R., Koretz, D. M., & Hamilton, L. S. (2004). *Evaluating value-added models for teacher accountability.* Santa Monica, CA: Rand Corporation.

Medley, D. M., & Shannon, D. M. (1994). Teacher evaluation. In T. Husén & T. N. Postlethwaite (Eds.), *The international encyclopedia of education* (2nd ed., Vol. 10, pp. 6015–6020). Elmsford, NY: Pergamon.

Mendro, R. L. (1998). Student achievement and school and teacher accountability. *Journal of Personnel Evaluation in Education, 12,* 257–267.

National Commission on Excellence in Education. (1983). *A nation at risk: The imperative for educational reform.* Washington, DC: U.S. Department of Education.

National Education Association. (1999, April). Should teachers and support staff be able to suspend students? *NEA Today, 17*(1), 43.

National School Boards Association. (2000). *Student testing and assessment: Answering the legal questions.* Alexandria, VA: Author.

No Child Left Behind Act of 2001, 20 U.S.C. § 6301 et seq. (2001).

Nye, B., Konstantopoulos, S., & Hedges, L. V. (2004). How large are teacher effects? *Educational Evaluation and Policy Analysis, 26*(3), 237–257.

Olson, L. (2004a, October 13). Wyoming signs innovative test contract with Harcourt Assessment. *Education Week*, p. 20.

Olson, L. (2004b, November 17). "Value added" models gain in popularity: Growth yardstick appeals to states. *Education Week*, pp. 1, 14–15.

Olson, L. (2004c, November 24). States weigh "value added" models. *Education Week*, p. 13.

Popham, W. J. (2003). Using data to improve student achievement: The seductive allure of data. *Educational Leadership, 60*(5), 48–51.

Rice, J. K. (2003). *Teacher quality: Understanding the effectiveness of teacher attributes*. Washington, DC: Economic Policy Institute.

Rivkin, S. G., Hanuschek, E. A., & Kain, J. F. (2001). *Teachers, schools, and academic achievement*. Amherst, MA: Amherst College Press.

Sanders, W. L., & Horn, S. P. (1994). The Tennessee Value-Added Assessment System (TVAAS): Mixed-model methodology in educational assessment. *Journal of Personnel Evaluation in Education, 8*, 299–311.

Sanders, W. L., & Horn, S. P. (1998). Research findings from the Tennessee Value-Added Assessment System (TVAAS) database: Implications for educational evaluation and research. *Journal of Personnel Evaluation in Education, 12*, 247–256.

Schalock, H. D. (1998). Student progress in learning: Teacher responsibility, accountability and reality. *Journal of Personnel Evaluation in Education, 12*(3), 237–246.

Schalock, H. D., Schalock, M., & Girod, G. (1997). Teacher work sample methodology as used at Western Oregon State University. In J. Millman (Ed.), *Grading teachers, grading schools: Is student achievement a valid evaluation measure?* (pp. 15–45). Thousand Oaks, CA: Corwin.

Stiggins, R. J. (2004). *Student-involved assessment for learning* (4th ed.). Upper Saddle River, NJ: Prentice Hall.

Stronge, J. H. (2002). *Qualities of effective teachers*. Alexandria, VA: Association for Supervision and Curriculum Development.

Stronge, J. H., & Tucker, P. D. (2000). *Teacher evaluation and student achievement*. Washington, DC: National Education Association.

Stronge, J. H., & Tucker, P. D. (2003). *Handbook on teacher evaluation: Assessing and improving performance*. Larchmont, NY: Eye on Education.

Tucker, P. D., & Stronge, J. H. (2001). The ultimate accountability: Use of student learning measures in teacher evaluation. *American School Board Journal, 9*, 34–37.

Tucker, P. D., & Stronge, J. H. (2005). *Linking teacher evaluation and student achievement*. Alexandria, VA: Association for Supervision and Curriculum Development.

Wenglinsky, H. (2002, February 13). How schools matter: The link between teacher classroom practices and student academic performance. *Educational Policy Analysis Archives, 10*(12). Retrieved May 17, 2005, from http://epaa.asu.edu/epaa/v10n12/

Wright, S. P., Horn, S. P., & Sanders, W. L. (1997). Teacher and classroom context effects on student achievement: Implications for teacher evaluation. *Journal of Personnel Evaluation in Education, 11*, 57–67.

Wynne, E. (1972). *The politics of American education*. Berkeley, CA: McCutchan.

Portfolios in Teacher Evaluation

8

Kenneth Wolf

Teaching portfolios are increasingly popular tools for both evaluation and professional development. Portfolios are currently in use in a variety of settings—in university teacher education programs to foster the growth of pre-service teachers (Borko, Michaelec, Timmons, & Siddle, 1997; Lyons, 1999; Delandshere & Arens, 2003), with the National Board for Professional Teaching Standards to certify and reward teaching excellence (National Board for Professional Teaching Standards, 1989; Ballou, 2003), and in school districts to hire and evaluate teachers (McNelly, 2002; Theel & Tallerico, 2004).

Why have educators turned to teaching portfolios? Proponents contend that portfolios present authentic views of learning and teaching over time, offering a more complete and valid picture of what teachers know and can do (Shulman, 1988; Wolf, 1991, 1996). Moreover, they believe that portfolios promote professional development by providing teachers with a structure and process for documenting and reflecting on their practice.

Although portfolios have many attractive features, their use can have significant liabilities as well. Portfolios can be time-consuming to construct, cumbersome to store, and difficult to score. Nevertheless, the potential of portfolios for addressing assessment needs as well as advancing professional learning suggests that administrators should consider a role for teacher portfolios in their school-based evaluation and staff development programs.

In this chapter we provide principals and other school administrators with an overview of teaching portfolios so that they can make informed choices

AUTHOR'S NOTE: The author gratefully acknowledges the contributions of Gary Lichtenstein and Cynthia Stevenson to this chapter in the first edition of the book. Thanks also to Janet Junkin and Nancy Hall for contributing examples from their teaching portfolios.

about their use. We begin by defining teaching portfolios and discussing issues related to their design. Next, we present examples from actual teaching portfolios. We conclude by offering recommendations for putting portfolios into practice.

WHAT IS A TEACHING PORTFOLIO?

In its most basic form, a teaching portfolio is a collection of information about a teacher's practice. Portfolios can come in many different shapes and sizes, but in practice they often take the form of scrapbooks filled with photographs of classroom life, along with affectionate notes from students and parents. Although this kind of portfolio may be eye-catching and heartwarming, it does not effectively advance either evaluation or professional development goals.

The problem with portfolios such as these is that they are not connected to professional content standards that describe what teachers should know and be able to do, nor are they explicitly linked to a teacher's individual teaching philosophy or a school's improvement plan. In addition, these types of portfolios often lack examples of student or teacher work that illustrates the ways in which teachers have acted on the professional content standards and their philosophies and goals. Moreover, there is no explicit reflection on the teaching and learning portrayed in such portfolios nor any explanation of the context in which these events occurred. Furthermore, these portfolios are typically constructed without input from colleagues.

What might be a more productive vision for portfolios? Drawing on the work of Lee Shulman (1992), we offer the following:

A teaching portfolio is the structured documentary history of a carefully selected set of coached or mentored accomplishments, substantiated by samples of student work, and fully realized only through reflective writing, deliberation, and serious conversation.

The key features of such a teaching portfolio are as follows:

- The portfolio should be structured around sound professional content standards and individual and school goals.
- The portfolio should contain carefully selected examples of both student and teacher work that illustrate key features of the teacher's practice.
- The contents of the portfolio should be framed by captions and written commentaries that explain and reflect on the contents.
- The portfolio should be a mentored or coached experience, in which the portfolio is used as a basis for ongoing professional conversations with colleagues and supervisors.

WHAT PURPOSES MIGHT A TEACHING PORTFOLIO SERVE?

There are three main purposes of a teaching portfolio:

- To address evaluation requirements
- To advance professional growth
- To aid in employment searches

Although a carefully conceptualized portfolio can address all of these to some degree, each purpose suggests somewhat different design considerations. Portfolios that are used primarily for evaluation, for example, require greater structure than do those that primarily serve professional growth. For the evaluation portfolio, *fairness* is a chief concern. Consistency—in portfolio requirements and in the evaluation process—best advances this goal. With the professional development portfolio, however, *ownership* of the learning process is a major concern. Individual customization of the portfolio best serves this goal. For an evaluation portfolio, for example, the structure and contents should be specified in advance so that the requirements for completing the portfolio are clear and the evaluation process is consistent. On the other hand, for a professional development portfolio, latitude in choices concerning the focus and format of the portfolio is likely to increase learning, because each teacher will adapt the portfolio to his or her specific needs and goals.

A portfolio used in employment searches is shaped by still different forces. In all likelihood, those doing the hiring will have limited time to review the portfolio, and they will be strongly affected by their general impressions. In this situation, as Lichtenstein (1997) has found in his interviews with administrators, the portfolio author needs to pay greater attention to presentation issues, such as the attractiveness of the portfolio and the accessibility of the information.

Although we distinguish among these three types of portfolios in terms of their primary purposes to highlight the trade-offs inherent in each, we want to emphasize that a single portfolio can advance all three goals if the person responsible for conceptualizing the portfolio is clear about his or her purposes and thoughtful in designing it.

WHAT MIGHT BE INCLUDED IN A TEACHING PORTFOLIO?

The contents of teaching portfolios can be as varied as the people who construct them. A portfolio might include samples of student and teacher work, such as photographs of class projects, lesson plans, student assessments, and evidence of professional activities. In addition, a portfolio might include a variety of other information, such as letters of commendation from parents, evaluations from supervisors, and even teaching credentials and college transcripts. Any number of these items might be desirable, but which are essential? We recommend that the following items be included in every portfolio, regardless of its primary purpose:

- A statement of philosophy or teaching goals
- Samples of teacher work, such as lesson plans and student assessments
- Samples of student work, such as reading logs and student projects
- Captions that briefly explain the work samples
- Commentaries that reflect on the teaching and learning documented in the portfolio

In addition to samples of student and teacher work, captions and commentaries on those samples are essential. Captions provide contextual information about each item in the portfolio (see Figure 8.1). Commentaries are written accounts that elaborate on and interpret the portfolio contents.

Figure 8.1   Portfolio Caption Form

Title of evidence: _____

Date created: _____

Educator's name: _____

Description of context in which evidence was collected: _____

_____

Interpretation: _____

_____

Additional comments: _____

_____

In essence, then, a portfolio should be framed by a sound philosophy that is consistent with professional expectations and school goals, illustrated through samples of student and teacher work, and explained through captions and commentaries. Depending upon the purposes of the portfolio, however, additional information might be warranted. For example, an employment portfolio should probably contain a résumé, whereas an evaluation portfolio might include copies of previous evaluations. Such additional contents will vary across settings based on individual and school needs; the ingredients described above, however, are essential for all portfolios.

HOW MIGHT THE PORTFOLIO PROCESS UNFOLD?

The following steps might serve as a guide for teachers in building their portfolios:

- Prepare a philosophy statement.
- Set goals for the portfolio in consultation with a supervisor.

- Collect a variety of student and teacher work samples.
- Discuss the work samples with colleagues at regular intervals.
- Organize and caption the portfolio contents.
- Write reflective commentaries about the teaching and learning documented in the portfolio.
- Submit the completed portfolio to a supervisor for review.
- Receive feedback from the reviewing supervisor.
- Set new goals in light of the supervisor's feedback.

In this scenario, the teacher and his or her supervisor meet to set the goals and expectations for the teacher's portfolio. Throughout the school year, the teacher gathers a variety of work samples for possible inclusion in the portfolio. At regular intervals, the teacher uses these artifacts as departure points for discussions with colleagues about his or her teaching. The teacher prepares to submit the completed portfolio by organizing and captioning the portfolio contents and explaining through written commentary the significance of various items. Finally, the portfolio is formally evaluated by the teacher's supervisor, who rates the portfolio performance and provides written, and possibly oral, feedback to the teacher. The teacher then sets new goals in light of what he or she has learned. Although action is not a part of the portfolio process per se, it is assumed that the teacher will be constantly acting on what he or she is learning to improve classroom practice and students' learning.

HOW SHOULD A TEACHING PORTFOLIO BE EVALUATED?

Portfolios are exciting as assessment tools because they allow teachers to represent the complexities and individuality of their teaching in great detail. They are problematic, however, for the same reasons. Each portfolio is thick and unique, making evaluation a daunting task.

Ensuring that the evaluation process is manageable and fair requires that several elements be put into place in advance, including identification of sound content and performance standards for teachers, specification of the requirements for construction of a portfolio, and design of an efficient evaluation system. The establishment of these elements will increase the likelihood that the evaluation system will successfully meet the essential requirements of validity, reliability, and utility (Stronge & Helm, 1991).

Identification of Content and Performance Standards

The evaluation of a teacher's portfolio should be based on clear content standards (what teachers should know and be able to do) and performance standards (how well they should know and be able to do it). These standards should be spelled out in advance, so that teachers have clear targets for their performance. These standards will serve to guide teachers in the construction of their portfolios as well as reviewers in their evaluations.

We recommend the identification of a small set of content standards (about three to seven), with each of the standards composed of several statements that clarify its meaning. For example, the Douglas County School District in Colorado has three content standards (e.g., assessment and instruction) for evaluating a teacher's performance, each of which is explained with five statements that operationally define the standard (see Table 8.1).

Table 8.1 Professional Content Standards for Teachers: Douglas County School District, Colorado

Assessment and instruction

Outstanding educators

Act on the belief that all students can learn

Recognize, value, and adjust for individual differences, while maintaining an in-depth understanding of how students develop and learn

Implement a variety of instructional strategies

Motivate and engage students

Draw on multiple strategies for assessing student learning and development, and clearly communicate assessment results to students and parents

Content and pedagogy

Outstanding educators

Know the subjects they teach

Know how to teach those subjects to students

Know how subjects are related to one another across the curriculum

Can relate the subjects they teach to real-world applications

Are reflective practitioners who facilitate professional growth through self-assessment, and whose knowledge is based on both practical experience and professional literature

Collaboration and partnership

Outstanding educators

Collaborate with other school professionals

Work effectively with parents and community

Draw on school and community resources to benefit students

Contribute to the school, community, and profession in a variety of ways

Respect diverse individuals and groups

Along with content standards, performance standards need to be established as well. Performance standards address the question, How good is good enough? What level of performance is required for an "outstanding" designation, for example? Are the expectations different for beginning and experienced teachers? Determining these levels may take several exploratory efforts. During the development of these performance levels, we suggest that the emphasis of the portfolio process should be on professional growth rather than on high-stakes evaluation.

How many performance levels are desirable? Ratings can vary from satisfactory/unsatisfactory to a scale with multiple designations, such as accomplished/proficient/needs improvement. Ratings can be made at the overall performance level or for each of the content standards. We recommend a rating system that is as simple as possible to avoid the problems associated with making many fine (and probably unsupportable) distinctions about portfolio performance. Feedback to teachers, however, should be detailed and linked to the information in the portfolios, so that teachers have a clear understanding of the specific strengths and weaknesses in their performance as well as the reasons for their ratings.

Designing the Portfolio

To help ensure that the portfolio construction and review process is manageable, a portfolio should be focused on a few key areas of teaching rather than the entire curriculum, and should be slender in size rather than as thick as a metropolitan phone book. For example, an elementary school teacher might address aspects of only two content areas, such as mathematics and art, and link the two through a similar topic, such as patterns. Along the same lines, a secondary school teacher might choose two broad topics within his or her subject matter. For example, a middle school English teacher might document aspects of his or her writing instruction and literature discussions over a semester, and a high school American history teacher might focus on units on the American Revolution and the civil rights movement.

An alternative approach to focusing on a specific topic or subject matter might be for teachers at any level to conduct small-scale case studies on three diverse learners in their classrooms in which they investigate the students' learning across a variety of content areas and contexts. The point here is that the focus for the portfolio can productively vary, but trying to address too broad a scope within a single portfolio is more often a problem than is too narrow a focus.

Less is more, not only in terms of breadth of coverage but also in amount of information. A carefully selected collection of evidence can be used more productively by both teacher and administrator than can a file cabinet's worth of material. In any case, a portfolio already contains far more information than is available in most evaluation contexts. But how much is enough? Five to 10 teacher work samples, such as lesson plans and classroom tests, and a similar number of student work samples, such as homework assignments and self-assessments, might be sufficient, assuming they are carefully selected to illustrate their connection to the content standards and portfolio goals. Add a caption for each piece of information and one or two commentaries of two to three pages in length, and the portfolio evaluator has a wide range of information on which to base decisions and feedback.

Specification of Requirements

Another way to make the portfolio construction and evaluation process more manageable and fair is to specify the requirements for the portfolio in advance. This information might be packaged in a "portfolio construction handbook," which should include the following elements:

- Purposes of the portfolio
- Procedures for constructing the portfolio
- Timeline for completion and evaluation of the portfolio
- List of required and/or suggested portfolio contents
- Description of the evaluation process
- Evaluation criteria (content and performance standards)
- Description of the feedback and appeals process

As this list indicates, teachers should be provided with specific information about how to construct portfolios, including advice on the types and numbers of work samples that should be included and the length and structure of written commentaries. Timelines for submitting materials for review by mentors or supervisors should be explicit. In addition, the evaluation process should be described, so that teachers know who will participate in their reviews, what additional sources of information might be used, and what options teachers have for revising or remedying less-than-proficient performance appraisals. Clearly defined portfolio procedures allow teachers to spend more time reflecting on their instruction and less on trying to figure out how to "play the portfolio game."

Evaluating the Contents

Given the challenge of comprehensively reviewing a thick set of documents and materials, we recommend that administrators examining teacher portfolios follow a systematic review process that includes the following steps:

- Read the entire portfolio to get a sense of the overall performance.
- Review the portfolio in light of the content standards and teacher goals.
- Take notes about significant pieces of information in the portfolio.
- Assign a rating for the portfolio (if appropriate).
- Provide feedback to the teacher.

It is important that the reviewer examine the portfolio for each of the content standards. This can best be achieved by reading the entire portfolio first, and then reviewing the portfolio with each standard as a separate lens. During these cycles through the portfolio, the reviewer should note significant sources of evidence that will be used in the evaluation and as feedback to the teacher.

In addition, the reviewer should keep the teacher's goals for the portfolio in mind. A portfolio, although a thick collection of information, is still only a thin slice of a teacher's entire performance. Thus, it is unrealistic to expect a teacher to represent all that he or she knows and does within a single portfolio. The teacher's goals for the portfolio, which have been set in consultation with a supervisor, should provide the focus for the evaluation.

Whether the portfolio actually receives a rating (e.g., exemplary, proficient, unsatisfactory) will depend on the purposes of the program. In most cases, it may be unnecessary, and even undesirable, for the supervisor to rate the portfolio. Assigning scores to portfolios may focus conversations among teachers, and between teachers and administrators, on scores rather than on issues of teaching effectiveness. To offset this possibility, we recommend basing teacher evaluation on a variety of evidence—such as direct observation, parent feedback, and student achievement—in addition to the teacher-constructed portfolio. Using multiple measures also helps to allay the concern voiced by some administrators and teachers that a teacher might be an excellent portfolio maker but a poor teacher. We believe that this concern is exaggerated, but the perception itself is enough to undermine the credibility of the process. Hence, to offset the possibility of an ineffective teacher receiving a high rating, as well as to strengthen the credibility of the portfolio process, it is wise for administrators to draw on multiple sources of information beyond the portfolio in evaluating a teacher.

Although specific scores should probably not be assigned to portfolios, detailed feedback is critical. Ideally, feedback on a teacher's portfolio should be presented in both written and oral form. However, time constraints may limit the amount of energy that administrators can devote to the feedback process. It is important to remember that feedback from the administrator is not the only, or even the primary, source of information for the teacher about his or her practice. Regular portfolio-based conversations among teachers should be an integral and ongoing feature of the portfolio process.

EXAMPLES FROM TEACHING PORTFOLIOS

In this section, we present examples from two teachers' portfolios. The first examples come from the portfolio of Nancy Hall, a first-grade teacher in a preservice education program at the University of Denver in Colorado. Preservice teachers at the University of Denver are required to prepare portfolios as part of their professional preparation program. The second set of examples comes from the portfolio of Janet Junkin, an experienced middle school social studies teacher in the Douglas County School District in Colorado, who submitted this portfolio to the district's Outstanding Teacher Program. Teachers in the Douglas County School District are invited to present portfolios to qualify for a designation of "outstanding" and a $1,000 bonus for that school year.

An Elementary School Teacher's Portfolio

First-grade teacher Nancy Hall placed the table of contents shown in Table 8.2 in her portfolio. The first section of her portfolio provides background information about her experiences and perspectives, the second section presents direct evidence of her teaching, and the third section describes her future professional development plans and evidence of her professional expertise in one area of education (cooperative learning).

Table 8.2   Sample Portfolio Table of Contents

Section I

    Résumé
    Letters of Recommendation
    Educational Philosophy

Section II

    Unit Plan Overview
    Lesson Plan
    Reflective Summary
    Artifacts

Section III

    Professional Development Plan
    Professional Development Expertise

In a one-page statement of her philosophy of education, she described her academic instruction in the following way:

> My approach to teaching will incorporate the integration of the four academic disciples (math, social studies, science, and language arts), as well as the arts. For example, study of the tropical rain forest would include learning about the kinds of trees, animals, and weather patterns that are particular to those regions. The height of the jungle trees could be compared to the indigenous trees of Colorado. The word "tropical" would generate a geography lesson. There is [abundant] literature related to the rain forest that could lead to a discussion on social issues and ecology. Through art projects the classroom could be transformed into a multi-rain forest. Our daily lives are interconnected with things around us, and it makes sense that we approach education in the same manner.

Nancy Hall also incorporated several overviews of a unit that she taught on the rain forest. One overview was presented in the form of a calendar, with each day's activities briefly summarized. In another overview, she described each week's focus in greater detail. Here is her description of Week Three's events:

> This week the class will learn about biodiversity and why it's important. We will begin the study of rain forest animals and feature a different animal each day. The student will learn about the characteristics, classification, habits, and habitat of each animal. This week we will study the toucan, hummingbird, sloth and armadillo. I will incorporate [information about] the animals in the math journal problems.

She also included a lesson plan from the unit, examples of student work, assessments from the students about the value of the unit, and the university supervisor's visitation report on the lesson documented in the portfolio.

Nancy Hall then offered a one-page reflective summary of her lesson on the monkey. She noted the following strengths and weaknesses in her instruction:

> I felt that the lesson on the monkey went particularly well. It was successful because of the following reasons: the information itself was of interest and I planned two activities which require student participation. To demonstrate the sensitivity of finger tips and the precision grip that primates use, I blindfolded [a student] and had him pick up and identify beans, nuts, and raisins. I chose a few students to pantomime phrases I had written down to prove that communication is achieved through means other than words and that monkeys have this capacity. I have found interactive lessons to be rewarding and plan to involve the students in demonstrations of various concepts whenever possible.
>
> I didn't feel that the student surveys I provided gave an accurate picture of what the students thought about the lesson. I would not repeat the survey assessment. I felt that a better evaluation of the lesson were the reactions and information generated during the "think, pair, share." As the students verbalized information it was clear that they had listened, learned, and enjoyed the lesson.

A Middle School Teacher's Portfolio

Middle school social studies teacher Janet Junkin prepared a portfolio for her district's Outstanding Teacher Program. In her portfolio, she explained why she believed her performance met the district's criteria for "outstanding" for each of the three content standards. In this excerpt, she addresses the content standard "collaboration and partnership":

> I believe that my performance is outstanding in the area of collaboration and partnership because I believe and model the philosophy, "It takes a whole village to raise a child." Quality education occurs when

the school staff, parents, and community contribute to this process as a team. . . .

I visit my core students in their elective classes throughout the year for a variety of reasons. I enjoy seeing "my kids" in another setting. I value our elective program and I want the students to know this. This provides an avenue for collaboration with other teachers to benefit my students. . . .

Recruiting and working with parent volunteers through the magazine sale, geography bee, student council, team field trips, community service projects, and the cruise is a very positive experience for me and has accomplished many things to benefit our students. . . .

I draw on the community and private sector through phone calls, letters, and personal contacts. . . . These efforts provide my students with additional classroom resources as well as support for school-wide events.

To support her claim of outstanding performance in the area of "content and pedagogy," for example, Janet Junkin included information associated with a unit that she taught on Western Europe. In one activity, she asked the students to prepare an orientation brochure for American families who were about to move to Western Europe. Instructions that she gave to the students, which were documented in her portfolio, included the following:

You work for a major American corporation that is expanding its business overseas . . . to Western Europe. You have been promoted to the position of Director of Expatriate Orientation. You are to provide training and information for FAMILIES about to move overseas.

She asked the students to begin the assignment by first identifying the questions that they might address in the orientation brochure:

- Three questions YOU might ask if you found out your family was moving overseas
- Three questions your SIBLING might want answered
- Three questions one of your PARENTS might want answered

As evidence of what students had learned, she included one student's brochure, called "A Traveler's Guide to France," in her portfolio. The brochure gave information about topics such as attractions, climate, and holidays.

In addition to a variety of work samples from herself and her students, Janet Junkin also included surveys from students and their parents about her effectiveness as a teacher. These surveys, which were required for all teachers participating in the Outstanding Teacher Program, were mailed to 20 different families. The surveys were designed to parallel the content standards for the district's teachers. Excerpts from one family's responses to the 13-question survey are presented in Figure 8.2.

Figure 8.2   Client Survey, Douglas County School District

	Strongly Agree	Agree	Disagree	Strongly Disagree	Not Observed
1. This teacher believes that ALL students can learn	(SA)	A	D	SD	NO

Comments: *She offers extra opportunities and experiences for students such as the Geography Bee.*

	Strongly Agree	Agree	Disagree	Strongly Disagree	Not Observed
2. This teacher makes adjustments for individual differences among students.	(SA)	A	D	SD	NO

Comments: *They can choose what they want to do on projects.*

	Strongly Agree	Agree	Disagree	Strongly Disagree	Not Observed
3. This teacher uses a variety of strategies to meet my child's needs.	(SA)	A	D	SD	NO

Comments: *There are creative projects that help them learn.*

These surveys were anonymously returned directly to the teachers, who then included commentary in their portfolios about what they learned from the surveys. In her one-page reflection on the client surveys, Janet Junkin stated that she learned the following:

> My clients value guest speakers and a focus on current events. Biweekly progress reports are very time-consuming, but based on these surveys they are a very successful form of communication with my clients.

After she turned in her portfolio to her administrator, Janet Junkin received an overall rating as well as written feedback from her administrator about aspects of her performance for each of the district's three content standard (Table 8.3 presents an example of one of the standards). Based on her portfolio, Janet Junkin was awarded a designation of "outstanding."

Table 8.3   Administrator Feedback on Janet Junkin's Portfolio

Content Standard: Content and Pedagogy	
Areas of Strength	*Areas for Growth*
Uses wide variety of techniques. Connects to outside experiences. Celebrates diversity. Plans interdisciplinary units. Employs authentic assessment. Piloted district standards.	If possible, carry out interdisciplinary units with core teammates as well as with elective teachers.

The examples presented above from the portfolios of Nancy Hall and Janet Junkin are intended to suggest the possibilities for what might be included in a portfolio. Ultimately, the contents that are selected will vary, depending on the purposes of the portfolio, expectations for teacher performance, school improvement plans, and individual teachers' interests and needs.

PUTTING PORTFOLIOS INTO PRACTICE

In the following pages we offer some suggestions for putting portfolios into practice. We propose a series of steps that administrators might follow in introducing portfolios in their schools or districts, as well as considerations for creating a productive climate for teachers who are willing to try out portfolios:

1. Define the expectations for teacher performance.

2. Clarify the purposes of the portfolio.

3. Identify the products for the portfolio.

4. Develop guidelines for portfolio construction.

5. Establish procedures for portfolio evaluation.

Step 1: Define the expectations for teacher performance in a building or district. Before portfolios are actually introduced, it is critical that administrators first examine the expectations, or content standards, for teachers in their buildings or districts. What are teachers expected to know and be able to do? Are the expectations for performance for beginners different from those for experienced teachers? Many good examples of content standards currently exist (see Table 8.1, for example), and these can be adapted for use in other settings.

Step 2: Clarify the purposes of the portfolio. Decisions about the purposes of the portfolio will influence issues related to the portfolio design, construction, and evaluation. If the primary use of the portfolio will be for evaluation, then the portfolio process should be similar for all participants; otherwise, administrators may not be able to evaluate the portfolios in a fair and consistent fashion. On the other hand, portfolios that are intended primarily for professional development may be completely different from teacher to teacher in format and focus. In this instance, the administrator's primary responsibility is not to evaluate the portfolio but to provide feedback to the portfolio's creator. Clarity about these purposes will help prevent the portfolio process from becoming a paper chase for teachers or an evaluation nightmare for administrators.

Step 3: Identify the products for the portfolio. Although many different products can be productively placed in a portfolio, requirements (or recommendations) for the inclusion of certain types of information will allow teachers to discuss their instruction with each other more easily and will enable administrators to evaluate portfolios more efficiently. What types of information should be included in portfolios? We have offered a general list above, but an even more detailed set of products and specifications is recommended. For example, a school or district might require that each teacher submit a one-page narrative overview of three consecutive lessons and a two-page lesson plan for the second lesson in the series. Again, it is worth mentioning that if the portfolio is not being used for evaluation, the need for consistency in the type and number of portfolio products is much less critical.

As the portfolio products are being identified, it is important to link the products to the expectations, or content standards, for teachers. The question to be answered then is, What kinds of information in a portfolio can best provide insights into a teacher's performance for a particular standard? A matrix is a useful tool for examining the relationship between the portfolio products and content standards (see Table 8.4). For example, for what content standards might a lesson plan, student assessments, and parent feedback provide evidence?

Table 8.4   Matrix of Content Standards by Portfolio Contents

	Lesson Plan	Student Assessments	Parent Feedback
Assessment and instruction	X	X	
Content and pedagogy	X		X
Collaboration and partnership			X

Step 4: Develop guidelines for the portfolio construction process. It is important to establish guidelines for portfolio construction so that teachers will have to spend as little time as possible thinking about portfolio logistics and have as much time as possible for considering issues of teaching and learning. These guidelines should include such elements as the timeline for completing the portfolio, required or recommended contents, specifications for preparing information (e.g., date and caption each piece of information), and information about the evaluation process. This information might be presented in a handbook or in a series of one-page handouts.

Step 5: Establish procedures for evaluating the portfolio. In evaluating portfolio performance, a number of issues need to be addressed. Who will evaluate the portfolio—the principal, a trusted peer, a committee? How will the information be used—as part of an individual evaluation, for self-assessment, for discussion about school goals? What kind of feedback will a teacher receive—a score, written comments, a conference with a supervisor? Teacher confidence in the program will be greatly enhanced if evaluation-related decisions such as these are made well in advance.

Introducing the Use of Portfolios

Along with those described above, the following steps should be followed during the introduction of the use of portfolios in a school or district:

- Enlist volunteers.
- Start small.
- Keep the risk low.
- Encourage portfolio-based conversations.
- Use multiple measures of evaluation.

Enlist volunteers. A core group of enthusiastic volunteers should be identified who are willing to be carpenters constructing their own portfolios at the same time they are architects building the overall program. These teachers, then, will not only be trying out the process by preparing their own portfolios, they will also take leadership roles in tasks such as identifying the content standards and developing portfolio procedures. Many new ideas in education fail not because the concepts are flawed, but because they did not have teacher input or buy-in.

Start small. Begin by having teachers focus on only a single content standard or school goal, or on only a few types of portfolio products. Portfolios can quickly become unmanageable if a lot of information is collected without clear purposes and procedures for its organization and use. After the initial design issues have been worked out, and portfolios have been successfully introduced, then the focus of portfolios can be expanded to more content standards or multiple goals or a greater variety of information.

Keep the risk low. The portfolio pioneers should feel confident that the work that they do will, at a minimum, have no negative consequences. Clarity about the agenda of the program and the uses for the portfolios will help to establish an atmosphere of trust. Moreover, not only should the risk remain low, but providing incentives for teachers, such as release days or bonuses, will increase the likelihood of the program's taking root.

Encourage portfolio-based conversations. Portfolios provide an opportunity for teachers to work together to foster their professional development and to address difficult problems of practice. Administrators should promote these collaborative interactions through a variety of strategies, such as devoting a portion of faculty meetings to portfolio-based conversations or structuring schedules so that teachers have shared planning times. Wolf, Hagerty, and Whinery (1995) offer suggestions for organizing and conducting portfolio-based conversations among teachers.

Use multiple measures of evaluation. Like any assessment approach, portfolios have strengths as well as limitations. They may provide a clear view of a teacher's instructional strategies, for example, but give no information about that teacher's classroom management practices. Furthermore, portfolios are better at revealing strengths than they are at providing information about weaknesses. For these reasons, portfolios should be part of an overall evaluation system that might include classroom observation, evidence of student achievement, and client feedback.

CONCLUSION

In this chapter, we have defined the concept of a teaching portfolio and discussed the various forms that portfolios can take. We have also provided examples from actual portfolios. Finally, we have suggested steps that administrators might take in putting portfolios into practice.

In essence, we believe that all portfolios should contain carefully selected examples of teacher and student work, framed by commentaries and captions, and brought to life through extended conversations with colleagues and supervisors. We also emphasize that a portfolio's purpose drives many decisions about the specific contents of the portfolio, as well as the process for constructing and evaluating it.

Whether teachers are creating portfolios as part of a school evaluation plan or for their own professional development purposes, we believe that the process of carefully documenting and reflecting on selected aspects of one's practice enhances performance. Thus, although the purposes for creating portfolios may vary, all portfolios contribute to the same ultimate aim—to advance student learning through the professional development of teachers.

REFERENCES

Ballou, D. (2003). Certifying accomplished teachers: A critical look at the National Board for Professional Teaching Standards. *Peabody Journal of Education, 78*(4), 201–219.

Borko, H., Michaelec, P., Timmons, M., & Siddle, J. (1997). Student teaching portfolios: A tool for promoting reflective practice. *Journal of Teacher Education, 48*(5), 345–358.

Delandshere, G., & Arens, S. A. (2003). Examining the quality of the evidence in preservice teacher portfolios. *Journal of Teacher Education, 54*(1), 57–73.

Lichtenstein, G. (1997). *Portfolios for hire.* Unpublished manuscript.

Lyons, N. (1999). How portfolios can shape emerging practice. *Educational Leadership, 56*(8), 63–66.

McNelly, T. A. (2002). Evaluations that ensure growth: Teacher portfolios. *Principal Leadership, 3*(4), 55–60.

National Board for Professional Teaching Standards. (1989). *Toward high and rigorous standards for the teaching profession.* Washington, DC: Author.

Shulman, L. S. (1988). A union of insufficiencies: Strategies for teacher assessment in a period of educational reform. *Educational Leadership, 46*(3), 36–41. (ERIC Document Reproduction Service No. EJ 385 344)

Shulman, L. (1992). *Portfolios for teacher education: A component of reflective teacher education.* Paper presented at the annual meeting of the American Educational Research Association, San Francisco.

Stronge, J. H., & Helm, V. M. (1991). *Evaluating professional support personnel in education.* Newbury Park, CA: Sage.

Theel, R. K., & Tallerico, M. (2004). Using portfolios for teacher hiring: Insights from school principals. *Action in Teacher Education, 26*(1), 26–35.

Wolf, K. (1991). The schoolteacher's portfolio: Issues in design, implementation, and evaluation. *Phi Delta Kappan, 73,* 129–136.

Wolf, K. (1996). Developing an effective teaching portfolio. *Educational Leadership, 53*(6), 34–37.

Wolf, K., Hagerty, P., & Whinery, B. (1995). Teaching portfolios and portfolio conversations for teachers and teacher educators. *Action in Teacher Education, 17,* 30–39.

Teacher Self-Evaluation

Peter W. Airasian

Arlen Gullickson

Teacher self-evaluation is a process in which teachers make judgments about the adequacy and effectiveness of their own knowledge, performance, beliefs, and effects for the purpose of self-improvement. At the heart of teacher self-evaluation is the belief that teachers' main reasons for engaging in professional development activities come from their own experiences of what it means to be a teacher and from a personal need to understand, critique, and improve their own practice (Airasian & Gullickson, 1994a, 1994b; Hargreaves, 1995). In self-evaluation, it is the teacher who collects, interprets, and judges information bearing on personal practice. It is the teacher who frames criteria and standards to judge the adequacy of his or her beliefs, knowledge, skills, and effectiveness. It is the teacher who decides on the nature of professional development activities to be undertaken.

Self-evaluation is related to such concepts as the reflective practitioner, reflection on practice, teacher connoisseurship and criticism, teacher research, self-understanding, educational action research, and analysis of practice. All of these approaches encourage teachers to assess their own practice, based on the belief that if meaningful professional development is to occur, the focus must be in areas where teachers perceive the need for improvement (Sergiovanni & Starratt, 1988). Self-evaluation has been likened to a formative evaluation of one's practice, formative in the sense that the evaluation is aimed at examining and, if necessary, altering or improving practice (Airasian & Gullickson, 1994a; Barber, 1990; Kremer-Hayon, 1993). Some have viewed it as an informal type of action research based in and concerned with practice (Gitlin et al., 1992; Hatton & Smith, 1995; Osterman & Kottkamp, 1993).

Underlying teacher self-evaluation are the following beliefs (Airasian & Gullickson, 1994b; Osterman & Kottkamp, 1993):

- Teachers need professional growth opportunities.
- Teachers want to improve their practice and knowledge; teachers want and need information about their knowledge, performance, and effectiveness.
- Teachers are capable of assuming responsibility for much of their own professional growth and development, given time, encouragement, and resources.
- Collaboration enriches professional growth and development.

It is, however, necessary to point out that in spite of the importance and usefulness of teacher self-evaluation, it is only part of a viable, ongoing program of teacher evaluation. Self-evaluation is evaluation for teachers to help them become aware of, reflect on, analyze, and make decisions about their practice. However, in most school settings there is a need for other types of teacher evaluation, because teachers are accountable to many constituents besides themselves: (a) pupils and the community who are affected by their actions, (b) employers with whom they have contractual obligations, and (c) their profession, which has its own standards and expectations (Dwyer & Stufflebeam, 1996). Although self-evaluation can fulfill some of these accountability needs, it cannot fulfill them all; thus, other forms of teacher evaluation are necessary.

WHY IS TEACHER SELF-EVALUATION IMPORTANT?

At the time we first wrote on this matter we noted that the nature of teacher evaluation was changing in response to three trends: poor pupil achievement, bottom-up reform efforts, and new views of teaching and learning. First, the perceived poor performance of American students on national and international tests has been associated, in part, with unsatisfactory performance by teachers. Critics argue that improving the performance and quality of teachers is a crucial and critical prerequisite of improving student achievement (Carnegie Task Force on Teaching as a Profession, 1986). As a consequence, programs emphasizing the importance of careful preservice and inservice teacher evaluation, accompanied by raised standards for teacher certification, have been implemented in many states and school districts (Darling-Hammond, 1990; Dwyer & Stufflebeam, 1996; Grimmett, Rostad, & Ford, 1992).

Second, a 1990s emphasis in teacher evaluation was viewed as a bottom-up approach to educational reform (Glickman, 1992; Hargreaves & Fullan, 1992; Smith & O'Day, 1991). In contrast to the top-down reform approaches of the 1970s and 1980s (Milner, 1991), which were based largely on mandated, common evaluation strategies for all teachers in a state or district, bottom-up reforms are focused on the individual school or teacher and seek to make teaching more professional by providing varied and ongoing opportunities for professional development. There is a more balanced emphasis on summative and formative evaluations. This shift can be seen in efforts to do the following:

- Extend assistance to new teachers
- Broaden career opportunities for experienced teachers
- Make teachers more responsible for demonstrating their own competence
- Introduce portfolio evaluation to foster teacher reflection
- Provide opportunities for collegial and cooperative teacher activities, such as site-based management and action research

All these efforts are designed to help teachers play an informed and active role in assessing and advancing their own practice.

The bottom-up approach views teachers as influential educational decision makers and seeks to use evaluation to identify the professional development they need to enhance their own practice (Airasian, 1993). There is recognition that experience is a necessary but not sufficient prerequisite of teaching expertise. What distinguishes the expert teacher from the nonexpert is the former's ability to learn from reflection and experience (Berliner, 1987; Schön, 1987). Evaluation, including self-evaluation, is viewed as a major and important means of making teachers aware of their practice, challenging them to think about it, and encouraging them to analyze and evaluate it and implement changes as needed.

Third, the increased emphasis on teacher evaluation occurs in response to the growing attention accorded the teaching and learning of higher-level thinking skills. The view of teaching and learning one adopts has direct implications for what and how one teaches (Delandshire & Petrosky, 1994; Driver, Asoko, Leach, Mortimer, & Scott, 1994) and consequently for how one's teaching should be evaluated. A view of learning that conceives of individuals (including teachers) as constructors of their own knowledge (Bruner, 1990; Wertsch & Toma, 1995) rather than as passive recipients of others' knowledge calls for supervision and teacher evaluation models different from those currently in common use. The search is for models that can help teachers acquire a deeper personal understanding of the teaching-learning process and a reconstructed role perception of themselves as active promoters of that process (Carter & Doyle, 1987; Schön, 1988).

When we first wrote on this topic, we saw a growing balance between an external, inspectorial view of teacher evaluation and one in which responsibility is given to teachers to self-evaluate. While these same forces operate today, they are now heavily influenced by top-down forces aligned with the No Child Left Behind Act of 2001 (NCLB). NCLB has shifted public attention away from teacher-based self-evaluative responsibility back toward the inspectorial view of teacher evaluation. Yet, we believe that continued progress must include self-evaluative efforts on the part of teachers.

Stufflebeam and Shinkfield (1985) suggested that the most important evaluations of professionals are the ones conducted by the professionals themselves. Opportunities to explore their beliefs, knowledge, practices, and effects make teachers more likely to question their taken-for-granted expectations, norms, beliefs, and practices. Clandinin and Connelly (1988) emphasized that self-knowledge and self-understanding are the keys to professional growth and that the best way to improve these is to give teachers more control and responsibility for self-evaluation. Gitlin et al. (1992) argued that building upon notions such as the self-monitoring teacher and the teacher as classroom researcher represents the best way to give teachers a true "voice" in their practice. Kuhn (1991) emphasized the importance of thinking about one's theories and beliefs, not just applying them. Tom (1984) described an effective teacher as one who "is able to conceive of his teaching in purposeful terms, analyze a particular teaching problem, attempt the approach, judge the results in relation to the original purpose, and reconsider either the teaching or the original purpose" (p. 94). Gadamer (1975) noted that reflection on practice is a powerful method for bringing one's tacit, unquestioned beliefs and assumptions into the open to be self-examined. Although none of these commentators uses the term *self-evaluation* to describe the processes recommended, each recognizes the centrality of teachers' self-evaluation activities to their development and professional growth.

In sum, teacher self-evaluation is an important process for teachers to utilize for all of the following reasons (Airasian & Gullickson, 1995, 1996; McColskey & Egelson, 1993):

1. It is a professional responsibility to do so.

2. It focuses professional development and improvement at the classroom or school level, where teachers have their greatest expertise and impact. It grows from the immediacy and complexity of the classroom, as do teachers' motives and incentives.

3. It recognizes that organizational change is usually the result of individuals' changing themselves and their personal practice, not of top-down mandates.

4. It gives teachers "voice," that is, a stake in and control over their own practice.

5. It makes teachers aware of the strengths and weaknesses of their practice.

6. It encourages ongoing teacher development and discourages unchanging classroom beliefs, routines, and methods.

7. It treats teachers as professionals and can improve teacher morale and motivation.

8. It encourages collegial interactions and discussions about teaching.

WHAT IS THE ROLE OF REFLECTION
IN TEACHER SELF-EVALUATION?

Integral to teacher self-evaluation is reflection, the act of thinking about or pondering an idea, issue, or problem. Schön (1983, 1987) and others (Calderhead, 1988; Kuhn, 1991; Osterman & Kottkamp, 1993) have noted that teachers must reflect on their practice in order to understand, critique, and modify it; reflection is a central aspect of the process of constructing knowledge and developing professionally. Accountability to oneself is a fundamental aspect of professionalism because it implies a moral commitment to serve the interests of students and an obligation to review (i.e., reflect on) the nature of one's own practice in order to improve it (Eraut, 1993).

The work of Schön (1983, 1987, 1988) has contributed substantially to discussions about teacher reflection. Although we choose to focus on the work of Schön, we note that other, more detailed models of teacher reflection have been advanced (Hatton & Smith, 1995; Louden, 1991, 1992; Valli, 1992; Van Manen, 1991). These models extend—and to some extent complicate—Schön's conceptualization of reflection and appear to be more useful for studying the teaching *process* per se than teacher self-evaluation.

Schön proposed two ways in which teachers reflect on their practice: *reflection in action* and *reflection on action*. The former focuses on the spontaneous and tacit reflections and decisions teachers make when they are engaged in the process of teaching. During reflection in action, the teacher reflects on an activity that is in progress, lets the activity, in Schön's words, "talk back to" him or her, and makes an on-the-spot decision to alter or maintain the activity. The process is largely tacit and spontaneous.

Reflection on action takes place out of the activity of practice; it is consideration of an action, belief, or effect divorced in time from the factors that prompted the need for reflection. Reflection on action, with its temporal separation of activity and reflection, comes closer to the commonly held understanding of *reflection* than does reflection in action (Airasian & Gullickson, 1994b; Osterman & Kottkamp, 1993). The process is more conscious and reasoned. Note that both reflection in and reflection on action can produce teacher decisions, although the nature and consciousness of the decision-making process differ substantially for each. However, given the differences between the two—the former being tacit and spontaneous, deriving self-knowledge from in-practice reflection and the latter being conscious and planned, deriving self-knowledge from out-of-practice reflection—it is not surprising that they differ in many ways.

Reflection in Action

Given classroom complexity and uncertainty, teachers must learn much of their teaching repertoire from the concrete reality of their classroom practice—from the specific problems they must respond to and manage (Elbaz, 1990;

Ross, Cornett, & McCutcheon, 1992). From trial-and-error, self-evaluative experiences, teachers forge a "personal practical knowledge" that structures their teaching activities (Kleinsasser, 1992; Schwab, 1969). The world of the classroom demands that teachers have this practical knowledge to enable them to negotiate the practical problems they face.

Without experientially based personal knowledge, practical activities such as teaching cannot be fully understood or practiced. Experience creates problems for the practitioner and the necessity of finding solutions. In this scenario, the role of tacit/spontaneous reflection in action appears crucial and inevitable. The informal, experiential, trial-and-error nature of teachers' in-action activities is an important self-evaluation medium through which teachers become learners and constructors of their own practical knowledge and beliefs. The nature of classrooms leads teachers to initiate self-evaluation. "After all, it's the teacher's subjective school-related knowledge which determines for the most part what happens in the classroom; whether the teacher can articulate his/her knowledge or not" (Halkes & Olson, 1984, p. 1).

Although teachers' tacit, in-action reflections are important in shaping their practice and teaching beliefs, this approach has many characteristics that hamper its usefulness as a self-evaluation strategy for professional growth and development. We noted a number of these characteristics previously: The tacit, fleeting nature of reflection in action makes it difficult to study and model; the amount of time available to reflect on any particular action event is very small, leading to brief, often shallow, reflections and decisions; the fleeting nature of reflection in action can result in superficial, expedient decisions that lead to simplistic explanations and heuristics (Court, 1988; Elbaz, 1990; Farnham-Diggory, 1994). In addition, the bases for reflection in action are particular to each teacher, thereby encouraging the formation of idiosyncratic practice (Gilliss, 1988). In the extreme, idiosyncrasy can provide a justification for teachers to dismiss or fail to seek out information that might lead to improved practice.

The fact that reflection in action is a personal, spontaneous, tacit process means that it limits teachers' opportunity to seek or receive feedback from others or from the reflective episode itself (Kremer-Hayon, 1993). Only the teacher's fleeting impressions and "gut-level" instincts are available for him or her to identify weaknesses and make decisions about practice. Moreover, reflections in action focus on events and situations that arise spontaneously and unplanned (Cochran-Smith & Lytle, 1990; Kagan, 1992). In a real sense, what is reflected upon and evaluated in action is controlled not by the teacher, but by the spontaneous flow of events transpiring in the classroom. Thus, reflection in action is reactive, not proactive. There is no opportunity to identify procedures, alternatives, or options before action takes place. This reactivity serves to narrow one's view of practice. Finally, reflection in action, like all other self-evaluation approaches, shares an inherent and problematic characteristic: The teacher is both evaluator and evaluatee (Airasian & Gullickson, 1994b; Kremer-Hayon, 1993). Thus, even if a teacher overcomes the many limitations of reflection in action described above, he or she still must face the difficult barriers of personal biases and conflicts of interest in decision making.

Reflection on Action

Reflection on action involves a post hoc, conscious replay of an activity or event from practice. It is a conscious rather than a tacit process, and it is controlled by the teacher, not spontaneously occurring. The ability to revisit and linger over areas or events has many potential benefits for teachers. First, it permits conscious reflection related to practice; thus, it is accompanied by a degree of awareness of actual practice not usually available from reflection in action. Second, the time devoted to reflection on action can provide a deep, broad perspective on practice. Third, conscious reflection on classroom action and events plays nicely into the cyclical nature of teaching. Inevitably, teaching involves repeating many processes (e.g., lesson planning, grading, cooperative learning) and content topics (e.g., distinguishing use of *lay* and *lie*, rate/distance/time problems, balancing chemical equations) over the course of a week, month, or school year. Reflection on action can be a powerful tool for identifying, anticipating, and making changes in cyclical processes and content areas. In many cases, the alternatives identified by reflection on action at one point in time can be recalled and applied to the same process or topic at a subsequent point in time. It is for this reason many teacher education programs emphasize and develop experiences designed to spur preservice teachers' reflections on their classroom actions (e.g., Gore & Zeichner, 1991; Hatton & Smith, 1995; Valli, 1992).

However, like reflection in action, reflection on action has its limitations as a self-evaluation strategy. First and foremost, conscious reflection is not often associated with teaching, and teachers are not generally provided with instruction on how to be effective reflective practitioners (Elbaz, 1990; McNamara, 1990). As a consequence, teachers may consider the wrong information, weigh it improperly, ask the wrong questions of it, and make the wrong inferences when using it (Nisbett & Ross, 1980). These problems are accentuated by teachers' tendency to adopt simple, often superficial explanations for classroom events (Feiman-Nemser & Floden, 1986; Peterson & Barger, 1985).

Second, in order for reflection to lead to self-evaluation, it must result in a teacher decision. For many reasons, reflection may stop at the revisiting stage, without a decision or strategy being made or identified. Teachers are no different from other people who reflect on their activities and actions, insofar as a substantial number of both the reflections and decisions made from the reflections are forgotten from one day to the next. Self-evaluation resulting from reflection on action is highly dependent on the teacher's recall of things reflected on.

Third, reflection on action is practice driven. Even with conscious deliberation, reflection on action takes place in a closed system in which the teacher is both evaluator and evaluatee. Teachers' preexisting beliefs and experiences are a strong influence on the interpretive frameworks they use to label and categorize new reflective situations (Shulman, 1987). Frequently, such preconceptions preempt adequate teacher reflection on situations of concern (Wildman & Niles, 1987).

Because of the personal nature of reflection and self-evaluation, interpretation and decision making inevitably pit reason and objectivity against emotion and self-protection. This issue has been raised in a variety of ways by a number of commentators (Barber, 1990; Kuhn, 1991). Knowledge about teacher self-evaluation is not voluminous, but the studies noted above do show differences between teachers' own reflections, awareness, and self-evaluations and those made by the teachers' supervisors, peers, and students. Such findings raise questions about teachers' objectivity when it comes to judging their own practice. Another important concern is that incompetent or inexperienced teachers, regardless of the amount of conscious reflection they engage in, will produce reflections that prevent them from recognizing that they are performing at an unsatisfactory level or will be unable to identify means to improve even when they know their performance is unsatisfactory.

Thus, although reflection on action does provide a more deliberative, conscious examination of practice than that provided by reflection in action, it is clear that reflection of either type is laden with problems that inhibit its leading to satisfactory self-evaluation. It is important to point out that many of these problems are inevitable, because self-evaluation means that the teacher personally must be the reflector, interpreter, and decision maker regarding practice. So, limitations such as subjectivity, personal interpretations, and preexisting perceptions and beliefs will always be issues of concern in teacher reflection and self-evaluation. However, there is an approach that has promise for diminishing these and other problems of teacher reflection, an approach based on obtaining externally generated information about practice.

Enhanced Reflection

The availability of external information can enhance teachers' reflection by providing them with explicit information about practice (Airasian & Gullickson, 1995; Osterman & Kottkamp, 1993; Shulman, 1987). As we noted previously, the reflective process that occurs during both reflection in and on action engenders many factors that inhibit a teacher's ability to recognize problems, delineate their salient features, marshal appropriate evidence for their interpretation, and make informed, meaningful decisions. One way to improve reflection and awareness of practice is to supplement teachers' personal perceptions and recall with formal evidence about practice.

Of course, efforts to supplement teachers' reflection about their practice with more formal, "objective" information are not new. An early emphasis on teacher reflection, awareness of practice, and self-evaluation is found in Flanders's work on interaction analysis in the 1960s (see Bailey, 1981; Travers,

1983). This work gave credence and respectability to the systematic study of teachers' behavior and also emphasized the need for teachers to be able to operate independently in classrooms, where there is little opportunity for external feedback on their own teaching behaviors.

The model of stimulating teacher self-evaluation through an outside observer or recorder remains predominant today, especially in evaluations of teacher practice and development. The function of the external observer or recorder is to help the teacher see himself or herself as others see him or her. The intent is to "confront" teachers with external information about their practice so they will see it, reflect on it, compare it with their own personal perceptions of practice, and evaluate it in a more objective light than when the only information about practice is self-generated (Fuller & Manning, 1973).

The intent exemplified in this approach to teacher self-evaluation underlies other common teacher evaluation approaches, such as microteaching (Allen & Ryan, 1969), interpersonal process recall (N. Kagan, 1975), self-report (Bailey, 1981), self-study materials (Silver & Hanson, 1980), and observations of teachers by school principals or department heads. All of these approaches are intended to enhance teacher awareness, reflection, and, subsequently, self-evaluation with formal, externally generated, information about practice.

However, the most common approach—principal observation and evaluation of teaching—is not regarded highly by most teachers as a basis for their self-evaluation. The infrequency and brevity of the typical observation, the observer's lack of knowledge of the classroom culture, the lack of specific suggestions for improvement, and the lack of support for improvement efforts are all cited by teachers as reasons principals' observations and evaluations rarely stimulate self-evaluation (Duke & Stiggins, 1985; Jones & Airasian, 1996; Kottkamp, Provenzo, & Cohn, 1986).

A number of authors have compiled formal strategies that can be used to enhance teachers' awareness of practice and reflection. Angelo and Cross (1993) provided numerous examples of formal assessment strategies that can be employed by teachers to learn more about their practice. Kremer-Hayon (1993) described the context of teacher self-evaluation, the relationship between pedagogical knowledge and self-evaluation, qualitative and quantitative methods for conducting teacher self-evaluation, and sources of support needed for self-evaluation in schools to be viable. Pollard and Tann (1993) suggested a large number of reflective and self-evaluation activities aimed mainly at elementary school teachers. Saphier and Gower (1987) provided a thorough description of the knowledge base of teaching, with suggestions for areas in which to conduct self-evaluation. Haysom (1985) presented a number of self-evaluation strategies that relate to professional development. What is common among these and other sources (Airasian & Gullickson, 1996; Barber, 1987; Iwanicki & McEachern, 1983; McColskey & Egelson, 1993; Osterman & Kottkamp, 1993) is a reliance upon formal information gathering to support and enhance reflection in the hope that it will stimulate teacher awareness, recall, reflection, self-evaluation, and improvement.

Eight general strategies can be used to supplement and enhance teacher reflection, awareness of practice, and self-evaluation (Airasian & Gullickson, 1995):

- *Self-reflection tools:* These are designed to be completed by the teacher and allow him or her to evaluate performance in identified areas of practice, beliefs, and outcomes. Such tools usually take the form of checklists, rating scales, or questionnaires.
- *Media recording and analysis:* Media such as audio- and videotape may be used to record a sample of teacher performance for subsequent analysis by the teacher and/or peers. Microteaching is an example of media recording.
- *Student feedback:* This is gathered using instruments similar to self-reflection tools, except that pupils complete the forms instead of the teacher. Questionnaires, "minute surveys," and journals are examples of sources of student feedback.
- *Teacher portfolios:* Teachers prepare portfolios to provide evidence about their beliefs, knowledge, skills, and effectiveness. The process of collecting and analyzing portfolio pieces provides opportunity for self-evaluation. Note that a teacher portfolio can contain many of the self-evaluation strategies in this list.
- *Student performance data:* These include all student productions that can be used to help the teacher assess his or her own instructional effectiveness. Test results (classroom or standardized), essays, and projects are examples of student performance data.
- *External peer observation:* This involves a peer, colleague, or administrator's observing and describing particular aspects of another teacher's behavior, such as questioning behavior, lesson organization, and student feedback.
- *Journaling:* This requires the teacher to maintain and reflect upon a record of classroom events or activities with the intent of identifying recurring problems, successes, and needs.
- *Collegial dialogue/experience sharing/joint problem solving:* This encourages collaboration and interchange among teachers around common problems. Procedures, strategies, and perceptions are shared. Exposure to the ideas and practices of colleagues is a potent strategy for examining one's own practice.

Use of these external strategies for gathering information about practice enhances teacher reflection and self-evaluation in a number of ways. First, external information about practice takes the teacher out of the closed circle of reflection in and reflection on action (Iwanicki & McEachern, 1983; Kremer-Hayon, 1993). It allows teachers to be proactive, not just reactive, when examining and evaluating their practice. Second, the availability of formal evidence-gathering tools allows the teacher to focus on areas beyond immediate practice. For example, self-reflection tools are available that allow a teacher to examine basic teaching beliefs, knowledge of recent innovations, and instructional processes (Airasian & Gullickson, 1996; Angelo & Cross, 1993). Microteaching can identify many aspects of practice that might not be questioned or identified as problematic in the context of direct practice.

Third, and quite important, the availability of formal, external information about an area of practice provides a comparative basis against which a teacher can examine his or her own perceptions and interpretations: Is the teacher's personal view corroborated by external evidence garnered from peers, colleagues, students, media, or some other source? Without this comparative base, the teacher might overlook needed areas of improvement or misjudge areas of strength (Airasian & Gullickson, 1994b; Barber, 1990; Osterman & Kottkamp, 1993). When a teacher's self-defined standards and criteria can be compared with externally generated information in the form of student feedback, peer observation, self-reflection instruments, media recording, and the like, the teacher has an external, independent basis against which to compare his or her personal reflections and perceptions. Note that this comparison cannot be made without some form of external information. Note also that the comparison is most powerful when the teacher makes his or her own predictions about what the external information will show *before* that information is actually obtained. The potential of an externally based description of practice to enhance and corroborate teachers' personal awareness of practice is an important argument for using formal, external, "objective" awareness of practice as an extension of reflection and an integral part of teacher self-evaluation.

GETTING STARTED WITH SELF-EVALUATION

What is needed to carry out teacher self-evaluation for professional development? First and foremost, the impetus for involvement with self-evaluation must come from the teacher. Forcing teachers to self-evaluate destroys its purpose and success. However, there are many environmental conditions that affect teachers' willingness to participate in self-evaluation. It is these conditions that principals can manipulate to improve the climate and, thus, the likelihood that teachers will feel sufficiently comfortable and unthreatened to engage in self-evaluation.

Most of what has been written about teacher self-evaluation focuses on the teacher. This is natural because, as the name implies, teacher self-evaluation is a teacher-conducted activity. When peers, supervisors, principals, and students are mentioned in the context of teacher self-evaluation, it is usually as external reporters or observers who can provide objective information about teacher practice. We argue that such external information can foster and assist teacher self-evaluation, guide its use, and help sustain it when barriers threaten its use. Although external assistance can be provided by many persons, in most schools it is the principal who has direct authority and responsibility for providing motivation, guidance, and support for teacher activities.

As we noted previously, teachers regularly employ reflection in action during their teaching, less regularly employ reflection on action, and rarely engage in enhanced reflection on action. The challenge to principals is to increase the strongest of these three modes, enhanced teacher self-evaluation, to serve the development of teachers. We believe school principals are the best persons to help teachers address this challenge, by making sure that both they and their teachers (a) know what self-evaluation is and know some self-evaluation strategies teachers can use, (b) know the characteristics teachers must have to do viable self-evaluation, and (c) construct a school environment conducive to teacher self-evaluation. We turn now to strategies of self-evaluation and the teacher characteristics and school support structures needed for successful teacher self-evaluation.

STRATEGIES FOR TEACHER SELF-EVALUATION

The preceding sections have provided common understandings about what teacher self-evaluation is and why it is important. In this and succeeding sections, we address the issue of what a principal can do to get self-evaluation started. We present a few specific examples of self-evaluation strategies that can be shared with teachers to provide understanding of the nature and intent of self-evaluation. The examples are meant to be illustrative of possibilities, not exhaustive and all encompassing. The examples are excerpted from our *Teacher Self-Evaluation Tool Kit* (Airasian & Gullickson, 1996); interested readers are referred to this publication for additional examples.

Two fundamental criteria underlie the examples to be presented. First, the examples are formal, in the sense that they produce some tangible record or information for the teacher to use for self-evaluation. Although the nature and source of this information can vary considerably, the aim is to produce tangible information to use in analyzing and making decisions about practice. It is important to note, however, that the focus on formal approaches does not mean that the approaches have to be complicated, time-consuming, or controlled by others.

Second, the examples are aimed at helping teachers to obtain an awareness of their practice, including their beliefs, knowledge, activities, and effects. Much of the current discussion about teacher development emphasizes teacher reflection and introspection as the path to change and improvement. Although reflection and introspection are important aspects of professional development, they are insufficient to guarantee improvement. The missing link between reflection/introspection and the self-evaluation decisions that lead to professional development is an objective awareness of one's practice. Before we can meaningfully reflect on practice, we must have a clear awareness of that practice. Awareness is essential for change, and although reflection may help awareness, it does so much more productively when it is based on formal information about practice.

The following examples vary in many ways, but there are some common guidelines that apply to any self-evaluation approach: anonymity, focus, comparison, and multiple tools.

1. Self-evaluation strategies that obtain feedback from students should protect the anonymity of the student respondents. Maintenance of student anonymity protects them and encourages them to provide the honest feedback needed for viable self-evaluation.

2. In selecting areas to self-assess, teachers should focus on narrow aspects of teaching rather than more general ones. It is more productive and diagnostic to examine one's "questioning strategies" or "beliefs about learning" than it is to inquire about one's general "teaching competence" or "instructional approaches."

3. Whenever possible, it is advantageous to build a comparison into self-evaluations. Before administering a self-evaluation tool, teachers should attempt to predict what the main outcomes will be. If possible, these predictions should be made in writing. Then, when teachers get the actual results, they can compare them with their predictions.

4. No single strategy can provide all the information needed to self-assess teaching. Different self-evaluation strategies are useful for evaluating different areas, as is shown in the following examples.

Example 1: Examining Teacher Practice or Effects Using a Student Feedback Tool

The minute survey (Angelo & Cross, 1993) is a very flexible and simple strategy for getting feedback from pupils regarding various aspects of classroom activities. To conduct a minute survey, the teacher sets aside two or three minutes at the end of a class period to survey the students about some aspect of the lesson. The teacher then asks the students to answer one or two questions about the lesson (either by writing down their answers or, in early grades, raising their hands or making some other indication). Students respond anonymously. For example, the teacher might ask the students to address one or two of the following issues:

1. What are two things you learned from the lesson?

2. Write one question you would like to have answered about the lesson.

3. What part of the lesson would you like to know more about?

4. How confident are you about doing tonight's homework on this lesson?

5. Rate the success of the example presented to reinforce the lesson's main point.

6. Rate how well the reading assignment prepared you for today's lesson.

7. Solve one or two problems or calculations similar to those taught in the lesson.

There are, of course, many other questions a teacher could ask pupils about a lesson, an assignment, a homework exercise, a field trip, a video presentation, a demonstration, or even a test. However, to make the use of the minute survey most informative, the teacher should follow these guidelines:

1. Let students reply anonymously.

2. Keep the amount of writing requested of the students small. Don't ask students to write responses to four or five questions. The minute survey is meant to be completed in a short time; hence, it should focus on only one or two aspects of the lesson.

3. Before reading the responses, try to answer the questions yourself, based on your perception of the lesson. For example, what do you (the teacher) think will be the two most important things most students will say they learned, or the one question most students will want answered, or the degree to which the example you showed helped students to learn? Answering the questions yourself will provide a check of your observational impressions in light of students' actual responses.

4. Read the responses, compare them with your own predictions, and, depending on the responses, use the information to reteach, answer questions, reexplain, or move on to the next topic.

Example 2: Examining Practice Using Media, an External Observer, or Student Feedback

There are many ways for a teacher to obtain information about the nature and content of classroom discourse. He or she can have a colleague observe a lesson or two and provide information about who talks most, about what, the quality of questions asked, the reinforcement and encouragement given students, and so on. The teacher can also poll pupils to obtain their impressions of the nature and content of classroom discourse, or use media such as audio- or videotape to record and subsequently analyze discourse. One advantage of taping classroom interaction is that it provides a permanent record of performance that can be examined and reexamined. Often, when teachers are engaged and engrossed in the process of teaching, they are not aware of how much they talk, to whom, why, and with what purpose. This strategy also can be effective if a teacher collaborates with another person over time (McColskey & Egelson, 1993).

Regardless of the method used to obtain information on classroom discourse, it is useful for the teacher to do two things to increase the usefulness of the information:

1. State a set of questions he or she wants to answer before collecting information.

2. Answer the questions himself or herself before examining the information collected.

Sample questions that might guide analysis of discourse during a lesson include the following:

1. What proportion of time is spent in teacher talk?

2. Are there differences in the amount of talk from high- and low-ability students, from males and females, and so on?

3. What is the proportion of social/personal chat compared with "on-task" talk?

4. How many different students participate in discourse?

5. How much time is spent setting up and explaining the purpose of the lesson?

6. How much time is spent summing up and responding to student questions?

Example 3: Examining Practice Using a Self-Reflection Tool

The questionnaire presented in Figure 9.1 is intended to help teachers identify and reflect on their current and future professional development activities.

Example 4: Examining Practice or Knowledge Using a Self-Reflection Tool

Often, the simple task of rating oneself can lead to reflection about what one really knows or can do and what one needs to do to perform as well as one would like. In carrying out such self-ratings, it is better to rate specific areas of knowledge and skill than more general ones. The more specific the knowledge or skill, the easier it is to focus on its improvement, if necessary. Thus, rather than rating one's "assessment and evaluation skills" in general, an instrument such as the one shown in Figure 9.2 is useful for focusing on more detailed aspects of assessment and evaluation skills.

Example 5: Examining Teacher Effects Using Student Performance Data

This strategy is intended to promote teachers' thinking about both instruction and student learning. It is based on examination and reflection on

Figure 9.1 Sample of a Self-Reflection Tool

Answer each question by circling the term that best describes your level of agreement, and then list current and planned activities in the spaces provided.

1. I am actively involved in developing my command of the knowledge base of teaching.

   Strongly agree   *Agree*   *Disagree*   *Strongly disagree*

   Topics I am currently working on   *Topics I will work on next*

   _____   _____

   _____   _____

   _____   _____

2. I am actively engaged in reflecting on issues related to myself as a teacher and my professional role.

   Strongly agree   *Agree*   *Disagree*   *Strongly disagree*

   Topics I am currently reflecting on   *Topics I plan to reflect on next*

   _____   _____

   _____   _____

   _____   _____

3. I am actively engaged in developing my repertoire of specific teaching and assessment practices.

   Strongly agree   *Agree*   *Disagree*   *Strongly disagree*

   Practices I am currently learning   *Practices I plan to learn next*

   _____   _____

   _____   _____

   _____   _____

4. What is the one area of teaching in which you feel you most need professional development? What evidence leads you to identify this particular need?

Figure 9.2   A Self-Reflection Tool for Detailed Assessment of Knowledge and Skills

Rate your knowledge or skill as high, medium, or low for each of the following. For each skill, put an X under the appropriate rating category.

	Level of Knowledge or Skill		
Understanding or Skill	High	Medium	Low
My understanding of			
the effects of my grades on students			
biases in my grading procedures			
importance of grades to parents			
norm- versus criterion-referenced grades			
what my grades actually represent			
the fairness of my grading systems			
My skill at			
diagnosing students' prior knowledge			
providing relevant feedback			
preparing students for my tests			
linking my teaching to my tests			
including nonrote items in my tests			
scoring essay items fairly			

Select one area of knowledge and skill in which you rated yourself low, and write a plan for how you could go about improving that knowledge.

students' learning gains. It is predicated on the availability of chapter or unit tests that can serve as a pretest and a posttest. Most textbooks provide both end-of-chapter assessments and review assessments. The latter can serve the function of a preunit test and the former the function of a postunit test.

The teacher should take the following steps:

1. Plan your instruction on the unit or chapter as you normally would.

2. Administer the pretest to students before instruction begins.

3. Score the tests not just in terms of total score, but by objective as well.

4. Based on the students' scores, determine (a) how well your original lesson plan fits the information from the pretest and (b) how you might have to revise the plan based on the pretest information; then, (c) make a prediction of how the class will do after instruction.

5. Teach the subject, making revisions in your plan as needed.

6. Administer the posttest and score it.

7. Compare the students' pretest and posttest performance, examining both total score and individual objectives.

8. On the basis of the comparison, ask yourself the following: (a) How did the class as a whole do relative to your prediction? (b) In what areas (objectives) did the class learn well, and which need improvement? (c) Why did the class not learn some areas as well as others? What might explain the discrepancy in learning across objectives? (d) What can I do next time to improve learning of those objectives?

9. Examine the performance of the three pupils who scored lowest on the posttest. What was the nature of their mistakes, and what could you do next time or in the next unit to help them improve?

Once the teacher has collected and examined the pre- and posttest information, many additional questions and issues will be raised.

Example 6: Examining Knowledge Using a Self-Reflection Tool

The self-evaluation instrument presented in Figure 9.3 is designed to help teachers rate their knowledge of some educational processes or activities.

WHAT ARE THE CHARACTERISTICS OF SUCCESSFUL SELF-EVALUATION?

Although all forms of self-evaluation focus on teacher improvement, the most clear-cut aspect of fully implemented self-evaluation is its careful development

Figure 9.3   A Self-Reflection Tool for Examining Level of Knowledge

For each process or activity, indicate how familiar you are with *how it could be applied in a classroom* by circling the appropriate response.

How familiar are you with the classroom implications and applications of

Alternative assessment	very familiar	somewhat familiar	heard the term	unfamiliar
Inclusion	very familiar	somewhat familiar	heard the term	unfamiliar
Multiple intelligences	very familiar	somewhat familiar	heard the term	unfamiliar
Portfolios	very familiar	somewhat familiar	heard the term	unfamiliar
Inquiry teaching	very familiar	somewhat familiar	heard the term	unfamiliar
Action research	very familiar	somewhat familiar	heard the term	unfamiliar
Advanced organizer	very familiar	somewhat familiar	heard the term	unfamiliar
Constructivism	very familiar	somewhat familiar	heard the term	unfamiliar
Metacognition	very familiar	somewhat familiar	heard the term	unfamiliar

Which two of these processes/activities do you most want to learn more about?

_____

Where or to whom in your school or district would you go to get the information you want?

_____

and attention to detail at every stage of the self-evaluation process, from clear definition of the area to be evaluated to the collection and analysis of personal and external data. This form of teacher self-evaluation involves conscious planning and implementation, and generally leaves a paper trail of evidence (Kremer-Hayon, 1993; McColskey & Egelson, 1993). Other forms of teacher self-evaluation, such as reflection in or on action, generally do not (Hatton & Smith, 1995; Louden, 1992). However, although careful and conscious planning enhances the quality of self-evaluation, it also increases its complexity. There are, then, a number of characteristics that the successful self-evaluating teacher should possess and a number of obstacles that must be overcome.

Motive for Self-Evaluation

Successful self-evaluating teachers understand the need to take charge of their own practice and professional development (Hargreaves, 1995; Osterman & Kottkamp, 1993). Thus, as a starting point for self-evaluation, the teacher must have a commitment to practice and to his or her responsibility to understand, evaluate, and improve it. The initiative and desire for self-evaluation have to come from the teacher himself or herself. Principals, however, can directly encourage teachers to employ and model good self-evaluation practices.

Control of Self-Evaluation

If self-evaluation is truly to be self-evaluation, the teacher must assume control of the self-evaluation process. In particular, the teacher must be the one who carries out reflection and makes the ultimate decision about his or her practice.

Teacher control of self-evaluation does not preclude the possibility that others can help stimulate or initiate self-evaluation. A colleague's or administrator's viewing or reviewing aspects of the teacher's practice can be a powerful means of increasing the teacher's awareness of that practice (Anderson & Freiberg, 1995). Frequently, such awareness is created when an observer asks "why" questions. Why did you present the material that way? Why did you reject that student's argument when it seemed to have some merit? These externally generated questions focus on issues in the instructional process and may directly stimulate teacher reflection and self-evaluation.

Sharing control in the self-evaluation process can benefit the teacher, but it may also have undesirable effects. The benefits flow most directly from enhanced verifiability (e.g., when the teacher's perceptions are consistent with the perceptions of others) and the additional impetus given to self-evaluation. Undesirable effects result mainly from the teacher's perception of his or her own vulnerability in the evaluation situation.

Perceived Ability to Change Practice

Unless a teacher acknowledges responsibility for or the possibility of being able to improve an area of practice, the self-evaluation process is unlikely to be carried through. Once a teacher becomes aware of a problem in practice, he or she must make a decision about the possibility of altering or improving it. Values, beliefs, prior experience, and available school support systems influence the teacher's perceptions and decisions about both the problem and the possibility of its melioration (Grimmett & Erickson, 1988). If the teacher believes that the factors that underlie a problem are outside his or her control (whether or not they really are) or not worth the effort to change, the self-evaluation process will cease. Many factors related to teachers' personal development and characteristics (e.g., risk-taking tolerance, self-efficacy, dogmatism) as well as the resources and support for professional development available in the school can influence teachers' interpretations of problematic classroom occurrences or situations (Ashton & Webb, 1986; Bandura, 1991; Nais, 1988). For this reason, the principal must help build a school climate that encourages and supports professional development through teacher self-evaluation.

BUILDING A SUPPORT STRUCTURE FOR SELF-EVALUATION

Overcoming barriers to teacher self-evaluation is important and heavily dependent on both teacher and principal/administrator commitment. A school-based support structure should include the important features described below.

Awareness of Self-Evaluation and Encouragement for Teachers to Conduct Self-Evaluation

The concept and processes of self-evaluation should be brought to the attention of teachers and encouraged as a schoolwide practice. Encouragement is important, because few teachers initiate and regularly use formal self-evaluation activities in their classrooms. The principal can help inform teachers about self-evaluation by making written resource information available to teachers, discussing self-evaluation in meetings, and setting expectations for the conduct of self-evaluation. The main objective of these activities is to introduce and sustain a positive environment for self-evaluation, one that supports self-evaluation and a general focus on the importance of teachers' responsibilities for professional development.

Assistance to Teachers in Learning About Self-Evaluation

Most teachers receive little instruction in assessment and self-evaluation practices. If these practices are to be implemented, some form of education for teachers is necessary. At a first level, teachers need to be provided with information about self-evaluation options, opportunities, and pitfalls. At a second level, teachers need to be informed about basic ideas and information for planning, organizing, and implementing self-evaluation at the school and classroom levels. At a third level, teachers can be given opportunities to experience the use and exploration of specific techniques and strategies for carrying out self-evaluation.

School Policy That Establishes Self-Evaluation as an Integral Part of the School Structure

Few things are universally acclaimed and accepted from the outset. Most innovations need time and opportunity to become established and formal recognition to ensure longevity. Making self-evaluation an option within the formal structure of the school increases the relative importance of self-evaluation and enhances its long-term viability. Such recognition gives self-evaluation the exposure, standing, and credibility needed to encourage teachers to employ self-evaluation in their classrooms. Importantly, schoolwide guidelines can ensure that self-evaluation activities obtain the requisite resources, are conducted as part of the normal expectations for professional development in the school, are conducted appropriately, and are integrated with other aspects of instruction and evaluation.

Resources to Help With and to Encourage Teacher Self-Evaluation Processes

Self-evaluation can lead to its own reward of improved practice, but self-evaluation competes for time and attention against myriad other demands on teachers. How a principal chooses to allocate school resources sends an explicit message to teachers about what is valued and encouraged in the school. A clear indicator of the importance of any initiative is the willingness of the school administrator to apply resources to it. Resources can take the form of time, provision of physical facilities or aides, opportunities to visit with and learn from others, and a host of other possibilities.

Safeguards to Protect Teachers

Three safeguards will encourage teachers to participate in self-evaluation activities:

1. For self-evaluation to be most useful, it must be based on unbiased information. Bias is reduced when self-evaluation is conducted in an environment of support and trust, in which teachers can take an honest look at their practices without fear of sanction or penalty. It is also reduced when teachers learn to gather information that provides a basis for valid judgments about practice and when they obtain feedback from colleagues.

2. Self-evaluation is inherently risky. It is never easy to learn that there are weaknesses in one's practice or that one's beliefs about instruction are not borne out in the classroom. Negative information can be seized upon

by others and used to the detriment of the self-evaluating teacher. School policy should provide guidelines to protect the rights and self-efficacy of teachers engaged in self-evaluation. Concrete commitments that ensure privacy of self-evaluation information and protect teachers who identify weaknesses in their practice must be provided at the school level.

3. Care needs to be taken to ensure the voluntary nature of self-evaluation. In particular, it is important to keep self-evaluation information and processes separate from externally imposed, summative evaluations. If voluntary and imposed teacher evaluations are mingled, teachers are likely to lose the feeling of voluntarism and the sense of personal empowerment that are fundamental to self-evaluation.

CONCLUSION

Teacher self-evaluation has the potential to help teachers examine and improve their practice in many ways. However, in applying the suggestions outlined above, it is important to recognize that each application will reflect the special cultures, values, resources, and personalities of the contexts and professionals involved. Part of the usefulness of teacher self-evaluation is its potential to spur examination of a school's or teacher's context and practices to arrive at a strategy of teacher self-evaluation that best suits the setting of the involved teachers and administrators. If it is made meaningful to teachers and nurtured and supported by school administrators, teacher self-evaluation can give teachers a sense of ownership and pride in their practice and also improve instruction and learning in schools.

REFERENCES

Airasian, P. W. (1993). Policy-driven assessment or assessment-driven policy? *Measurement and Evaluation in Counseling and Development, 26*, 22–30.

Airasian, P. W., & Gullickson, A. (1994a). Examination of teacher self-assessment. *Journal of Personnel Evaluation in Education, 8*, 195–203.

Airasian, P. W., & Gullickson, A. (1994b, Fall). Teacher self-assessment: Potential and barriers. *Kappa Delta Pi Record, 31*(1), 6–9.

Airasian, P. W., & Gullickson, A. (1995). *Teacher self-evaluation tool kit.* Report submitted to the Office of Research, Office of Educational Research and Improvement, U.S. Department of Education, Washington, DC.

Airasian, P. W., & Gullickson, A. (1996). *Teacher self-evaluation tool kit.* Thousand Oaks, CA: Corwin.

Allen, D. W., & Ryan, K. (1969). *Microteaching.* Reading, MA: Addison-Wesley.

Anderson, J. B., & Freiberg, H. J. (1995, Winter). Using self-assessment as a reflective tool to enhance the student teaching experience. *Teacher Education Quarterly*, pp. 77–91.

Angelo, T. A., & Cross, K. P. (1993). *Classroom assessment techniques: A handbook for college teachers.* San Francisco: Jossey-Bass.

Ashton, P. T., & Webb, R. B. (1986). *Making a difference: Teachers' sense of efficacy and student achievement.* New York: Longman.

Bailey, G. D. (1981). *Teacher self-assessment: A means for improving classroom instruction.* West Haven, CT: NEA Distribution Center. (ERIC Document Reproduction Service No. ED 207 967)

Bandura, A. (1991). Self-regulation of motivation through anticipatory and self-reactive mechanisms. In R. A. Dienstbier (Ed.), *Nebraska Symposium on Motivation: Vol. 38. Perspectives on motivation* (pp. 69–164). Lincoln: University of Nebraska Press.

Barber, L. W. (1987, January). *Teacher evaluation.* Report submitted to the Teacher Quality Program, Indiana Department of Education.

Barber, L. W. (1990). Self-assessment. In J. Millman & L. Darling-Hammond (Eds.), *The new handbook of teacher evaluation: Assessing elementary and secondary school teachers* (pp. 216–228). Newbury Park, CA: Sage.

Berliner, D. C. (1987). Ways of thinking about students and classrooms by more and less experienced teachers. In J. Calderhead (Ed.), *Exploring teachers' thinking* (pp. 60–83). London: Cassell Educational Limited.

Bruner, J. (1990). *Acts of meaning.* Cambridge, MA: Harvard University Press.

Calderhead, J. (Ed.). (1988). *Teachers' professional learning.* Philadelphia: Falmer.

Carnegie Task Force on Teaching as a Profession. (1986). *A nation prepared: Teachers for the twenty-first century.* New York: Carnegie Forum on Education and the Economy.

Carter, K., & Doyle, W. (1987). Teachers' knowledge structures and comprehension processes. In J. Calderhead (Ed.), *Exploring teacher thinking* (pp. 147–160). London: Cassell Educational Limited.

Clandinin, D. J., & Connelly, F. M. (1988). Studying teachers' knowledge of classrooms: Collaborative research, ethics, and the negotiation of narrative. *Journal of Educational Thought, 22*(2A), 269–282.

Cochran-Smith, M., & Lytle, S. L. (1990). Research on teaching and teacher research: The issues that divide. *Educational Researcher, 19*(2), 2–11.

Court, D. (1988). "Reflection in action": Some definitional problems. In P. P. Grimmett & G. L. Erickson (Eds.), *Reflection in teacher education* (pp. 143–147). New York: Teachers College Press.

Darling-Hammond, L. (1990). Teacher evaluation in transition: Emerging roles and evolving methods. In J. Millman & L. Darling-Hammond (Eds.), *The new handbook of teacher evaluation: Assessing elementary and secondary school teachers* (pp. 17–34). Newbury Park, CA: Sage.

Delandshire, G., & Petrosky, A. R. (1994). Capturing teachers' self-knowledge: Performance assessment. *Educational Researcher, 23*(5), 11–18.

Driver, R., Asoko, H., Leach, J., Mortimer, E., & Scott, P. (1994). Constructing scientific knowledge in the classroom. *Educational Researcher, 23*(7), 5–12.

Duke, D. L., & Stiggins, R. (1985). *Teacher evaluation: Five keys to growth.* Washington, DC: NEA Professional Library.

Dwyer, C. A., & Stufflebeam, D. L. (1996). Teacher evaluation. In D. C. Berliner & R. C. Calfee (Eds.), *Handbook of educational psychology* (pp. 765–786). New York: Simon & Schuster/ Macmillan.

Elbaz, F. (1990). Knowledge and discourse: The evolution of research on teacher thinking. In C. Day, M. Pope, & P. Denicolo (Eds.), *Insights into teachers' thinking and practice* (pp. 15–42). London: Falmer.

Eraut, M. (1993). Teacher accountability: Why is it central to teacher professional development? In L. Kremer-Hayon, H. C. Vonk, & R. Fessler (Eds.), *Teacher professional development: A multiple perspective approach* (pp. 23–43). Lisse, the Netherlands: Swets & Zeitlinger.

Farnham-Diggory, S. (1994). Paradigms of knowledge and instruction. *Review of Educational Research, 64,* 463–477.

Feiman-Nemser, S., & Floden, R. E. (1986). The cultures of teaching. In M. C. Wittrock (Ed.), *Handbook of research on teaching* (pp. 505–526). New York: Macmillan.

Fuller, F. F., & Manning, B. A. (1973). Self-confrontation reviewed: A conceptualization for video playback in teacher education. *Review of Educational Research, 43,* 469–528.

Gadamer, H. (1975). *Truth and method.* New York: Seabury.

Gilliss, G. (1988). Schön's reflective practitioner: A model for teachers? In P. P. Grimmett & G. L. Erickson (Eds.), *Reflection in teacher education* (pp. 47–54). New York: Teachers College Press.

Gitlin, A., Bringhurst, K., Burns, M., Cooley, V., Myers, B., Price, K., Russell, R., & Tiess, P. (1992). *Teachers' voices for school change.* New York: Teachers College Press.

Glickman, C. D. (Ed.). (1992). *Supervision in transition: The 1992 ASCD yearbook.* Alexandria, VA: Association for Supervision and Curriculum Development.

Gore, J., & Zeichner, K. (1991). Action research and reflective teaching in preservice teacher education: A case study from the United States. *Teaching and Teacher Education, 7,* 119–136.

Grimmett, P. P., & Erickson, G. L. (Eds.). (1988). *Reflection in teacher education.* New York: Teachers College Press.

Grimmett, P. P., Rostad, O. P., & Ford, B. (1992). The transformation of supervision. In C. D. Glickman (Ed.), *Supervision in transition: The 1992 ASCD yearbook* (pp. 185–202). Alexandria, VA: Association for Supervision and Curriculum Development.

Halkes, R., & Olson, J. K. (Eds.). (1984). *Teacher thinking: A new perspective on persisting problems in education.* Lisse, the Netherlands: Swets & Zeitlinger.

Hargreaves, A. (1995). Renewal in the age of paradox. *Educational Leadership, 52*(7), 14–19.

Hargreaves, A., & Fullan, M. G. (Eds.). (1992). *Understanding teacher development.* New York: Teachers College Press.

Hatton, N., & Smith, D. (1995). Reflection in teacher education: Towards definition and implementation. *Teaching and Teacher Education, 11,* 33–49.

Haysom, J. (1985). *Inquiring into the teaching process: Towards self-evaluation and professional development.* Toronto: Ontario Institute for Studies in Education Press.

Iwanicki, E. F., & McEachern, L. (1983). Teacher self-improvement: A promising approach to professional development and school improvement. *Journal of Staff Development, 4,* 62–77.

Jones, A., & Airasian, P. W. (1996). Through their eyes: Teacher self-assessment. *Midwestern Journal of Education Research, 4*(1), 12–16.

Kagan, D. M. (1992). Professional growth among preservice and beginning teachers. *Review of Educational Research, 62,* 129–169.

Kagan, N. (1975). *Interpersonal process recall: A method of influencing human interaction.* Mason, MI: Mason Media.

Kleinsasser, A. M. (1992). Learning how to teach language arts: A cultural model. In E. W. Ross, J. W. Cornett, & G. McCutcheon (Eds.), *Teacher personal theorizing: Connecting curriculum practice, theory, and research* (pp. 53–66). Albany: State University of New York Press.

Kottkamp, R. B., Provenzo, E. F., & Cohn, M. M. (1986). Stability and change in a profession: Two decades of teacher attitudes, 1964–1984. *Phi Delta Kappan, 67,* 559–567.

Kremer-Hayon, L. (1993). *Teacher self-evaluation: Teachers in their own mirrors.* Boston: Kluwer Academic.

Kuhn, D. (1991). *The skill of argument.* New York: Cambridge University Press.

Louden, W. (1991). *Understanding teaching: Continuity and change in teachers' knowledge.* New York: Teachers College Press.

Louden, W. (1992). Understanding reflection through collaborative research. In A. Hargreaves & M. G. Fullan (Eds.), *Understanding teacher development* (pp. 178–215). New York: Teachers College Press.

McColskey, W., & Egelson, P. (1993). *Designing teacher evaluation systems that support professional growth.* Greensboro, NC: Southeastern Regional Vision for Education.

McNamara, D. (1990). Research in teachers' thinking: Its contribution to educating student teachers to think critically. *Journal of Education for Teaching, 16*(2), 147–160.

Milner, J. O. (1991). Suppositional style and teacher evaluation. *Phi Delta Kappan, 72,* 464–467.

Nais, J. (1988). What it means to "feel like a teacher": The subjective reality of primary school teaching. In J. Ozga (Ed.), *Schoolwork: Approaches to the labour process of teaching.* Milton Keyes, UK: Open University Press.

Nisbett, R. E., & Ross, L. (1980). *Human inference: Strategies and shortcomings of social judgment.* Englewood Cliffs, NJ: Prentice Hall.

No Child Left Behind Act of 2001, 20 U.S.C. § 6301 et seq. (2001).

Osterman, K. F., & Kottkamp, R. B. (1993). *Reflective practice for educators: Improving schooling through professional development*. Newbury Park, CA: Corwin.

Peterson, P. L., & Barger, S. A. (1985). Attribution theory and teacher expectancy. In J. B. Dusek (Ed.), *Teacher expectancies* (pp. 159–184). Hillsdale, NJ: Lawrence Erlbaum.

Pollard, A., & Tann, S. (1993). *Reflective teaching in the primary school* (2nd ed.). London: Cassell Educational Limited.

Ross, E. W., Cornett, J. W., & McCutcheon, G. (Eds.). (1992). *Teacher personal theorizing: Connecting curriculum practice, theory, and research*. Albany: State University of New York Press.

Saphier, J., & Gower, R. (1987). *The skillful teacher*. Carlisle, MA: Research for Better Teaching.

Schön, D. A. (1983). *The reflective practitioner: How professionals think in action*. New York: Basic Books.

Schön, D. A. (1987). *Educating the reflective practitioner*. San Francisco: Jossey-Bass.

Schön, D. A. (1988). Coaching reflective teaching. In P. P. Grimmett & G. L. Erickson (Eds.), *Reflection in teacher education* (pp. 19–30). New York: Teachers College Press.

Schwab, J. (1969). The practical: A language for curriculum. *School Review, 78,* 12.

Sergiovanni, T. J., & Starratt, R. J. (1988). *Supervision: Human perspectives* (3rd ed.). New York: McGraw-Hill.

Shulman, L. S. (1987). Knowledge and teaching: Foundations of the new reform. *Harvard Educational Review, 57,* 1–22.

Silver, H. F., & Hanson, J. R. (1980). *Teacher self-assessment*. Moorestown, NJ: Hanson Silver & Associates.

Smith, M. S., & O'Day, J. (1991). Systemic school reform. In S. H. Fuhrman & B. Malen (Eds.), *Politics of education association yearbook, 1990* (pp. 233–267). London: Falmer.

Stufflebeam, D. L., & Shinkfield, A. J. (1985). *Systematic evaluation*. Boston: Kluwer-Nijhoff.

Tom, A. R. (1984). *Teaching as a moral craft*. New York: Longman.

Travers, R. (1983). *How research has changed American schools: A history from 1840 to the present*. Kalamazoo, MI: Mythos.

Valli, L. (1992). *Reflective teacher education: Cases and critiques*. Albany: State University of New York Press.

Van Manen, M. (1991). *The tact of teaching: The meaning of pedagogical thoughtfulness*. Albany: State University of New York Press.

Wertsch, J. V., & Toma, C. (1995). Discourse and learning in the classroom: A sociocultural approach. In L. P. Steffe & J. Gale (Eds.), *Constructivism in education* (pp. 159–174). Mahwah, NJ: Lawrence Erlbaum.

Wildman, T. M., & Niles, J. A. (1987). Reflective teachers: Tensions between abstraction and realities. *Journal of Teacher Education, 38*(4), 25–31.

Using Multiple Data **10** Sources in Teacher Evaluation Systems

Kenneth D. Peterson

The use of multiple data sources for teacher evaluation presented in this book is important because each view adds depth to the complex picture of teacher quality. Also, no single data source, such as client surveys or pupil achievement, works well (i.e., is reliable, valid, and feasible) and is available for every teacher in a school district. To the five key sources described in Chapters 5 through 9 can be added the following techniques for documenting teacher quality: peer review of instructional materials, teacher tests, systematic observation by independent educators from outside the school district, National Board for Professional Teacher Standards (NBPTS) certification, documented payoffs from Action Research or School Improvement participation, administrator report of teacher functioning in the school, and evidence unique but pertinent to an individual teacher.

The rich data about teacher performance and results provided by these sources open many doors for both administrators and teachers. Complex information about teachers can be used to enhance a sense of school mission accomplishment, teacher assignments, school improvement projects, a focus on pupil achievement, teacher status, teacher security, school and district public relations, and district planning.

The use of multiple data sources makes possible another innovation in teacher evaluation: *variable data sources*. This development is significant because data gathering can be tailored to actual specific performances, match the circumstances of each teacher, and employ different data sources for different teachers according to availability and appropriateness. Not all teachers are evaluated the same way, because not all of them foster learning the same way or have the same opportunities to present their data. Teacher acceptance of evaluation increases when teachers see it to be more pertinent to their situation, less dependent on a single individual, under some teacher control, and fair. Fairness is not that all teachers are evaluated the same way, but that each has a chance to document his or her specific merit, value, and impact.

Good use of multiple data sources results in

- Credible and respected information
- Support for student payoffs
- Pertinent information for stakeholders and audiences
- A stimulant for still more teacher evaluation activity

This chapter will discuss using multiple data sources beyond just having a more elaborate filing system. Rather, good data use calls for variety, choices, decisions, deliberation, and resources of time, personnel, and money. Good use of teacher evaluation data calls for imagination, initiative, and collective and individual action.

WHAT DOES THE USE OF MULTIPLE DATA SOURCES FOR SUMMATIVE TEACHER EVALUATION LOOK LIKE?

Teachers and administrators have many choices in using multiple data sources for teacher evaluation. Educators can vary the number and kind, the mode of presentation, and the location of interpretation and judgments. These variations can be at an individual teacher level, school site, or district level of agreement.

The following three scenarios, of many possible ones, describe increasing levels of uses in complexity. In the first scenario, individual principals and teachers begin to incorporate multiple data sources into conventional, principal-dominated evaluation. The next two scenarios rely on more views and judges, increased control for credibility, and more teacher participation. The following sections of this chapter will present details of issues introduced in these scenarios.

Using Multiple Data Sources Scenario 1: Simple Uses

In this scenario, the principal is the sole judge and reporter of teacher performance for both staff development (formative) and employment retention (summative) evaluation purposes. The principal uses a form of clinical supervision with an annual planning conference, one or more classroom visits, and a final summary conference. The principal may conduct walk-through visits (Downey, Steffy, English, Frase, & Poston, 2004) for monitoring, formative feedback, or information for summative evaluation.

In addition to the above, more traditional (Glickman & Kanawati, 1998) evaluation, individual teachers elect to collect and bring to the conferences one or more of the following:

- client surveys (student and/or parent),
- summaries of pupil achievement gain,
- peer teacher reviews of classroom materials,
- teacher test scores,
- lists of professional activity,
- systematic observation, reported by outside person,
- documentation of participation and payoffs of teacher involvement in action research or school improvement projects,
- National Board for Professional Teaching Standards (NBPTS) certification,
- portfolio, and/or
- self-evaluation.

Each data source has some provision for credibility (e.g., another teacher helped in the data collection and scoring and can vouch for accuracy of results). Teachers control data at two points: (1) they elect to have data collected, and (2) they inspect results before deciding to have them used in evaluation. Teachers maintain their own files and credibility checks. Some of these data sources must be repeated each year (e.g., professional activity, student surveys) while others are done once with results lasting four to seven years before repeating (e.g., teacher tests, systematic observation); NBPTS is done once for the career. The principal includes the teacher-supplied data in the conferences and final report.

Using Multiple Data Sources
Scenario 2: Moderately Complex Uses

The principal submits the annual teacher summative report. Then, the principal negotiates details (e.g., data sources, timing) of evaluation with each teacher for the year. Clinical supervision by the principal is one optional data source, although either the principal or teacher can require clinical supervision as the evaluation mode. Principals conduct monitoring walk-through visits of teachers not involved in clinical supervision.

Teachers are required to select a total of four data sources each year if they elect not to participate in clinical supervision. The teacher keeps data and credibility checks in a private dossier folder, separate from a personnel file. The dossier (Peterson, Stevens, & Mack, 2001) contains compressed teacher data (e.g., survey results, test scores) from all previous teacher evaluations.

Using Multiple Data Sources Scenario 3: Complex Uses

Both the principal and a district-level, teacher-dominated panel (e.g., four teachers, two administrators, one parent, one older high school student) separately review teacher dossiers for formative and summative evaluation. Alternatively, the teacher may elect not to participate in a panel review, but rather have a traditional principal-controlled clinical supervision model used. Principals conduct monitoring walk-through visits of teachers not involved in clinical supervision.

The district panel makes recommendations for additional assignments for additional pay (e.g., student teacher assignments, department and grade level chairs, textbook adoption committees). A school district evaluation unit is responsible for technical advice to teachers, data procedures and forms, data collection, credibility credentialing, and storage of data. Teachers inspect results before deciding which specific data to include in their dossier. Teachers can examine contents of dossier and ask for additions or deletions. Principal reports, with or without classroom visits, are one optional data source for review. Teachers must select at least four data sources per year to add to their cumulative professional dossier.

WHY USE MULTIPLE DATA SOURCES?

Multiple data sources are used in teacher evaluation because teaching is so complex that no one source sufficiently captures the role or performance (Peterson, 2004). Also, no single data source is valid or feasible for each and every teacher in a school district. Rather, multiple and variable data sources are needed to accurately and fairly evaluate all teachers, taking into account their setting, style, actual performance (not mere compliance with an overgeneralized model), and documented results.

Having the best objective data available improves the necessarily subjective decision making of summative teacher evaluation. For example, the well-designed and -administered client surveys described in the Chapter 6 are most likely more accurate than administrator reports of client satisfaction that may be based on inadequate sampling, hearsay evidence of several glowing (but unrepresentative) testimonials, or, conversely, a few disgruntled students or parents. While most administrators balance these fairness and validity issues, good survey data help make the judgment process more accurate and objective. Likewise, the impressions of administrators who are not subject matter specialists are strengthened by the data source of peer review of materials by third party, neutral but expert teachers currently having the same student age and subject assignment. Finally, multiple data sources expand the evaluation beyond teaching processes to include teacher preparation and student outcome results.

Gathering additional objective data has benefits beyond better data for decision making. They can take pressure off administrators as the single data source. Many principals would prefer walk-through supervision, along with other pertinent sources of performance information, rather than comprehensive conferences and visits called for when the administrator is the only source of information. Multiple data sources include more stakeholder views and, thus, enjoy more support from educators, parents, and legislators. For example, client surveys engage students and parents, peer review of classroom materials involves colleague teachers, and pupil achievement data satisfy all audiences about ultimate payoffs.

Finally, there are sociological reasons for using multiple data sources. Teachers are more supportive and involved in teacher evaluation when they feel that it is pertinent to their own performance and fair in its use of information in their individual case. Teachers behave more profoundly and responsibly when they share the authority involved in personnel evaluation (Peterson & Chenoweth, 1992).

ARE SOME DATA SOURCES BETTER THAN OTHERS?

Definitely! Some, like adjusted pupil gain, are more compelling evidence of teacher quality than are others. Some have more utility and validity in individual cases. Some data sources, for example, peer visits to classroom or graduate follow-ups, should not be used at all (Peterson, 2000). Experts do not completely agree on priority use among all data sources, but there are some general principles about selecting and using evidence of teacher quality.

Teacher Data Need to Be Well Designed and Gathered

All data sources need to be logically sound, well designed, and researched based. Instruments and procedures must be the best available, not hastily assembled by inexperienced individuals or ad hoc committees. The expert advice presented in this book on classroom observation, surveys, pupil gain data, and portfolios is extremely important. The research basis for each data source should show us how the procedures and instruments work in small-scale trials, give norms for performance, and report client satisfaction. Research findings on empirical applications of evaluation procedures are required, not merely those borrowed from other educational inquiries (e.g., "teacher effectiveness" studies).

Teacher Data Can Be Payoff (Outcome), Process (Methods, Materials), or Preparation (Training, Experience)

In general, the priorities for teacher data sources are payoff first, process second, and preparation third. The most compelling case for quality teaching can be made if there is evidence that the students are learning in both the cognitive and affective domains. When it is impossible to get good tests or affective measures for individual teachers, then processes and materials of teaching can be important clues to teacher quality. Finally, there is a level of preparation to teaching—teacher knowledge of subject matter and pedagogy, experience, and degrees or programs completed—that is an indication of teacher quality. The most complete teacher evaluations include all three levels as a complex view of individual quality.

We wish we could have these types of data for all teachers, but it's often not possible. In individual cases data are not available, too expensive, or not pertinent. In these situations, other data sources are valuable for highlighting their particular view of possible teacher excellence, standing in when desirable data sources are not available, and making a more complete picture of individual teacher excellence.

Three Important Data Sources

While various data sources, when used properly, can play a valuable role in teacher evaluation, among the most desirable data sources are student value-added achievement, student report, and peer review of instructional materials. Our main concern with teacher quality is that students are learning. Once this is established, a quick check with student surveys confirms that students are supportive of the learning and are not being damaged by practices such as unethical treatment or overintensive test preparation that kills interest. Generally, high levels of learning are associated with good attitudes in students, but it is best to check high achievement with student attitude. Finally, once we know that students are learning, we still need to know if *what* they are learning is valuable; well-used peer teacher reviews of teaching materials are an excellent judge of curriculum quality.

Pupil achievement is the single most compelling data source about teacher quality. Debates about teaching processes/methods or staff development are less important when there is clear evidence that students are learning well. It is hard to argue for an evaluation *system* that does not take student learning data into account well beyond mere principal report of adequacy. Catalogs of teacher performance descriptions are no substitute for using good student achievement data in a system *when they are available*. Pupil achievement has been argued for as a good stand-in for other goals, for example, interest in subject matter or positive attitudes about school or future interest in subject (Wright, Horn, & Sanders, 1997).

As important as student learning data are, their use for determining teacher quality is not without controversy (Berk, 1988; Sacks, 1999). Table 10.1 presents the considerable limitations to universal and sole use of pupil gain to evaluate teachers.

Table 10.1 Limitations to Universal and Sole Use of Pupil Gain Data to Evaluate Teachers

---

Good tests not available for all subject areas, all teachers in a system

Multiple-year data or gains adjusted for prior achievement are needed, but not available in all systems

Good tests and multiple-year data not available for primary grade teachers

Many achievement test programs are inadequately accurate at high and low ends

Experts do not agree that high-stakes achievement testing focus always best

Experts do not agree that achievement stands in well for all other objectives

---

It is difficult to collect technically defensible pupil achievement data for all teachers. Good tests are not available for all. Many systems of student achievement documentation are insufficient for teachers of PreK–3 students, subject areas where good tests are not available, teachers of high turnover student populations, and teachers of extremely high or low performance students.

Educators may not agree on the goals directly measured by the tests. Some value-added systems assume that series of classes are isomorphic while other experts do not agree. For example, general science, biology, chemistry, and physics may or may not be parallel. Gains are influenced by combinations of teachers before and after. Results of some teachers may take years to show. High-stakes measures of pupil achievement shape the instruction, but other values—citizenship, artistic development, caring, and physical fitness and nutrition—all are important school outcomes that may be ignored in a districtwide, oversimplified academic testing program (Sacks, 1999).

The multiple and variable data source approach rounds out this estimate of teacher effectiveness with student learning and provides a substitute when pupil achievement data are not available. Other data sources add to the pupil gain data evidence that the content taught is of high quality (peer review of materials), that students have positive attitudes (pupil survey), and that the results are not some interaction combination of location and student assignment. It addresses teachers in the system for whom gain data are not available. It gives voice to teachers who claim importance for evidence along with pupil achievement.

Some Attractive Data Sources Are Not Recommended

Potential data sources require expert scrutiny before adoption (Peterson, 2000). Not all possible or even attractive sources have proved themselves. Rather, they must pass tests of logical connection to teacher effort or results and to empirical success. For example, graduate follow-ups have been found to be unreliable because of low return rates. Peer visits to classrooms have shown lower reliability than administrator visits. Faculty opinion polls are reliable but inaccurate (low validity).

WHAT OPTIONS AND DECISIONS ARE CREATED BY USING MULTIPLE DATA SOURCES?

When a teacher, principal, or school district decides to use multiple data sources, the increased complexity of teacher evaluation requires thoughtful management of the additional information to be employed. Table 10.2 presents 15 issues for the use and management of multiple teacher data sources. Some of these are decided by individual teachers, some by building administrators, some by new district-level organizational groups formed to manage complex data (e.g., Evaluation Unit, Evaluation Board), and all by professional deliberation and agreement in the district.

Just the use of multiple data sources in teacher evaluation opens up possibilities; it increases the number of issues a school district needs to face. Just as there is no "one size fits all" set of teacher data sources, there is no single recommendation for addressing the issues presented in Table 10.2 for all settings.

Table 10.2   Options/Decisions for Using Multiple Data Sources in Teacher
Evaluation

Which data on teachers are to be gathered in the school district?
How are the data to be used?
Who gathers the data?
Use same data on all teachers, or vary by individual teacher?
Who selects data on individual teachers?
Who owns the data?
How are the data organized, presented?
How are the data stored, maintained?
Who interprets the data?
How will the data gathering be paid for?
How can multiple data sources increase the uses for teacher evaluation?
Who provides leadership on data development, gathering, use?
Who resolves disputes over process or results?
How does the use of multiple data sources affect the sociology of educators?
How does the use of multiple data sources affect the politics of educators?

The best advice is to expand slowly (on the order of five years), use teacher volunteers, build on successes, solve problems as they emerge, and deliberate to set development goals, timetables, and evaluations of the evaluation system itself.

School districts may find that a "Teacher Evaluation Board" consisting of teachers, administrators, parents, older students, community representatives, and education departments (university and state) can be a central place of debate, advocacy, planning, coordination, staff development, local R&D on data sources, and policy recommendation. This group can keep a focus on teacher evaluation in the midst of all other tasks facing a school district. The Board can be charged with addressing all the issues of Table 10.2.

HOW ARE MULTIPLE SOURCE
DATA USED IN A SCHOOL DISTRICT?

A key area of management concerns how the teacher data will be used. This happens on three levels of use: individual teachers, local schools, and school district. Individual teachers may have their own uses, which vary by individual (e.g., security or promotion). Schools may have purposes for school improvement, action research projects, teacher leadership assignment, or accountability. A district can use data aggregated, if not identifiable to an individual teacher, for public relations, district planning, teacher assignment, and staff development.

How Are Individual Multiple Data Sources Chosen?

Data gathering can be chosen as school district policy and can be school based, teacher collectively controlled, or individual teacher controlled. The best teacher evaluation programs will include elements of each of these and should be well discussed and defined in each district.

School District Selection of Data Sources

The data sources chosen for inclusion in a school district pool should be extensive, varied, and proven in order to provide flexibility, variety, complete coverage, and validity. The district pool should be the largest possible in order to have sufficient numbers of subgroups within the districts from which to choose. Some sources should be excluded because of logic (validity), feasibility, or lack of empirically demonstrated success. Also, when sources are selected by the district, the specific forms and procedures need sanctioning because individual teacher or school student reports do not work equally well or compare well across the district.

To this point we have argued for teacher choice of data sources. However, there can be some situations where a district may mandate data gathering as a part of administrator action, such as with an unsatisfactory teacher. For example, if a teacher is having trouble with student complaints, a survey probably is not needed to document and pinpoint the problems. However, the district norms and expectations are good tools for this purpose for principals.

Individual Principal or School Selection of Data Sources

Individual principals or schools can effectively encourage the broadest use of data sources as approved at the district level. They can select among these for their own local purposes, such as school improvement or action research. They can advocate for broadest use of a school-focus initiative, such as pupil achievement. Individual teacher data can be made anonymous and aggregated at a school level. Care should be taken to avoid unfair school comparisons, unintended identification of individual teachers, or misuse of data by outsiders (Read, 1973).

Principals are in a good position to encourage growth of good teacher evaluation (Peterson, 2004; Peterson & Peterson, 2005). Principals can lead professional deliberation in their own schools about reasons and practices for expanded teacher evaluation. They can encourage teachers to become more involved in their own evaluation and to advocate for better evaluation in the school district. Principals can include teacher-controlled data in their own individual teacher summative evaluations. They can use teacher evaluation data in school planning and improvement projects. Finally, principals should look to increase the evaluation of their own practice in order to lead.

Teacher Selection of Own Data Sources

The individual teacher can select the most pertinent and fair combination of data sources, especially for purposes of selecting material to be included in a dossier or portfolio. Of course, teachers should consider which data sources make the best case for documenting competence and excellence. In addition, teachers can get experience with different data sources, and possible improvement in data sources that do not meet expectations, because the teachers can control whether or not the results will be kept and, if so, who will use them.

Teacher selection of data collection and use is a permissive system, with a seeming problem of conflict of interest: Won't teachers just select those things that make them look good? Yes, of course. But at the same time they will be choosing sources that match their professional, expert judgment of what is valid in each their individual case, and satisfying their own senses of acceptability and fairness. Teacher ownership and buy-in are very important in the design and functioning of practical but complex teacher evaluation systems. We have found that most teachers, rather than collecting only the mandatory minimum, will call for additional data for inspection (Peterson, 1989).

If teacher choice works well for teacher involvement, the question remains whether teacher choice is good assessment for accountability. Teacher choice of multiple data sources is a *best case* system, but the logic of review and judgment is the same as for the conventional teacher evaluation *fixed case* system in which one size (set of data sources) fits all. There are superior, adequate, and unacceptable best cases (categorical analysis). There are better best cases and weaker best cases (ordinal or ranking analysis). Best cases can be rated on scales (interval analysis).

Another critique of teacher choice is that poor teachers may cover up the mediocre or even bad data sets. However, the principal is the first monitor of bad practice, and an elaborate, multi-data source evaluation system rarely is needed to show up the problems. Also, a truly bad teacher has trouble finding *any* indicators of quality.

HOW ARE COMPLEX TEACHER EVALUATION DATA PRESENTED?

The best format for presenting complex teacher evaluation data depends on the use and audiences for the results. Data may be for individual teachers or aggregated for schools or districts. Two formats for individual teacher data are professional portfolios and dossiers.

Data Aggregation at School or District Level

Teacher evaluation data can be aggregated at a school or district level to determine ranges and expected practices. For example, student surveys can be gathered across the district and analyzed by student age groups. Studies have shown consistent patterns of positive attitudes toward teachers (Peterson, 2000). These norms can give a sense of expectations and provide positive information for public relations (Blair, 2004) and districtwide accountability.

Portfolios and Dossiers

Portfolios are well suited to individual teacher displays, personal teacher reflection, documentation of professional growth, and personnel decisions such as job searches. Portfolios are individualized, vary in format and content, and reflect the organization of the individual teacher. Portfolios are incorporated into NBPTS certification processes. Shulman (1992) described teacher portfolios as "fully realized through reflective writing, deliberation, and serious conversation."

Dossiers are page-limited collections of compressed and career-long teacher evaluation data (Peterson et al., 2001). Dossiers may be limited in size to 12 to 15 pages containing compressed results of test scores, activity listings, survey results, peer reviews of materials, and other data summaries. Photo reduction of documents aids in space management. Dossiers are not portfolios or scrapbooks of teacher work, testimonial letters, collections of student work, photographs, unit plans, or statements of educational philosophy. Dossiers are designed for ease in analysis and comparison, contain materials not open to wide interpretation, and are intended to be practical to store and access.

Portfolios and dossiers are separate from the personnel files, which are necessarily kept by the school district. Teachers ultimately are responsible for the contents and use of their teacher evaluation dossier or portfolio documentation.

WHO INTERPRETS THE DATA FROM MULTIPLE SOURCES?

Who is to interpret the rich data of multiple sources depends on the purpose of their use. For example, teacher development, retention, tenure (or other job security), school improvement, or public relations call for different persons or roles within a district to judge information about teacher quality. The task is to match the data with the appropriate expert. This could be an individual teacher, a principal, a curriculum supervisor, a personnel director for a district, a superintendent, or an expert panel assembled for the review and decision. In every instance the persons must be expert, informed, and experienced; have the best objective data available; and have inevitable biases balanced by the views of others. People who evaluate teachers should themselves be evaluated for the quality of their work.

Complexity of Interpreting Teacher Evaluation Data

Interpreting complex teacher evaluation data is an expert, subjective procedure. For example, Coker, Medley, and Soar (1980) produced evidence that classroom observation of teachers on categories such as "contacts students when off task," "asks questions," and "takes student's views into account" all are widely (and wildly) open to subjective perception and meaning. However, expert, informed interpretation of complex data is a necessary part of teacher evaluation. The task is much like interpreting fingerprint matches (Federal

Bureau of Investigation, 1979), jury resolution of legal cases (Lloyd-Bostock, 1989; Peterson, 2000), personnel hiring (Eder & Harris, 1999), or interpretation of mammograms or military intelligence photographs (Gladwell, 2004). In all of these instances, the best objective evidence (fingerprints, forensic evidence, and testimony; résumés, recommendations, and interviews; radiological prints, photographs, and radar images) requires expert subjective analysis and interpretation that cannot be reduced to brief descriptions or component catalogs but that, when done well, serves important practical uses.

Interpreting teacher evaluation data is not as simple as ranking teachers by student test scores or by comparing faculties on parent survey results. Rather, expert consideration of the context can be crucial in determining value. Training, experience, and a track record of good discernment all are required for those persons who interpret teacher data.

Individual Teacher Interpretation

Individual teachers interpret their own data in a variety of ways. They look for high levels of success, and may at first be disturbed by less than perfection. District norms may give them some helpful perspective. Year-to-year patterns are meaningful to teachers looking for improvement or a record of good work for security of employment. Some will look for reassurance, a few for improvements. Some teachers use complex data to examine their practice: for example, to acquire and use strategies to improve parent relations reflected in parent surveys.

Interpretation of aggregated teacher data raises interesting issues of comparison. It can be very difficult for teachers to accept other than outstanding results when, of course, "average" findings will be most common. There are so many good teachers in a district that it is difficult to tell individual teachers that class means as much as 1.5 standard deviations *below* district means can still represent good teaching. The norms simply will be very high; for example, Peterson and Stevens (1988) reported a mean of 4.57 (SD = 0.42) on a 5-point scale of overall student satisfaction of teachers in their large sample! The best advice for individual teachers is to avoid norm comparisons; but where unavoidable, consider and report only categories of *well functioning* and *needs attention*. Much attention must be paid to educating teachers about comparing individual data.

Individual Principal Use

Principal use of teacher data is appropriate for (a) including in annual individual teacher summative evaluation and (b) school improvement programs. The close monitoring of teachers, particularly with frequent walk-throughs, makes for good interpretation of data. Principals can look for patterns that either (a) support their general administrative opinion of the teacher or (b) open up new ways of looking at their teachers.

District Analysis

School district analysis can be done where individual teachers and schools are not identifiable. This analysis may include data gathered where the teacher chooses not to have the data included in individual summative evaluation. No permanent record should be kept that can identify these teacher-rejected data with that teacher.

WHAT ARE THE COSTS OF USING MULTIPLE DATA SOURCES?

Scriven (1973) described the need for "comprehensive cost" analysis in good educational evaluation. He included for consideration side effects, comparisons, installation, displacement, morale, and time. Teacher evaluation surveys, peer reviews of materials, systematic observation, and teacher tests have predictable costs (Peterson, 1989; Thompson, 1980), as shown in Tables 10.3 and 10.4. Standard F-3 of the *Personnel Evaluation Standards* (Joint Committee, 1988) requires that "adequate time and resources should be provided for personnel evaluation activities, so that evaluation plans can be effectively and efficiently implemented" (p. 79).

Teacher use of district-supported data gathering may be limited to a reasonable level. Individual teachers can share costs for data sources beyond requirements for adequate evaluation. Some very expensive data sources, most notably outside systematic observation, can be limited by a lottery drawing procedure to pick district-sponsored teachers each year.

Table 10.3   Costs of Teacher Data Sources (after Peterson, 1989)

	$ per Student	$ per class (N = 25)	$ per Teacher	Teacher Time[1]	Staff Time[1]	Administrator Time[1]
Student survey	.17	4.25	8.50[2]	10	30	—
Parent survey	.65	16.25	32.50[2]	10	30	—
Principal report	—	—	—	10	—	2 hrs
Teacher tests	—	—	41.00	3 hrs	5 hrs[3]	—
Professional activity	—	—	2.00	1 hr	—	—
Peer review mtls	—	—	29.00	12 hrs	8 hrs[3]	—
Systematic observation	—	—	85.00	2 hrs	16 hrs	1 hr
Pupil gain	.50	12.50	25.00	3 hrs	10	10

SOURCE: Used with permission of Kenneth D. Peterson.

NOTES:

1. Minutes, unless indicated as hours

2. Assumes 50% elementary teachers (1 class) and 50% secondary (3 classes each)

3. One time per year cost for all district teachers

Table 10.4   Dollar Costs to District for Teacher Data Sources (after Peterson, 1989)

	$ Cost per Teacher	Usage in District[1]	Frequency by Teacher[2]	Source Cost per Teacher[3]
Student survey	8.50	0.85	0.667	4.34
Parent survey	32.50	0.75	0.667	14.63
Teacher tests	41.00	0.40	0.143	2.35
Professional Activity	2.00	0.90	1.000	1.80
Peer review mtls	29.00	0.33	0.143	1.37
Systematic observation	85.00	0.80	0.143	9.72
Pupil gain	25.00	0.70	0.667	10.50

TOTAL Dollar Cost per Teacher in District = $44.70

SOURCE: Used with permission of Kenneth D. Peterson.

NOTES:

1. Estimated decimal percentage of teachers who would elect this data source

2. Yearly decimal fraction, for example, 0.143 = once each seven years; 0.667 for two of every three years

3. Source cost/teacher = cost/teacher × usage × frequency

District requirements for teacher contributions can be made on a sliding scale based on district availability and use by teachers. Districts may fully pay for data sources to get them established, but then begin to share costs when usage is high and beyond necessary teacher evaluation purposes.

WHAT NEW USES FOR TEACHER EVALUATION ARE ENABLED BY USING MULTIPLE DATA SOURCES?

Enhanced use of teacher evaluation data is the most important stimulus to increase the amount and variety of evaluation activity. The expense, disruption, and sociological challenge of serious teacher evaluation are hard to defend unless the uses of the data are greatly expanded beyond conventional practice. In turn, expanded use is the greatest driver to enlarge the program. Table 10.5 presents new uses for teacher evaluation using multiple data sources; these uses are briefly discussed in this section.

Expanded Annual/Biennial Summative Evaluation

Teacher data can be added to the administrator report with the agreement of the principal and teacher.

Table 10.5   New Uses for Teacher Evaluation Enabled by Multiple Data Sources

Expanded annual/biennial summative evaluation
Teacher authoritative reassurance
Teacher leadership
District and school planning: staff development, hiring
Staff development
School improvement, action research
Achievement gap teacher assignment
Teacher tenure, promotion schemes
School, district accountability
Public relations

Teacher Security

Sociologist Lortie (1975) identified "endemic uncertainty" as a hazard of school teaching. Extensive and credible performance data can reassure teachers of needed and quality work, and documentation of career-long accomplishments can be a source of security (Peterson & Chenoweth, 1992).

Teacher Leadership

Teacher leadership can be chosen formally in a school as department chairs, grade-level leaders, textbook and curriculum selection, hiring committees (Peterson, 2002), mentors for beginning teachers, mentors for teachers under remediation, and teachers on special assignment are selected by dossier or portfolio review. Any of these positions can be appointed based on panel review—a true use of competitive merit in schoolteacher assignment and pay.

Teacher Tenure

Extensive data over the first three years of teaching provide a basis for a very positive recognition of competence that can be acknowledged with some kind of regular teacher or tenure status. This decision can be based upon a certain number of data accomplishments of certain standards.

Teacher Promotion Systems

Teacher ranks and pay can be based upon data showing accomplishment. Promotion systems like those in postsecondary education recognize accomplishment and status. For example, titles like Professional Teacher, Senior Teacher, and Master Teacher can be conferred for successful data review at

3 years, 7 years, and 14 years. The promotions do not have to be mandatory, or competitive, or limited. There can be opportunities for annual review for teachers not succeeding at first review. Salary ranks, in addition to current annual "step" increases, add an element of merit to teacher pay without the drawbacks of merit pay.

Merit Pay

It is quite clear that simple merit pay schemes (i.e., direct pay for short-term performance) are not appropriate for teacher assignment settings (Peterson, 2004). Rather, additional pay for school leadership by merit or promotion by merit are appropriate monetary rewards differentially given for meritorious performance and documentation.

District, School Planning

District leaders can use aggregated district data (e.g., student or parent surveys) to plan staff development, publicity campaigns, school schedule or organization, or instruction/curriculum changes.

Staff Development

District inservice can be tied to individual teachers who want to improve their results. For example, teachers looking to improve parent surveys often are interested in workshops, consultations on parent relations, and communication training sessions.

School Improvement

Individual school improvement projects can be planned and documented. Principal and teacher planning teams agree on goals, activities, and how to document results.

Achievement Gap Teacher Assignment

It is possible to document the track record of some teachers who have had great success in closing the achievement gap (Peterson, Deyhle, & Watkins, 1988; Peterson, Bennet, & Sherman, 1991). These teachers can be identified, assigned to work together in large teacher teams at sites of need, and paid an outstanding salary for their results.

Teacher, School, and District Accountability

State and national report cards can be based upon aggregated teacher data from multiple sources. Documentation of sustained high performance meets the needs of many external audiences. Selective improvement in a given area can be a valuable goal to document with individual teacher performance.

Public Relations

School districts are in competition with charter and private schools as well as builders of roads and prisons. All of these competitors have well-developed arguments for their priority over public schools in terms of public resources and decision making. Significantly increased activity based on data of actual teacher performance in the district makes a difference in the support of the public. Use of survey results, teacher background and preparation, test results, action research findings, peer reviews of materials, and promotions and assignments based upon merit all contribute to the case for public support of schools and educators.

Both aggregated results showing positive views and accomplishments and individual case studies may be publicized. Districts can be aggressive in developing solid relationships with print and video reporters and editors. They can develop publicity tools that work, organize news events for maximum impact, understand what makes "news," market story ideas to the media, respond to crisis reports, and better understand the people who work in the media (Blair, 2004; Warner, 2000).

Specific public relations using teacher evaluation data include

- News conferences
- Press releases
- District newsletters
- Parent night meetings
- Teacher presented "truth squad" presentations to civic organizations (e.g., Kiwanis Clubs, local NAACP chapters, political parties)

WHAT LEGAL ISSUES ARE ADDED BY USING MULTIPLE AND VARIABLE DATA SOURCES?

The use of teacher-controlled multiple and variable data sources for teacher evaluation has a number of legal implications that are positive for school districts. For example, there is a shift in burden for establishing validity (including reliability) of data sources under teacher direction. When a school district imposes a kind of data gathering, there is a responsibility for the district to defend the acceptability of the data. When teachers choose, *they* are making the claim for validity, which the district chooses to accept. For example, many teachers would challenge the validity of determining teacher quality on *all* teachers in a district by using standardized test scores of teachers. However, it is quite another situation when *some* teachers choose to include their own test scores, with the agreement of other teachers and the school district. These same teachers are not then in a position to legally challenge the use of teacher tests or to challenge their validity.

HOW DOES THE USE OF MULTIPLE AND VARIABLE DATA SOURCES AFFECT THE SOCIOLOGY AND POLITICS OF EDUCATORS?

The social and political issues of teacher evaluation may do more to improve teacher practice than application of subject matter or pedagogical understandings. It also is the case that the very best technically designed teacher evaluation systems can be expected to fail in a district if time and careful sociological development are not taken for their introduction.

Sociology is the study of *how* teachers act in their occupational setting (psychology explains *why* these actions occur). Much of the literature of teacher evaluation ignores these realities in favor of technical descriptions of validity and legal considerations. Sociologists (Johnson, 1990; Lortie, 1975; Waller, 1932/1967; Wolf, 1973) have described the importance of such dynamics as power, status, reassurance, and authority in the work lives of classroom teachers. All of these factors are greatly affected by the kind of teacher evaluation practiced in the district. There are reasons for teacher evaluation that make teachers look the same, with a few critical exceptions, and that do not single out exemplary practice. There are important needs within a school for day-to-day feelings of equity, teamwork, and protection from comparisons and striving. This is one reason that merit pay schemes are inconsistent with the equity required in a well functioning school.

Sociologists describe teaching as an isolated job, with virtually no feedback to teachers about their value and impact other than the appearance of interest on the faces of students. There are no mechanisms like clear immediate results, returning clients, high and performance-based salary, discretionary time, and high social status to assure teachers of a needed and effective job. Thus, according to researchers in this area, the most important use of teacher data is *authoritative reassurance*—believable evidence to teachers themselves that they are doing a needed and effective job.

Likewise, the politics of teacher evaluation is a critical dimension for understanding teacher evaluation. Good, complex data and analysis must be balanced against the uses of the data in the political and economic arenas of society. For example, teacher status is deliberately restricted because of the economic need for uniform and limited salaries and the social need for uniform assignments of teacher talent and effectiveness across school settings. The political reality of deliberate restriction of teacher talent and accomplishment within any market conditions is remarkable. The use of compelling multiple and variable data source teacher evaluation can form a basis for differential assignment and pay of demonstrably effective teachers in high-need situations (e.g., achievement gap schools).

HOW CAN EDUCATORS MOVE FROM
SINGLE TO MULTIPLE DATA SOURCES?

Decisions to move from single data source evaluation (e.g., principal report) require local discussion, decision making, and adoption. There are cultures to be dealt with (e.g., which teachers are at the top of the pecking order) and careful transitions to be made over time with the sociology of teacher evaluation and the complexity of the technical procedures in mind. Stage-wise development of multiple data source use over perhaps five years is required for success (Peterson & Chenoweth, 1992). It is best to begin with pioneer volunteers, adjust procedures to make them successful, and then to build on successes. Pioneers must be protected and be seen as successful by other teachers. A long-term perspective of teacher evaluation improvement allows districts to start with positive and lenient practices and results. Future success of an innovative teacher evaluation system requires the development of a local capacity of experience, knowledge, successful innovation and adaptation, infrastructure, and instruments/procedures.

Principal leadership is essential in the improvement of teacher evaluation. Individual principals can provide wise advice to individual teachers on selection of data sources. Principals can protect delicate feelings and relationships, and they can demonstrate their own use of multiple data sources. In addition, principals can supply patience, assistance with interpretation, and local problem solving.

CONCLUSION: HOW SHOULD WE STUDY
THE USE OF MULTIPLE DATA SOURCES?

Study of complex teacher evaluation is needed at the local district level as a part of innovation in teacher evaluation and in the larger educational research world (Peterson, 2004). Current research on such an important topic as teacher evaluation is woeful. For example, not much has changed since Danielson (1996), a decade ago, wrote that "the ingredients required for clean research studies— educational goals, assessment measures, and control over extraneous variables— are compromised. Consequently, hard, empirical research in education is scanty" (p. 22).

Educators need small-scale clinical studies of materials, procedures, judgments, costs, and arrangements for teacher evaluation. Necessary arrangements include deliberative bodies, technical support, and cooperation of school districts. There are needs for sociological studies and political analysis, as well as techniques for teacher assessment. All of these inquiries should be conducted with multiple research teams who not only innovate but also replicate other studies.

We should look in research reports for levels of client satisfaction, not merely for polemics of what educators *ought* to do. A good rule of thumb is that teacher satisfaction with innovations ought to be in the low 80%. This level is high enough to support and foster development, but also low enough to indicate a push at some teachers who resist good change. It is reasonable to expect some level of dissatisfaction; after all, no one wants to look bad at doing something they care very much about, and teachers are a population vulnerable to criticism.

Local district studies beyond those of academic researchers are required for refining evaluation procedures. Development of teacher evaluation should be based on the experience of volunteers. Volunteers are pioneers with their own purposes in evaluation who will take the teacher initiative required to build good teacher evaluation practices in the district. R&D requires support at a district administration level, including lobbying for funding. If educators are serious about teacher evaluation, they will have to be serious about supporting it.

Teacher quality and how to determine it are crucial concerns of education, surely as important as work in how students learn, instructional techniques, or curriculum content. However, not as much talent has gone into development of teacher evaluation as many other important areas of education. Support for public education depends on clear, rational, compelling evidence that public school teachers are effective. Our theoretical understanding of teacher quality is at the basis of teacher education and staff development. Evaluation of teacher education and staff development depends on documenting changes in teacher quality. All of these are reasons for significant support of teacher evaluation development, including the use of multiple data sources, by school districts, principals, teacher organizations, and individual teachers.

REFERENCES

Berk, R. A. (1988). Fifty reasons why student gain does not mean teacher effectiveness. *Journal of Personnel Evaluation in Education, 1,* 345–363.

Blair, J. (2004). *Building bridges with the press: A guide for educators.* Bethesda, MD: Education Week Press.

Coker, H., Medley, D. M., & Soar, R. S. (1980). How valid are expert opinions about effective teaching? *Phi Delta Kappan, 62*(2), 131–134, 149.

Danielson, C. (1996). *Enhancing professional practice.* Alexandria, VA: Association for Supervision and Curriculum Development.

Downey, C. J., Steffy, B. E., English, F. W., Frase, L. E., & Poston, W. K. (2004). *The three-minute classroom walk-through.* Thousand Oaks, CA: Corwin.

Eder, R. W., & Harris, M. M. (Eds.). (1999). *The employment interview handbook.* Thousand Oaks, CA: Sage.

Federal Bureau of Investigation. (1979). *The science of fingerprints.* Washington, DC: U.S. Department of Justice.

Gladwell, M. (2004, December 13). The picture problem. *New Yorker,* pp. 74–81.

Glickman, C. D., & Kanawati, D. G. (1998). Future directions for school supervision. In G. R. Firth & E. F. Pajak (Eds.), *Handbook of research on school supervision* (pp. 1248–1257). New York: Simon Schuster & Macmillan.

Johnson, S. M. (1990). *Teachers at work.* New York: Basic Books.

Joint Committee on Standards for Educational Evaluation. (1988). *The personnel evaluation standards: How to assess systems of evaluating educators.* Newbury Park, CA: Sage.

Lloyd-Bostock, S. (1989). *Law in practice: Applications of psychology to legal decision making and legal skills.* Chicago: Lyceum.

Lortie, D. C. (1975). *Schoolteacher: A sociological study.* Chicago: University of Chicago Press.

Peterson, K. (2004). Research on school teacher evaluation. *NASSP Bulletin, 88*(639), 60–79.

Peterson, K. D. (1989). Costs of school teacher evaluation in a career ladder system. *Journal of Research and Development in Education, 22*(2), 30–36.

Peterson, K. D. (2000). *Teacher evaluation: A comprehensive guide to new directions and practices* (2nd ed.). Thousand Oaks, CA: Corwin.

Peterson, K. D. (2002). *Effective teacher hiring: A guide to getting the best.* Thousand Oaks, CA: Corwin.

Peterson, K. D., Bennet, B., & Sherman, D. F. (1991). Themes of uncommonly successful teachers of at-risk students. *Urban Education, 26,* 176–194.

Peterson, K. D., & Chenoweth, T. (1992). School teachers' control and involvement in their own evaluation. *Journal of Personnel Evaluation in Education, 6,* 177–189.

Peterson, K. D., Deyhle, D., & Watkins, W. (1988). Evaluation that accommodates minority teacher contributions. *Urban Education, 23*(2), 133–149.

Peterson, K. D., & Peterson, C. A. (2005). *Effective teacher evaluation: A principal's guide.* Thousand Oaks, CA: Corwin.

Peterson, K. D., & Stevens, D. (1988). Student reports for schoolteacher evaluation. *Journal of Personnel Evaluation in Education, 1,* 259–267.

Peterson, K. D., Stevens, D., & Mack, C. (2001). Presenting complex teacher evaluation data: Advantages of dossier organization techniques over portfolios. *Journal of Personnel Evaluation in Education, 15*(2), 121–134.

Read, L. F. (1973). An assessment of the Michigan Assessment. In E. House (Ed.), *School evaluation: The politics and process.* Berkeley, CA: McCutchan.

Sacks, P. (1999). *Standardized minds.* Cambridge, MA: Perseus Books.

Scriven, M. (1973). *Handbook for model training program in qualitative educational evaluation.* Berkeley: University of California Press.

Shulman, L. S. (1992, April). *Portfolios for teacher education: A component of reflective teacher education.* Paper presented at the annual meeting of the American Educational Research Association, San Francisco.

Thompson, M. S. (1980). *Benefit-cost analysis for program evaluation.* Beverly Hills, CA: Sage.

Waller, W. (1967). *The sociology of teaching.* New York: John Wiley. (Original work published 1932)

Warner, C. (2000). *Promoting your school: Going beyond PR* (2nd ed.). Thousand Oaks, CA: Corwin.

Wolf, R. (1973). How teachers feel toward evaluation. In E. House (Ed.), *School evaluation: The politics and process* (pp. 156–168). Berkeley, CA: McCutchan.

Wright, S. P., Horn, S. P., & Sanders, W. L. (1997). Teacher and classroom context effects on student achievement: Implications for teacher evaluation. *Journal of Personnel Evaluation in Education, 11,* 57–67.

Part III

Implementing the Teacher Evaluation System

Conducting a Successful Evaluation Conference

11

Virginia M. Helm

Henry St. Maurice

The evaluation conference in the school setting has for several decades tended to be tied directly to classroom observation, which occurred infrequently and, in so-called clinical supervision models, followed a highly prescribed pre- and post-observation format. In an era of intensified global competition among educational, industrial, and service sectors, the limitations of performance evaluation based solely on formal observations have become increasingly apparent. Questions of validity and reliability, of course, prevail, but so do concerns about evaluators' parochialism, subjectivity, and bias. Specifically, there is widespread recognition that performance evaluations of any employee must depend on data beyond those found in brief exhibitions. Evaluators must report those data in the most effective manner, and evaluatees must produce significant improvement wherever deemed necessary, as soon as practicable.

Because relatively little has been written in education literature about how to conduct an evaluation conference—excepting volumes of research on the above-mentioned so-called clinical supervisory pre- and post-observation conferences—we have turned to the literature of business and the professions, where the evaluation conference (also called a performance appraisal interview) is based on nearly four decades of theory, research, and practice. In the past two decades, since the advent of total quality assurance and participative management approaches that distribute responsibilities—if not authority—among managers and employees, traditional hierarchical approaches to evaluation in professions and businesses have been generally supplanted (Heneman

235

& Milanowski, 2003). Many studies and implementations have shown that peer involvement in work processes usually leads to peer input in performance evaluation; emphasis on customer satisfaction often leads to customer input in performance evaluation (Glickman, Gordon, & Ross-Gordon, 2004). Although supervisors usually retain responsibility for developing final, summary evaluations, they do so based on input from a wide variety of sources, often including self-appraisal by employees being evaluated. The literature on performance appraisal in professions and businesses reflects a unanimous understanding of the evaluation conference as only one component in an ongoing communication and feedback cycle that is informal, timely, and specific (Buzzotta, 1988; Derven, 1990; Meyer, 1991; Nathan, Mohrman, & Milliman, 1991; Pennock, 1992). This feedback cycle shifts a supervisor's role from one of boss and judge delivering an annual pronouncement about the employee's performance to that of coach or mentor, where a supervisor is in frequent contact with the employee, offering regular—even daily—encouragement, praise, and constructive criticism immediately after observing specific actions or behaviors. Nonetheless, we want to note here that although the evaluation conference described in this chapter reflects contemporary approaches to performance evaluation, much of what we discuss remains applicable to so-called clinical supervision conference as well. Although the education community has also recognized the desirability of diversifying the range of materials and inputs submitted for the supervisor's consideration in constructing the final evaluation (see McGreal, 1988; Popham, 1988; Scriven, 1988), recent policy initiatives present enormous challenges to participatory management approaches to educational evaluations, as we will briefly discuss in the next section.

HOW HAVE FEDERAL STANDARDS CHANGED TEACHER EVALUATION?

Federal Public Law 107-110 (U.S. Department of Education, 2001), titled "No Child Left Behind" (NCLB), stipulated more exacting standards-based accountability measures than ever before required by federal laws and policies on education. NCLB changed the terms of educational evaluation by focusing accountability measures on high-stakes standardized testing of students and teachers. Specifically, for federal aid, state and local education agencies are held responsible for

> developing systems to measure the effectiveness of specific professional development programs and strategies to document gains in student academic achievement or increases in teacher mastery of the academic subjects the teachers teach. (U.S. Department of Education, 2001)

How do standards-based accountability provisions in NCLB affect teacher evaluation conferences? Following are some policy statements and research findings with implications for teachers and evaluators in the one-on-one, face-to-face conferences in which they discuss and review teacher quality.

Policy makers recognize that NCLB has set rigorous standards for teachers as well as along with students. The Education Commission of the States (2004) summarized,

> The goal of improving student learning through the improvement of teaching is at the heart of a professional model of accountability. Such a model regulates the qualifications and performance of teachers and school leaders. . . . The professional model also includes regular peer and administrator evaluation to ensure that teachers engage in appropriate professional practice. In instances where they do not, the model provides mechanisms for intervention and termination.

Professional development policies and practices, in particular instructional supervision leading to teacher evaluation, have come under unprecedented scrutiny. Processes once dubbed a "private cold war" (Blumberg, 1980) are now more public and heated.

Advocacy of professional development for improving student achievement is not new. In their report on NCLB, "No Dream Denied," the National Commission on Teaching and America's Future (NCTAF, 2003) concluded,

> Countless studies confirm the elements that make staff development effective . . . professional development for teachers cannot be "one size fits all." As in business and other professions, the best development opportunities provide teachers with "just in time" and "just what's needed" help. Such a pattern merits a greater focus on assessment literacy. This process requires not just time, but analytical tools and an understanding of the instructional options and resources available. (p. 30)

Implementation of NCLB drove assessment literacy to the forefront of professional development and therefore intensified ongoing debates over accountability. At issue were such questions as, Would student test scores supplement or supplant such time-honored evaluation data sources as individual observation, reflective self-study, local survey, and criterion-referenced assessments of teaching knowledge, skills, and dispositions? Would local, state, and federal funds support a wide variety of accountability measures, including value-added assessments, or would policy stipulations and budget affordability determine methods of accountability? As Berry (2004) stated, "the debate is really about whose knowledge should be taught and in what ways, what standards will be enforced in the teaching profession, and how they will be paid for" (pp. 9–10).

At this writing, research studies are under way to validate the effectiveness of teacher professional development in terms of NCLB standards, including evaluation based on tests of student achievement (Milanowski, 2003; NCTAF, 2004). Previous studies have shown that evaluation, along with preparation, certification, and induction, is a dependent variable in increased student achievement on National Assessment of Educational Progress (NAEP) tests (Darling-Hammond & Sykes, 2003). More analysis is needed of data from thousands of schools in which educators work in the enterprise of public education. Among the hordes of researchers searching for evidence of effective evaluation (e.g., Heneman & Milanowski, 2003), some have studied the effects of evaluation conferences (e.g., Tsui, Law, & Shum, 2001), but so far none can be found that correlate qualities and quantities of teacher evaluation conferences with student achievement. To the contrary, recent studies indicate strong preferences by both teachers and evaluators for multiple measures of effectiveness and various standards for accountability; as Tsui et al. concluded, a supervisory conference that is considered effective by its participants apparently depends on "a long-term relationship that fosters mutual trust, understanding of and respect for each other's work" (p. 343).

Such qualitative aspects of evaluative conferences have prominent places in research and practice. As Holland (1998) summarized in her review of the literature of supervision processes and techniques, there is "wide divergence" among theories and practices of supervision and evaluation, leading to a "crossroads" of choices, not consensus. Current supervisors' tendencies toward heterodoxy—even when orthodoxy is stipulated—do not seem diminished by NCLB policies. For example, a leading supervision textbook (Glickman et al., 2004) presents a continuum of supervisory behaviors for conferences, from "directive" to "nondirective," denoting the latter as more democratic and having greater potential for effecting durable improvement (pp. 133–134), without mention of any necessity for directive evaluation based on accountability systems stipulated in NCLB. As such, this and many other theories and practices of evaluative conferences seem deliberately out of step with federal policy for reasons that have yet to be fully described.

One possible reason that scholarly literature on evaluative conferences has not readily endorsed NCLB stipulations as a basis for practice may be a sense of déja vu. In the 1980s, school supervision in the United States was dominated by so-called clinical models deploying strict quantitative standards and benchmarks and advocating accountability systems based entirely on them. The most widespread such model was developed and marketed by Hunter (1980) and became prescribed supervisory practice in many schools and even states (Holland, 1998, p. 401ff.), despite disclaimers (Hunter, 1984) about its zealous implementation. Hunter's methods were often criticized for scientism and disparaged for inadequacy by theorists, researchers, and practitioners; they had fallen into disfavor and disuse by the late 1990s (Holland, 1998), just before similar methods become encoded in NCLB. Without wishing for resumption of debates known for two decades as "paradigm wars," it is possible to foresee renewed contentiousness over NCLB stipulations for teacher evaluation. It is also possible that those stipulations could eventually be labeled obsolete, as seems to have happened to Hunter's methods of supervision and evaluation.

Finally, persuasive indications that policies implementing NCLB might not substantially change theories and practices of evaluative conferences can be found in a broad consensus among theories, policies, and practices of instructional supervision and evaluation. As teacher evaluators have adopted theories and practices of human relations, derived from long-term and widespread studies in clinical and social psychology, along with quality assurance processes developed worldwide in professions and businesses, general agreement has emerged on valid theories and effective practices for evaluative conferences. Emphases on mutual communications, shared goals, and collaborative processes emerged from diverse kinds of research informed by widespread forms of practice, not legislated mandates. For human resource professionals, the norm for evaluative conferences incorporates multiple measures across time, shared decision making, and individualized goals. It seems unlikely that such consensus would have followed any legislative mandate, and that any mandate could replace a consensus with diametrically opposed practices such as high-stakes one-shot measures targeting specific goals.

Therefore, we can conclude that NCLB has yet to have significant effects on the purposes and practices of teacher evaluation recommended in this volume, and that specific stipulations in NCLB would have deleterious effects opposed by our recommendations in this chapter on evaluative conferences. We concur with the broad goals of NCLB, to improve student achievement and develop accountability systems for teachers and administrators, but do not at this writing find compelling theories and conclusive research evidence to support stipulating any one set of standards and benchmarks to measure progress toward those worthy goals. Along with changes of federal administration, NCLB will be reviewed and revised. Policy debates, theoretical discussions, and research studies will continue; results remain to be seen.

WHAT ARE THE PURPOSES OF THE EVALUATION CONFERENCE?

Despite being a site of contested policy implementation, the evaluation conference nonetheless serves multiple purposes for practitioners of professional development. As early as 1960, MacGregor (cited in Downs, 1990) identified three purposes that still hold true today:

- *Administrative:* to document performance for use in personnel decision making
- *Informative:* to inform the employee about his or her work performance
- *Motivational:* to motivate employees to higher levels of performance

A good evaluation conference can also serve problem-solving, strategy-developing, and goal-setting functions (Anderson & Barnett, 1987; Krayer, 1987; Losyk, 1990/1991; Meyer, 1991), as will be seen in the discussion that follows.

What has changed since 1960, however, when MacGregor identified the administrative, informative, and motivational purposes served by the evaluation conference, is that the conference is now understood as part of the ongoing feedback and communication that characterize good supervisory "coaching" (Somerick, 1993). Essentially the evaluation conference confirms what has been communicated throughout the evaluation period. With regular feedback letting the teacher know where he or she has excelled and where there are concerns, there should be no surprises in the summary evaluation conference (Derven, 1990; Mancision, 1991; Pennock, 1992).

PREPARING FOR THE EVALUATION CONFERENCE

The success of any evaluation conference depends on one simple but often overlooked factor: careful preparation—not only by the principal but also by the teacher. Primary responsibility for planning, of course, rests with the principal.

Preparation begins with the principal's setting a tentative time for the conference and checking with the teacher for any schedule conflicts. When selecting a location, the principal should look for a neutral conference room rather than using his or her office or the teacher's classroom. The principal should then provide the teacher with written notice of the date, time, and location of the evaluation conference, along with a copy of any evaluation form that is to be used and instructions to the teacher suggesting that he or she complete the form as part of a self-appraisal activity, which might also include the teacher's analysis of any external factors or conditions that have affected his or her ability to meet expectations. If the teacher has been keeping a portfolio or otherwise collecting data for evaluation purposes, he or she should also be asked to organize and prepare the material for submission—preferably several days to a week prior to the evaluation conference. The following list summarizes the eight steps a principal should take to prepare for an evaluation conference:

1. Set date, time, and place of evaluation conference after confirming with the teacher his or her availability at that time.

2. Give the teacher a copy of the evaluation form, requesting that he or she use it for self-appraisal, if applicable.

3. Ask the teacher to organize, review, and submit any performance documentation collected.

4. Ask the teacher to be prepared to discuss successes, unmet challenges, factors interfering with his or her best performance, and what the principal or school system can do to help the teacher achieve his or her goals.

5. Review any job description and previous evaluation along with any performance goals that were set for the evaluation period.

6. Complete a tentative evaluation and prepare notes summarizing the teacher's successes and concerns.

7. Plan a "script" for addressing concerns tactfully.

8. Prepare questions to enable the teacher to provide meaningful analysis of his or her strengths and areas for improvement.

If there is a job description for the teacher, the principal should review that carefully, along with a copy of the previous evaluation, to refresh his or her memory of any goals that were set during the last evaluation conference and any areas in which the teacher was expected to improve performance. If the principal has kept any documentation about the teacher's performance (critical incidents log, notes from informal drop-ins or observations, calendar), he or she should review those also.

Finally, the principal should tentatively complete the evaluation form used by the school or district. This will give the principal a clearer idea of the teacher's strengths and successes as well as any problem areas and unmet expectations or goals. Where there are deficiencies, it is crucial that the principal be prepared to articulate clearly, yet tactfully, the nature of the problems and some specific examples of behaviors or outcomes in which those deficiencies were exhibited. In addition, the principal should develop some specific suggestions for improvement. Jotting down all of these ideas in advance of the evaluation conference will ensure that the principal is focused and thorough during the conference, as well as enhance the likelihood of communicating with tact when discussing any performance problems or deficiencies. If possible, the principal should conduct all of this review and appraisal several days or even weeks before the evaluation conference, to allow time to step back and regain objectivity and distance on the situation.

The teacher also must invest some time and effort in preparing for the evaluation conference. Ideally the principal will have provided the guidelines for such preparation, as described above, but in the absence of such guidelines, a teacher can maximize the benefits of the evaluation conference by taking the following steps:

- Collect, organize, and analyze any documentation generated during the evaluation period (sample assignments, tests, student work, pictures of displays, etc.).
- Review the job description (when available), previously set goals or objectives, and district or school mission statements.
- Complete a copy of the evaluation form provided by the principal.
- Identify major strengths and successes of the year.
- Identify any unmet expectations or goals and analyze possible reasons for failure to meet them, paying careful attention to factors both within and outside the teacher's control.

- Identify areas for growth (improvement or new directions) and possible goals or objectives for the next year.
- Identify how the principal or school system can help the teacher achieve greater effectiveness.

As the foregoing lists of activities necessary for effective preparation for an evaluation conference indicate, this conference is ideally an opportunity for reflection not only on the teacher's performance but also on the climate and conditions in which the teacher works. It can—and should—become an opportunity for joint problem solving and for the principal to obtain valuable insight from the teacher about the "health" of the school. And, as we emphasize throughout this chapter, the evaluation conference should not be an isolated, once-yearly event; rather, it should be a structured conversation and reflection that is part of the ongoing and usually less formal feedback process characterizing the principal's working relationships with teaching staff.

CONDUCTING THE EVALUATION CONFERENCE

When the teacher arrives, the principal should do everything possible to establish a comfortable, relaxed atmosphere. To minimize authority barriers, the principal can sit next to the teacher, or both parties might sit in chairs on either side of an end table. The principal should have arranged in advance to remain uninterrupted by calls or visitors during the conference. Such prioritizing lets the teacher know how important he or she is and how important the conference itself is.

Many researchers suggest that the evaluator (in this case, the principal) invite the employee (the teacher) to share his or her self-appraisal first (Alexander Hamilton Institute, 1995; Buzzotta, 1988; Pennock, 1992). Research has demonstrated that evaluation conferences based on the employee's self-review "were significantly more constructive and satisfying to both parties than those based on the manager's appraisal. It also resulted in significant improvement in job performance" (Meyer, 1991, p. 72).

If the principal shares his or her evaluation first and then asks, "What do you think?" the teacher is in an awkward position and may well respond with a shrug and the only viable reply: "I'll go along with that." This pretty well closes the discussion, precluding exploration of facts or issues. An additional advantage of allowing the teacher to speak first is that when the teacher has not met certain predetermined expectations or has experienced performance problems that he or she is willing to admit, the principal is spared the awkwardness of initiating such criticism. Because we are all more willing to accept self-criticism than criticism from others, allowing the teacher to identify problem areas first can also defuse some of the emotional content of the conference and reduce the natural defensiveness that interferes with receptivity to suggestions for improvement (Stronge & Helm, 1991). Clearly, if there are performance problems the teacher refuses to recognize, the principal must be willing to convey his or her concerns. If the principal has taken time in advance to prepare how to convey those concerns, this will greatly enhance the effectiveness of the evaluation conference.

To the extent that specific performance goals or objectives were set at the previous evaluation conference, the principal may open the conversation by asking the teacher to review the major goals and then indicate how close he or she came to accomplishing those goals. For example: "Eric, last year we agreed on two major goals you would pursue. Let's review what those were and the extent to which you believe you achieved those goals." Another opening might be to ask the teacher to summarize major strengths or major successes during the evaluation period: "What have you felt particularly pleased with in your classroom teaching this semester?" This question is open-ended but invites— even requires—specifics.

After focusing on and commending the teacher's strengths and accomplishments, the principal can comfortably shift the focus by asking the teacher in what areas he or she might have done a better job or might be able to do a better job in the coming year. At this point, the principal may also ask what he or she can do to help the teacher achieve success in those areas cited for improvement.

In situations where the teacher has not attained a specific goal or level of performance, the principal should ask for an explanation. For example:

Principal: Cheryl, one of your goals for the year was to send fifty percent fewer students to my office for disciplinary action. How close do you think you came to reaching that goal?

Teacher: Well, Ms. Principia, I wasn't counting, but I'm afraid I didn't make the kind of improvement I had hoped to make.

Principal: What factors do you think made progress slower than you expected?

Teacher: I've given it some thought in preparation for this evaluation conference, and I think part of the problem was that I had a much larger number of at-risk students in my class this year. Instead of five out of twenty-five, I had twelve—that really makes a difference, you know.

Principal: Yes, Cheryl, we understand that it does. You didn't come to me for any additional assistance—did you contact the special education consultant or teacher for some suggestions for behavior modification?

Here, the principal shows that she has listened and understands, but also conveys awareness that the teacher bears some responsibility for taking initiative to solve her own problems.

Admittedly, explanations may sometimes consist of making excuses, in which case the principal must prod the teacher to go beyond making excuses. The principal might continue: "Ed, not hearing the alarm clock doesn't justify your frequent tardiness—which is unacceptable. What ideas do you have for getting yourself to school on time?"

Sometimes, however, there will be times when legitimate mitigating circumstances, such as those in Cheryl's scenario above, should be taken into account in the final evaluation. Furthermore, the principal's asking the teacher to discuss the context and external or environmental factors affecting his or her performance may reveal some important information about the school or classroom environment that can be the basis for problem solving to remedy the situation.

WHAT ARE THE CHARACTERISTICS OF EFFECTIVE EVALUATION CONFERENCES?

The literature of performance appraisal reveals several components of effective evaluation conferences. Specifically, the five elements described below are central.

Two-Way Communication

Numerous studies have shown that the more an employee (i.e., the teacher) participates in the evaluation conference, the more satisfied he or she will be with the conference and the supervisor (principal) (see, e.g., Anderson & Barnett, 1987; Krein, 1990; Webb, 1989). Principals who listen more than they talk will obtain more useful information about teachers' performance and development needs. Encouraging substantial contributions by the teacher also ensures greater commitment of the teacher to the process, which in turn improves the likelihood of success during the next evaluation cycle.

Balanced Review of Past Performance and Future Goals

We in education have too frequently focused on past or present performance. As we emphasize setting performance goals or developing professional growth plans, we must devote more of the evaluation conference to development of those goals and plans for future professional growth. Again, applying lessons taken from research literature in education, business, and other professions, principals are well advised to encourage teachers to take the initiative in identifying the goals and plans that are most meaningful to the school. This serves a dual purpose: (a) It ensures ownership of the goals selected for the teacher to pursue during the next evaluation period, and (b) it contributes to the teacher's positive perceptions about the evaluation conference itself (Downs, 1990).

Recognition of Teacher Strengths and Successes

This component is one that hardly needs repeating, given that principals already realize the impact of such recognition on motivation and morale. What is important to remember, however, is that the more specific the commendations, the more meaningful they are to the receiver. Keeping a "critical incidents log" of particular events or successes throughout the year can aid the principal in developing a list of examples to reference when making generalized comments. (Presumably, the principal also will have commended the teacher at the times the successes occurred.)

Identification and Analysis of Problems Affecting the Teacher's Performance

Few teachers will meet or exceed all goals or expectations set the previous year, assuming the goals and expectations are adequately rigorous. Where there are disappointments (failures) in meeting those expectations, the principal should encourage the teacher to first identify and then analyze the reasons for these unmet goals or performance expectations. The purpose is to understand the context for these failures and then to move immediately toward identifying solutions to the problems that interfered with maximum effectiveness. The principal should be especially quick to ask what he or she can do to help resolve the problem(s) identified. The principal can also ask what the teacher believes he or she can do to contribute to solving the problem. Realistically, we should add that where the principal has identified performance problems overlooked or unconfessed by the teacher, he or she will, of course, need to present those concerns to the teacher tactfully and then pursue the joint problem solving discussed earlier.

Teacher Initiation of Goals for the Next Evaluation Cycle

Allowing the teacher to be actively involved in the goal-setting process has been shown to be a more powerful catalyst for later performance than a general discussion about goals (Anderson & Barnett, 1987). Creating a sense of ownership in the goals or job expectations may be the most potent factor, not only in commitment to those goals but also in the teacher's perception of the success of the evaluation conference (Klein & Snell, 1994). The principal can facilitate the teacher's goal setting by asking questions that derive from the conversation about achievements and areas for growth (which might be areas for improvement or development of new skills/knowledge) earlier in the conference. Again, the principal should be prepared to offer a couple of goals on those occasions when a teacher is unwilling or unable to suggest some.

To reiterate, the characteristics of an effective evaluation conference can be summarized as follows:

1. Two-way dialogue, a majority of which is teacher talk

2. Balanced review of past performance and planning for the next evaluation cycle

3. Principal's recognition of the teacher's strengths and successes

4. Identification and analysis of problems affecting the teacher's performance

5. Teacher initiation of goals for performance improvement for the next evaluation cycle

HOW CAN PRINCIPALS FACILITATE PRODUCTIVE TEACHER TALK?

As mentioned earlier, the more the teacher contributes to the evaluation conference, the more likely the event will be perceived by both principal and teacher as effective. A good talking ratio has been suggested as 80% teacher, 20% principal (Alexander Hamilton Institute, 1995).

We have already suggested as good openers (after any initial small talk) questions that elicit the teacher's perception of his or her strengths and successes or the teacher's review of previously established goals/objectives and the extent to which he or she has achieved them. Some teachers, however, may be reticent about speaking in the conference, whether because of shyness, anxiety, or possibly even resentment. A principal who responds to such reticence by doing all of the talking, however, will be left worse off than before the conference, and so will the teacher. No productive dialogue having occurred, the teacher will feel no ownership in the event or its outcome, nor will that teacher have any reason to be committed to any goals or expectations set solely by the principal. How can a principal get such a teacher to talk? A number of useful strategies are discussed below (Alexander Hamilton Institute, 1995).

Silence

Silence can be effective because it is not judgmental or offensive. When the teacher makes a negative statement (e.g., "This class is making me crazy" or "I think these evaluations are a waste of time"), a response of silence by the principal invites the teacher to say more. If the principal can wait in silence, the teacher will often go on to provide details. By not responding judgmentally, the principal does not put the teacher on the defensive. It takes a lot of fortitude to use this strategy, because we are all conditioned to fill silences. The principal who can let that conditioning compel the teacher, however, may gain valuable information as well as be perceived as an excellent listener.

Staying on Track

Although it is true that we have emphasized the importance of teacher talk, it is equally important that the teacher talk about performance-related issues. Thus, the principal is responsible for directing the conversation and keeping it going. He or she must continually probe for specific information and ideas, in part by avoiding questions that produce "yes," "no," or "I guess so" answers. The question, "Do you think you're doing a good job in the classroom?" is a start, but it is not as effective as, "How do you feel you're doing in the class-room?" Even more effective would be such questions as, "What aspects of teaching do you feel you do especially well?" and, "What do you do in the class-room that you feel especially good about?" These questions invite not only a list of several behaviors but almost inevitably a brief discussion of the importance or results of those behaviors. Closed-ended questions producing all but useless answers tend to begin with "Did you," "Will you," or "Can you," as well as "How many" or "When."

Open-Ended Questions

Open-ended questions invite expansive, thoughtful, and informative answers. For example, if the principal asks, "Why do you think you're having trouble keeping students in their seats?" the question encourages the teacher to state the cause, making him or her less defensive than if the principal had offered the same explanation. The principal can then go on to ask, "How would you suggest we deal with this?" This question makes teacher and principal part-ners in solving the problem.

Drawing Out Explanations

When a teacher gives a cursory answer, the principal can invite further detail by making such requests as, "Give me the details," "Please explain that," "Say a little more," or "Tell me a little more about that." To invite somewhat more thoughtful reflection on a teacher's decisions, a principal might ask, "How did you happen to choose that strategy?" or "What was your rationale for choosing that approach?" Usually the most reticent teacher will be able to con-tinue with such prodding, but the principal may still need to exercise the silence strategy to accomplish the goal of obtaining a fuller explanation.

Presenting a Problem

Another way a principal might obtain an open-ended response is to present a real or hypothetical problem to the teacher and ask for a possible solution. "Suppose we were to say that we need to reduce the number of students you send to the office by 50% next year. What might each of us do to accomplish this goal?" An alternative might simply be to establish the goal as a schoolwide goal or as a goal for a hypothetical teacher. Such questions not only help the principal assess the teacher's approach to problems but also lead to realistic goal setting for the next year.

Active Listening

Active listening goes beyond the silence approach discussed above, and it takes a variety of possible forms. Responsive listening entails both verbal and nonverbal responses, such as nodding the head, smiling, or saying "I see," or "I understand." Empathic listening, on the other hand, entails restatement to the speaker, indicating that one understands what he or she has said. For example, the teacher may say, "The worst part of the job is grading exams and projects. The reason my semester grades are late so often is because the grading is so unpleasant." The principal might then reply, "You really find it that unpleasant to do?" No judgment has been communicated, but the teacher knows the principal has heard and understands the teacher's feelings about the task. Conveying judgment, advice, or sarcasm will be less effective. For instance,

- *Judgment:* "We need those grades turned in on time so that all the report cards can be sent out on schedule."
- *Advice:* "You'd better start getting those grades in on time or you're going to be in serious trouble."
- *Sarcasm:* "I thought you must enjoy grading, since you are so reluctant to end the process by turning the grades in."

These kinds of responses are guaranteed to make the teacher defensive and resistant to suggestions or recommendations for improvement.

Other Listening Skills

Following are a few additional suggestions for principals to improve their genuine listening during the evaluation conference (Alexander Hamilton Institute, 1995):

- Remember to talk less. You'll learn more.
- Don't make hasty judgments. Seek instead to probe for real reasons behind problems or behind stated explanations.
- Read the nonverbal cues. When there is a discrepancy between what the teacher says verbally and what the body language indicates, the principal should inquire directly about that discrepancy.
- Don't interrupt. Even if the principal has figured out what the teacher is going to say, it is rude and conveys disinterest in the teacher to finish the sentence for him or her or to interrupt with a response before the teacher has finished.
- Acknowledge ideas. There is a difference between accepting and acknowledging a teacher's idea. Acknowledging the idea, and even going beyond to state its benefits or impacts, conveys the principal's receptivity to ideas, which will help ensure continued sharing of ideas.
- Ask for clarification. An excellent way of communicating to a teacher that he or she is being carefully listened to is to ask for clarification or expansion where the description is vague or general. Such follow-up can produce valuable recommendations or suggestions.

Use of Pronouns

It is important for evaluators to be aware of possible evaluatee responses to statements dealing with performance problems. Generally the literature suggests avoiding *you* and *your* statements, which can sound judgmental and make people defensive. For example, the statement "Your grading standards are too unrealistic" will only make a teacher resistant to suggestions for change. An alternative approach might be to say "Many of your students feel that your grading standards are so high that there is no point in trying." Here, the principal places the emphasis on the students' perceptions. This might lead into an open-ended question or request for an explanation designed to get at the root of the problem: "We appreciate any teacher who sets and holds to high standards for their students. It is not the easy thing to do. But we would be interested to learn your rationale for setting standards so high that no student earns an A." Now the teacher has an opportunity to reflect on why he or she gives lower grades than other teachers, and the principal may be able to probe further by asking how effectively this approach enables the teacher to achieve the expressed goal.

Some authorities suggest replacing *you* statements with *we* statements, but it seems there is a spectrum from *you* through *we* to *I*, or to a *we* question. "You ought to start your classes as soon as the bell rings" places the emphasis on the teacher and what he or she should do. "*We* want you to start your classes as soon as the bell rings" changes the emphasis to the principal and what he or she wants. But an even more effective approach would be to say, "We all benefit when teachers start their classes on time. Is there anything we on the staff can do to help you do this more often?"

Focus on Results or Impact

In the case of a teacher who frequently starts classes late, the principal might explain, "When you start your classes as soon as the bell rings, your students will be more likely to arrive on time, get in their seats, and spend more time on task. It's a good way to communicate your expectations and minimize student disruption." Or in the case of a teacher who consistently turns in grades late, the principal might ask, "Have you ever thought about the consequences to the system when a teacher turns grades in late?" By shifting the focus from the teacher's behavior to the impact or results of that behavior, the principal enables the teacher to look at the issue more objectively and less defensively.

CONCLUDING THE INTERVIEW

Principals hardly need reminding of the importance of concluding an evaluation conference on a constructive, encouraging note. After summarizing the teacher's main accomplishments and strengths and reviewing one or two areas targeted for professional growth in the next year, the principal should conclude with a couple of additional statements or questions designed to bring closure to the interview and to motivate the teacher toward continued dedication. For example, the principal might ask, "Carol, before we finish, do you have any questions about the appraisal or about our expectations for you next year?" Then, the principal might conclude,

> Carol, you make an invaluable contribution to our school community. Your dedication and your competence are recognized by many others besides myself. You're to be commended for your willingness to try out the new science curriculum next year. If you run into any difficulties, we hope you'll drop by—you know we'll provide whatever support we can.

Or, if it has been necessary to emphasize some areas for remediation, the principal may reshape the conclusion along these lines:

> Kent, your subject-area competence is unquestioned. Your students like you, and we know you have unrealized potential at this point. As you work on classroom discipline, please feel free to contact me for additional help or chat with one of your colleagues down the hall. I am confident that we'll be seeing far fewer of your students in my office next year.

SUMMARY

The most successful evaluation conference is a dialogue between principal and teacher, not a monologue by the principal. That dialogue, in fact, should contain much more teacher talk than principal talk. This conference is a more structured component of an ongoing supervisory system that approximates the coaching function, with regular, immediate, and specific feedback. Both principal and teacher must spend time reviewing and reflecting on the previous evaluation period in order to maximize the time spent in conferencing. Discussion is not limited to the "what" of teacher performance but also explores the "why" and "how" of that performance; it also focuses on the larger context in which the teacher's performance must be appraised. As such, the conference can also become an excellent forum for problem solving, as teacher and principal identify constraints on or obstacles to the teacher's maximum performance. The focus is not limited to the past, however. It should also include significant emphasis on the future and on any areas the teacher or principal has identified as new opportunities for professional growth or improvement. Finally, the evaluation conference should make it clear that the principal is committed to providing assistance and support as the teacher undertakes new challenges or attempts to correct performance deficiencies.

Despite policies that seek to limit discussions of teacher quality to measurements linked to mandated standards and benchmarks, evaluation conferences characterized by the features described above will be successful because the teacher will have participated as a professional, will feel appreciated and valued, and will have offered many of the major insights and much of the direction for the coming year. The principal and teacher will leave the conference with renewed appreciation for each other and fresh awareness of a mutual commitment to the school community and the learning enterprise.

REFERENCES

Alexander Hamilton Institute. (1995). *Effective interviews for every situation*. Ramsey, NJ: Modern Business Reports.

Anderson, G. C., & Barnett, J. G. (1987). Characteristics of effective appraisal interviews. *Personnel Review, 16*(4), 18–25.

Berry, B. (2004). Recruiting and retaining "highly qualified teachers" for hard-to-staff schools. *NASSP Bulletin, 87*(638), 5–27.

Blumberg, A. (1980). *Supervisors & teachers: A private cold war*. Berkeley, CA: McCutchan.

Buzzotta, V. R. (1988). Improve your performance appraisals. *Management Review, 77,* 40A3.

Darling-Hammond, L., & Sykes, G. (2003). Wanted: A national teacher supply policy for education: The right way to meet the "Highly Qualified Teacher" challenge. *Education Policy Analysis Archives, 11*(33). Retrieved October 28, 2004, from http://epaa.asu.edu/epaa/v11n33/

Derven, M. (1990). Assessment: The paradox of performance appraisals. *Personnel Journal, 69,* 107–111.

Downs, T. M. (1990). Predictors of communication satisfaction during performance appraisal interviews. *Management Communication Quarterly, 3,* 33–354.

Education Commission of the States. (2004). *The teacher professionalism model: Summary*. Denver, CO: Author. Retrieved October 28, 2004, from http://www.ecs.org

Glickman, C., Gordon, S., & Ross-Gordon, J. (2004). *SuperVision & instructional leadership: A developmental approach* (6th ed.). Boston: Pearson Allyn-Bacon.

Heneman, H., III, & Milanowski, A. (2003, June). Continuing assessment of teacher reactions to a standards-based teacher evaluation system. *Journal of Personnel Evaluation in Education, 17,* 173–195.

Holland, P. (1998). Processes and techniques in supervision. In G. Firth & E. Pajak (Eds.), *Handbook of research on school supervision* (pp. 397–408). New York: Macmillan.

Hunter, M. (1980). Six types of educational conferences. *Educational Leadership, 37,* 409.

Hunter, M. (1984). Knowing, teaching and supervising. In P. Hosford (Ed.), *Using what we know about teaching*. Alexandria, VA: Association for Supervision and Curriculum Development.

Klein, H. J., & Snell, S. A. (1994). The impact of interview process and context of performance appraisal interview effectiveness. *Journal of Managerial Issues, 6,* 160–175.

Krayer, K. J. (1987). Simulation methods for teaching the performance appraisal interview. *Communication Education, 36,* 276–283.

Krein, T. J. (1990). Performance reviews that rate an "A." *Personnel, 67*(5), 38–41.

Losyk, B. (1990/1991). Face to face: How to conduct an employee appraisal interview. *Credit Union Executive, 30*(4), 24–26.

Mancision, J. (1991). The appraisal interview: Constructive dialogue in action. *Health Care Supervisor, 10,* 41–50.

McGreal, T. L. (1988). Evaluation for enhancing instruction: Linking teacher evaluation and staff development. In S. J. Stanley & W. J. Popham (Eds.), *Teacher evaluation: Six prescriptions for success* (pp. 1–29). Alexandria, VA: Association for Supervision and Curriculum Development.

Meyer, H. H. (1991). A solution to the performance appraisal feedback enigma. *Academy of Management Executive, 5,* 68–76.

Milanowski, A. (2003). The varieties of knowledge and skill-based pay design: A comparison of seven new pay systems for K-12 teachers. *Education Policy Analysis Archives, 11*(4). Retrieved October 28, 2004, from http://epaa.asu.edu/epaa/v11n4/

Nathan, B. R., Mohrman, A. M., Jr., & Milliman, J. (1991). Interpersonal relations as a context for the effects of appraisal interviews on performance and satisfaction: A longitudinal study. *Academy of Management Journal, 34,* 352–369.

National Commission on Teaching and America's Future. (2003). *No dream denied.* Washington, DC: author. Retrieved October 28, 2004, from http://www.nctaf.org

National Commission on Teaching and America's Future. (2004). *Strengthening and sustaining teachers project.* Washington DC: Author. Retrieved October 28, 2004, from http://www.nctaf.org

Pennock, D. (1992). Effective performance appraisals (really!). *Supervision, 53*(8), 14–16.

Popham, W. J. (1988). Judgment-based teacher evaluation. In S. J. Stanley & W. J. Popham (Eds.), *Teacher evaluation: Six prescriptions for success* (pp. 56–77). Alexandria, VA: Association for Supervision and Curriculum Development.

Scriven, M. (1988). Evaluating teachers as professionals: The duties-based approach. In S. J. Stanley & W. J. Popham (Eds.), *Teacher evaluation: Six prescriptions for success* (pp. 110–142). Alexandria, VA: Association for Supervision and Curriculum Development.

Somerick, N. M. (1993). Strategies for improving employee relations by using performance appraisals more effectively. *Public Relations Quarterly, 38*(3), 37–39.

Stronge, J., & Helm, V. (1991). *Evaluating professional support personnel in education.* Newbury Park, CA: Sage.

Tsui, A. F., Law, Y., & Shum, M. (2001). Roles and relationships in tripartite supervisory conferencing processes. *Journal of Curriculum & Supervision, 16*(4), 322–344.

U.S. Department of Education. (2001). *No Child Left Behind act.* Washington DC: Author. Retrieved October 28, 2004, from http://www.ed.gov/policy/elsec/leg/esea02/index.html

Webb, C. (1989). Room for improvement: Performance evaluations. *Wilson Library Bulletin, 63*(6), 56–57, 125.

Additional Sources

Armentrout, B. W. (1993). Eight keys to effective performance appraisals. *HR Focus, 70*(4), 13.

Bushardt, S. C., Jenkins, J. M., & Byrd, P. C. (1990). Less odious performance appraisals. *Training and Development Journal, 44*(3), 29–35.

Goodale, I. G. (1992). Improving performance appraisal. *Business Quarterly, 57*(2), 65–70.

Latting, J. K. (1992). Giving corrective feedback: A decisional analysis. *Social Work, 37,* 424–430.

MacLean, J. C. (1994). Personnel evaluation in education: A model for job-specific criteria. *Clearing-House, 68*(1), 47–51.

Marien, B. A. (1992). Quality in R&D: Putting TQM into the performance review process. *Research-Technology Management, 35*(5), 39–43.

Plachy, R. J., & Plachy, S. J. (1993). Focus on results, not behavior. *Personnel Journal, 72*(3), 28–33.

Sandler, L. (1990). Two-sided performance reviews. *Personnel Journal, 69,* 75–78.

Dealing Positively With the Nonproductive Teacher

12

A Legal and Ethical Perspective on Accountability

Mary Jo McGrath

T he educational battle cry across the nation is *"No Child Left Behind!"* Yet accountability for producing that result is sending shock waves through the field of education, with people lining up for and against the means used to accomplish the end. Putting politics and varying opinions of the federal legislation aside, accountability for student achievement is an explosive and multifaceted dynamic in its own right.

Accountability involves the school district's organizational systems, as well as the individual behavior of the principal, the teacher, and the student. From a principal's leadership perspective, being accountable for student success calls into play responsibility for one's own professional effectiveness, the discomfort of holding others accountable for their performance results, and the paramount responsibility of answering to parents and the community for the quality of our children's education.

A broad and highly informative perspective on the issue of accountability, particularly as it relates to employee and managerial performance, can be found in the American judicial system and its educational law analysis and decisions. The judiciary has a long history of wrestling with accountability and determining what is appropriate and fair when passing judgment on a teacher's continued employment. From extensive inquiry, the courts have delineated practical criteria that provide sound guidance on what behaviors, on the part of both employees and management, determine quality performance and powerful administrative leadership.

Equally as important as these practical criteria governing actions is an assessment of the ethics of the culture and climate in which those actions are taken. For most people, *accountability* is a frightening word, implying "feet to the fire for failures." The fear people experience around accountability elicits blaming behavior to avoid responsibility, even among the most committed and ethical people.

For true progress to occur and excellence to become reality, these two tracks, practical criteria and workplace ethics, must merge into a cohesive management approach that balances the whole. Competent administration of successful schools must include both the skill and the courage to manage for the utmost success of students and staff.

In this chapter, I present the criteria for accountability and their companion ethical factors, and discuss how they should be incorporated into the day-to-day practices of school administrators. If this holistic approach is adopted, educators are much more likely to succeed in their efforts to be accountable and to realize the goal of quality education for all students.

THE LAW: PREDICAMENT OR OPPORTUNITY?

The decision to terminate a permanent teacher's employment based on faulty performance is reached after a multitude of events has taken place. These events involve all aspects of the school community, including administration, students, peers, and parents. Many aspects of the legal process are involved, often including lawyers, a trier of fact, and judicial review.

An assessment of the appropriateness of a teacher's dismissal also encompasses an analysis of many personal influences in the teacher's life: his or her health, marital difficulties, extended family complications, and the like. Particularly nerve-racking for the principal, teacher dismissal includes a close look at the competence of the administrator in the areas of leadership, supervision, documentation, and evaluation. The legal criteria that have arisen around this area of employment law have evolved to weigh and balance the whole when reaching a judgment on appropriate action.

As Marshall (1995) notes, "The unexamined application of Newtonian laws to social systems caused us to design . . . linear system(s) . . . when in fact human systems are complex, dynamic and organic" (p. 11). The multidimensional, dynamic nature of educational institutions is recognized in the law, and the legal criteria are designed to consider the interrelationships within the whole.

Teacher dismissal opens the door to detailed scrutiny of almost every aspect of a teacher's life, personal and professional, as well as scrutiny of the entire school site's functioning. Competent performance of an administrator in the area of evaluation and accountability is not just a matter of observing classroom performance, accumulating input from portfolios or other means, and writing comprehensive summary evaluations. It is also a matter of being attuned to the entire organism that constitutes a teacher as a whole human being, as well as a school as an organic organization.

This systemic approach can be viewed as a predicament or an opportunity. Perhaps the highest measure of administrator competence is the fair, ethical, and professional treatment of employees and how successfully the administrator incorporates such treatment into day-to-day practices that hold people to account for excellence in education. When professional administrators realize that the judicial process surrounding teacher dismissal considers the whole of the situation from an educational, legal, and ethical perspective, they may be stimulated to learn what factors are taken into account and how best to incorporate those factors into their everyday routines.

HOW DOES THE LAW OF ACCOUNTABILITY CONSIDER THE WHOLE?

Typically, we hear the phrase *the law* and we think two things: Trouble is brewing, and we are going to get tied up doing things that are irrelevant to getting the real job of educating students done. Recently, one educator challenged the usefulness of the law as applied to education, pointing out that the legal system seems to be the only societal system in more trouble than education. In reality, the law of accountability applied to teacher evaluation and termination is very broad, flexible, and—believe it or not—user-friendly.

It is important to distinguish between the procedural aspects of the law, which apply to such things as hearing rights and appellate review, and the criteria that have evolved within the law related to the actual components of a teacher's performance and employment. Though the procedural protections can seem to be a ghastly maze, the substantive guidelines are based in thoughtful reflections that have emerged over time as courts have confronted poorly performing teachers and their impact on the students they educate. The judicial standards are in tune with the fundamental essence of the law, which is meant to address the question, "When people join together in an educational community, what should the rules be so that everyone thrives?" Viewed in this light, the legal criteria may be seen as a fit for educator temperament, which most often is that of nurturing caregiver, not quasi-lawyer and case builder.

There are three primary legal criteria that govern the area of teacher performance and retention: due process, just cause, and fitness for service. These concepts are used collectively to determine the appropriateness of the supervision and evaluation processes and, in the cases where necessary, whether a teacher should be removed from the classroom and his or her employment be terminated. What is even more important is that these criteria provide excellent guidance for the smooth functioning of the school as a dynamic organism. These legal concepts are discussed below in terms of their technical definitions and their translation for everyday use by administrators.

Due Process = Don't Surprise People

The assessment of the presence of due process on a day-to-day basis involves asking the question, "Is the teacher receiving notice of problems and an opportunity to correct them?" In legal terms, due process requires that a person receive notice of the charges against him or her, an opportunity to review any documentary evidence, and the chance to respond (Alexander & Alexander, 1985; *Cleveland Board of Education v. Loudermill*, 1985). The practical essence of this legal concept is to give employees a contemporaneous opportunity to be informed of and to correct deficiencies when they are originally noted by the administrator. Said in common parlance, people should not be surprised and blindsided by deficiencies that show up in their summary evaluation reports.

An administrator should avoid at all costs the practice of creating hidden personal files on employees—files filled with anecdotal notes and records of things the administrator has observed or heard about concerning employees as they go about their duties. Often an administrator will fail to inform an employee that such information exists until a situation deteriorates. Sometimes an employee will see a reference to a complaint based on behaviors observed many months earlier, or a past parent complaint, for the first time during a final evaluation. If an administrator is keeping such a hidden file, the teacher has the right, legally and ethically, to know about it and its contents.

In order to observe fairness and not surprise an employee after the fact, administrators must follow these four steps in the maintenance of any tangible material on the employee:

1. The employee must be informed that the material exists and is being retained.

2. The employee must be informed of his or her right to comment in writing and have the comment included with the original material.

3. This notification must be done in a timely fashion, meaning within a reasonable amount of time so that the employee can remember pertinent facts about the event recorded and respond to the concerns stated.

4. The source of the information must not be anonymous or unidentified to the employee (*Miller v. Chico Unified School District*, 1979). (It is acceptable for client surveys [e.g., parent/student surveys] to be designed to be anonymous.)

Just Cause = Be Fair

Just cause fundamentally means, "Be fair." This legal concept has been interpreted by arbitrators and judges as requiring in all cases an assessment of the totality of the circumstances. In any individual case of contested evaluation or termination, everything about the situation is taken into account, from employee conduct to management response. Key questions asked in judicial review are as follows:

1. What did the teacher do or not do?

2. How did those behaviors affect the school community, including pupils, coworkers, staff, administrators, and parents?

3. What context was the teacher working within? (a) Were the supervisor and school district acting in good faith, clearly pointing out problem areas and diligently and honestly striving to assist in improvement? (b) Were there unforeseen difficulties operating as extenuating circumstances that need to be considered?

The courts have ruled that for determining the propriety of the termination of an employee, the terms *just cause* and *good cause* have been difficult to define and depend on the circumstances of each case. Essentially, these terms connote a fair and honest cause or reason, regulated by good faith on the part of the party exercising the power (*Moore v. May Dept. Stores Co.*, 1990). The actions of the employee alone are rarely enough to warrant termination. They are considered in the context of the actions of management.

Fitness for Service = Don't Be Nitpicky

The fitness for service criterion takes into account many different factors that, when taken together, answer the question, "Was the disruption significant to the educational process or was it inconsequential?" (See *Morrison v. State Board of Education*, 1969.) If the answer is that it was inconsequential, the likelihood that an evaluation can be thrown out is high, and the likelihood that dismissal will occur is low.

In determining fitness for service, courts take a look at matters that actually show that a teacher should not continue in the classroom because of the harm being generated (*Bassett Unified School District v. Commission on Professional Competence*, 1988; *Morrison v. State Board of Education*, 1969). These factors fall into the eight categories described below.

Harm Caused by the Conduct

The courts look to see whether the conduct engaged in by the teacher actually resulted in harm, that is, disruption of the educational process or impairment of teacher-student relationships. Harm may be detected in several areas—not just to students, but also in negative impact on the school district, the teachers, classified staff, administration, and/or the community. Without a showing of harm, it is nearly impossible to terminate a teacher.

On a regular basis, it is important for the administrator not only to specify the behavior a given employee is engaged in that is considered less than satisfactory, but also to track that behavior to its impact on students, staff, and others. The administrator should ask himself or herself, "What do I say, in my professional opinion, is the impact on students, teachers, staff, administration, community, parents, or others?" He or she should then record the answers in the documentation, along with a specific description of the behaviors observed. This factor is governed by the principle that having an employee be considerate of his or her impact on others is essential to the employee's understanding that what he or she does affects other people and matters to the smooth functioning of the whole.

Notoriety of Conduct

Courts may look at the notoriety of the teacher's conduct in considering the seriousness of any disruption caused by the teacher's behavior. What this means on a practical level is that the administrator should determine whether the improper conduct is known to others and whether it is disrupting the teacher-student or teacher-parent relationship or impairing the reputation of the school district. Here the question the administrator should ask is, "What are the comments from others (coworkers, faculty, administration, community, students, parents, public) about the impact or effects of this behavior/incident/ pattern of conduct?" The guiding ethical principle is that people are accountable for the reputations they generate by their actions and are answerable to others for their effectiveness. The administrator must be sure that complaints received are not secreted away, but shared contemporaneously with the employee. Also, the administrator must follow any parent complaint procedure established in his or her school district.

Proximity or Remoteness in Time

The courts look to see whether the conduct charged against an employee is recent. If the conduct occurred so long ago that it can be said to be stale, the remoteness of the conduct will argue against its inclusion in the evaluation or dismissal of the employee. Note that if the administrator responds to situations in a timely fashion, the issue of proximity in time will not be a problem. Being timely with the communication of problems to the employee goes along with the notice requirements detailed above in regard to the retention of documentation. To check themselves on timeliness, administrators should ask the question, "What is today's date? Is it near in time to the incident/conduct at issue?" The ethical principle here involves the administrator's effort to be aboveboard in the management of issues, disciplining himself or herself to handle things as they come up, and not procrastinating.

Extenuating or Aggravating Circumstances

The fitness for service criterion examines whether there is something happening surrounding the activity of the teacher that would either explain the conduct or be an additional aggravating circumstance, rendering the conduct even more of a problem. An example of the former would be if an employee's spouse has just suffered a very severe illness or the loss of a job. An example of the latter would be a case in which the employee has been continually advised of the requirement to be at school on time and there has been continuing failure to improve performance. The question the administrator should ask here is, "Were there any extenuating circumstances (identified by the administrator or the employee) that are external to the employee that are affecting performance?" The principles of awareness and compassion should lead managers to make judgments that take into account the whole of the circumstances and factor them into the solution.

Motive for Conduct

It is crucial to determine early in the process whether the teacher has any attitudinal justification for how he or she is behaving. If this factor is ignored, at the time of trial an understandable "excuse" may be given that undermines the district's ability to obtain a dismissal. The employee should be asked at the investigative conference regarding the conduct why he or she has engaged in the behavior, and any response should be recorded in the conference memorandum. The administrator should answer the question, "What statements or conduct reflects the internal motivation or attitude of the individual about this conduct/incident/pattern of conduct?" On an ethical basis, the administrator is assessing the employee's will to address the issue and whether he or she can be counted on to bring forth a commitment to its resolution.

Prior Help Given

An important factor is whether an employee has been notified of the improper conduct *and* provided assistance in an effort to remediate the problem. A key aspect here is whether the teacher made any effort to correct the situation, particularly after receiving help, advice, or direction from the administration. Also important is whether the administration has provided assistance appropriate to correction of the deficiencies; usually, this is understood to include the district's paying for such training and providing release time. The administrator should determine the following: Did the individual have any training, inservice, teacher preparation, course work, or the like that relates to the focus of the communication? Principled management requires that the administrator consider whether he or she has provided the remedial assistance needed so the employee can succeed.

Likelihood of Recurrence

Determination of the likelihood of recurrence of the same type of conduct seems to require a crystal ball. It is reasonable and necessary to speculate or predict into the future based on conduct that has occurred in the past. When the administrator has identified that a pattern of performance is occurring, he or she should point this out in a memorandum to the employee, using words to the following effect: "I am concerned that your conduct is likely to recur based on the fact that to date you have failed to take any steps to rectify the situation." This type of language places the determination of likelihood of recurrence in the administrator's hands. The administrator should answer the question, "Is there a continuing pattern of conduct that persists despite attempts at remediation?" The principle here is that the administrator should be sure to consider the current incident in the context of overall performance and not overreact to a single incident (unless the single incident is truly flagrant or harmful to students or others).

Chilling Effect on Legal Rights

Demands on teachers should not violate any rights they have as employees under federal, state, or other relevant laws or collective bargaining provisions. Whenever a request is made of an employee, it should be educationally sound and supported by sufficient reason, not just a preference of the administration that has no demonstrable, educational rationale. The pertinent question is, "What are the rights of the individual balanced against the rights of the people who may be affected or harmed by the conduct?" Weighing the competing rights of all parties brings into play the principle of balance and justice, allowing for a wise, informed decision.

Incompetence/Unsatisfactory Performance as a Basis for Dismissal

Incompetence has been described as "a relative term which may be employed as meaning disqualification, inability or incapacity. The term can refer to lack of legal qualifications or fitness to discharge the required duty" (Gifis, 1984). Incompetence or unsatisfactory performance must be proved by a pattern of conduct rather than a single instance of behavior. Proof of charges of incompetence can come from good classroom observations, reviews of portfolios, client surveys, student outcomes, and other related evidence of performance, documented over the period of time in question, as well as thorough summary evaluations. Other evidence and testimony of students and parents can also be important.

The most important factor in proving a case of incompetence/unsatisfactory performance is the ability to show that the individual has been specifically notified of the areas that are deficient, provided a remediation plan by his or her supervisor, and given the assistance and time needed to correct these inadequacies in classroom performance (McGrath, 1993). In such cases the administrator's credibility and effectiveness are at issue. The administrator should be shown as a compassionate and helpful partner to the teacher in his or her attempts to improve teaching performance.

Other important sources of information in incompetence cases are parent and student complaints. It is essential that when a parent indicates a concern about a teacher, the administrator request that the parent put his or her concerns in writing. If the matter is resolved satisfactorily and does not form the basis of an ongoing pattern, the document probably will be of little importance. If there is an ongoing pattern of incompetent conduct, however, the document will prove to be invaluable. It will be used to refresh the recollection of the parent as to what his or her concerns were at the time. The parent complaint procedure of the school district must, of course, be followed.

A frequently asked question is, "What weight is given to the complaints of students?" A single complaint by a student regarding the competence of a teacher does not carry much weight. However, an ongoing pattern of complaints received by the administration against a particular teacher will help document that there is an ongoing pattern of incompetence or unsatisfactory performance. Additional sources of information, such as tests, quizzes, transfer requests, nurse's referrals, and disciplinary referrals, will probably also be needed to show a pattern of conduct.

Remediation Plans Are Crucial to Success

Any employment action taken against an employee should be preceded by an honest effort to remediate the deficient performance, unless the offense is so egregious that it calls for immediate dismissal (Frels, Cooper, & Reagan, 1984). Remediation plans should address the following questions:

1. What specific conduct or behavior must improve?

2. What resources will be provided to address the directed change (e.g., workshops, counseling, monitoring, mentoring, retraining, written technical assistance)?

3. What measures will be used to determine if the individual has been successful in meeting the directive(s) for change?

4. Is it appropriate to give a warning that disciplinary action will be taken if the behavior does not improve?

5. How will the administrator and the employee know if the requirements have been satisfactorily met?

6. When will the administrator communicate again with the employee to check progress?

7. Has the administrator listed any pertinent attachments, such as letters from parents or copies of previous memos to the individual on the behavior/conduct/incident in focus?

WHAT IS THE ARCHITECTURE OF ACCOUNTABILITY?

To understand the interrelatedness of the myriad elements that are part of employee performance and the legal analysis, it is helpful to use the metaphor of a building. To stay in the spirit of the topic, imagine an old schoolhouse. This metaphorical schoolhouse is made up of a floor, walls, and a roof (see Figure 12.1). The "architecture of accountability" can be viewed as similar to the structure of that schoolhouse. Consider the floor to be made up of the teacher's classroom and other work-related performance. The materials used to assess the quality of *performance output* consist of the following:

- *Performance standards* clearly communicated to all employees
- *Accountability records* of systematic monitoring of performance
- *Classroom observations* performed with objectivity and skill
- *Evaluation documents* that assess the whole, indicating patterns and setting forth plans where needed

These four elements are summed up in the acronym PACE.

Continuing the metaphor of the schoolhouse, the next part to consider in the architecture of accountability is the walls, which represent the *environmental impact* of the performance output. This part of the structure is made up of the impact of the teacher's performance as measured by the following:

- *Student* information, taking into account achievement and the variables that affect performance
- *Peer and parent* observations and opinions of the effect of the performance being measured
- *Administrative* factors that arise as a result of the teacher's performance, such as delayed reports or increased staff workload
- *Community relations,* as affected by the reputation the teacher and school have earned based on performance
- *Extenuating circumstances* that influence the performance

These elements are summed up in the acronym SPACE.

Finally, the roof of the schoolhouse is made up of the *management/staff relationship* and reflects the interpersonal skills of the manager as assessed by the following factors:

- *Commitment to success* of the teacher demonstrated by management
- *Assistance* provided to the teacher to accomplish remediation
- *Resources* allocated to the teacher's success
- *Encouragement* reflected in consistent feedback provided to the teacher

These elements are summarized by the acronym CARE.

If the jobs of supervision and evaluation are addressed, including all the elements represented in the architecture of accountability, administrators will succeed on many levels. They will be managers who are up-front, fair, and

Figure 12.1 The Successful Schoolhouse: The Architecture of Accountability

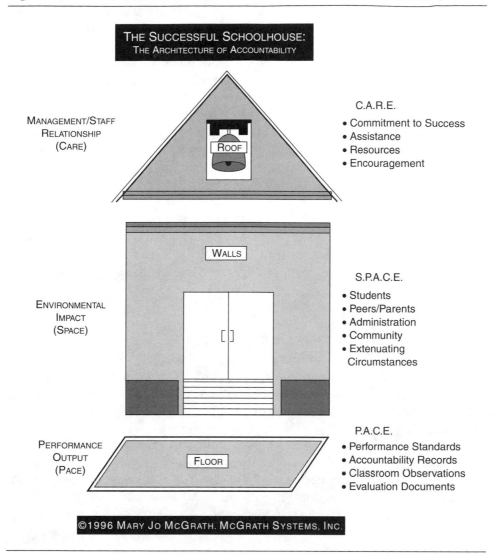

SOURCE: McGrath Systems, Inc. Copyright 1996 by Mary Jo McGrath. Reprinted by permission.

balanced, and will be complying with all aspects of the law of accountability. They will be both legally fit and principled.

EVALUATION AND DOCUMENTATION: WHY ARE THEY SO IMPORTANT?

An administrator's opinion that a given teacher should not be in the classroom will not be accepted at face value. The burden of proof is on the school district, which must prove by a preponderance of the evidence that the teacher should be dismissed, meaning that it is 51% more likely than not that the district's charge is true. The difficulty of that task is reflected in the percentage of cases in which school districts' decisions to terminate particular employees have not been upheld (Bridges, 1992).

Regardless of the difficulty, the needed action is systematic documentation of any existing problems, which leads to remediation or substantiates the case for dismissal. This documentation needs to be created in a systematic and contemporaneous fashion, as events occur. The primary vehicles for recording those actions are (a) accountability records of incidents that occur regarding work performance and their impact; (b) classroom observations, which memorialize a teacher's performance at a particular time and place; and (c) summary evaluations, which should pull together in a periodic fashion all the factual data regarding performance (McGrath, 1993).

In a teacher termination proceeding, the evidence presented must accurately substantiate the school district's decision to proceed to dismissal. Weak, inaccurate, careless, nonexistent, or procedurally improper evaluations and documents can greatly reduce the strength of a school district's position during a termination hearing.

Administrators who are assigned to evaluate teacher performance should receive extensive training in both supervision and evaluation processes. A simple truth is that the person on "trial" in a dismissal case is not necessarily the teacher, but rather his or her immediate supervisor. Insinuations and outright attacks on the administrator are frequent, and it is essential to establish administrator competence and credibility. One good way of establishing an administrator's competence is through an assessment of the quality of documentation he or she has produced.

Careful planning and teamwork among the supervising administrator, the administrator in charge of personnel, the superintendent, the governing board, and the attorney for the school district are essential. It takes a team and a commitment of resources to equip administrative staff to do the job of supervision, evaluation, and, on rare occasions, dismissal.

UNDERSTANDING THE CULTURE AND ETHICS OF ACCOUNTABILITY

Punishment Is Not the Way to Alter Culture

For any significant advancement to occur in the quality of education or in the enhancement of the environment in which teachers work, a transformation must occur. We must shift from a culture in which accountability is seen as punitive to one in which it is experienced as an opportunity for full self-expression and contribution. We tend to focus on the "doingness" of what should happen to remove ineffective teachers, training administrators in how to document unsatisfactory performance and apply progressive discipline. In the meantime, we have virtually ignored the "willingness" of educators to hold themselves and others accountable for the results that indicate quality education. In addition, we have largely ignored the culture and climate in which that willingness arises.

After a career of grappling with the issue of accountability and training administrators in effective supervision and evaluation, Bridges (1992) notes, "The challenge for scholars and practitioners alike is to find an answer to this fundamental question. 'How do we create organizational environments in which people willingly own, rather than deny or sidestep, performance problems?'" (p. 179).

Accountability Should Be an Opportunity, Not a Punishment

We can accomplish only so much when we set out to convince people to do what we want them to do, then they're going to do it their own way. School systems that mandate managers' strict supervision and evaluation of employees may experience success in the removal of unsatisfactorily performing people. However, long-term systemic change in the culture of accountability is highly questionable and may be negatively affected by a concentrated drive to rid the system of ineffective performance, especially if that drive fails to include increased communication with and acknowledgment of the successful teachers who make up the bulk of the teaching staff.

An example of such partial success is found in the case of a North Carolina school district that initiated a drive to rid its system of incompetence. The school board did a truly fine job of coordinating the efforts of administrators, legal counsel, and mentor teachers to provide an approach to identifying and evaluating less-than-satisfactory performers. Through this approach, the district identified 134 teachers who needed significant improvement and within two and one-half years removed 61 of those teachers, most through resignations and 4 through the formal dismissal process. Another 10% of the identified teachers lifted their performance to a standard at or above acceptable performance. The district was apparently successful, except that now it reports an unexpected backlash—the "fear factor." Effective employees expressed fear that they would be "next" and sought the protection of their union from this perceived onslaught on their ranks. Although they were consulted in designing the approach and agreed with the need to remove incompetence from their ranks, when it became a reality, it struck a nerve deep within.

This kind of reaction to the imposition of accountability is a phenomenon discussed by Argyris (1991):

> Many professionals have extremely "brittle" personalities. When suddenly faced with a situation they cannot immediately handle, they tend to fall apart. . . . There is no better example of how this brittleness can disrupt an organization than performance evaluations. . . . Indeed, a poor evaluation can reverberate far beyond the particular individual involved to spark defensive reasoning throughout an entire organization. (p. 25)

Argyris attributes this brittleness to a very common fear of failure. In studies he conducted with more than 6,000 people, he determined that the defensive reasoning individuals use to place the blame for failure outside of themselves is universal (Argyris, 1994).

Bridges (1992) has noted that his own analysis of the problem of managing the incompetent teacher underestimated the significance of one variable—owning the problem: "What I did not fully appreciate was how the responses of both teachers and administrators reflected a failure to own the problem. Nor did I realize how resistant people are to owning their problems and doing something about them" (p. 177). Grove (1985) identifies five steps to problem solving: ignore, deny, blame others, assume responsibility, and find a solution. He maintains that the process gets stuck at the "blame others" stage and therefore provides no insight into the organizational conditions that nurture or thwart problem ownership.

CONCLUSION

We must recognize that the current paradigm of accountability, which is linear rather than multidimensional and dynamic, flies in the face of people's innate understanding of the complexity of human behavior. This mismatch may result in administrators' not using such evaluation systems for the real management and assistance of their employees. Rather, they may use such systems only to "do what they're told," to satisfy school district requirements of evaluation. They do their real management of people "off the record," where they can employ their recognition of the whole person in context, both personal and professional.

What if we redefined accountability as an opportunity to learn from the natural outcome of shared vision, values, and commitment to the group's goals, considering the group to be an integrated, whole, dynamic organism? What if we deeply grounded our behaviors in principles and ethics that enhanced relatedness while calling for growth and excellence? Could excellence in education become a reality for all?

Teacher dismissal is the ultimate statement of accountability. It is the final process in which a school district calls a teacher to account for his or her failure to perform satisfactorily and stands accountable for its part in the failure to remediate the situation. Perhaps a key reason it is so difficult to take the step to terminate employment is that the current paradigm holds failure as an invalidation of the person's "self" that results in the need for punishment.

Another possible paradigm includes the view that accountability represents an opportunity to be part of the whole, to matter and to make a positive difference with our life's work, and if not where we are, then somewhere else. If we are failing and unable to course correct, we are being "told" we are in the wrong place to make the contribution we want to with our lives. Argyris (1994) notes that "people genuinely strive to produce what they intend. They value acting competently. Their self-esteem is intimately tied up with behaving consistently and performing effectively" (p. 79).

This interpretation of failure takes a great deal of maturity of self and cultural evolution. It is the end product of a shift in paradigm that we are only now glimpsing. The individual being terminated from employment may never reach this view of the whole situation, but the trier of fact and decision makers must, because (a) on a personal basis they need to feel good about what they are doing, (b) they need for their actions to fit with their values and principles of how people should be treated, and (c) legally, the judicial system is designed to ensure fair treatment of public employees, procedurally and substantively.

The law of accountability is not limited in its usefulness to when a teacher is to be terminated. We can learn and incorporate the legal criteria, and their ethical and principled underpinnings, for what they are—clear guidelines as to what factors need to be in place to determine (a) whether a human being has been treated well in the workplace, and (b) what the future should be for that person based on his or her accountability for producing excellence in education.

REFERENCES

Alexander, K., & Alexander, D. M. (1985). *American school law* (2nd ed.). St. Paul, MN: West.

Argyris, C. (1991). Teaching smart people how to learn. *Harvard Business Review, 69*(3), 20–30.

Argyris, C. (1994). Good communication that blocks learning. *Harvard Business Review, 72*(4), 77–85.

Bassett Unified School District v. Commission on Professional Competence, 201 Cal. App. 3d 1444 (1988).

Bridges, E. M. (1992). *The incompetent teacher: Managerial responses.* Washington, DC: Falmer.

Cleveland Board of Education v. Loudermill, 105 S. Ct. 1487 (1985), 721 F.2d 550 (Ct. App. 1983).

Frels, K., Cooper, T. T., & Reagan, B. R. (1984). *Practical aspects of teacher evaluation.* Topeka, KS: National Organization on Legal Problems of Education.

Gifis, S. H. (1984). *Law dictionary.* Woodbury, NY: Barron's.

Grove, A. (1985). *High output management.* New York: Vintage.

Marshall, S. P. (1995). The vision, meaning and language of educational transformation. *School Administrator, 1*(52), 8–13.

McGrath, M. J. (1993). When it's time to dismiss an incompetent teacher. *School Administrator, 50*(3), 30–33.

Miller v. Chico Unified School District, 24 Cal. 3d 703 (1979).

Moore v. May Dept. Stores Co., 222 Cal. App. 3rd 836 (1990).

Morrison v. State Board of Education, 1 Cal. 3d 214 (1969).

Teacher Evaluation and Professional Development $\mathbf{13}$

Stephen P. Gordon

Teacher evaluation and professional development are two leadership functions that historically have not been done well in our schools. All one needs to do is ask teachers from several schools what they think of the two functions as currently practiced and you will receive informal verification of this analysis, often in rather blunt terms. The most disturbing aspect of the current state of affairs is that we now have a strong knowledge base of what we need to do to improve teacher evaluation and professional development, with concrete models of effective teacher evaluation systems and professional development programs to point to. One necessary step in improving teacher evaluation and professional development is to disseminate the knowledge base on a wider level. The prior chapters in this book provide a range of theoretical, research, and practical knowledge on teacher evaluation. This chapter adds knowledge on effective professional development to this mix and makes connections between these two important functions—teacher evaluation and professional development.

The debate among scholars and practitioners about whether summative evaluation (as the basis for personnel decisions) and formative evaluation (as the basis for professional development) should be integrated or kept separate is addressed early in the chapter. Types of evaluation data that are more and less useful for professional development and school improvement are described. An argument is made that—for the sake of both professional development and school improvement—our concept of teacher evaluation should be expanded to the team and school level. The research on general characteristics of successful professional development programs is reviewed briefly. Twelve frameworks for professional development are presented, and the use of multiple frameworks in a professional development program is described. The chapter concludes with a prediction that teacher evaluation, professional development, and school improvement are all moving toward the same common denominator of improved student learning, along with suggestions on how teacher evaluation can be enhanced to foster professional development and school improvement.

WHAT IS THE FORMATIVE-SUMMATIVE CONTROVERSY?

The very *meaning* of summative and formative evaluation is a point of controversy, with some authors considering formative evaluation the long-term process of gathering evaluation data and summative evaluation the synthesis of those evaluation data in order to make personnel decisions (Beckham, 1985), while others describe formative evaluation as the basis for professional development and summative evaluation as the basis for personnel decisions (Danielson & McGreal, 2000). It is the latter pair of definitions around which the really significant controversy swirls: Should formative evaluation (for professional development) and summative evaluation (for personnel decisions) be integrated or be kept separate? Those who favor integrating the two say that they must be combined for the unity of the purpose and coherence needed for an effective evaluation system. Those who favor separating them consider their purposes to be fundamentally different, and argue that the trust, openness, and collegiality needed for professional development is endangered when summative evaluation is tied to formative evaluation for professional development.

Whether formative and summative evaluation are integrated or kept separate ultimately is a philosophical issue that must be addressed at the district and school level. It seems to me, however, that there are some propositions that both sides of the summative-formative controversy can readily accept. First, both formative and summative evaluations are necessary. Second, formative and summative evaluation must be consistent and coordinated with each other. Third, formative evaluation (at least), professional development, and school improvement must be integrated if student learning in our schools is going to improve. To those three straightforward propositions I will add a fourth that applies to either integrated or dual track teacher evaluation systems: Some types of evaluation data are more useful than others as a basis for professional development. This last proposition warrants further discussion.

WHAT EVALUATION DATA ARE MORE AND LESS USEFUL?

As indicated in other chapters in this book, evaluation of teaching has a variety of specific purposes beyond the broad categories of summative and formative. Certain types of evaluation data tend to be more appropriate for some purposes than for others, although in many cases a particular type of data can serve several purposes. Based on my work with districts and schools in a number of states as well as my own research, I'm confident that the types of data described here as more useful will lead to more meaningful and successful professional development. It is my guess that many proponents of both integrated and dual track evaluation systems will agree with the distinctions that are made.

Evaluation Data Focused on Teaching and Learning Rather Than Other Areas

The improvement of teaching and learning is the heart and soul of successful professional development programs. It makes sense, then, that teacher evaluation data focused on teaching and learning are the most valuable data for professional development. Here the phrase *teaching and learning* is used in the broad sense, including the curriculum that teachers convey, teaching practices, student assessment, and the relationship of all of these to student learning. Although the classroom certainly is a primary source for gathering data on teaching and learning, teachers' work on instructional teams and teachers' participation in schoolwide instructional improvement efforts also are valuable foci for teacher evaluation. Even though the gathering of evaluation data in other areas (meeting clerical responsibilities, assisting with extracurricular activities, etc.) might be necessary foci for teacher evaluation, these other types of data tend to be far less useful as input for professional development.

Evaluation Data Relevant to Local Standards Rather Than External Standards

Successful professional development programs focus on school improvement goals (Gordon, 2002; Joyce, Calhoun, & Hopkins, 1999). Effective teacher evaluation systems are based on school goals (Danielson & McGreal, 2000; Stronge & Helm, 1991). Taken together, these findings support aligning the school's improvement goals, teacher evaluation standards, and professional development program.

Evaluation Data That Are Contextual Rather Than Context Free

Teacher evaluation that is most useful for professional development gathers and analyzes data within the local context. This means considering the community that the school serves, the school culture, the school's mission and improvement goals, and the curriculum and instructional program. Teachers' career histories, levels of expertise, teaching styles, and instructional goals and concerns also must be taken into account. Finally, students' cultural backgrounds, prior learning, current needs, and learning styles should be considered. Analysis of context should influence the types of evaluation data collected and how evaluation data are interpreted. Consideration of contextual factors can create a serious headache for the legal expert who is focused on specific evaluation criteria and uniform application. From a professional development standpoint, however, contextualized teacher evaluation provides highly valuable input for teacher development.

Deep, Rich Evaluation Data Rather Than Efficiently Gathered, Simple Data

Teacher evaluation data that leads to successful professional development is by necessity deep, rich data. To assist professional development, teacher evaluation must go beyond identifying effective and ineffective practices or professional and unprofessional behavior. Evaluation data must help teachers, administrators, and staff developers to understand *why* things are as they are, and to examine the relationships of various aspects of teaching to each other and to student learning. Using multiple data sources and multiple data gathering methods goes a long way toward assuring the evaluation data will be deep and rich. Multiple data sources can include teachers, students, parents, classroom lessons, teachers' written reflections, teacher portfolios, student achievement data, student work products, teaching artifacts, and so on. Multiple data gathering methods can include self-assessments, conferences, classroom observations, videotaping, surveys, interviews, document review, and examination of artifacts, to name a few. Gathering a variety of data must be accompanied by collaborative analysis of the data by evaluators and teachers, as well as mutual agreement on the meaning of the data for the teachers' professional development.

Cumulative Data Based on Long-Term, Continuous Data Gathering Rather Than "One-Shot" Evaluations

Successful professional development is long-term and continuous (Glickman, Gordon, & Ross-Gordon, 2004; Gordon, 2000, 2002). This means that teacher evaluation that informs and measures professional development must involve long-term, continuous data gathering and analysis. Continuous teacher evaluation becomes a critical feedback loop for professional development. Teacher evaluation and professional development, if done well, become complimentary parts of a continuous improvement cycle.

LEVELS OF TEACHER EVALUATION AND PROFESSIONAL DEVELOPMENT

Conventional thinking about teacher evaluation and professional development is focused on individual teachers. Although individual evaluation and development are critical to improved student learning, there is a long line of evidence pointing to the need to evaluate teaching and promote professional development at the team and school level as well. Collegial analysis and evaluation of teaching are characteristics of improving schools (Little, 1982; Wasley, Hampel, & Clark, 1997; Joyce et al., 1999). In fact, evidence suggests that teachers in improving schools identify shared instructional goals, develop common technical knowledge, and take collective action to improve teaching and learning (Rosenholtz, 1989). Successful schools also focus on school development as a whole rather than on isolated teaching practices (Hopkins, Ainscow, & West, 1994). Collaborative inquiry and professional development, with small workgroups connected to the larger school community, increase the likelihood of school improvement (Joyce et al., 1999). Individual teacher evaluation, evaluation of instructional teams, and schoolwide evaluation of teaching are so interrelated they all need to be part of a single evaluation system linked to professional development and school improvement. Let us examine more closely teacher evaluation and professional development at the individual, team, and school level.

Individual Teacher Evaluation and Professional Development

From a professional development perspective, individual teacher evaluation needs to focus on the teacher's pedagogical, cognitive, and ethical development (Gordon, 2002), all of which have direct implications for the quality of teaching and learning at the classroom and school levels. Pedagogical development needs to be fostered in a number of specific areas, including

- building subject matter knowledge;
- understanding the district and school curriculum;
- diagnosing student learning needs, teaching methods, and student assessment; and
- working with parents to improve student learning.

Cognitive development involves growth in decision-making capacity in planning for teaching, during teaching, and in postanalysis of teaching. Ethical development includes things like developing commitment to educating the whole child, inclusion, and social justice. With the body of evidence we now have on the value of collaborative teams and schoolwide instructional improvement efforts, individual teacher evaluation should include such areas as collegiality, contributions to collaborative work, and connecting classroom practice to school improvement. The goal of individual teacher evaluation and professional development is to create reflective practitioners who work on continuous improvement of teaching and learning in their own classrooms and as members of the school community.

Team Evaluation and Professional Development

Examples of instructional teams are grade-level teams, content-area teams, interdisciplinary teams, inclusion teams, and so on. McGreal (in Brandt, 1996) proposed that teams of teachers evaluate their teaching in light of school goals and develop team instructional improvement plans consistent with those goals. McGreal also recommended that instructional leaders assume the role of facilitator in the evaluation process, meeting with the team periodically. Teachers in PreK–12 education historically have not worked together in instructional improvement teams; thus professional development in group process skills often is a necessary starting point for team development. Other professional development activities can focus on assisting teams to assess their instructional performance, plan and implement improvement activities, and evaluate results.

Schoolwide Evaluation of Teaching and Professional Development

A few years ago, several colleagues and I were asked to carry out a schoolwide evaluation of teaching at an elementary school. Part of the evaluation included classroom observations of every teacher in the school. We focused on what was taking place during classroom lessons. What instructional methods were teachers using? What were students doing during lessons? What teacher-student and student-student interactions were occurring? Based on these observations, as well as a variety of other data gathered during the evaluation, we determined that every teacher in the school except one relied almost exclusively on lecturing, oral questions at the lower end of Bloom's taxonomy, and independent seatwork. Teachers and administrators were amazed at the lack of variety in teaching methods indicated by the data we had gathered. Subsequently, we recommended that the school consider providing professional development to its teachers on alternative models of teaching and how to match and adapt different teaching models to particular content and students.

Every school has common instructional problems that can be identified by schoolwide evaluation and addressed through schoolwide professional development. As Glickman and colleagues (2004) noted,

> Clearly, one characteristic of successful schools is that each teacher has "a cause beyond oneself." Teachers do not view their work as simply what they carry out within their own four walls. In successful schools, teachers see themselves as part of the larger enterprise of complementing and working with each other to educate students. For successful schools, education is a collective rather than an individual enterprise. (pp. 51–52)

WHAT ARE THE GENERAL CHARACTERISTICS OF SUCCESSFUL PROFESSIONAL DEVELOPMENT PROGRAMS?

The research on professional development has increased dramatically over the past several years (see Birman, Desimone, Porter, & Garet, 2000; Boyer, Crowther, Fast, Kasselman, Nolte, & Wilson, 1993; Guskey, 1995; Norton, 2001; Richardson, 2000; Sparks & Hirsh, 2000). My own national study on characteristics of successful school-based professional development (Gordon, 2000) is consistent with this research. Characteristics of successful programs found in this study include the following:

1. An atmosphere of support, trust, and mutual respect fostered by the principal;

2. Encouragement of teachers to assume leadership roles in planning, delivering, and assessing professional development;

3. Linkage of professional development activities to teachers' classroom experiences and needs;

4. Voluntary participation in specific professional development activities, combined with professional norms fostering participation;

5. Opportunities for self-directed learning within collaborative professional development programs (a balance of individual and collective learning);

6. A diversity of learning activities;

7. Active, constructivist learning experiences;

8. Integration of efforts to improve classroom teaching and learning with whole-school improvement; and

9. Career-long, continuous professional development; professional development as a "way of life."

As one reviews the characteristics of successful professional development, the complimentary nature of quality teacher evaluation and quality professional development becomes apparent.

The general characteristics of successful professional development reported above are necessary but insufficient ingredients for professional development that improves teaching and schools. Specific frameworks for professional development must be matched with the professional needs identified by the evaluation of teaching at the individual, team, and school level. The mixing and matching of such frameworks is the nuts and bolts of successful professional development programs.

WHAT ARE ALTERNATIVE FRAMEWORKS FOR PROFESSIONAL DEVELOPMENT?

Each of the professional development frameworks[1] discussed here has been used effectively to improve teaching at the individual, team, or school level, and in many cases at all three levels. It is doubtful that any school will wish or be able to use all 12 frameworks; however, schools with advanced professional development programs tend to use a variety of frameworks within their overall professional development program.

The evaluation of teaching at the individual, team, and school levels can provide vital information to assist in the selection of frameworks to use in a school-based professional development program. In addition, teacher evaluation is critical to the assessment and improvement of an existing professional development program. Based on the evaluation of teaching, professional development frameworks can be added, modified, or dropped from the program, and the relationship of multiple frameworks can be reconfigured. Table 13.1 provides an overview of the 12 frameworks.

Table 13.1 Overview of Alternative Professional Development Frameworks

Framework	Description
Training	Skill development, classroom application, assessment, reflection, peer support throughout
Coteaching	Teachers plan lesson together, teach lesson together, collaborate in post-lesson analysis
Lesson study	Group identifies gap between desired and actual practice, sets goal, carries out series of study lessons
Clinical supervision	Pre-conference, classroom observation, post-conference
Peer coaching	Peers engage in coaching cycles to transfer training skills to classroom, learn about teaching, or foster reflective decision making
Study groups	Small groups of teachers explore professional literature, provide collegial support, or work collaboratively to improve curriculum and instruction
Action research	Individual or group identifies focus area, gathers data, designs action plan, implements plan, evaluates results
Reflective writing	Includes journal writing, case writing, autobiography
Teacher induction and mentoring	Induction programs support beginning and new-to-the-district teachers, often include mentoring by experienced teachers
Intensive assistance	Special assistance for teachers not meeting performance expectations
Self-directed professional development	A teacher conducts a self-analysis of professional needs, then plans, implements, and assesses an individualized professional development program
Portfolio development	Can be for projects, the school year, or career; includes artifacts and reflections on beliefs, experiences, self-assessment, professional growth, and so on

Training

Training is the most widely used professional development framework. Joyce and Showers (1980, 1981, 1982, 1983, 1988) developed a widely accepted training model that consists of presentation of the new skill's underlying theory, demonstration of the new skill, teacher practice with feedback, and peer coaching as the teacher transfers the new skill to the classroom. Another training model, developed by Stallings (1989), calls for teachers to analyze observation data on their teaching to become aware of improvement needs, then develop new skills using a variety of experiential activities. Stallings's model provides teachers with opportunities to modify new skills for application in their own classrooms. Teachers then try out new skills in their classrooms and assess effects. Teachers also observe each other's classrooms, gathering and analyzing data on classroom application. Follow-up training sessions allow teachers to share application problems and discuss possible solutions. Both the Joyce and Showers and the Stallings training models, thus, call for a cycle of skill development, classroom application, assessment, and reflection, with peer support provided throughout. Indeed, there is general agreement across the training literature that training should be job embedded, experiential, and reflective, with follow-up to assist classroom application (Gordon, 2002). The best training programs include entire teams or faculties developing skills to meet common improvement goals. Effective training programs, however, also provide for individualization, assisting teachers to transfer new skills to their own content areas and students.

Coteaching

Coteaching traditionally has involved a regular classroom teacher and a special education teacher teaching a class that includes special education students. Coteaching, however, can involve any two teachers and can be an excellent framework for professional development. Coteaching means that teachers plan a lesson together, teach the lesson together, and collaborate in a post-lesson analysis. One version of coteaching involves teachers with equal decision-making responsibility teaching together as they try out a new teaching strategy. Another version consists of a teacher who has developed expertise in a new teaching strategy teaching a lesson with a teacher who is in the process of learning the strategy. This version calls for the expert teacher to initially take the lead in planning, teaching, and analyzing lessons. The two teachers coteach several lessons using the new strategy, with the less skilled teacher gradually moving toward equal decision-making responsibility with the expert. Either version of coteaching can be adopted on a team or schoolwide level. Long-term coteaching programs can provide for periodic changes in teaching partners, increasing the breadth of collegiality and collaboration.

Lesson Study

Lesson study is a professional development framework widely used in Japan that is gaining increasing popularity in the United States. The process begins with an instructional team or the entire faculty identifying a gap between desired practice and actual practice, then agreeing on a research goal to bridge the gap. The research goal is sufficiently broad to apply to all of the teachers who are participating in the lesson study. The teachers collaboratively carry out a series of "study lessons" or "research lessons" designed around the research goal. The study lessons are not so much concerned with specific content to be taught or specific instructional techniques as they are with movement toward the broad research goal (Lewis, 2002).

The first stage in a study lesson is for the teachers to collaborate in a detailed lesson plan. This lesson plan includes planned activities, but also anticipates alternative student responses to each step in the lesson, and provides alternative strategies for modifying the lesson to address or incorporate student responses (Fernandez & Chokshi, 2002). One teacher delivers the lesson while the other teachers observe, gathering data through videotaping, observation notes, or examination of student work (Lewis, 2002).

All of the teachers engage in a debriefing session following the lesson. The teacher who taught the lesson often begins with a presentation, after which all participants discuss the lesson and the data that were gathered during the lesson. Over time, the entire group revises the lesson, and another teacher teaches the revised lesson to a new group of students. Teachers observe the second lesson, gather new observation data, and hold another debriefing session. At the end of the process, teachers share their learning and the group writes a reflective report. Fernandez and Chokshi (2002) recommended that the group engage in two or three study lesson cycles a year, with each cycle lasting three to four weeks. Lesson study helps teams and schools to meet broad instructional improvement goals, but also results in individual professional development as teachers apply what they have learning to their daily teaching (Audette, 2004).

Clinical Supervision

Clinical supervision, although it has the same structure as a traditional evaluation cycle (pre-conference, classroom observation, post-conference), was not originally conceived as a vehicle for summative evaluation. In authentic clinical supervision, the teacher and supervisor agree during the pre-conference to gather descriptive, nonjudgmental data on a specific aspect of the lesson to be observed. An observation instrument that will assist in the gathering of the agreed-upon data is selected during the pre-conference (a district's standardized evaluation form thus is inappropriate for clinical supervision). A wide variety of systematic observation instruments has been developed for use in clinical supervision. Some examples include categorical frequency, performance indicator, visual diagramming, selected verbatim, and focused questionnaire (Glickman et al., 2004). However, if none of the available instruments match the agreed-upon focus of the observation, the supervisor and teacher are free to design a tailored observation instrument.

The supervisor gathers only the agreed-upon data during the classroom observation, then shares the observation data with the teacher during the post-conference. The teacher and supervisor collaboratively interpret the data and discuss how the teacher can improve the selected aspect of his or her teaching in future lessons. It is important to note that clinical supervision is intended to be ongoing. For example, the post-conference for one clinical cycle can morph into the pre-conference for the next cycle.

Clinical supervision can be a powerful framework for professional develop-ment, but it does consume a great deal of a supervisor's time. Thus, it probably is best used as a tool for the development of selected individuals, and in combi-nation with other frameworks that address other development needs. Although teacher evaluation and clinical supervision are separate processes, teacher evaluation can lead to the selection of clinical supervision as a professional development framework, provide an initial direction for clinical supervision, and serve as a formal measure of improvement fostered by clinical supervision.

Peer Coaching

There actually are several different types of peer coaching, all of which involve teachers observing each other's teaching and engaging in reflective dia-logue on lessons observed. One type of peer coaching mirrors clinical supervi-sion, with a teacher rather than a supervisor assuming the role of the observer. This version is referred to as "responsive coaching" (Gordon, 2002) or "colle-gial coaching" (Garmston, 1987).

A second type of peer coaching is called "technical coaching" (Garmston, 1987). The purpose of technical coaching is to transfer skills learned in train-ing programs to the classroom. This version of peer coaching, developed by Bruce Joyce and Beverly Showers, calls for interspersing workshop training with classroom-based coaching. Teachers learning new skills observe each other teaching, then provide assistance with technical feedback, application to the classroom situation, adaptation to students, and personal facilitation. Joyce and Showers have conducted extensive research indicating that combining workshop training with classroom-based coaching enables teachers to inte-grate new skills into their teaching repertoires and results in improved student learning (Joyce & Showers, 1980, 1981, 1982, 1983).

Joyce and Showers developed a new model of peer coaching in the 1990s called peer coaching study teams. Teachers in schools adopting this model of peer coaching agree on school improvement goals and become members of small teams that develop curriculum and instruction to meet school goals. Team members plan and implement change, support each other during the change process, and gather and analyze data to measure effects on student learning. The newer Joyce and Showers's model still calls for teachers to observe each other's lessons, but for the purpose of learning about teaching rather than providing feedback (Joyce & Showers, 1995; Showers & Joyce, 1996).

A fourth type of peer coaching, cognitive coaching, has the goal of fostering teachers' reflective decision making (Costa & Garmston, 1994). Teachers practicing cognitive coaching seek to improve each other's decision making in planning for lessons, teaching lessons, reflecting on lessons taught, and applying learning to future teaching. Cognitive coaching has three steps: planning conference, observation, and reflecting conference.

Which type of peer coaching is most appropriate for a school depends on the instructional needs of the school. Responsive coaching can meet needs for improved collegiality at the same time it addresses the improvement needs of individual teachers. Technical coaching is best used as follow-up for a team or school-wide skill development program. Peer coaching study teams can link wider school improvement efforts such as changes in the curriculum or instructional program to classroom teaching. Cognitive coaching is best matched with goals to improve teachers' reflection and decision making. Regardless of the specific model chosen, peer coaching is an ideal framework for integrating individual, team, and school-wide professional development.

Study Groups

The study group is a generic framework that takes many forms. Study groups might focus on reading and discussing professional literature, exploring new models of teaching, or improving student assessment. Study groups can continue for years, often changing their focus and activities as they evolve (Murphy, 1992; Rich, 1992).

Despite the many forms that study groups can take, there are a number of common characteristics of successful groups. Optimal group size is six to eight members. Most schools find that groups made up of teachers from different content areas and grade levels are preferable to homogeneous groups. Diversity in race, ethnicity, and gender also is important. The group should support experimentation and risk taking among its members. Items for reflection and dialogue should be provided in each group session. Considering the tendency of study groups to evolve, leaders need to be flexible and willing to foster development toward new group foci and activities.

Study groups, despite their focus on common topics, can assist individual professional development. In groups studied by Keedy and Rogers (1991), individual teachers identified yearlong foci for improving their teaching and were assisted in their improvement efforts by study groups that met throughout the school year. Group members established "game plans" to be implemented during two- to four-week periods between group meetings. At each meeting, teachers updated their study group on progress they had made since their last meeting. The study groups fostered dialogue and reflection as they assisted individual teachers in planning, assessing, and revising improvement efforts.

Study groups also can assist in schoolwide efforts to improve teaching. For example, an elementary school studied by Boggs (1996) established a broad goal of "more student-directed classroom environments that meet the needs of all the learners" (p. 14). Seven study groups were formed, each with a specific topic (special learning needs, multiple intelligences, etc.) related to the school's broad goal. The study groups participated in various activities (reading literature, taking courses, developing curriculum, designing learning activities) as they worked to bring about a change.

Action Research

Action research, often carried out by study groups, has its own rich history as a professional development framework. Action research can be done by individual teachers, teams, or on a schoolwide basis. The first step in the action research cycle is to identify a focus area. The focus area is concerned with a practical problem in the immediate work setting. The second step is to gather data on the focus area. Reviewing student achievement data or student work products, classroom observations, parent surveys, and student interviews are just a few ways of gathering data on the focus area. There are two reasons to gather data at this stage of action research: first, to find out more about the focus area and underlying causes of the problem, and second, to gather baseline data to be used as measures of progress later in the research process. In addition to gathering on-site data, literature related to the focus area often is reviewed to better understand the problem and potential solutions. After review of on-site data and literature, an action plan is designed to solve the problem. Typically, an action plan includes objectives, improvement activities, and a plan to measure results. The next step is the implementation of the action plan, and the final step is the gathering of evaluation data to measure results. Based on the results, the action research might be concluded, continued, or revised.

An example of action research that cuts across both individual and team professional development is the ABC (Assessment by Collaboration) program used in several schools in the Round Rock (Texas) Independent School District. Teachers join small teams, with each team selecting a common focus area (called a "banner question" in the ABC program). Teachers on each team develop individual research plans related to the team's focus area but designed to meet their own instructional needs. Throughout the school year, teams meet on a regular basis to assist members with data analysis, action planning, and classroom change. Building administrators attend team meetings as facilitators. Between team meetings, administrators are available to conduct classroom observations and confer with teachers on their action research. At the end of the school year, teachers meet individually with the administrator assigned to their team to review progress toward improvement goals.

Action research for the improvement of teaching often takes place at the school level, with the faculty selecting a schoolwide focus area. Focus areas for schoolwide action research tend to be general enough to apply to all teachers in the school. Some examples of schoolwide focus areas are "assisting at-risk students," "addressing diverse learning needs," "enhancing the use of technology," and "implementing cooperative learning in all classrooms." Different teams may address different aspects of a schoolwide action research project. Schoolwide action research should allow individual teachers the flexibility to work out their own classroom applications of the school's action plan.

Reflective Writing

Reflective writing is an underused but powerful professional development framework. Reflection on practice is a key to the improvement of teaching (Ash, 1993; Langer & Colton, 1994; Moss, 1997), and writing is a wonderful vehicle for promoting reflective practice. Writing can help teachers reflect on the curriculum, their students, and their teaching (Bolton, 2001). Shared or collaborative writing can improve teaching at the individual, team, and school level.

Journal writing is the most common form of teacher writing. Teachers' journals can be structured or unstructured, private or shared. Journal writing can be structured by providing teachers with topics or questions to be addressed. Let us assume, for example, that a group of science teachers is implementing a new inquiry-based curriculum and they are keeping journals during the implementation process. They might be asked to make journal entries once a week on each of the following questions:

1. What new inquiry strategies did you try this week?

2. How satisfied are you with the way you implemented the strategies?

3. What was the effect of the strategies on students and student learning?

4. The next time you use the same strategies, what will you do differently?

Instructional leaders working with teachers who have not previously practiced reflective writing may wish to begin the process with structured questions and then gradually reduce the level of structure until teachers are ready to organize their own written reflections on teaching.

Another form of reflective writing is case writing. Cases are descriptions of practice intended to promote professional growth. A powerful way to use cases is to have teachers write and discuss their own cases (Richert, 1991). Ackerman and colleagues described a process in which teachers write cases about real-life professional experiences. The process begins with teachers' writing cases like stories, with characters and dialogue. Next, teachers split into triads and read their cases to one another. Other members of the triad ask the writer clarifying questions in order to better understand the case. The teachers in the triad attempt to frame the case's central issue, identify possible actions, and discuss consequences of alternative actions. The triads merge into groups of six to reflect on the process of writing, reading, listening to, and discussing the cases.

The groups of six then report discussions and conclusions to the entire group (Ackerman, Maslin-Ostrowski, & Christensen, 1996).

A third example of reflective writing is autobiography. "Collaborative biographies," as described by Raymond, Butt, and Townsend (1992), integrate teacher autobiographies, team reflection, and a team improvement project. Teachers write about their current work context and teaching practice, their past personal and professional lives, and their preferred professional futures. Final autobiographies are written only after exploratory writing and group dialogue on each topic. Teachers in the team develop individual professional development plans based on their autobiographies. Next, the team as a whole identifies common concerns, then plans and implements a team project designed to address individual and group concerns.

Teacher Induction and Mentoring

Teacher induction refers to the overall program for supporting beginning teachers and, in many schools, new-to-the-district teachers. Mentoring, although it should not be equated with teacher induction, often is a key component of a teacher induction program. Unlike other professions in which mentoring relationships are voluntary and evolve naturally, mentor teachers tend to be experienced teachers formally assigned to support new teachers. The debate over whether a teacher induction program and teacher evaluation should be merged—and whether mentors should participate in summative evaluation of new teachers—reflects the larger debate over whether formative and summative evaluation should be merged. However, there is little disagreement that induction, mentoring, and teacher evaluation should be coordinated and complementary.

A comprehensive teacher induction program includes a number of components (Gordon & Maxey, 2000). Before the beginning of the school year, new teachers need to be oriented to the school district, the community the school serves, the campus, the curriculum, the school's professional community, and the students. Regardless of the quality of their preparation program, beginning teachers usually do not start their careers as experts. Ongoing assistance is needed to help teachers further develop teaching skills and to adapt skills to the school's curriculum and to the teacher's students. New teachers need to have their roles and responsibilities (both formal and informal) explained to them at different points throughout the school year. Finally, it is critical to provide moral support to new teachers as they deal with pedagogical, cultural, and emotional problems typically experienced by new teachers. A teacher induction program needs to be well planned, coordinated with the school's overall professional development program, and continuous throughout the school year.

Assigned mentors can be key players in a school's induction program. Because of the importance of the mentoring role, the school should establish selection criteria and a selection process that will assure only expert teachers highly motivated to assist new teachers become mentors. Working with beginning teachers is not the same as working with students, so even the most expert teachers need their own professional development on the needs of beginning teachers and how to assist adult learners. Mentors themselves need ongoing support, including released time to work with new teachers. Finally, mentors should be rewarded for their work with new teachers, monetarily if possible, but certainly through acknowledgment by their professional community.

Despite the power of mentoring, a teacher induction program needs to go beyond assistance from an assigned mentor. The best approach to assisting beginners is a team approach, with the support team including the mentor, a school administrator, and other professionals who work closely with the new teacher. The mentor and school administrator can work together to coordinate assistance provided by the support team.

Intensive Assistance

There are, unfortunately, some teachers—experienced as well as inexperienced—who are not meeting performance expectations and need special assistance if they are going to survive professionally while providing students the quality education they deserve. The district has the right and responsibility to terminate tenured teachers who do not meet district-defined responsibilities, but only after a good-faith effort to help those teachers improve. Intensive assistance is *intensive* in two ways. First, there is an intense, specific focus on the inadequate professional behaviors identified through summative evaluation. Second, school personnel concentrate significant time and energy on assisting the unsatisfactory teacher to improve in the targeted areas. Intensive assistance is a professional development effort completed prior to disciplinary procedures, with the intent of making disciplinary procedures unnecessary.

Danielson and McGreal (2000) provided a general process for intensive assistance. First, the teacher is made aware of the area of concern. Second, a specific plan of assistance is developed, including the improvement goals, strategies, timelines, progress indicators, resources needed, and support to be provided. Third, the administrator and teacher set a specific date to review progress. Fourth, at the time of the review, a decision is made that the concern is resolved, the intensive assistance will be continued with a revised plan, or the teacher will be moved to a disciplinary phase.

Other professional development frameworks discussed above can be integrated into the process for intensive assistance proposed by Danielson and McGreal. Training, coteaching with an expert teacher, clinical supervision, and coaching by an expert teacher are especially effective frameworks to include in a plan of intensive assistance. A combination of these frameworks often is desirable. Intensive assistance is neither necessary nor possible for an entire team or school, as it is needed for perhaps 5% of teachers. However, the intensive assistance framework can be a vital component of the school's larger professional development program.

Self-Directed Professional Development

At the other end of the continuum from intensive assistance is self-directed professional development, in which a teacher plans, implements, and assesses an individual improvement project. One model for self-directed development (Gordon, 2002) begins with a self-analysis phrase in which the teacher gathers data on her or his professional development needs and adult learning styles. To identify professional development needs, the teacher analyzes at least three different types of job-based data, usually including a combination of data from the teacher's recent evaluation cycles and additional data that the teacher gathers independently. To learn her or his adult learning styles, the teacher can complete self-administered, self-scoring inventories, then compare results. In a reflective essay, the teacher discusses her or his professional development needs and adult learning styles. The second phase of the model calls for the teacher to write an individual improvement plan. The plan includes improvement objectives related to self-assessed needs, activities the teacher will complete to reach the objectives, a plan for self-assessing progress, a timeline, and a list of needed resources. The third phase of the plan is implementation, and the fourth phase is evaluation of results.

In many schools, teachers are required to connect their individual goals to team and school goals. Thus, the process becomes a type of formative evaluation for the individual, team, and school. Self-directed professional development may be integrated with other professional development frameworks, including frameworks that require collaborative work. What makes *self-directed* professional development self-directed is not that the teacher engages in solitary activities, but that the teacher makes her or his own decision at each stage of the process—including needs assessment, planning, implementation, and post-assessment. The teacher might decide that her or his individual development is best served by attending group training, partnering with a colleague for peer coaching, joining a study group, and so forth.

Portfolio Development

Portfolios can be used for teacher evaluation, professional development, or both. There are at least three types of portfolios that place a heavy emphasis on professional development (Gordon, 2002).

Project Portfolios document and enrich self-directed improvement projects with artifacts and reflections on each phase of the project.

Comprehensive Annual Portfolios include entries in several areas, such as educational philosophy, curriculum development, instruction, student assessment, collaboration with parents, and professional service. This type of portfolio includes artifacts and reflections on self-assessment and professional growth in each chosen area.

Career Portfolios can use artifacts and reflections to review a teacher's career phases and professional accomplishments. In addition, they can describe and illustrate current beliefs, practices, and concerns. Career portfolios also can be used to identify long-range professional development goals and plans to achieve those goals.

A few years ago, I carried out a case study of a portfolio program in Leander (Texas) Middle School. This program provides a good example of using portfolios to enhance teachers' professional development. Every teacher in the school (as well as every administrator and staff member) completed a portfolio based on an individual improvement project. Teachers were prepared to work with portfolios at team meetings that addressed topics such as how to self-assess professional development needs, select an improvement topic, plan professional development activities, and develop a portfolio. One requirement was that each teacher's improvement topic be related to school and district improvement goals. The portfolios that teachers developed followed a PDSA cycle (Plan, Do, Study, Act), with a different portfolio section for each stage of the cycle. The "Plan" section documented self-assessment and planning. Learning activities, changes in practice, and collegial support were addressed in the "Do" section. The "Study" section included data on teacher and student growth resulting from improvement activities. The "Act" section was based on an end-of-year portfolio conference with a school administrator. At the end of the year, a "portfolio fair" was held in which administrators, teachers, and staff shared their portfolios with the school community.

Portfolio development also can serve as a framework for team and school development. Teams can develop group portfolios on collaborative instructional improvement projects. Bernhardt (1994) recommended that schools develop portfolios including such components as student achievement and school assessment data, improvement plans, improvement activities, and evaluation of improvement efforts. Teachers throughout the school can collaborate on the development of school portfolios. Collaborative development of school portfolios not only facilitates school improvement, but also is a form of professional development for participating teams and individuals.

USING MULTIPLE PROFESSIONAL DEVELOPMENT FRAMEWORKS

A school initiating its own professional development program might wish to start with a single framework that will meet the needs of the greatest number of teachers. However, the more sophisticated programs I have examined use multiple frameworks. Multiple frameworks can be integrated, differentiated, or both. A program with integrated frameworks might begin with teachers' forming study groups to explore new instructional strategies. The study groups could lead to a commitment to attend training on promising new strategies. Between training sessions, teachers might engage in peer coaching to transfer new skills to their classrooms. The teachers could continue the study groups to provide collegial support to one another or they could integrate new instructional strategies into their teaching repertoires. They also might keep reflective journals on their progress. There are endless variations on how professional development frameworks can be integrated to foster teacher and school improvement. The combination and relationship of frameworks depends on school improvement goals, teachers' instructional needs, and teachers' level of comfort with various frameworks.

Multiple frameworks also can be used as components of differentiated professional development programs. Common school improvement goals sometimes require differentiated professional development to meet different teacher improvement needs and learning styles. For a simple example, if two teachers both need to improve their classroom management skills, one might benefit most from a training program with peer coaching follow-up, while the other might benefit most from belonging to a study group on classroom management and coteaching lessons with colleagues who form the study group. What connects different professional development frameworks in a differentiated program is a common focus on the same school improvement goals. Whether a program integrates frameworks, differentiates frameworks, or develops some combination thereof, the use of complementary frameworks can create a powerful professional development program.

CONCLUSIONS: CONNECTING TEACHER EVALUATION, PROFESSIONAL DEVELOPMENT, AND SCHOOL IMPROVEMENT

The current emphasis on accountability in K–12 education—and the focus of the accountability movement on student achievement—means that teacher evaluation, professional development, and school improvement are heading for a common denominator: the improvement of student learning. To elaborate on the movement within each of the three areas:

- Although *teacher evaluation* will continue to examine things like subject matter knowledge, instructional behavior, and meeting of assigned responsibilities, it will examine these aspects of teaching *in relation to student learning,* which will become the primary focus of teacher evaluation.
- Although *professional development* programs will continue to address teachers' perceived needs, development of teachers' knowledge and

skills, and changes in teachers' attitudes and dispositions, it will address these aspects of professional development *in relation to student learning*, which will become the primary focus of professional development.

- Although *school improvement* programs will continue to build collective visions, develop collegial cultures, and foster schoolwide change, they will address these aspects of school improvement *in relation to student learning*, which will become the primary focus of school improvement.

The common denominator of student learning means that teacher evaluation has the potential for a significant impact on teachers' professional development, both through identifying professional development needs and providing data to help assess and modify professional development programs. However, if teacher evaluation is going to foster professional development, it will need to possess some characteristics that have not been present in conventional teacher evaluation programs.

- Teacher evaluation will need to focus on team evaluation and schoolwide evaluation of teaching as well as individual teacher evaluation. For the purposes of professional development and school improvement, individual, team, and schoolwide evaluation cannot be separated.
- Teacher evaluation will need to place as much emphasis on formative evaluation as it does on summative evaluation. The debate over whether formative and summative evaluation should be integrated or separate will continue for the foreseeable future, but formative evaluation— whether integrated with or separate from summative evaluation—must receive more emphasis than it has received historically if evaluation is going to significantly influence teacher professional development and school improvement.
- As discussed earlier in this chapter, teacher evaluation must rely on multiple data sources and multiple data gathering methods if it is to provide sufficient data to inform professional development and school improvement. A single evaluation rating scale or checklist is of little value to a professional development program.

A teacher evaluation program that meets the above criteria can provide critical input and feedback for a professional development program. Figure 13.1 shows the interactive relationship of teacher evaluation and professional development, with both contributing to the ultimate goal of school improvement.

Figure 13.1 Relationship of Teacher Evaluation, Professional Development, and School Improvement

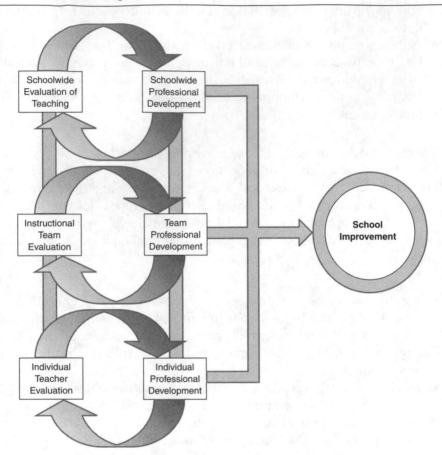

NOTE

1. For in-depth discussions of alternative professional development frameworks, see Gordon (2002).

REFERENCES

Ackerman, R., Maslin-Ostrowski, P. M., & Christensen, C. (1996). Case stories: Telling tales about schools. *Educational Leadership, 53*(6), 21–23.

Ash, T. (1993). *Reflective teaching. What am I doing? Why am I doing it this way? Instructional strategies series No. 11.* Regina, SK: The Saskatchewan Instructional Development and Research Unit and the Saskatchewan Professional Development Unit.

Audette, A. (2004). Lesson study: Teachers learning together. *New England Reading Association Journal, 40*(2), 31–34.

Beckham, J. C. (1985). *Legal aspects of employee assessment and selection in public schools.* Topeka, KS: National Organization on Legal Problems of Education.

Bernhardt, V. L. (1994). *The school portfolio.* Princeton Junction, NJ: Eye on Education.

Birman, B. F., Desimone, L., Porter, A. C., & Garet, M. S. (2000). Designing professional development that works. *Educational Leadership, 57*(8), 28–33.

Boggs, H, (1996, October). *Launching school change through teacher groups: An action research project.* Paper presented at the annual conference of the Midwestern Educational Research Association, Chicago.

Bolton, G. (2001). *Reflective practice: Writing and professional development.* Thousand Oaks, CA: Sage.

Boyer, K., Crowther, S., Fast, D., Kasselman, J., Nolte, S., & Wilson, D. (1993). *Outcome based staff development.* Topeka: Kansas State Board for Education.

Brandt, R. (1996). On a new direction for teacher evaluation: A conversation with Tom McGreal. *Educational Leadership, 53*(6), 30–33.

Costa, A. L., & Garmston, R. J. (1994). *Cognitive coaching: A foundation for renaissance schools.* Norwood, MA: Christopher Gordon.

Danielson, C., & McGreal, T. L. (2000). *Teacher evaluation to enhance professional practice.* Alexandria, VA: Association for Supervision and Curriculum Development.

Fernandez, C., & Chokshi, S. (2002). A practical guide for translating lesson study for a U.S. setting. *Phi Delta Kappan, 84*(2), 128–134.

Garmston, R. (1987). How administrators support peer coaching. *Educational Leadership, 44*(5), 18–26.

Glickman, C. D., Gordon, S. P., & Ross-Gordon, J. M. (2004). *SuperVision and instructional leadership: A developmental approach.* Boston: Allyn & Bacon.

Gordon, S. P. (2000, November). *Professional development for teacher and school renewal: Alternative pathways, common characteristics.* Paper presented at the University Council for Educational Administration Annual Convention, Albuquerque.

Gordon, S. P. (2002). *Professional development for school improvement: Empowering learning communities.* Boston: Allyn & Bacon.

Gordon, S. P., & Maxey, S. (2000). *How to help beginning teachers succeed.* Alexandria, VA: Association for Supervision and Curriculum Development.

Guskey, T. R. (1995). Professional development in education: In search of the optimal mix. In T. R. Guskey & M. Huberman (Eds.), *Professional development in education* (pp. 114–131). New York: Teachers College Press.

Hopkins, D., Ainscow, M., & West, M. (1994). *School improvement in an era of change.* New York: Teachers College Press.

Joyce, B., Calhoun, E., & Hopkins, D. (1999). *The new structure of school improvement: Inquiring schools and achieving students.* Philadelphia: Open University Press.

Joyce, B., & Showers, B. (1980). Improving inservice training: The messages of research. *Educational Leadership, 37*(5), 379–385.

Joyce, B., & Showers, B. (1981). Transfer of training: The contribution of "coaching." *Boston University Journal of Education, 163*(2), 163–172.

Joyce, B., & Showers, B. (1982). The coaching of teaching. *Educational Leadership, 40*(1), 4–8, 10.

Joyce, B., & Showers, B. (1983). *Power in staff development through research on training.* Alexandria, VA: Association for Supervision and Curriculum Development.

Joyce, B., & Showers, B. (1988). *Student achievement through staff development.* New York: Longman.

Joyce, B., & Showers, B. (1995). *Student achievement through staff development: Fundamentals of school renewal* (2nd cd.). White Plains, NY: Longman.

Keedy, J. L., & Rogers, K. (1991). Teacher collegial groups: A structure for promoting professional dialogue conductive to organization change. *Journal of School Leadership, 1*(1), 65–73.

Langer, G. M., & Colton, A. B. (1994). Reflective decision making: The cornerstone of school reform. *Journal of Staff Development, 15*(1), 2–7.

Lewis, C. (2002). Everywhere I looked—Levers and pendulums. *Journal of Staff Development, 23*(3), 59–65.

Little, J. W. (1982). Norms of collegiality and experimentation: Workplace conditions of school success. *American Educational Research Journal, 19*(3), 325–340.

Moss, C. M. (1997, March). *Systematic self-reflection: Professional development for the reflective practitioner.* Paper presented at the annual meeting of the American Education Research Association, Chicago.

Murphy, C. (1992). Study groups foster schoolwide learning. *Educational Leadership, 50*(3), 71–74.

Norton, J. (2001). Grounded in research. *Journal of Staff Development, 22*(3), 30–32.

Raymond, D., Butt, R., & Townsend, D. (1992). Contexts for teacher development: Insights from teachers' stories. In A. Hargreaves & M. G. Fullan (Eds.), *Understanding teacher development* (pp. 143–161). New York: Teachers College Press.

Rich, S. J. (1992). Teacher support groups: Providing a forum for professional development. *Journal of Staff Development, 13*(3), 32–35.

Richardson, J. (2000). Learning benefits everyone. *Journal of Staff Development, 21*(1), 54–59.

Richert, A. E. (1991). Using teacher cases for reflection and enhanced understanding. In A. Lieberman & L. Miller (Eds.), *Staff development for education in the 90's* (pp. 113–132). New York: Teachers College Press.

Rosenholtz, S. J. (1989). *Teachers' workplace: The social organization of schools.* New York: Longman.

Showers, B., & Joyce, B. (1996). The evaluation of peer coaching. *Educational Leadership, 53*(6), 12–16.

Sparks, D., & Hirsh, S. (2000). *A national plan for improving professional development.* Oxford, OH: National Staff Development Council.

Stallings, J. (1989, March). *School achievement effects and staff development: What are some critical factors?* Paper presented at the annual meeting of the American Educational Research Association, San Francisco.

Stronge, J. H., & Helm, V. M. (1991). *Evaluating professional support personnel in education.* Newbury Park, CA: Sage.

Wasley, P., Hampel, R., & Clark, R. (1997). The puzzle of whole-school change. *Phi Delta Kappan, 78*, 690–697.

Author Index

Subject Index

**CORWIN
PRESS**

The Corwin Press logo—a raven striding across an open book—represents the union of courage and learning. Corwin Press is committed to improving education for all learners by publishing books and other professional development resources for those serving the field of PreK–12 education. By providing practical, hands-on materials, Corwin Press continues to carry out the promise of its motto: **"Helping Educators Do Their Work Better."**